D1476880

Western Mayfly Hatches

FROM THE ROCKIES TO THE PACIFIC

Rick Hafele
Dave Hughes

FLY PATTERN PHOTOGRAPHS BY JIM SCHOLLMEYER
ILLUSTRATIONS BY RICHARD BUNSE
FLIES TIED BY JOHN CHILDS

Western Mayfly Hatches

From the Rockies to the Pacific

Rick Hafele
Dave Hughes

Frank Amato
PORTLAND

Dedication

To Dr. Norm Anderson, Rick's major Professor,
who introduced us both to aquatic insects, and instilled
a sense of wonder that has kept us looking at them.

About the Authors

RICK HAFELE has worked in Oregon for over 25 years as an aquatic biologist specializing in aquatic insects. He received his Bachelor of Science degree in biology in 1973 from Western Washington University at Bellingham, Washington, and in 1979 his Master of Science degree in aquatic entomology from Oregon State University at Corvallis, Oregon. Through both his professional work and his fly-fishing, Rick has studied the aquatic insects of creeks, streams, rivers, and lakes from Alaska to California, and from the Pacific Coast through the Rockies. Rick has written articles for scientific and technical journals, and has penned the Aquatic Entomology column for *American Angler* magazine for over 20 years. He is the co-author of *Western Hatches* (with Dave Hughes, Frank Amato Publications, 1981) and *Aquatic Insects and Their Imitations* (with Scott Roederer, Johnson Books, 1995). Rick is a member of the North American Benthological Society and Oregon Trout, and has been awarded life membership in the Federation of Fly Fishers and the Flyfisher's Club of Oregon for his contributions to flyfishing literature. He lives in Portland, Oregon with his wife Carol.

DAVE HUGHES is a professional flyfishing writer and photographer, an amateur aquatic entomologist, and editor of *Flyfishing & Tying Journal*. He was born and raised in Astoria, Oregon and has lived in the West all of his life. He has traveled and fly-fished the Western states and provinces for more than thirty years. His hobbies include collecting, identifying, and photographing all stages of the aquatic insects that trout eat. Dave is author of more than twenty books about fly-fishing, including *Trout Flies* (Stackpole Books, 1999) and *Western Streamside Guide* (Frank Amato Publications, 1986, revised in 1997). His articles have appeared in most of the major fishing magazines. He is a contributing editor to *Field & Stream*. Dave is a member of Trout Unlimited, a life member of the Federation of Fly Fishers, in 1983 was founding president of Oregon Trout, and in 1992 was awarded life membership in the Flyfishers Club of Oregon for his contributions to flyfishing literature. His home club is the Rainland Flycasters in Astoria, Oregon. He lives in Portland with his wife, flyfishing writer Masako Tani, and daughter Kosumo.

All inquiries should be addressed to:
Frank Amato Publications, Inc. • P.O. Box 82112 • Portland, Oregon 97282
503-653-8108 • www.amatobooks.com

Fly Plate Photography: Jim Schollmeyer
Book Production: Tony Amato/Jerry Hutchinson

SB ISBN: 1-57188-304-5 • SB UPC: 0-81127-00138-5
HB ISBN: 1-57188-305-3 • HB UPC: 0-81127-00139-2
Limited HB ISBN: 1-57188-337-1 • Limited HB UPC: 0-81127-00171-2
Printed in Singapore

1 3 5 7 9 10 8 6 4 2

Contents

Acknowledgements

We would like first to thank those few close friends with whom we have done most of our exploring in the world of trout and mayflies, and in the world of words written about them: Richard Bunse, Jim Schollmeyer, and Ted Leeson. In addition our wives Carol Horvath and Masako Tani, who often outfish us, deserve special thanks for their unwavering support.

Second, our thanks go to all of those, both scientists and anglers, who have collected and studied the mayflies, and who have shared their knowledge by publishing their results. Any personal knowledge of such wonderful works of nature as the mayflies is the result of the efforts of countless others who have been fascinated by their dance.

Finally, we would like to thank those who have contributed so much to *Western Mayfly Hatches*: photographer Jim Schollmeyer, artist Richard Bunse, John Childs for tying the flies, Ronn Lucas, Sr. for tying the Polly Rosborough patterns, Tony Amato and Jerry Hutchinson for their layout and design skills, and Frank Amato for taking on its publication.

A Note About the Fly Patterns

Based on the belief that there are plenty of fly patterns already out there, we rarely originate them ourselves, preferring instead to search out patterns and carefully attribute them to those who did originate them. We followed that prescription twenty years ago in *Western Hatches*, and will do our best to do it once again here in *Western Mayfly Hatches*. In our work on the first draft, however, we ran into a bit of a buzz saw.

While working with books and magazines as sources, and carefully attributing flies to those who wrote about them, we suddenly bumped into two patterns, for a specific stage of a particular insect, that were clearly right out of our own *Western Hatches*, with no attribution to the originators we'd credited in that earlier work. That presented a problem in credibility, since we'd been listing the author of that source as the originators of many patterns that likely were from other tiers.

As a consequence, we've listed *originators* in this book if we know them, have listed *sources* where we've found patterns and want you to be able to look up the source for further reading, but we don't know for sure if the source is the orignator. If we do not know the originator and have taken the dressing from our own sources, then we have left the space blank. Normally this means it's an old or traditional pattern, but in some cases it means we don't know the originator for sure and don't want to give credit to the wrong person. Wrong attributions lead to quarrels. So do missing attributions. We apologize to any originators who are not properly credited on account of this decision.

Introduction: Lessons Learned

The goal of *Western Mayfly Hatches* is to introduce the mayflies important in fly-fishing the western states and provinces, to show how to recognize them, to help in the selection of fly patterns to match them, and to provide information on the best presentation methods to take trout with those matching patterns.

At one time we operated under the philosophy that if you could identify a mayfly on which trout were feeding, then select the one right fly to match it, you'd be able to take trout with that fly, during that hatch, anytime, anywhere. Our search, in all of our fishing, was always directed toward that one precise right fly for each of the hatches we encountered. We've learned that there is rarely one single right fly for any hatch.

A mayfly species can vary in size and color from stream to stream. The style of fly that works best for a single species will change as you move from one water type to another—from smooth water to rough water or vice versa. The preferences of trout, for a particular stage of the mayfly, or for one style fly over another, often change from hour to hour and even moment to moment, at times capriciously. You catch two or three trout on a size-16 Olive Compara-dun during a *Baetis* hatch, and are sure you've got the world worked out, when suddenly the trout refuse it. If that's the only fly you carry to match that hatch, you're in for a long afternoon.

Our fly pattern philosophy has worked out over twenty years to something like this: it's best to carry three, four, or even more styles of flies for a particular hatch that you fish often, so that when you fish different water types, or trouts' tastes change, you're able to offer them something that floats a little differently on the surface or in it, or that even dips beneath it.

We've learned that observation is the key to matching hatches. It's far more important than identification. You can collect an insect, observe its size, form, and color, and choose a matching pattern for it without ever

The original *Western Hatches.*

knowing its Latin name. Observation cuts in many directions. A close observer might notice rising trout that a casual fisherman might miss. This happens often with small mayflies. If you fail to watch the water you might not even notice there's a hatch to match. In the opposite direction, observation cuts toward general conditions of the wind and weather. If the air is cold and the weather a bit brutal, it could easily be a day when the best bet is to turn over some stones, notice which nymphs might predominate in the diet of trout down there, and then roll a nymph imitation along the bottom. It's unlikely you'll have a hatch to match in such nasty weather, but your observations will still add to your action.

We've learned that conditions on a stream or lake, from day to day or from hatch to hatch, are rarely the same twice. We're just like you: we'd like to catalog the hatches, know that on the seventeenth of May every year we're going to get a heavy blue-winged olive hatch on the Deschutes, and on the fourth of July we'll always be able to sneak off and fish a green drake dressing with great success on one of our secret little hill streams. Those are hatches that nature has roughly scheduled, but as often as not they fail to happen on specific days, or even weeks. Fortunately, nature almost always offers surprise hatches to replace them, which can be just as good, and are often better. Certainly the mystery of it all adds to the fun.

We've learned that trout and hatches can both be fickle. At times they're predictable and at times they're not. You've got to please trout with what they want, when they want it. You've got to match hatches when and where they happen, not where and when you've read that they happen. We've learned that it's always best to go to any stream, river, or stillwater prepared for anything that might happen, rather than going prepared only for the one great hatch we hope will happen.

We've learned that the more you know about mayflies and their hatches, the more trout you'll catch, and the more fun you'll have fishing.

—*Rick Hafele*
—*Dave Hughes*
Portland, Oregon
January, 2004

The time you spend observing trout, insects, and conditions of wind and weather are never wasted, and usually result in things noticed that lead to many more trout caught than you'd get by just rushing in and beginning to cast without taking time to look around.

Part I

MATCHING MAYFLIES

Chapter 1

A Philosophy for Matching Hatches

Any book about western angling entomology must deal with a unique set of western conditions. Chalk-stream hatches in England have long been identified to species, timed to the moment, and matched to perfection. Knowledge of our eastern mayfly hatches now approaches the same point. As more hatches are catalogued, and matching fly patterns codified, eastern anglers begin to arrive at their streams with a fair knowledge of what insect might hatch, and a certain confidence that they've got the right pattern to match it.

We western anglers may never enjoy quite such a complete catalogue of mayfly hatches and patterns on our own waters. The West is a vast landscape. It has great geographic differences, from desert tailwaters in the Southwest to rainforest streams in the Pacific Northwest, from alpine lakes in the High Sierra to the big and sometimes brutal blue-ribbon trout rivers in Montana. Elevation can differ by thousands of feet on a single river system. Mayfly inhabitants change along this gradient according to the changing conditions of the river. Climatic variations are sharp: the knife-edge crest of a mountain chain can be the dividing line between a fertile forest environment and a desert just as rich, but only where waters flow.

Mayflies adapt to the conditions that surround them. Through millions of years, and therefore millions of mayfly generations, the wide variety of western conditions has given rise to an equally wide variety of mayfly species. Taxonomists, who have catalogued the insects of England and are on their way toward understanding the aquatic life of our eastern waters, are still struggling to fit together the unruly insect puzzle of the West.

This diverse collection of western hatches should lead western anglers toward a different approach to hatch matching. You must be prepared to collect and observe the mayflies you encounter in your own fishing. You will be helped immensely by the basic knowledge necessary to classify your own collected specimens to useful levels. Finally, you must be informed well enough to select a matching pattern, and at times must even be creative enough to invent your own. Not every hatch has been collected, identified, matched, and written about in our still-wild West.

There are four logical steps in matching any hatch: 1. identify it as far as possible, 2. understand it as well as you can, 3. select a fly pattern to match it and the water where you'll fish it, and 4. present that fly in the manner of the living insect.

Identification is not always necessary in order to match a mayfly. Generations of anglers fished successfully without ever knowing a single Latin name. However, some level of identification is almost always helpful. *Western Mayfly Hatches* was written to help you discover which level is most useful for each hatch, and then to show you how to identify a collected mayfly to that level.

Identification is based on a hierarchy of names that allows scientists to group organisms from broad general groups down to specific species. It consists of six main categories: Phylum, Class, Order, Family, Genus and Species. An example of these categories for two common mayflies follows. Note that genus and species names are always italicized.

Green Drake	*Trico*
Phylum: Animal	Animal
Class: Insecta	Insecta
Order: Ephemeroptera	Ephemeroptera
Family: Ephemerellidae	Leptohyphidae
Genus: *Drunella*	*Tricorythodes*
Species: *grandis*	*minutus*

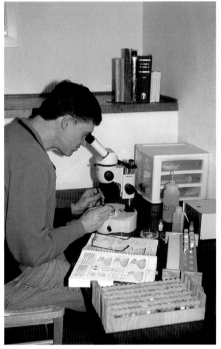

Spending time at a microscope, with a book of keys open alongside it, is the only way to identify most mayflies to species.

What is the most useful level of identification for an insect you're about to match, mayfly or anything else? It is that level at which all members of a genus or species live in the same type of habitat and exhibit the same behavior. For most mayflies this is the genus level. For example, if a hatch of mayflies occurs on a slow, marshy river, the ability to identify that hatch to the genus *Siphlonurus* will enable you to fish it just as effectively as if you identified it to species. Different *Siphlonurus* species vary in size and color; they do not vary in shape or behavior. A pattern can be selected or created based on observation of the natural, and presented with the action that is consistent throughout the genus.

Identification to species is intriguing. It is a quest that spurs your authors into pouring over textbooks and peering through microscopes when they should be fishing. It gives us great satisfaction to identify a mayfly to species. Only occasionally does it increase our ability to match the hatch.

Some western hatches are so famous they have long been identified to species. An example is the western green drake (*Drunella grandis* and *D. doddsi*), famous on Idaho's Henry's Fork of the Snake and many other rivers, some of them made famous in part by the presence of the famous hatch. Where such identifications have been made, and specific patterns have evolved to match them, it's useful to identify these insects to species, and they will be discussed in detail at that level.

Many western mayflies, however, are still uncatalogued to species even by professional taxonomists. The western angler must not yet look for books filled with species lists, matching patterns, and detailed daily and hourly emergence charts except for specific stretches of specific waters. It is possible, over many seasons, to catalog hatches on a home stream or home lake. Even then it's likely you'll bump into surprises. It's best to learn to collect your own hatches, on your home waters or throughout your travels, identify them to family or genus in all cases and to species in some, and to select or create matching patterns for them.

Understanding an insect means knowing what you can about its hatch cycle, habitat preference, and behavior. Mayflies have adapted in unique ways to specific water conditions. Where and how each executes its life within its water type tells you where and how to fish patterns selected to match it.

Selection of ***matching*** patterns should be based on the size, form, and color of the natural. The type of water in which the mayfly hatches must be cranked into this equation. If it's a fast-water hatch, you might need to imitate it with a rough-hackled dry fly. If it emerges on spring-creek flats, a dressing without hackle that lowers the body into the surface film is more likely to fool trout.

Presentation of the selected imitation is based on the movement, or lack of it, revealed by the stage of the mayfly you're matching. If you understand a mayfly's habitat and behavior, you will know where trout find it, and the way it will be moving when a trout takes it. You'll therefore know how your imitation should be fished to imitate it. Most of the time this presentation will amount to a dead drift, especially with a dry fly. But a nymph fished on the swing or another dead-drifted along the bottom can be every bit as imitative, depending on the insect it imitates.

Reassessment of what you are doing becomes a fifth and final part of matching any hatch. If what you try at first fails to fool trout, which will often be the case, go back through the parts of matching the hatch, again in the same logical order, and try to determine where you might have gone away from what the trout want. Collect another specimen, observe its size, form, and color, and see if you've identified it to the correct order, family, genus, or even species. Make sure you understand its behavior, and what stage the trout might be taking. Check your pattern selection, and try one that presents a different silhouette on the water, or switch to one that fishes a different level, say an emerger rather than a dry. Make sure your rigging is right, and that your presentation is correct for the insect you are imitating and the fly you are fishing.

Such careful reassessment is just as important as the original process of matching a hatch. If you don't take time to do it, however briefly, the alternative is a panicked series of fly changes that rarely solves a hatch. In truth, adding a couple of feet of tippet, or switching your casting position, and therefore the way your fly arrives before the trout, can contain the solution to refusals just as often as changing flies.

Western Mayfly Hatches was written to make your study of mayflies, whether casual or serious, more enjoyable, and therefore to make your fishing more productive. We hope it will prompt you to practice stream tactics a lot more often, and to enjoy them more when you do. We also hope you will develop an appreciation for the environment of the trout, and know that fishermen are only a small and occasional part of it.

Chapter 2

Collecting and Observing Mayflies

Western Mayfly Hatches is designed to be most useful at streamside, or back home at the tying vise, with an insect in hand. When you find a mayfly that trout feed on selectively, an effective imitation is necessary for consistent success. But you can't match a mayfly until you capture one and have a close look at it. There is a great deal of difference between the appearance of an insect taken in at a glance at three feet and the same insect observed carefully at the distance a trout sees it just before it eats it: an inch or two off the end of its nose. Colors change when you get up close. Shapes are not what they seemed at longer range. The underside of the mayfly dun, always the side seen by trout as they tip up to take one, is almost always a different shade, usually lighter, than the backside, seen by the fisherman unless the insect is collected and turned over.

Just as there are certain tools and tactics for catching fish, so too are there certain tools and techniques for capturing aquatic insects. We will break these into four categories: 1. What will fit conveniently in a fishing vest; 2. What will fit in the trunk of a car; 3. What is best left to be used at your home; and 4. None. Since it's the simplest, we'll discuss the last first.

None: This is for the angler whose vest carries an inventory to rival a tackle house catalog, with little room left for additions, or the opposite, one who goes so light that any addition is not a consideration. We will tell you a couple of ways to collect insects with just techniques, no tools. The best way, and among the most fun, is to catch a fish. If you plan to kill it for dinner anyway, a sin we sometimes commit ourselves when the law allows it and trout are both abundant and healthy, then always take the time to slice open its stomach and examine the contents. This is the surest way to know what that trout has been eating.

We do not advocate killing trout just to see what they've been taking. We feel it's a bit of a waste, however, to kill a fish you plan to eat without bothering to see what it's been eating. Pay special attention to insects taken recently. These will be near the front of the throat; stomach acids will not have decomposed them or changed their colors. If a trout has been feeding selectively, then what is up front is what you want to match.

Another collecting method requiring no equipment is to carefully lift rocks, gravel, debris, moss, and other substrate from the bottom with your hands. The advantage of this method is that you can see exactly what habitat the collected specimens prefer. The major disadvantage is that many nymph types will let go their grip the instant they're disturbed, and swim or drift away before you get a chance to notice them. Another disadvantage is that you are limited to collecting areas shallower than the length of your arm, or the extent to which you're willing to get wet. However, this method is always "at hand," and you should always employ it. A few minutes spent hoisting and examining streambed stones should become your standard practice whenever you fish new waters, or when you approach any old and familiar waters after a while away.

Vest Pocket Equipment: A few small collecting tools will fit easily in one pocket of your fishing vest and greatly aid you when you're stymied

You can often learn which bug to match simply by hoisting rocks off the stream bottom, and examining them to see what is clinging to them.

by a hatch and would like a close look at whatever is causing the problem. We always carry five items: an aquarium net, tweezers, a small white jar lid, a magnifying loupe, and three or four alcohol-filled vials. It's also rare for us to fish for trout without small travel binoculars dangling around our necks, to bring distant observations into closer view.

The small aquarium net is for capturing specimens off the surface. It will be appreciated most by those who have seen a dun emerge or spinner fall and float gracefully down the current to their waiting hand, only to have it slip between their fingers and float away. It can be very difficult, and constantly frustrating, to try to lift insects off the water with your fingers. A tiny net costs less than a couple of dollars at a pet supply store. It is handy in a thousand situations and is seldom in the way. Buy one and you'll use it more often than you'd ever believe.

Tweezers are used to transfer specimens from the aquarium net to vials, or to hold them so you can get a better look at them. Choose soft-sprung tweezers with fine points. Stiff tweezers are clumsy and damage insects. Some flyfishing supply houses list *nymph tweezers*. They are perfect for collecting. We constantly carry tiny Swiss Army knives. The tweezers inserted in these knives are not perfect, but are usually adequate and are ever-present.

A small white jar lid, such as those found on pickle or condiment jars, is perfect for observing nymphs, and tucks flat into a vest pocket, taking up almost no room. If you collect a sample that is a mixture of debris with naturals mixed in, you can put it all in the lid, add water, and the insects will be easy to spot as they swim or crawl out of the debris against

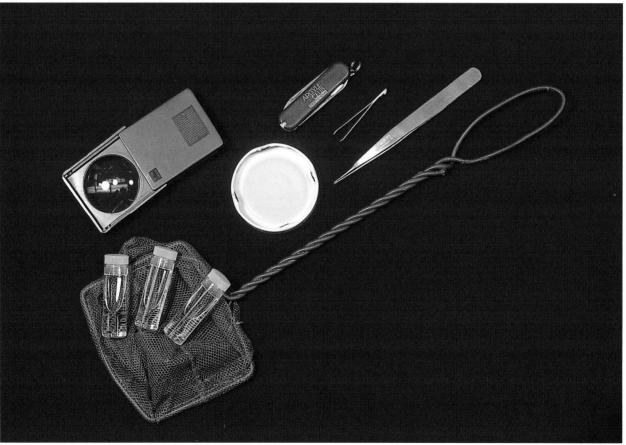

A few small items carried in your vest can make collecting rewarding, and at times keep frustration to a minimum.

the white background. A white jar lid is also perfect for examining stomach contents. Squeeze the mess into the lid, add water, and stir it with your tweezers. Any usable specimens will untangle so it's easy to tell what the trout has been eating. The least-digested specimens will be those eaten most recently, and will also be those most complete and therefore easiest to observe and match.

We've discovered the usefulness of small 10X magnifying loupes available from most nature stores, and surprisingly from cutlery stores. These cost twenty to thirty dollars, and will open a very close view of an insect's minute parts to you. Most of the features that are described in this book for recognizing the insects at various levels can be observed with a 10X loupe. For streamside work, it might be too powerful. You'll be able to classify most mayflies to genus in the field with an inexpensive—five to ten dollars—collapsing magnifying glass in 4X to 6X. We recommend you carry such a glass at all times.

Vials filled with alcohol are used to preserve collected specimens. Be sure to observe the colors of any insect before putting it in the vial. Alcohol washes colors out quickly, as do all other convenient preservatives. Ethyl alcohol, either denatured or not, diluted to about 80% strength with water, is best for insect preservation. Denatured ethanol is available from drugstores. Rubbing alcohol (isopropyl) will also work, but it makes the specimens brittle. When you observe them later their legs, wings, tails and antennae will be broken off. Because the number of tails is critical to identification of mayflies, it's best to stay away from rubbing alcohol unless you're unable to find anything else. One- to three-dram vials with rubber or plastic stoppers will work well for storing your specimens. We are not fond of vials with screw-on caps as they almost always leak, going empty over long periods of time in storage, and the necks are narrow, making removal of specimens very difficult. Vials are available from biological supply houses and some university bookstores.

We often, though not always, carry a medicine bottle or film cannister with holes poked in it for air, and a bit of fiberglass screening in the bottom for traction. This is perfect for keeping live winged specimens. It is especially valuable if you are interested in taking duns or spinners back to the tying bench, or in getting duns to molt into spinners under your kind care, so you can observe both stages of the insect. Coax the duns into the container without touching their wings. If you compress their wings, it will scar them and prevent the insects from molting successfully. Put no more than three or four duns in each container or they will damage each other. Keep them out of direct sun. In a day or two they will make the final molt, and you can observe or even photograph the spinners and know without doubt that they're the same species. If you desire to send mayflies to professional entomologists for exact identification, they'll need male spinners. Hatching them from known duns is one way to get spinners, and also to be sure that they're linked to the duns, which is most likely the stage you're trying to identify and match.

A stomach pump is handy to see what a trout has been taking without having to kill it. The pump must be used very gently, however, or the fish might be injured. In truth, we're both sensitive to what it might be like to have a tube jammed down our own throats to extract what we've been eating lately, and neither of us use stomach pumps, though we do not condemn you if you do.

Binoculars that are small enough to carry conveniently while fishing provide a surprising benefit in matching hatches. They let you spy into the feeding lanes of trout without wading out to see exactly what they're

Don't kill trout just to take stomach samples; but if you kill one for other reasons, don't fail to examine what it's been eating. The trout that provided this sample appeared to be feeding on an obvious hatch of *Callibaetis* duns, but the autopsy revealed it had taken a smattering of *Callibaetis* spinners, an emerger, two caddis pupae, and a predominance of *Callibaetis* nymphs. It had eaten no duns.

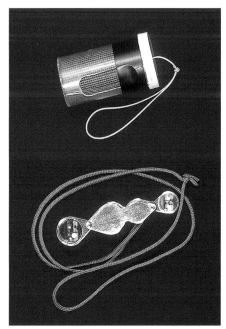

A portable "rearing chamber" made from a medicine bottle and window screening (top), and a loupe with a 10X lens at one end and 15X lens at the other (bottom), are excellent, though not necessary, additions to your fishing vest.

Collecting with a kick screen net will reveal a full sample of which insects the bottom holds.

taking. This can give you a rough idea of what's out there, and will often reveal something, say a minute mayfly, where you thought there was nothing. Binoculars will also let you sort out masking hatches. It's quite common to be frustrated by trout feeding on a hatch of size-16 mayflies, only to put the binoculars up and discover a fleet of size 20s mixed among them. It seems that the smaller ones are almost always preferred by selective trout, which appear to be taking the larger ones but are not.

Car-Trunk Items: We always keep either a commercial hoop kick net, made specifically for collecting aquatic insects, or a simple handmade kick-screen net in the car to collect bottom samples, and a flat-bottomed white pan in which to observe them. We also carry an aerial net, additional alcohol-filled vials, and pre-cut labels.

The best commercial kick net is a bit expensive ($35-$50) and available only from a few biological supply houses. It will have a handle like a broom, with a twelve- to eighteen-inch heavy-wire hoop attached. The bottom of the hoop, where it contacts the streambed, is straight. It will have a twelve-inch-deep bag made of 24 to 32 meshes-per-inch netting sewn to the hoop, reinforced with canvas around the opening.

It's easy and almost as effective to make your own kick-screen net. Simply cut a three-foot-square section of fiberglass window screening and staple the ends to 3/4-inch dowels four feet long. Leave three inches of dowel exposed at the bottom end of each leg, below the screening, to dig into the stream bottom.

To use the commercial hoop net or your kick-screen net, hold it firmly on the bottom in a current, then stand upstream and shuffle your feet in the substrate. Kick gravel and weeds, and try to work under some larger stones and lift them up, roll them over, with your toes. The most tenacious insects will be dislodged and swept into the net. This method is not hit-or-miss like hand collecting, where the most agile insects simply swim away. Most everything that lives down there will be caught in the net. When you are finished, lift the net carefully from the water in the upstream direction so nothing can swim out, and take it ashore to examine it. On a rich river there will be an incredible array of critters flipping, crawling, and running across the meshes.

A long-handled hoop net can also be used to sample lakes and ponds. Swish it through vegetation, over the bottom, or along undercut banks. It will often come up squirming with exactly the animal you need to imitate. Your favorite fly shop or catalog will stock various collecting nets that fold neatly and store easily. Some are designed to carry conveniently in the back pocket of your vest. You can also buy a mesh net the right size to fit inside the hoop of your landing net, perfect if you carry a net when you're fishing. Since neither of us does, we're stuck with the aquarium net we carry in a vest pocket and the larger kick nets we carry in the rig.

No matter what you use for bottom sampling, always be sure to sample a wide variety of habitats. In running water, collect from riffles, runs, pools, margins, and vegetated areas. You'll find different insects in each. In stillwaters, sample the shallows, then the deepest part you can reach. Sweep clean gravel bottoms as well as bottom muck and decaying leaf packs. Be sure to swish the net through any rooted vegetation such as watercress and cattail stalks.

Use a white freezer pan, enamel tray, or plastic photo developing tray to examine the larger bottom samples you'll take with these nets. As with the white jar lid already mentioned for the vest, nymphs can be observed as they swim or crawl against the white background. Simply

Place your sample in a white pan or tray to sort out what you have collected.

shake the sample out of the net and into the pan, debris and all. Add water and watch patiently while the living beasts separate themselves out from inanimate pebbles, twigs, and vegetation.

A light aerial collecting net is best for sweeping duns and spinners out of the air, though a heavier hoop kick net will also work, but not as well. You can swing a light net with more speed, which is often necessary to capture dancing mayflies. A standard butterfly net with a deep bag is perfect for this. Try to make or buy one sturdy enough so you can beat brush with it. Swishing it through streamside grass and leaves, over conifer boughs, and across ferns will sometimes turn up quiescent mayflies on which trout might have been feeding recently, or might be about to feed upon soon. Thrashing sagebrush is one of our favorite sports along our home Deschutes, and often reveals the predominant insect that has been hatching, and therefore what trout have been eating, though it will be a stonefly or caddis as often as a mayfly. Match those if that's what you find in the meshes of your net.

Aerial collecting can also be accomplished with a quick swipe of your hat. A baseball cap works best, but we're not about to advise you to switch hat styles for this reason alone. Try what you wear and see how it works. Mayflies captured in an aerial net or hat will usually be stunned for a moment, then attempt to fly away. Either observe them quickly or coax them into your medicine bottle or film cannister.

Things Best Left at Home: Your budding insect collection will be kept at home. It will include the specimens, vialed and labelled, that you have collected over the years. It is amazing how valuable these will become as they accumulate over time.

How do you organize the collection? That's a problem we have not entirely solved. Ours is tangled. Looking at it theoretically, the best system would lay out the mayflies in the order they're covered in this book. If possible, keep specimens of each of the important stages of the hatches you encounter and find it important to match. The vials might be kept in boxes, drawers, or even on display. But do try to keep them organized.

Ideally a type-specimen collection, which is a systematic cataloguing of a perfect sample of each stage of each identified insect, is kept in disciplined order. Gathered and catalogued over many seasons, this sort of collection would have wonderful value. It would be a challenge, and also a pleasantry, to fill in the blanks as the seasons went along. It would be a benefit to have a fine specimen as a base point, as a visual and virtual reference, whenever you collected from a new piece of water, and wanted something to which you could compare the new samples you've gathered. Of course, you'd want to have a photograph as well, since the specimens themselves would have lost their true colors.

The most important part of any collection, next to the insects themselves, is the labels with them. No collection has any merit if you cannot look at it and know when and from what water each insect was taken. A correct label is made on white note-card paper with No. 2 lead pencil. Ink runs when wet. Each vial must be labelled, and each label should have the following information: county, state, stream or lake, exact location, date of collection, and the collector's name. On the back write the order, family, genus, or species, never taking it to a level where you are guessing.

Guesses are fine for your files or notebooks, when identified as guesses, but not for the label itself. Somebody might see the specimen and take your stab at its identity for granted when it might well be wrong. That

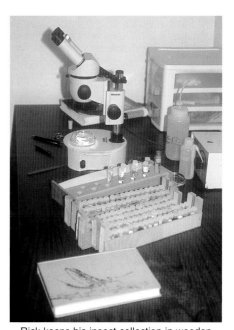

Rick keeps his insect collection in wooden trays that are easy to build yourself.

SAMPLE OF A CORRECT LABEL

Front:
Clatsop Co., Oregon
Youngs River 2 miles above falls
15 Sept., 1995
Coll. by D. Hughes

Back:
Order: Ephemeroptera
Family: Ephemerellidae
Genus: *Drunella*
Species: *doddsi*
Det. by R. Hafele

sort of mistake is what makes fly-fishermen, in their role as amatuer entomologists, unpopular with professional entomologists.

Place the finished label inside the vial with the specimens. At the same time be sure the vial is filled to the top with alcohol. An air bubble rolling back and forth as the vial is moved or examined can be just as damaging as a pebble. Each vial should be labelled on the day the collection is made. If you wait you will forget the pertinent data.

Your collection will be more valuable if you start a small card file system. Number each vial and cross reference it to a numbered card. Data that will not fit on the label can go on the card: weather, water and air temperatures, fishing conditions, time of emergence, and patterns which effectively matched the specimens. A notebook can be used instead of a file to record the same information. If you work with a computer, set up a system for cross-referencing and recording vital information. You'll soon be able to write the book on your own hatches, and that will be the most valuable book to your own fishing.

When collecting aquatic insects, always show the same respect for the environment that you do when you're fishing. Most healthy western rivers won't be hurt by collecting any more than they are by wading to fish them. But we have fragile systems, too. Show them respect, collect minimally and discriminately, and they will stay healthy and productive. It's also a good idea to check fish and game regulations, as some states require a permit, usually free, to collect aquatic insects.

Respect the insects as well. They are lives. Don't hesitate to collect and preserve those that will inform your tying and fishing. But release back into their own environment any that you have no reason to keep. It's a bit like catch and release in fishing. You can also use the release of captured specimens to improve your fishing. Place a mayfly nymph that you've netted back into the water where you collected it, after you've observed its size, form, and color, and watch the way it swims or crawls away, or simply freezes and tumbles with the current. The way it moves, or does not, will tell you how to fish its imitation.

Chapter 3

Recognizing Mayflies

Mayfly nymphs are far more varied than the adults that spring from them. This makes sense. The immature stages must adapt to many different aquatic environments, from stillwaters and placid flats to bounding riffles and brutal cascades, in order to survive in them. They take on a variety of forms. The adults live in the single atmospheric environment, and have one mission: to procreate and die, usually very quickly. Adult mayflies are much more similar in function, and therefore structure, than mayfly nymphs.

Mayflies, like all insects, are identified by the differences in their structures. Mayfly nymphs can be separated, at most of the levels important to fly-fishermen, much more easily than adults, due to those greater differences in adaptations. If you identify a nymph, then associate it with the dun that emerges from it, you've identified the dun by association. This is a valid, scientific means of establishing the identity of an insect.

A further advantage of this method is that cast shucks of mayfly nymphs retain their identifying characteristics, even after the dun has escaped. Thus when you're standing in a stream, fishing for trout, and mayflies suddenly begin emerging all around you, but you're not sure what they are, you can put the brakes on your fishing for a moment, get out your aquarium net, and collect the cast shucks that will be drifting either where the duns are hatching or collecting in shallows and sidewaters.

With experience and the magnifying glass or loupe we've advised you to carry, you can identify a cast shuck to the most important level, usually genus, and get right back to fishing with some certain knowledge about the hatch over which you're casting. Preserve those shucks in a vial, along with three or four duns, and you might be able to identify them right to species when you get them home and are able to reference their characteristics to this book.

In much the same way, if you would like to determine what the spinner looks like, collect a few duns without damaging them, and keep them in rearing chambers for a couple of days. These need be no more than film cannisters or Styrofoam cups with holes punched in the lids. When the duns make that final molt, you'll have spinners that are clearly the same species.

Since professional entomologists make most positive identifications of mayfly species by referring to male spinners, usually by dissecting their reproductive parts, these spinners that you collect can have value to science. Their value is increased if you've kept careful labels in all vials, and if you've collected nymphs or cast shucks, duns, and then the associated spinners.

The value to you, as an angler, is the knowledge that the presence of a certain nymph will lead to a hatch of a specific dun, which can be matched with a particular fly pattern. The certainty of that dun also predicts the spinner fall that will follow. Association is one of the most valuable tools you can acquire as a curious fly-fisherman.

It's often overlooked that before you can identify an insect to species, it's necessary to identify it to order, family, and genus. These

If you can associate a mayfly dun with the cast nymphal shuck from which it just emerged, then it's often easier to identify the shuck to genus than it is to identify the dun. The shuck will retain all of the key characterstics of the nymph.

seem like minor details, but in truth they're not. A mayfly nymph and stonefly nymph of the same size, especially if small, will often have nearly the same shape, and move in much the same manner. At first glance it's easy to mistake a stonefly nymph for a mayfly.

The first step in learning to identify any insect, to any level, is to get beyond that first casual glance and begin observing the individual characteristics, the separating features, of whatever insect you've collected and would like to classify. That's where a magnifying glass or loupe helps, though it's not always necessary. That's also where we hope this book helps.

From many years teaching our workshop "Entomology and the Artificial Fly," which eventually became the notes and basis for *Western Hatches*, we came to realize that the most elemental question was always the same: "Is this a mayfly, stonefly, caddis, or something else?" That question is the rule rather than the exception, especially with nymphs. It's also where all identification must begin, for the professional entomologist as well as for the angler.

The purpose of this chapter is to unravel the basics, and help you separate mayflies from other insects with which you might confuse them. With an understanding of the life cycles of insects and some of their anatomical features, recognizing mayflies will become second nature, usually taking no more than that first streamside glance. That glance, given some knowledge and experience behind it, will automatically take in the important details that separate the orders.

Knowledge of life cycles and the basics of insect anatomy will provide the groundwork for identifying the families, genera, and species discussed in the following chapters. It will also help you understand and appreciate some of the remarkable adaptations aquatic insects have made to their unique environment.

Few animals undergo greater changes during their development than aquatic insects. The transformation of the worm-like caterpillar into the beautiful butterfly is familiar to us all. But the changes that occur among aquatic insects are more amazing. Immature stages live under water. They are used to slow changes in temperature, and get their oxygen directly from the water. Adults are not only different in form, but also in their adaptations to the conditions around them. They emerge into a terrestrial environment, with rapidly fluctuating temperatures, and must breathe in a gaseous as opposed to a liquid environment. The transition appears to be abrupt, taking place at emergence, but is actually accomplished over a long period of time, through the slower process of metamorphosis.

Metamorphosis refers to the changes that occur during an insect's life cycle. Despite the great diversity among aquatic insects, their life cycles can be grouped into three types of metamorphosis: *no metamorphosis, incomplete metamorphosis*, and *complete metamorphosis.*

Insects with no metamorphosis (ametabolous) do not change in form during their life cycle. Only a few primitive insects have no metamorphosis; none are important to fishermen. Those with incomplete metamorphosis (hemimetabolous), including mayflies and stoneflies, have three distinct stages of development: egg, nymph, and adult. Insects displaying complete metamorphosis (holometabolous) have four distinct stages of development: egg, larva, pupa, and adult. This group includes caddisflies and midges among others.

Incomplete metamorphosis probably evolved first, and thus is more primitive than complete metamorphosis. Incomplete metamorphosis does not allow for as much dramatic change in form between the aquatic and terrestrial stages of the insect. In other words, insects with incomplete metamorphosis look more alike in nymph and adult stages than those with complete metamorphosis, which with their extra pupal stage go through a more dramatic transformation.

An insect's outer covering, or *exoskeleton*, limits the growth of all immature insects, including mayfly nymphs. A new exoskeleton is formed periodically under the old one, which is then sloughed off, or molted. After each molt, growth proceeds to the limit of the new exoskeleton, then another molt occurs. The stages of growth between molts are called *instars*.

During each instar there is an increase in nymphal size. Various external changes also occur in insects with incomplete metamorphosis. Most noticeable is the development of wing pads, encasing the developing wings of the eventual adult. Look for them on fairly mature nymphs. Wing pads will not be developed at all, or at least not enough to notice, on early-instar nymphs.

Mature nymphs of some aquatic insect orders with incomplete metamorphosis resemble their forthcoming adult stage. This is especially true for the stoneflies: add wings to the nymph and it would look much like the adult. It is less true of mayflies. The mayfly nymph resembles the dun that will emerge from it only in superficial ways.

Complete metamorphosis is a later evolutionary development, with room for more change between the initial aquatic stage and the aerial adult. This has the benefit of allowing the immature stage to exploit a broader range of aquatic environments.

The initial stages of complete and incomplete metamorphosis are similar. After the egg incubates for a varying period, the immature insect—called a *larva* in orders with complete metamorphosis, a *nymph* in orders with incomplete metamorphosis—hatches and begins feeding. Larval and nymphal growth again proceed in a series of instars separated by molts.

As a worm-like caddis larva grows larger from instar to instar, its external features remain nearly the same. There is little or no resemblance to the adult stage, just as there is no similarity between a caterpillar and a butterfly. No development of external wing pads takes place. This lack of wing pads easily distinguishes larvae from nymphs, though you must remember that only mature nymphs display visible wing pads.

When mature, typically after eight or nine months, the larva does not transform directly into an adult caddis. Instead it changes into a pupal stage, still in the water. The caddis pupa is usually protected by a case lined with silk, fastened to the bottom, but the larvae of some aquatic insect orders hide in the substrate or even crawl out of the water and burrow into soft soil nearby before transformation to the pupal stage takes place.

Adult characteristics take shape during pupal development. External wing pads appear, legs change shape, antennae increase in size, and the reproductive organs develop. When the pupa is mature and time for emergence arrives, it cuts its way out of the pupal cell and swims or floats to the surface, often buoyed on the journey by a bubble of gas extruded between the pupal and adult exoskeletons.

In both complete and incomplete metamorphosis, variations in the duration of each stage, habitat preferences, and behavior are great between

A mayfly nymph will have visible wing pads throughout most of its underwater life, but they'll usually be the same color as the rest of the insect.

As the same nymph nears emergence, its wing pads darken. In your sampling, pay most attention to specimens nearest emergence, because they are most active, and most likely to be fed on by trout. They're also the most likely to produce fishable emergences of duns the same day, or in the next few days.

AQUATIC INSECT ORDERS WITH INCOMPLETE METAMORPHOSIS:
Ephemeroptera (Mayflies)
Plecoptera (Stoneflies)
Odonata (Dragonflies and
   Damselflies)
Hemiptera (Waterboatmen and
   Backswimmers)

AQUATIC INSECT ORDERS WITH COMPLETE METAMORPHOSIS:
Trichoptera (Caddisflies)
Megaloptera (Alderflies and
   Dobsonflies)
Coleoptera (Beetles)
Diptera (Midges, Mosquitoes, and
   Craneflies)

and sometimes even within each insect order. These differences will be detailed for each mayfly genera in later chapters.

Basic Insect Anatomy

The biggest stumbling block for amateur entomologists is the terminology used by professionals. You don't need to learn a new language; you do need to learn a few new words. Insects are different from all other animals. No others have six legs, four wings, and ten-segmented abdomens. Describing the unique features of insects, in order to be able to identify them, requires some special terms.

The difference between two taxonomic categories can be small, resting on the number of tails or the number of segments in each leg. Understanding a bit of basic insect anatomy is easy, and essential in order to distinguish between them. With a little fireside study added to a lot of streamside practice, recognizing the different orders and even families of aquatic insects will become second nature, and will often take but a glance at the characteristics—the unique features—of a specimen in order to recognize it to order and often family as well.

Certain characteristics of anatomy separate insects from other organisms that you might also collect in the aquatic environment. A typical insect can be recognized by:

1. Three major and usually distinct body divisions: head, thorax, and abdomen.
2. Three separate and usually distinct thoracic segments: prothorax (first, closest to the head), mesothorax (second), and metathorax (third).
3. Ten abdominal segments, though this number is reduced in some groups.
4. Six legs, one pair on each thoracic segment. (Some immature insects lack legs.)
5. Four wings, in two pairs, in most adult insects, though a few groups, including some important mayflies, have one pair, and rare insect groups lack wings.

Checking for these obvious characteristics will quickly separate insects from the few organisms with which they might be confused, such as crustaceans, spiders, mites, or underwater worms.

You are most likely to have trouble separating mayfly nymphs from stonefly nymphs. We've listed the characteristics of each below. If you ever collect an insect that you think is a mayfly nymph, but you cannot get it to fit any group in this book, check your original assumptions: assess the features of the natural against the following descriptions, and you might be surprised to discover it's a stonefly nymph. It has happened to one of your authors more often than he cares to confess.

Mayflies (Ephemeroptera)
Nymphs
1. Three tails, except members of the genera *Epeorus* and *Ironodes*, plus some species in the *Baetis* complex, which have only two.
2. Each leg with a single claw at the end.
3. Gills, usually plate-like, on abdominal segments only.

Note: It's possible to mistake mayfly nymphs for some small stonefly nymphs, but mayflies have gills on the abdomen, and stoneflies have them on the thorax if they have visible gills at all. Mayfly nymphs always have a single tarsal claw; stoneflies always have two.

Adults (both dun and spinner stages)
1. Two or three long tails.
2. Wings held vertically; front pair large and triangular, hind pair reduced or absent.
3. Body usually slender and delicate.

Stoneflies (Plecoptera)
Nymphs
1. Two stout tails of varying length.
2. Two claws at the end of each leg.
3. Gills often absent; when present appear on thorax.
Note: It's possible to confuse some smaller stonefly groups with mayfly nymphs, but again, stonefly gills are absent or on the thorax, not the abdomen, and there are two tarsal claws at the end of each leg.

Adults
1. Two tails. May be short and 1-segmented or long and multi-segmented.
2. Long antennae.
3. Four wings of equal length, held flat over the abdomen when at rest.

While it's easy, and becomes easier as you go along and look at the insects from time to time in the normal course of your fishing, separating the orders of insects is no place to make a mistake. Once you've identified an insect wrong at the highest level, it's impossible to key it out at any of the lower and more useful levels.

Once you're certain you've placed a mayfly specimen into the correct order, Ephemeroptera, then it's time to move on to the following chapters, and see where it fits into the world of mayflies, fly-fishing, and flies. It won't be long before you recognize mayflies, both nymphs and adults, at first sight, and you'll soon skip this chapter.

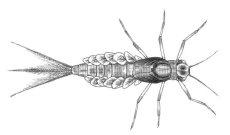

Mayfly nymph.

Mayfly adult.

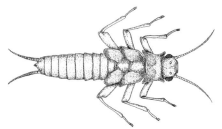

Stonefly nymph.

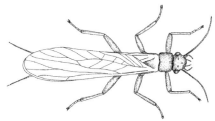

Stonefly adult.

COMMON ORDERS OF AQUATIC INSECTS

Nymphs and Larvae

Adults

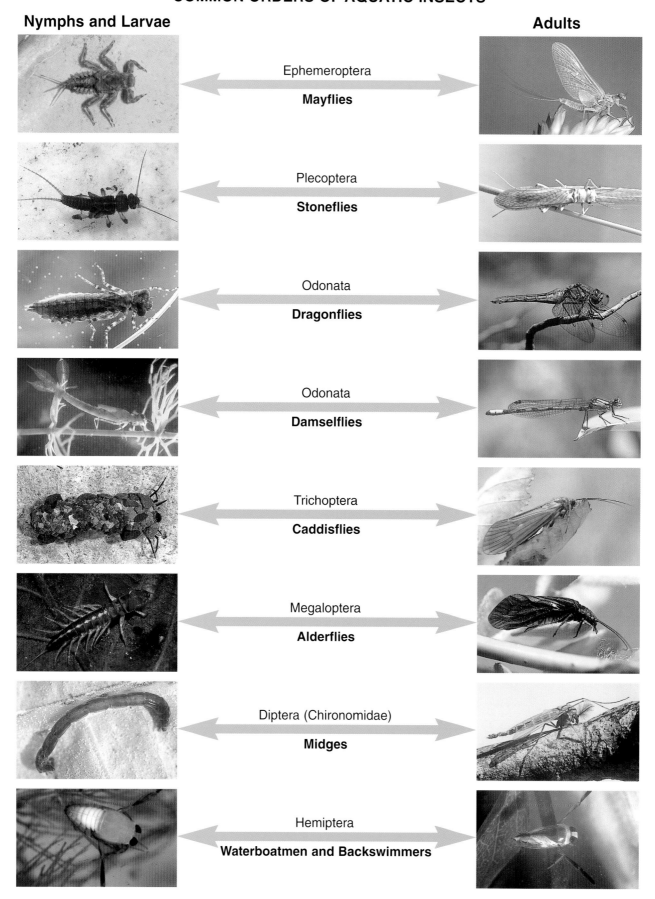

Ephemeroptera
Mayflies

Plecoptera
Stoneflies

Odonata
Dragonflies

Odonata
Damselflies

Trichoptera
Caddisflies

Megaloptera
Alderflies

Diptera (Chironomidae)
Midges

Hemiptera
Waterboatmen and Backswimmers

Chapter 4

About Mayflies

Mayflies were one of the earliest aquatic insect groups to evolve. In fact, they are one of the oldest of all insect groups, with their origins estimated to be some 270 million years ago, in the Permian era. The Ephemeroptera of today are considered some of the oldest examples of winged insects still surviving. We often muse that mayfly duns or spinners, looking much like those of today, might have landed to perch on the head of a *Tyrannosaurus rex* or the horn of a Triceratops, just as today they land on the hats of fly-fishers. Mayflies existed for some 200 million years before the first trout-like fish ever showed up to take floating duns off the surface.

Many ancestral characteristics are retained in present-day members of the mayfly order. Primitive wing venation, for example, gives their wings a fluted, accordion-like structure. These wings provide good vertical lift but poor forward flight. This results in the well-known rising and falling, yo-yo like dance of mating mayflies.

Their primitive wing-to-body attachment fixes the wings in the vertical position when they're at rest. Dragonflies and damselflies are the only other groups of insects that cannot fold their wings down flat on top of the abdomen when not in flight. The most unusual primitive characteristic of mayflies is their two separate winged stages: dun (subimago) and spinner (imago), with the final molt between. No other living insect has two distinct winged stages.

During their long evolution, mayflies adapted to almost every freshwater habitat. They are found throughout the world except for Antarctica, the extreme Arctic, and most small ocean islands. More than 600 species have been identified in North America, over 200 from the western United States and Canada. Great Britain has just forty-eight species. Mayflies are a perfect example of the complexity of western hatches.

Mayflies have incomplete metamorphosis. Their eggs are laid at the surface and sink to the bottom, or in a few cases the adult female dives or crawls to the bottom and deposits them there. Each egg is covered with a sticky substance, or with fine coiled filaments, that hold it to the substrate. Mayfly eggs hatch from a few minutes to several months after oviposition, the length of time varying widely with the species. Newly hatched nymphs are approximately 0.5mm long, about twice the width of the period at the end of this sentence. They begin feeding immediately on rooted plants, algae, or mosses. They are the primary herbivores of lakes and streams. Biologists often refer to mayflies as the cows of the freshwater ecosystem.

Mayfly nymphs can be grouped into four categories, *swimmers*, *crawlers*, *clingers*, and *burrowers,* based on their shape and behavior. These four mayfly divisions are not taxonomic. Instead they are based on the different behaviors of the nymphs, which are reflected in their shapes. Swimmer mayfly nymphs dart about like little minnows in both streams and stillwaters. Crawler nymphs move slowly about on the stream bottom, usually on the undersides of stones and in the cracks and crevices between them. Clinger nymphs are flattened and live compressed against bottom stones, always in moving water, often in the

The mayfly is the only insect with a final transformation from the dull-winged dun...

...to the glassy-winged and reproductive spinner.

PHOTOS BY KENSHIRO SHIMAZAKI, FROM HIS 1997 BOOK "A FLY FISHER'S VIEW (COURTESY OF FURAINOZASSHI MAGAZINE, JAPAN).

This remarkable set of photos shows three Japanese ephemerillid mayflies, closely related to our pale morning duns, lesser green drakes, and western green drakes, emerging by leaving the nymphal shuck on the bottom and rising to the surface as a dun (top photo), by escaping the nymphal shuck in the water column just short of the surface (middle photo), and by escaping the nymphal shuck in the surface film itself (bottom photo). The most interesting thing these photos revealed to your authors, is the closely-held posture of the dun wings after it has escaped the nymphal shuck, in top and middle photos. The wings are not "unfurling in the water, tossed by the currents" as we'd previously supposed. These photos indicate that the prolonged time spent on the surface by many mayfly duns is due to the need to erect the wings with fluids pumped into viens in the wings, and then for this fluid to harden before they're able to fly.

These photos were published in Kenshiro Shimazaki's beautiful and ground-breaking book *A Fly Fisher's View,* and are published here through the courtesy of Dave's favorite Japanese fly-fishing magazine, *FURAINO-ZASSHI.*

swiftest currents. Burrower nymphs dig tunnels into stream or lake beds, or bury themselves in bottom silts.

These four separate mayfly nymph types, because of their various behaviors and the different water types in which they live, make themselves available to trout in different ways in the nymph stage, and in some cases in the dun and spinner stages as well. They form the basis for the separate parts of any book about matching mayfly hatches. Your knowledge, and as a consequence your catch, will both be improved if you learn to identify nymphs as mayflies, and then to one of these four categories (see identification charts on pages 28 and 29). Each group will be covered in a separate part in this book.

As mayfly nymphs grow they molt twenty or more times. The typical nymph matures in about one year, although some require two or even three years and others only two or three months. Mature mayfly nymphs, those ready to emerge into winged adults, can be recognized by their large, dark wing pads.

Transformation from the nymph to the subimago, or dun, may occur on or near the bottom, in or a few inches under the surface film, or entirely out of the water on protruding plant stems, logs, or rocks. If it happens in the water, whether on or under the surface, the newly-winged duns remain on the surface until their wings are dry and they are capable of flight.

The change from nymph to dun is called an *emergence* or *hatch* by anglers. It can occur at any time of day, or even after dark. The exact time of emergence depends on the species, the time of year, and the weather on the day the hatch happens. Early afternoon emergence is typical during the cooler days of spring and fall; morning or evening emergence is more common during hot weather in summer.

Mayfly duns fly to streamside vegetation after emergence and hide like miniature winged mummies until their final molt to the imago, or spinner, stage. In some groups this holdover area is no farther than the nearest bank-side grasses. In others it is far enough up and over streamside trees and into the surrounding hills that even after a heavy hatch you'll search but find no duns nearby.

Mayflies are not capable of mating until after the molt to the imago, or spinner. This final transformation takes place from a few minutes to several days after emergence as subimagos, with the average being one to two days.

Spinners, after casting the dun skin, have shinier, more reflective body colors than duns, and have *hyaline*, or clear, wings rather than the opaque-colored wings of the duns. Both duns and spinners live solely for reproduction. They are unable to eat, having lost all functioning mouthparts during their emergence from the nymph. They have no digestive organs. Their abdomens become repositories for eggs in the females, sperm in the males.

Male spinners gather in swarms, doing their up-and-down dance, waiting for receptive females to enter the swarm. This might take place at any time of day, depending on the species involved and the weather of the moment. Swarms generally form over water or along the edges of the stream, but at times form miles from the nearest stream or lake. Mating mayflies often mistake nearby asphalt roads for the streams from which they emerged, which is unfortunate for the eggs of the next mayfly generation.

When a female flies into a swarm of males, they all rush to be the one to fertilize her. On rare occasions, when a mating swarm is heavy,

MAYFLY LIFE CYCLE

In the typical mayfly life cycle, all growth takes place in the nymph stage, over a period of nearly a year. When mature and ready for emergence, nymphs generally move to favorable positions along the streambottom or near the banks, and in some cases gather in great numbers for a massed hatch.

*Actual emergence can take place in one of three ways. The nymph can leave the streambottom, as in **A**, swim and drift toward the surface, where emergence can be a few inches beneath the surface or, as illustrated, in the surface film itself. Many mayfly groups emerge from the nymph stage along the bottom, as in **B**, and the dun struggles to the surface, buoyed by gases trapped in the new wings. Some mayfly species defend themselves against trout predation during emergence by crawling out on protruding sticks, reed stems, or rocks, as in **C**, where emergence takes place on land rather than the water.*

*After the dun emerges from the nymphal cuticle, it sits on the water or streamside structure until its wings are inflated, at which time it flies to vegetation and usually remains hidden for one or two days—there are exceptions that mate in half an hour and others that live up to four days. At the end of this waiting period, the dun casts its outer skin, molting into the reproductive spinner, as in **D**.*

*Mating takes place in the air **E**, usually in swarms, or spinner flights, after which most females return to vegetation briefly. They return to the stream or stillwater and drop their eggs in clusters, or dip to the surface, as in **F**, and wash them into the water. After laying their eggs the females drop to the water, surrender to the spent-wing position, and die. In some species the females are joined on the water by the males, though as many or even more males return to vegetation and expire where trout cannot get at them.*

Each of these parts of the life cycle must be fished differently, and with different sets of flies. Each manner of emergence presents different challenges to the angler attempting to take trout feeding selectively while a hatch is happening. If you're observant, you'll solve most situations easily.

you'll see what looks like a comet driving through it. This is a single female and the rush of males surrounding her, each striving to be the fortunate one to pass on its DNA. Mating occurs in the air, in flight. Copulation is rapid, fertilization being completed in the time it takes the male and female to fall a few feet in the air. Some females then fly to streamside vegetation to wait while their eggs ripen, which may take less than an hour in many species to a couple of days in others. A few species are ready to lay eggs immediately after mating.

The eggs are laid in clusters of several hundred each. They may be dropped from a few feet above the water or let loose on the water's surface as the females dip their abdomens to the water. In a few cases, the females crawl under water, down the sides of rocks or logs, and deposit their eggs directly on the bottom.

After all of their eggs have been released, flying females usually fall to the water's surface and die. Their wings are at first held upright, like those of duns, but as they lose energy the dying spinner's wings collapse through a forty-five-degree position, called *semi-spent*, to the most common position, with their wings flat on the surface, or *spent*. The process of egg-laying and dropping to die on the water's surface is known as a spinner fall. The number of spent spinners on the surface can be prodigious, and many are sipped from the surface by feeding trout. Others are swept beneath the surface in riffles and broken runs, to drown

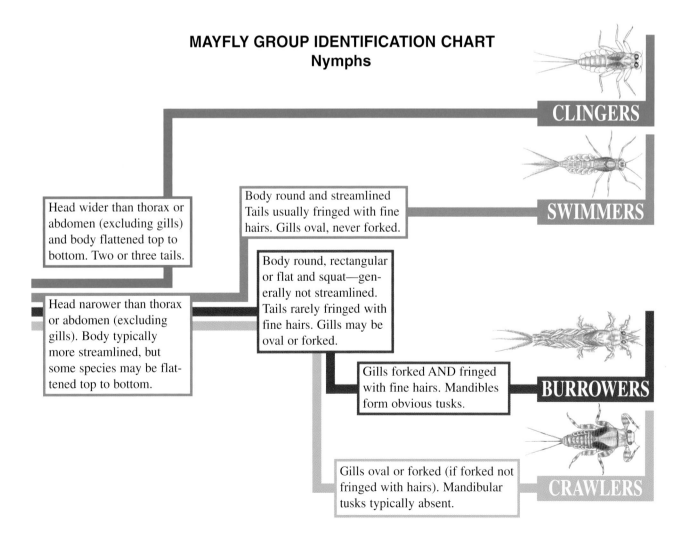

MAYFLY GROUP IDENTIFICATION CHART
Nymphs

CLINGERS

SWIMMERS

BURROWERS

CRAWLERS

Head wider than thorax or abdomen (excluding gills) and body flattened top to bottom. Two or three tails.

Head narower than thorax or abdomen (excluding gills). Body typically more streamlined, but some species may be flattened top to bottom.

Body round and streamlined Tails usually fringed with fine hairs. Gills oval, never forked.

Body round, rectangular or flat and squat—generally not streamlined. Tails rarely fringed with fine hairs. Gills may be oval or forked.

Gills forked AND fringed with fine hairs. Mandibles form obvious tusks.

Gills oval or forked (if forked not fringed with hairs). Mandibular tusks typically absent.

if they have not already expired on the surface. These submerged spinners are often eaten by trout feeding just inches deep.

Male spinners, after mating or failing to, generally fly back to streamside vegetation before dying. When trout feed on spinners it's common to mistake the males in a swarm for the insects the trout are taking. Trout almost always feed on females. Male and female mayfly spinners of the same species can be quite different in color and slightly different in size or shape. It is critical, when matching mayfly spinners, that you collect specimens of females off the water, and base your imitation on them, rather than collecting and matching the more visible males in the air.

The combined mayfly winged stages, dun and spinner, may live as briefly as a few hours, or as long as a week or two, but normally it's two to three days. The order derives its name, Ephemeroptera, *short-lived winged insects*, from this ephemeral existence as aerial adults.

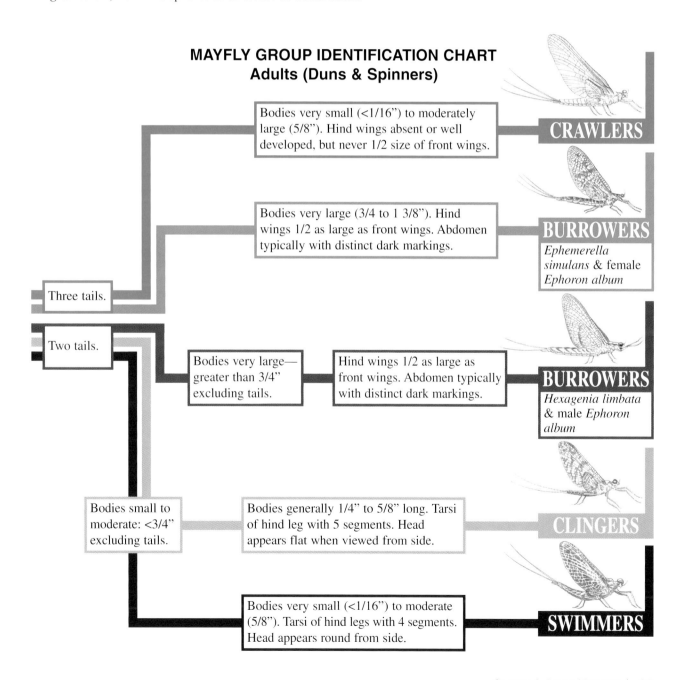

MAYFLY GROUP IDENTIFICATION CHART
Adults (Duns & Spinners)

Three tails.

Bodies very small (<1/16") to moderately large (5/8"). Hind wings absent or well developed, but never 1/2 size of front wings. → **CRAWLERS**

Bodies very large (3/4 to 1 3/8"). Hind wings 1/2 as large as front wings. Abdomen typically with distinct dark markings. → **BURROWERS** *Ephemerella simulans* & female *Ephoron album*

Two tails.

Bodies very large— greater than 3/4" excluding tails. Hind wings 1/2 as large as front wings. Abdomen typically with distinct dark markings. → **BURROWERS** *Hexagenia limbata* & male *Ephoron album*

Bodies small to moderate: <3/4" excluding tails.

Bodies generally 1/4" to 5/8" long. Tarsi of hind leg with 5 segments. Head appears flat when viewed from side. → **CLINGERS**

Bodies very small (<1/16") to moderate (5/8"). Tarsi of hind legs with 4 segments. Head appears round from side. → **SWIMMERS**

Chapter 5

Timing and Importance of Mayfly Hatches

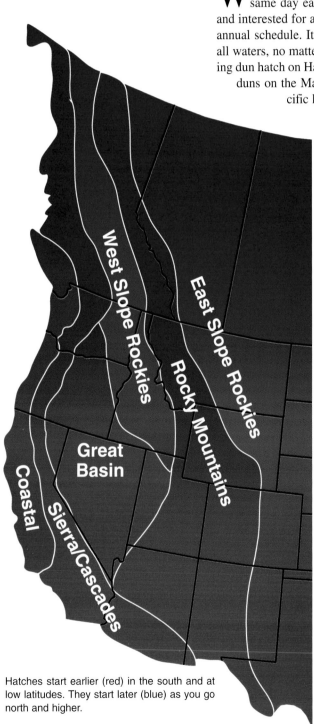

Hatches start earlier (red) in the south and at low latitudes. They start later (blue) as you go north and higher.

We'd all like mayfly hatches to be a bit more predictable, to begin on the same day each year, peak a precise number of days later, keep trout up and interested for a known number of days or even weeks, then taper off on an annual schedule. It would be nice if each species hatched at the same time on all waters, no matter how distant and scattered, so the arrival of the pale morning dun hatch on Hat Creek in California meant trout would be sipping the same duns on the Madison in Montana. Vacations would be planned around specific hatches, but we've found it's better to be prepared and happy to meet any hatch that might be happening, rather than try to aim trips at specific hatches on certain waters, only to be disappointed when we get there and the insects are not.

The West is too large, too varied, and has too many mayfly species to fit them all, or even any one of them, into neat little blocks of days on any calendar. Even if it weren't for more than a thousand miles in north-south latitude and nearly ten thousand feet of difference in elevation, annual weather cycles would make it impossible to predict any hatch precisely. A warm winter and spring might move a hatch up a week or two; a cold winter and spring might delay it that much more.

Still, there is some predictability to hatches. Given similar weather conditions, they'll hatch at somewhat similar times from year to year. They'll hatch earlier at low elevations, where things warm up earlier, and later at high elevations, where warmth arrives later. They'll begin sooner in the south than they will in the north, given that the elevation remains the same.

We've arrived at a map of the West that we hope will help you understand hatch timing, though we don't intend it as a tool on which to predict the right time to take your vacation. But it might help you understand that if you fish an important hatch of blue-winged olives in early April in the southern Rocky Mountains, you might be able to fish the same hatch a month or so later in the northern Rockies. If you have hot fishing over pale morning duns along the coast in June, you won't be surprised to bump into the same insect enticing trout in July on streams along the Front Ranges, in the far eastern part of our extensive West.

Daily emergence timing tends to depend on the weather, and seasonal changes in daily temperatures. If we were to write a general rule, it would be that a given hatch tends to come off in the warmest part of the day in the cool days of late spring and late fall, and tends toward morning or evening in the hotter days of late spring, summer, and early fall. But many insects have short emergence periods, and come off at the same times of day through-out their entire hatch. Other insects prefer certain times of day and rarely vary from them, for example Tricos in the morning hours and brown drakes at or after dark. So we've drawn up an emergence table for each insect covered, placed with the data on that insect in each appropriate chapter. The sample shown here is of the *Baetis* complex, a drawn-out and important hatch that dis-plays the typical behavior of hatching at mid-day when the season is cool, and late in the day when the weather is warm.

The shadings of this emergence chart show when the hatch is most impor-tant, which does not mean that it's at the best time of day for anglers, rather that it's most abundant and therefore most likely to be fed upon selectively by trout. In the sample you'll notice that hatches of *Baetis* tend to be heaviest in late win-ter and early spring, then again in the center of fall. So they're most abundant at those times of year when they're hatching in the warmest part of the day, and of less importance when they're hatching toward evening.

Like the earlier map showing approximate emergence times over the geog-raphy of the West, these daily emergence times must be viewed only as rough guidelines. If you encounter trout feeding selectively on any insect, at any time of day, that's when it's most important, and that's when you'd better match it. In our unruly West, exceptions are the rule, not the proof of the rule.

When an insect hatch is happening, and trout are focusing on it and ignoring all else, including your imitations that fail to match it, then that hatch, no matter how rare and obscure, is the most important hatch in all the world to you. That's

BAETIS COMPLEX EMERGENCE TABLE

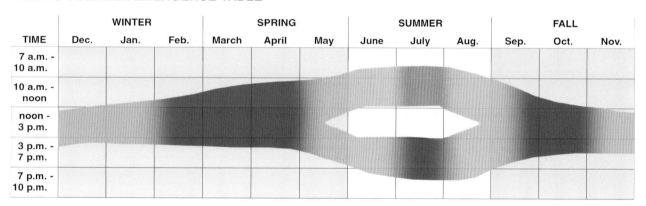

TIME	WINTER			SPRING			SUMMER			FALL		
	Dec.	Jan.	Feb.	March	April	May	June	July	Aug.	Sep.	Oct.	Nov.
7 a.m. - 10 a.m.												
10 a.m. - noon												
noon - 3 p.m.												
3 p.m. - 7 p.m.												
7 p.m. - 10 p.m.												

why you carry all those flies in your boxes, including some you rarely or never use. But there are western mayfly hatches that you're almost certain to run into if you get out on the water even a few days a year. You don't need to schedule any trips to find trout feeding selectively on blue-winged olives. If you fish ponds and lakes, then you'd have to almost calculate your timing carefully to avoid *Callibaetis*.

We've constructed a Hatch Importance Ranking Table (see page 34) to give you an idea of which hatches you're most likely to encounter, and at the same time point out which might be less important to imitate. The ratings are based on distribution, behavior, and timing. These factors combined affect how available to fish different hatches are, and thus their importance to fishers. The criteria, however, are subjective. We travel a lot, and run into some of the insects everywhere. If you fish a specific set of home waters, and one of the rarest mayflies happens to be important there, you'll think we're full of fish pellets and be right about it. In general, however, insects that are the most widespread, abundant, and available to trout are the ones you should imitate in the range of flies that you carry constantly in your boxes. Those that are important only at rare times, or on scattered waters, are less important to imitate, again unless you bump into trout taking them selectively, at which time you might be able to buy the right flies locally, take time to tie them, or even modify something else already in your fly box so that it works in this emergency.

Key Characteristics of a Hatch

After considerable debate we came up with nine characteristics that we felt most influenced an insect's importance to fly-fishers. We also devised a way to score these characteristics on a scale from one to five, so we could compare the importance of different insects in a consistent manner.

When combined, a single importance rating score can be calculated. Granted, it's a subjective process. However, a lot of understanding about these traits does exist, and it's possible to make good estimates, so that we can at least remove some of the mystery behind why a few hatches are called "super" and most others are not.

Distribution
• Widespread (5 points): These insects are abundant over a wide range of habitats and a broad geographic area in the West.
• Common (4 points): Common species occur across a wide area and range of habitats, but not always in large numbers.
• Scattered (3 points): These are species that occur in more limited types of habitats and therefore scattered locations.
• Isolated (2 points): These insects may be abundant, but only occur in small isolated areas.
• Rare (1 point): Found only in isolated areas and are never abundant.

Abundance during emergence
• Heavy (5 points): Adult emergence is concentrated and produces heavy hatches with strong surface feeding activity by fish.
• Abundant (4 points): Adult emergence is concentrated, but not as heavy or consistent as above.
• Modest (3 points): Adult emergence is not highly concentrated, but still enough to produce surface-feeding activity.
• Trickling (2 points): Trickling hatches are sparse and typically produce sparse or inconsistent surface-feeding activity.
• Individual (1 point): In these cases adult emergence is sporadic at best, resulting in little or no surface activity.

Emergence type
• Mid-water/slow (5 points): This refers to those species that emerge in open water with slow current, and are readily available to feeding fish.
• Mid-water/fast (4 points): While still important and available to fish, species that emerge in fast water are a little less easily taken by fish.
• Edges/slow (3 points): Some species emerge only along the edges of streams or lakes, perhaps to avoid feeding fish. When this occurs in areas with slow currents fish are still able to locate and feed on them.
• Edges/fast (2 points): When emergence along the edge of a stream or river occurs in fast water fish will rarely be able to feed on them.
• Crawl out (1 point): Adults emerge after the nymphs have crawled out of the water. Fish feed only on duns blown in by the wind.

Emergence time
• Mid-day (5 points): Those species that emerge from 10 a.m. to 3 or 4 p.m. have evolved to fit the biorhythm of anglers.

- Early or late with long emergence period (4 points): Only emerge in the morning or evening, but their activity lasts several hours, giving anglers plenty of time to fish over them.
- Early or late with short emergence period (3 points): Emerge in the morning or evening, but only for a short time period.
- Dawn or dusk (2 points): Have pushed their emergence to the last or first rays of light in the evening or morning.
- Night (1 point): We know a few artists who prefer working—and fishing— all night, but for us these species just deserve a "1."

Emergence duration:
- Multiple seasons per year (5 points): The more often fish and anglers find a species emerging, the more important it will be to imitate.
- Well-defined long hatch period (4 points): Species with well-defined long hatch periods are just a step behind those with multiple hatches.
- Well-defined short hatch period (3 points): A short hatch period means anglers are more likely to miss the best fishing. But if you hit it at the right time you won't really care.
- Poorly-defined long hatch period (2 points): A good emergence one day, then nothing for a week, then another 3 days of good fishing.
- Poorly-defined short hatch period (1 point): It's simply too difficult to predict when these species will hatch to make them important.

Nymph behavior/availability
- Excellent (5 points): Nymph behavior is active and makes them readily available to fish.
- Good (4 points): Nymphs are available, but not as frequently.
- Moderate (3 points): Nymphs are only occasionally available to fish.
- Slight (2 points): Nymphs are only rarely available to fish.
- Poor (1 point): Nymphs are almost never available to fish.

Emerger behavior/availability
- Excellent (5 points): Emergence behavior is active and makes them readily available to fish.
- Good (4 points): Emergence behavior exposes species to fish, but not as frequently as those above.
- Moderate (3 points): Emergers only occasionally available to fish.
- Slight (2 points): Emergers rarely available to fish.
- Poor (1 point): Emergers almost never available to fish.

Dun behavior/availability
- Excellent (5 points): Duns remain on the surface long periods and in open water and are readily available to fish.
- Good (4 points): Duns are available but not as readily as those above.
- Moderate (3 points): Duns are only occasionally available to fish.
- Slight (2 points): Duns are only rarely available to fish.
- Poor (1 point): Duns are almost never available to fish.

Spinnner behavior/availability
- Excellent (5 points): Spinners remain on the surface for long periods and in open water and are readily available to fish.
- Good (4 points): Spinners available but not as readily as those above.
- Moderate (3 points): Spinners are only occasionally available to fish.
- Slight (2 points): Spinners are only rarely available to fish.
- Poor (1 point): Spinners are almost never available to fish.

HATCH IMPORTANCE RANKING CRITERIA

CRITERIA/SCORE	5	4	3	2	1	
Distribution: (within Western waters)	widespread	common	scattered	isolated	rare	
Abundance:	heavy	abundant	modest	trickling	individual	
Emergence type:	mid-water/slow	mid-water/fast	edges/slow	edges/fast	crawls out	
Emergence time:	mid-day	early and/or late over long period	early and/or late over short period	dawn or dusk	night	
Emergence duration:	multiple seasons per year	well-defined long hatch period	well-defined short hatch period	poorly-defined long hatch period	poorly-defined short hatch	
(Behavior/Availability) Nymph:	excellent	good	moderate	slight	poor	
(Behavior/Availability) Emerger:	excellent	good	moderate	slight	poor	
(Behavior/Availability) Dun:	excellent	good	moderate	slight	poor	
(Behavior/Availability) Spinner:	excellent	good	moderate	slight	poor	
Totals:						

Excellent: readily available to trout; **good:** often available to trout; **moderate:** sometimes available; **slight:** infrequently available; **poor:** rarely available.

HATCH IMPORTANCE RANKING TABLE

HATCH	Importance Rating	Distribution	Abundance	Emergence Type	Emergence Time	Emergence Duration	Availability: Nymph	Availability: Emerger	Availability: Dun	Availability: Spinner
Baetis	43	5	5	4.5	5	5	5	5	5	3.5
Ephemerella inermis	41.5	5	5	4.5	5	4	4.5	5	5	3.5
Callibaetis	41	5	4.5	5	5	5	3	5	5	3.5
Smaller *Drunella*	35	4	4	5	5	3.5	3	4	4	2.5
Rhithrogena	34	4.5	4	4	5	4	2.5	4	5	1
Trichorythodes	33	3.5	5	5	3	4.5	1	3	3	5
Paraleptophlebia	33	4	4	3	5	5	2	3	4	3
Greater *Drunella*	32	3.5	3	4.5	5	3	3	4	5	1
Hexagenia limbata	28	2	4	5	2	3	1	4	4	3
Siphlonurus	25.5	3	5	1	2	3	3.5	1	2	5
Heptagenia complex	26	4.5	3	3.5	3	2	2	3	3	2
Timpanoga	25	3	3	3	5	3	1	2	4	1
Epeorus	25	4	2	4	5	2	1	2.5	3	1.5
Serratella tibialis	24	3	2	4	5	2	1	2	3	2
Cinygmula	23	3	2.5	3.5	4.5	1.5	1	2	3	2
Ephemera simulans	21	1	3	3.5	2	2	1	3.5	2.5	2.5
Ameletus	20	3	2	1	5	2	2	1	2	2
Attenella	19	1.5	1.5	3.5	3	2	1	2	3	1.5
Caenis	18	2	4	1	2	3	1	1	1	3
Isonychia	15	2	2.5	1	2.5	2	2	1	1	1
Leptophlebia	14	1	1.5	2.5	2.5	1.5	1	1	2	1
Ephoron album	13.5	1	3.5	3	1	1	1	1	1	1
Caudatella	13.5	1	1	3.5	3	1	1	1	1	1

Most Important	40-45
Very Important	30-39
Modest Importance	20-29
Rarely Important	<20

This table rates the importance for all the mayflies covered throughout the book. Individual hatch importance tables are provided for each hatch in the chapters that follow.

Part II:
MAYFLY SWIMMERS

Introduction

Swimmer mayfly nymphs are active in the water, darting from place to place in aquatic plants and algae, submerged brush tangles, around sunken logs, in undercut banks, and along the open stream bottom, swimming from stone to stone. They are shaped by this agile lifestyle. The body is slightly tapered from head to tail, streamlined like a fish for efficient movement through water. The tails of most swimmer nymphs are fringed with fine interlocking hairs. When these tails are held together they form a paddle-like surface, which supplies much of the swimming insect's thrust.

The swimming motion of these nymphs is an up-and-down flipping, much like the tail movement of a dolphin or whale. This gives you one clue to quick recognition: when they're seined in a net or held in your hand, swimmer nymphs frequently flip and flop like minnows removed from water. When you collect insects and wonder what they might be, tweezer them into your palm, or even better a small white dish, add a few drops of water, and note their reaction. If they look and act like little fish out of water, they're very likely to be mayfly swimmer nymphs.

This recognition gives you a dramatic jump in your selection of appropriate imitations, and also informs you how to present those imitations. Slender, sparsely tied patterns, fished with subtle twitches or a swinging retrieve to capture the swimming movement of the naturals, work best for swimmers.

Swimmer mayfly nymphs are found in all fishable trout habitats, from slow pools, rapids, and riffles in all types of moving water, to nearly all lakes and ponds. Their numbers will be greatest where they have rooted vegetation or abundant algae for food, plus some sort of shelter from the blunt force of the current in moving water. Spring creeks and tailwater flats with moderate flows, and any moving water with lots of undercut banks, usually offer dense hatches of swimmer mayflies. They are also present in numbers sufficient to cause selective feeding by trout in many less vegetated and swifter freestone riffles and runs. Their wide distribution over such a wide variety of water types, combined with their active habits and often great numbers, makes swimmers one of the most important insect groups to both fish and fishermen.

Duns and spinners that emerge from swimmer nymphs have only two tails, as opposed to the three tails found on most mayflies in the nymph stage. This feature—two tails in the winged stages—is shared with all clinger and some burrower adults. It does, however, eliminate the crawlers, which always have three tails in both nymph and winged stages. Such significant features as two or three tails, which instantly allow you to narrow things down and eliminate large categories from consideration, are exactly the kinds of hints to look for as you begin to identify mayfly hatches in the following chapters.

Important Swimmers:
Family: Baetidae
> **Genus:** *Acentrella*
> *Baetis*
> *Callibaetis*
> *Diphetor*
> *Plauditus*

Family: Siphlonuridae
> **Genus:** *Siphlonurus*

Family: Ameletidae
> **Genus:** *Ameletus*

Family: Isonychiidae
> **Genus:** *Isonychia*

Chapter 6

Baetis (Blue-Winged Olives)

The family Baetidae represents the most complex and challenging family of mayflies for entomologists, and one of the most important to a fly-fisher's success. To entomologists this family is in taxonomic flux, some might even say chaos. In recent years major revisions have been made at the genus and species levels. For entomologists this creates a taxonomic challenge that only a few specialists of this family have the knowledge to handle. For anglers it creates a patchwork of new and sometimes confusing scientific names, names like *Acentrella, Diphetor,* or *Plauditus,* and the disappearance of old familiar names such as *Pseudocloeon.*

Sixteen genera and more than 60 species of Baetidae occur in the West. The distribution and importance of many species are poorly understood, largely due to the difficulty of telling one from another. To deal with this unruly group, your authors have highlighted some of the major genera and hatches, but have also lumped most into a catchall we call "the *Baetis* complex." Such complexity also accounts for much of the mystifying range of colors, sizes, and hatch periods of the mayflies known to most fly-fishers simply as *Baetis.*

FAMILY: BAETIDAE

Major Genera: *Baetis, Acentrella, Diphetor, Plauditus*
Western Species: 26 currently identified in the above genera
North America: 43
Key Western Species:
> *Baetis tricaudatus* (synonym: *Baetis vagans*)
> *Baetis bicaudatus* (synonym: *Baetis minimus*)
> *Acentrella turbida* (previously *Pseudocloeon turbidum* and
> > *P. carolina*)
> *Diphetor hageni* (previously *Baetis hageni;*
> > synonym *Baetis parvus*)

Other Important Western Species:
> *Diphetor devinctus* (previously *Baetis devinctus*)
> *Baetis flavistriga* (synonym: *Baetis phoebus*)
> *Plauditus parvulus* (previously *Pseudocloeon parvulum*)
> *Plauditus punctiventris* (previously *Baetis punctiventris;*
> > synonyms *Pseudocloeon edmundsi* and *P. anoka*)
> *Plauditus propinquus* (previously *Labiobaetis propinquus;*
> > synonym: *Baetis propinquus*)

Common Names: Blue-Winged olives, little olives, little blue duns, BWOs.

It's easy to tell from the above list of important western species why we refer to this group as the *Baetis* complex, or simply by their common name, blue-winged olives, often shortened to BWOs. *Complex* is an appropriate term. For anglers wishing to pin every hatch down to species, this group can be a big problem. More taxonomic changes are expected over the next few years. Fortunately for anglers, trout haven't been paying attention. They still feed on members of the complex whenever they get a chance at them, without bothering to identify them to species. Patterns devised under the old classifications work as well now as they did before. The insects themselves, while sporting new names, display the same old shapes, sizes, and colors, and hatch on their old waters according to the same annual and daily schedules.

We've listed the taxonomic revisions to help you correlate species names used in previous scientific and angling works to species names used today. The term *synonym* refers to names once used to describe separate species that are now considered a single species despite color and size differences throughout their range. The term *previously* indicates a species that has retained the same species name, but has been reclassified into a different genus, sometimes an old one, sometimes a new one.

The important thing to remember in dealing with the *Baetis* or blue-winged olive group is that fly patterns effective for one species will be just as effective for others. You will need to change the size and color as you encounter different species, but that is often just as true within the same species as you move from one stream to another, or even as you collect a single species from different sections up and down the same river system. We feel that the *Baetis* complex constitutes the most important group of western mayfly hatches. That makes it just about the most important of all western hatches. Blue-winged olives are so diverse, and so prolific, hatching on so many water types over such a long period of time, that they cause selective feeding more often than any other aquatic insect group. Perhaps only the chironomids, or midges, come close in diversity, abundance and availability. That is why we consider the *Baetis* complex so important.

Emergence and Distribution

The *Baetis* complex is a large and widely distributed group, found in great numbers in all of the western states and provinces, though only in moving waters. Although we've listed nine species above as being most important, any obscure species in the complex that has minor, sporadic, or local importance can hatch on any western water you happen to be fishing, and will be very important when it does if trout feed selectively on it. With proper adjustments in the size and color of your imitations, you'll always be able to match such a hatch with the same patterns you use for the more famous species.

Most of the time, you'll encounter one of the listed species. But you'll run into other members of the group often enough that we recommend you be content with identification to the *Baetis* complex level, for the best

***Baetis* Complex**   **HATCH IMPORTANCE SCORE: 43.0**

CRITERIA/SCORE	5		4		3		2		1	
Distribution: (within Western waters)	widespread	5.0	common		scattered		isolated		rare	
Abundance:	heavy	5.0	abundant		modest		trickling		individual	
Emergence type:	mid-water/slow	4.5	mid-water/fast		edges/slow		edges/fast		crawls out	
Emergence time:	mid-day	5.0	early and/or late over long period		early and/or late over short period		dawn or dusk		night	
Emergence duration:	multiple seasons per year	5.0	well-defined long hatch period		well-defined short hatch period		poorly-defined long hatch period		poorly-defined short hatch	
(Behavior/Availability) Nymph:	excellent	5.0	good		moderate		slight		poor	
(Behavior/Availability) Emerger:	excellent	5.0	good		moderate		slight		poor	
(Behavior/Availability) Dun:	excellent	5.0	good		moderate		slight		poor	
(Behavior/Availability) Spinner:	excellent		good	3.5	moderate		slight		poor	
Totals:		39.5		3.5		0.0		0.0		0.0

understanding of the insect that is hatching in front of you, and then focus your effort on finding an appropriate imitation and fishing it with the most productive presentation. In our own fishing, when faced with an obvious blue-winged olive hatch, we get busy enjoying our fishing and don't worry much about which species it might be within the complex.

Hatches in this complex can occur at any time throughout the year, depending on the species, geographic area, and current weather conditions. Several species have two or three generations per year. Adults of these species emerge in the winter and spring, many times repeating in summer, and then following with a final emergence in late fall. The number of generations, and their exact timing, depends on the species and on the water temperature regimens of the particular stream in which they're found.

Because of the large number of species, their multiple generations, and the varying habitats in which they thrive, it's impossible to predict hatch periods for blue-winged olives across the entire West. They must be studied and timed on specific waters before they can be predicted with any degree of accuracy. Their abundance and diversity make them important at one time or another in almost every western river and stream.

In our own fishing, we have found members of this complex to be most important in early spring, before runoff, with a short period of importance in early summer, just after runoff, followed by a resurgence of importance in fall. We've fished their hatches as early as February on tailwater streams, most often in April and May on spring creeks, tailwaters, and pre-runoff freestone streams, and again in September and October on all types of moving waters. But these things must all be calculated against the fact that the seasons begin and end in western states and provinces at different times as altitude and latitude change.

A species that hatches beginning in February or March in California, Arizona, or New Mexico and has three generations per year in those states, might begin in May or June in Montana or Alberta, and have just two generations. That's why you can encounter *Baetis* hatching on any day during the trout fishing season, and will find yourself to be a far luckier fisherman if you're prepared for their hatches at all times.

Daily emergence times of the various species in the blue-winged olive complex change somewhat with the seasons, but are typically in the warmer parts of the day. In early spring, they'll hatch from early to late afternoon, when the air and water are warmest. Mid-summer hatches might move toward morning or more commonly evening, when conditions are cooler. Fall hatches move back toward the warmest hours again, occurring between late morning and early afternoon.

It is well documented, among scientists and anglers alike, that the heaviest and most prolonged hatches of members of this complex occur

BAETIS COMPLEX EMERGENCE TABLE

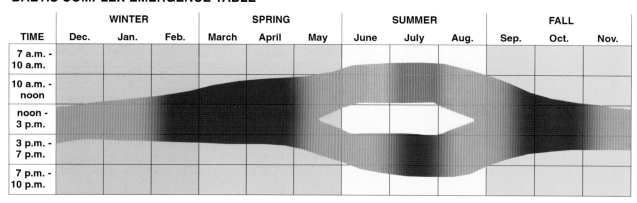

TIME	WINTER			SPRING			SUMMER			FALL		
	Dec.	Jan.	Feb.	March	April	May	June	July	Aug.	Sep.	Oct.	Nov.
7 a.m. - 10 a.m.												
10 a.m. - noon												
noon - 3 p.m.												
3 p.m. - 7 p.m.												
7 p.m. - 10 p.m.												

A typical *Baetis* day on the South Fork of the Snake River: cloudy and dark, with occasional rain.

on cool, overcast, and even wet and snowy days. On sunny and warm days the hatch is often truncated into a brief time span. This is common throughout the mayflies, and among other aquatic insects as well. On a cloudy day you'll get a trickling hatch that can go on for two to four hours, with trout up and feeding all that time. On a bright day the hatch will often be heavy, but might last only half an hour to an hour. If you fail to notice the small blue-winged olives on the water, and the almost invisible sipping rises with which trout often feed on them, the hatch might be nearly over before you are ever aware that it started.

Because of their small size, hatches of *Baetis* and related genera are easily overlooked by fishermen. Fish rarely make the same mistake. Many writers have noted that trout prefer to eat certain insects, seeming to consider them delicacies. When a hatch of small blue-winged olive mayflies occurs simultaneously with that of a larger insect, trout often ignore the bigger meal and become selective to members of the *Baetis* complex. It's easy to fish imitations of whatever is larger, and not realize you aren't catching anything because that's not what the trout are taking. They're feeding on the diminutive *Baetis*.

Some fishermen consider duns the most important stage of this complex. Studies of trout stomach contents, however, show that the nymphs are a consistent and important food item for stream trout nearly every week of the year. Trout also feed heavily on nymphs during pre-hatch activity, and become selective to spinners whenever they fall in great abundance. Because of their small size, emerging naturals are often trapped in the surface film during the transition from nymphs to duns. If enough of them are caught in this *cripple* condition, trout will at times concentrate on them, feeding in the surface film, ignoring nearby floating duns. You must be aware of this when it happens, and you need fly patterns to match emergers as well as nymphs, duns, and spinners in order to fish this hatch effectively.

Baetis nymph.

Acentrella nymph.

Nymph Characteristics

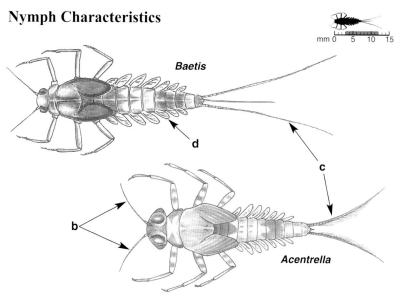

a. Streamlined, swimmer shape. Thorax varies from slender and not much wider than head (*Diphetor*) to rather wide and squat and clearly wider than head (*Acentrella*). Abdomen slender and tapered.

b. Antennae long, two or more times longer than width of the head.

c. Two or three tails often fringed with fine interlocking hairs. In species with three tails, middle tail is typically shorter than outer two.

d. Small, single, and generally oval-shaped gill plates on abdominal segments 1-7 or 2-7.

e. Hind wing pads minute or absent.

f. Color pale olive to olive-brown, or tan to dark brown.

g. Small; length, excluding tails, 3-12mm (1/8-1/2 in.).

Dun Characteristics

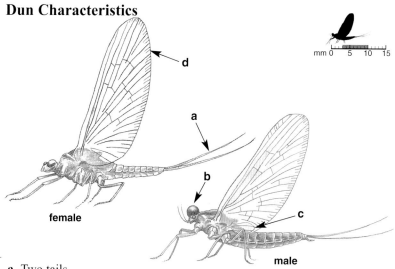

Baetis dun - male.

Baetis dun - female.

a. Two tails.

b. Eyes of male large and *turbinate*. Positioned to look directly upward. Each eye of male is divided into two segments.

c. Hind wings of both sexes very small, long and narrow, or absent.

d. Trailing edge of forewings with short, paired veinlets along outer margin of wing.

e. Color various shades of pale to dark olive, brown, or gray. Wings pale gray to dark slate gray.

f. Small; length, excluding tails, 3-l0mm (1/8-3/8 in.).

Spinner Characteristics

a. Two tails.

b. Eyes of male large, divided, and turbinate.

c. Hind wings of both sexes very small, long and narrow, or absent.

d. Forewings clear. Trailing edge of forewings with short, paired veinlets along outer margin of wing.

e. Male with abdominal segments 2-6 often clear and translucent white, or brown. Female uniform in color, normally light brown to reddish-brown.

f. Small; length, excluding tails, 3-10mm (1/8-3/8 in.).

Habitat and Behavior

Nymphs in the *Baetis* complex are found in most flowing-water habitats. In freestone streams, they live in quiet pools, slow eddies, and even white-water rapids, but are most common in shallow, sun-struck riffles, where algal and diatom growth is most prolific.

Though they are found in fishable numbers in freestone waters, these nymphs often reach their greatest abundance in gentle tailwater and spring-creek currents, with their beds of rooted vegetation and myriads of tiny microniches. Think about Silver Creek, the Bighorn, the Bow, the South Platte, Fall River, the San Juan, or the Deschutes, all famous for their *Baetis* hatches. They're as geographically widespread as you can get in the West, and are not at all alike in character. But all have areas of moderate currents tamed by nature or by dams, and all have excellent growth of aquatic plants and diatoms. Each has heavy and extended blue-winged olive hatches. Most of these streams and rivers have several species of the complex, all hatching in abundance.

In some mountain streams at high altitudes, members of the *Baetis* complex might be the only mayflies present. *Baetis bicaudatus*, a species particularly adapted to small, cold streams, thrives in such mountain environments. In larger, warmer streams, *B. tricaudatus* tends to dominate along with other species such as *Diphetor hageni*. Species of *Acentrella* prefer slower sections of streams, and can thrive in areas with more sand and silt than most other mayflies. Still other species in the complex may be found in limited lake environments, restricted to areas where inlet or outlet streams form currents that enter or exit the stillwater, or along weedy edges where wave action agitates the water and keeps the oxygen content relatively high.

Behavior of nymphs in the *Baetis* complex is predicted by their nature as swimmers. Quick pulsing movements of the abdomen combined with flips of the tails propel them in short bursts of three to five inches. Rapid darts from rock to rock, or from plant to plant, are common for these tiny nymphs. When they stop swimming they immediately cling to the substrate, facing upstream, often in the full force of a fairly heavy current. Their active behavior causes them to be a common component of stream drift and trout diets.

Baetis complex nymphs feed on diatoms or small detrital material that they scrape from the surface of submerged vegetation or rocks. The nymphs go through as many as twenty-seven instars. Mature nymphs, those ready for emergence, are easy to recognize by their dark, well-developed wing pads.

To emerge, a *Baetis* nymph releases its hold on the substrate and floats or swims to the surface, drifting downstream with the current as

Baetis spinner - female.

Baetis spinner - male.

The gentle flows of Oregon's Crooked River, a tailwater, are typical of prime *Baetis* habitat.

it does. After breaking the barrier of the surface film, the dun bursts quickly out of the nymphal cuticle. The dun normally leaves the surface immediately, but on cold days we have seen them float as far as fifty feet before getting airborne.

The surface film, formed by the tension of molecular bonding, can be a substantial barrier for so tiny an insect, especially on smooth currents and calm days. Fast, broken water breaks up the barrier of the surface film. Wind does the same thing. When members of the blue-winged olive group hatch on glassy flats, many fail to make it through the film. The result is a high percentage of cripples, stuck partially in their nymphal shucks, unable to complete emergence. When an abundance of these are present, at least some trout focus their feeding on them, refusing fully-formed duns and your best imitations of those duns. At such times, you need to notice the cripples, and you need to fish emerger imitations. That is among the reasons that we emphasize observation as the most important tool of all in any hatch-matching kit.

Seven to twelve hours after emergence the duns molt to spinners. Mating flights usually occur at mid-day, from late morning to early afternoon, although swarms have also been observed in late afternoon and evening. After copulation, the females of many species in the complex land on protruding rocks or sticks and crawl under water. These lay their eggs in rows on the submerged part of the objects which they've crawled down. After depositing their eggs they either crawl back up to air, or let go and are swept downstream, usually to death, often in the form of a feeding trout. This submerged egg-depositing behavior is unique, among mayflies, to members of this complex.

Other species in the complex lay their eggs on the water's surface. The females die soon after all eggs are laid. When spent on the water, these tiny, almost transparent, empty hulls are at times ignored by trout, at other times sipped patiently by them. The small insects and the subtle rises to them will be almost invisible. You'll often be frustrated by such rises until you move out among them, displace the trout, and suspend your aquarium net half in and half out of the surface film for a few minutes. You'll need your magnifying glass to examine what you find in the meshes.

You wouldn't think a trout, especially a big one, would ever bother to eat something so empty of nutrition. But the spinners are trapped there in the thousands, and trout don't have to work very hard to take them. Back out of that feeding lane, let the trout settle down, match those fragile spinners, and you might get some pleasant surprises.

Imitation

One beauty of the *Baetis* complex is the way you can reduce their complexity by considering them all one group, to be matched with color and size variations of the same set of flies. One problem with the same complex is the broad spectrum of water types in which they live. You need to carry imitations that float on riffles, others that combine flotation with a fairly accurate and unobstructed silhouette of the natural to fish on somewhat uneasy water, and finally you need flies that show the almost exact form of the insect on water so smooth that flotation is never a problem, but rejection by snotty trout is more than the average result of a cast.

This is the hatch, or more accurately the tangle of hatches, where the failure of our "one precise right fly" theory became most evident. John Gierach, author of that brilliant bunch of books that began with

Many *Baetis* females swim to the bottom to deposit their eggs on submerged rocks and logs.

Trout Bum (Pruett, 1986), has written about what he calls the *progression* of a blue-winged olive hatch. As the day goes along, you might begin by rolling a *Baetis* nymph along the bottom because you know lots of them are down there, and that trout like to eat them. Then you'll find a few trout rising higher in the water column, following the insects, and you'll switch to the same nymph fished shallow. You'll begin to notice duns, and trout feeding on them, and will be rewarded by changing to a dry fly. But some trout will get finicky and you'll notice they're taking only cripples, so you'll go to an emerger. And so forth, right through to the late-afternoon spinner fall.

John is right. If you stick with one fly pattern through a blue-winged olive hatch, you'll deal with some trout but a lot more disappointment. If you pay attention to what's going on, carefully observe how things change as the hatch progresses, and change flies as they do, you'll continue to catch trout throughout the hatch, and perhaps feel like you've solved something new each time you do.

NYMPH IMITATIONS

Baetis and related nymphs range from size 14 down to 24. The most common sizes are 16 to 20. Colors of the naturals vary from pale olive to dark olive-gray and dark olive-brown to brown. Their imitations should be tied slender on 1X short to 1X long hooks, usually unweighted to maintain their slender taper.

In our own fishing, we find that trout feed routinely on these small nymphs even when there is no hatch activity. Many times a small *Baetis* imitation will take far more trout in non-selective situations than a larger nymph, especially in waters where good numbers of the naturals are found. When a good hatch does occur, fish will feed selectively on the tiny nymphs during the early stages of the hatch.

The following nymphs are excellent imitations, to be used during *Baetis* complex activity. They're also very effective searching patterns, to be used whenever you feel that nymphing might entice trout and no other method seems like it has much promise, and no specific fly pattern is indicated. If you lack confidence that trout will be able to see such small flies down in the depths, try one as a dropper, on a short tippet tied right to the hook bend of whatever larger fly you decide to try. You'll be surprised how often the smaller fly is taken instead of the large one.

Pheasant Tail (Originator: Frank Sawyer)

Hook:	Standard nymph, 1X long, size 14-24.
Weight:	Scant turns of undersized lead wire, or omit.
Thread:	Brown 8/0.
Tails:	Pheasant center tail fibers.
Rib:	Fine copper wire, counterwound over abdomen.
Abdomen:	Pheasant center tail fibers, as herl.
Wingcase:	Pheasant center tail fibers.
Thorax:	Pheasant center tail fibers, as herl.
Legs:	Tips of thorax fibers.

Though the Pheasant Tail as given is more imitative of the natural nymph, many tiers and writers consider the Pheasant Tail Flashback the more effective pattern. We are drifting toward agreeing with this, and recommend you at least try the above pattern with Pearl Flashabou in place of pheasant-tail fibers for the wingcase.

Baetis Nymph

Hook:	Standard nymph, 1X long, size 14-24.
Weight:	Underweight or omit.
Thread:	Olive 8/0.
Tails:	Olive-dyed mallard flank or partridge fibers.
Abdomen:	Light olive to dark olive-brown fur dubbing.
Wingcase:	Mottled turkey tail or dark goose primary feather section.
Thorax:	Sightly darker fur than abdomen.
Legs:	Olive-dyed mallard flank or partridge fibers, or thorax fur picked out.

This is a standard nymph imitation for members of this complex, for those who feel the need to get more accurate than the Pheasant Tail. Tie a few in medium olive-brown, in sizes 16, 18, and 20, to carry as a preventative measure. They'll probably work when you get into a hatch of any of the species, and find trout more eager for nymphs than they are for emergers or duns. But always try to collect specimens during such times. Observe their size and colors carefully, and vary this dressing as necessary to match what you've found on the waters you fish yourself.

Recall that a single species in this complex can vary in color from stream to stream, and even as you go from section to section of the same stream. It's likely trout will accept this nymph dressing in its medium range of colors, most of the time, because they are accustomed to seeing the naturals arrive in a range of colors. Size and form are more important, though you do want to get the colors of your imitation within the range of what the trout see, and therefore will accept.

Krystal Flash *Baetis* Nymph (Originator: Rick Hafele)

Hook:	Tiemco 2457, 1X short, size 16-20.
Weight:	None
Thread:	Olive 8/0.
Tails:	3 to 6 light gray hackle fibers.
Abdomen:	4 to 6 strands of peacock Krystal Flash, or a color to match your own naturals, tied in at hook bend, twisted into a fine rope, and wrapped up hook shank.
Wingcase:	Mottled turkey tail or strands of dark brown to black Krystal Flash.
Thorax:	Tan to dark brown fur dubbing with guard hairs picked out.

This little nymph sinks well even when unweighted because of the Krystal Flash body, yet the loosely dubbed thorax retains some life-like action. Fished deep or just under the surface, it presents a realistic impression of the natural when tied in the appropriate size and color. It is also durable and easy to tie.

Presentation

The prehatch restlessness of these swimming nymphs makes them available for some time before the duns appear on the surface. *Baetis* nymph patterns are most effective as searching dressings, or when fished over feeding trout just before a hatch or during the early stages of an emergence. However, John Juracek and Craig Mathews, in their detailed *Fishing Yellowstone Hatches* (Blue Ribbon Flies, 1992), report that during heavy *Baetis tricaudatus* hatches on their waters, trout will continue porpoising and tailing to nymphs throughout the entire hatch.

Their book is one of the most thorough studies of regional trout stream insects that we have seen for western waters. The hatches they cover are not restricted to their streams and rivers. Reading the book will inform your fishing wherever you fish. It is also a fine model for the way regional trout stream insects should be studied, matched, and reported.

During the hours when no blue-winged olive hatch is happening, small nymphs can be fished with a free drift on or very near the bottom, using the split-shot and strike-indicator method. In the hour or so just before a hatch, the same flies can often be fished with some success on the traditional wet-fly swing, just inches deep. Mend line to slow them to the speed restless naturals might move in their aborted feints toward the surface and back down.

When duns appear, but you desire to continue fishing a nymph, rig with a long leader and present the fly with upstream casts, just as you would fish a dry fly to rising fish. The small imitations should be allowed to sink just beneath the surface film. It might be necessary to treat all but the last few inches of your leader with fly floatant. This not only keeps the fly near the surface, but helps in detecting subtle takes. When fishing this way we often tie a tiny yarn indicator into the leader five or six feet up from the fly. Set the hook to any movement of the indicator, or to any visible rise anywhere near it.

We often fish unweighted nymph imitations for this complex as droppers on two to three feet of tippet tied to the hook bend of the dry fly we've chosen to imitate the dun. That way both stages are covered, and the trout are offered a choice. You can then gauge which fly they like most. If one is dominant over the other, you can switch to the single fly.

When fishing such small flies, it's best to be armed with your finest presentation outfit. Our own preference is for rods in the three- to four-weight class, eight to nine feet long. You can use even lighter gear if you anticipate windless conditions. Short and accurate casts, and the most delicate presentations, are required to fish nymphs successfully with dry-fly tackle and techniques.

EMERGER IMITATIONS

Because *Baetis* and related species are so small, and hatch so often on smooth currents, they are susceptible to getting stuck in the surface film, the dun half in and half out of the nymphal shuck. They are helpless in this position, and trout often feed selectively on them.

Your imitations of this stage should float flush in the film, and should represent both the emerging dun, or at least its wings, and the trailing shuck. It's critical to carry flies for this stage of this group. We fish emergers during *Baetis* complex hatches as often as we do nymph and dun dressings.

Baetis Emerger

Hook:	Standard dry fly, 1X fine, size 16-24.
Thread:	Olive 8/0.
Tails:	Blue dun hackle fibers, split.
Abdomen:	Pale olive to olive-brown fur or synthetic dubbing.
Wings:	Ball of gray synthetic dubbing, as knot.
Thorax:	Slightly darker dubbing than abdomen.
Legs:	Blue dun hackle fibers.

When tying this fly, dub the wing knot material to your thread, hold it directly above the fly body, then slide the synthetic down the thread, locking it in place with a turn of thread around the hook shank while holding the knot upright with your fingers. When fishing it, treat just the knot with floatant, and fish the fly suspended from the surface film. You can also dress the entire fly and fish it flush in the film.

Darrel Martin, author of *Fly-Tying Methods* and *Micropatterns,* playing a fish in typical slow, meandering *Baetis* water. At times, fishing a nymph pattern before the hatch starts, or even after it's going and trout seem to be feeding on duns, can be very productive.

Krystal Flash *Baetis* Emerger (Originator: Rick Hafele)

Hook:	Tiemco 2457, 1X short, size 16-22.
Thread:	Olive 8/0.
Tail:	Olive or tan CDC fibers as long as hook shank.
Body:	4 to 6 strands of tan, olive, or mix of olive and tan or olive and brown Krystal Flash tied in at the hook bend, twisted into a fine rope and wrapped up the hook shank.
Wing:	Gray CDC fibers.
Thorax:	Tan to dark brown dubbing with guard hairs picked out.

This pattern is similar to the Krystal Flash nymph, but with the addition of CDC it floats perfectly in the surface film, and represents the key elements of an emerger stuck there: the trailing shuck and unfolding wings. You can vary its colors to match those of any blue-winged olive hatch you encounter.

BWO Trailing Shuck Dun (Originator: Bill Black)

Hook:	TMC 900, Mustad 94845, size 16-20.
Thread:	Olive 8/0.
Tail:	Olive CDC fibers topped with olive Z-Lon.
Body:	Olive dubbing.
Wing:	Dark dun CDC fibers.
Topping:	Brown partridge fibers.
Head:	Dark brown dubbing.

Bill Black's dressing represents the dun struggling to free itself from the still-trailing nymphal shuck.

Olive Sparkle Dun (Source: Juracek and Mathews)

Hook:	Standard dry fly, 1X fine, size 16-24.
Thread:	Gray 8/0.
Wing:	Natural deer hair, tied Compara-dun style.
Tail:	Olive-brown Z-lon.
Body:	Gray-olive fur or synthetic dubbing.

This is a standard emerger dressing, and represents the process as it nears completion: the dun is fully formed, but the nymphal shuck is still attached. When fishing it you're representing both the emerger and dun, in a sense offering trout a choice in a single fly. If we were restricted to a single fly style during hatches of this entire complex, this might be it. We'd vary the body colors if we found we needed to, but the truth, as Juracek and Mathews point out in *Fishing Yellowstone Hatches*, is that trout are less critical to color during these hatches than they are to other aspects of fly pattern and presentation. At times, however, you might find trout picky about color, and find it beneficial to observe a specimen closely and match it exactly.

Presentation

You'll be required to fish at your most delicate when you present emerger dressings to selective trout during blue-winged olive hatches on smooth currents. No trout will be more careful in their feeding, nor will any be more lazy in their refusal to move out of a narrow feeding lane to take a natural, or its imitation. You'll nearly always be fishing these patterns on slow-moving water with a smooth surface. If those were not the prevailing conditions, these little insects would not be getting stuck in the surface film.

Before casting, take up a position as near to the rising trout as you can without alerting them to your presence. Put as many conflicting

A *Baetis* just beginning the process of emerging from the split nymphal shuck, in the surface film.

currents behind you as possible, rather than leaving them between you and the trout, water across which your line must lie. If you're stalking a pod of rising trout, rather than a single rising fish, single out a trout, time its rise rhythms, and cast to it carefully, rather than casting at random to the pod of lifting and subsiding noses.

Try to align yourself either across stream from the trout, in position for a reach cast, or upstream and slightly off to the side of the trout, in position for a downstream wiggle cast. Both of those options allow you to show your fly to the trout ahead of your line and leader. Be as accurate and gentle with each cast as you can. It might take a long time, and many casts, before the moment becomes perfect and the trout is ready to rise at the instant your fly drifts exactly down its narrow feeding lane.

If you find it necessary to make an upstream presentation, place the fly onto the water just a foot or two upstream from the position of the fish. That allows a minimum of leader, and no line, to fly through the air over the head of the fish. Trout holding high in smooth water, focused on feeding on an abundance of tiny natural insects, are unhappy about things that suddenly fly over their heads. It reminds them of kingfishers and ospreys, and usually sends them sailing.

Emerger dressings become important when you fish the smoothest currents, over the fussiest fish, such as those on Montana's Bighorn River.

DUN IMITATIONS

When an emergence of blue-winged olives is strong, and fish are feeding on the surface, floating dun patterns generally become more effective than nymphs, or at least more fun to fish, and are easier to see than most emerger dressings. *Baetis* complex duns range in size from 14 through 24. The most common sizes are 18 and 20. The color spectrum is similar to that of the nymph, with pale-olives, dark-olives, and brownish-olives prevalent.

The following list of dun imitations reflects the fact that these insects hatch over a wide range of water types. Your imitations must show different things to trout depending on the water type in which the fish feed on the naturals.

Olive Quill Dun (Originator: A. K. Best)

Hook:	Standard dry fly, 1X fine, size 16-24.
Thread:	Olive 8/0.
Tail:	Medium dun spade hackle fibers.
Body:	Olive-dyed hackle stem.
Wings:	Medium dun hen hackle tips.
Hackle:	Medium dun.

Though this is a hackled dressing, and should be most effective on slightly rough water, we've fished with A. K. Best on his favorite Frying Pan River, and seen him coax trout as selective as trout get to this fly on water as smooth as water gets. We're A. K. fans, and believe the book that lists this dressing, *A. K.'s Fly Box* (Lyons and Burford, 1996) stands among the best about fly-fishing and flies.

The tiny duns of this complex can at times be matched successfully with other hackled patterns, including some traditionals such as the Adams and Blue-winged Olive. They were devised for eastern hatches, but trout in western waters don't consider that a fault. Try them, especially if you're carrying them when a BWO hatch starts and you have none of the listed flies to match it. You could also do well with standard midge dressings—nothing but tail, body, and hackle—in the right sizes and colors, or at times just the right sizes but the wrong colors.

Olive Hairwing Dun (Originator: René Harrop)

Hook:	Standard dry fly, 1X fine, size 16-24.
Thread:	Olive 8/0.
Tails:	Blue dun hackle fibers, split.
Abdomen:	Olive fur or synthetic dubbing.
Hackle:	Blue dun, five turns over thorax, clipped on bottom.
Thorax:	Olive fur or synthetic dubbing.
Wing:	Natural or light-gray dyed deer or yearling elk hair.

René Harrop, the famous professional tier from St. Anthony, Idaho, is and always has been right on the cutting edge of fly-pattern design. *Field & Stream* once polled its writers, asking which single fly they would choose if they were restricted to it for all of their fishing. The Hughes half of the authors of this book chose René Harrop's Olive Hairwing Dun, first because of the number of hatches that it matches as you run up the sizes—BWOs, lesser green drakes, green drakes, and various caddis—and second because it can be tugged under and fished wet. In an emergency, it can be stripped of its wings and fished as an adequate olive nymph.

This fly is excellent as a blue-winged olive dun imitation because it floats well enough to fish riffles and runs, but lowers the body into the water low enough to be a fine imitation on smooth water. If we're fishing two flies during a *Baetis* hatch, one for duns and the other for nymphs or emergers, this is likely to be the lead fly, serving as an indicator and also suspension for the other. When fished in tandem with another fly, a hair-wing dun usually takes at least as many trout as whatever trails it.

Olive Quill Parachute (Originator: A. K. Best)

Hook:	Standard dry fly, 1X fine, size 16-24.
Thread:	Olive 8/0.
Wingpost:	Dense white or gray turkey flat segment.
Tails:	Medium dun spade hackle fibers, splayed.
Body:	Olive-dyed hackle stem.
Hackle:	Medium dun, wound parachute.

This A. K. Best dressing gives you the parachute option, which is handy to have when matching a hatch that occurs on such a wide variety of water types. That post, especially when you use white turkey flats, gives you visibility that you do not have with any other of these small dun dressings. In his book, A. K. recommends what he calls turkey T-base feathers, which are smaller and of higher quality than typical flats.

BWO CDC Biot Compara-Dun (Originator: Shane Stalcup)

Hook:	Standard dry fly, 1X fine, size 16-24.
Thread:	Olive 8/0.
Tails:	Blue dun hackle fibers, split.
Abdomen:	Olive-dyed goose or turkey biot.
Wing:	Gray CDC topped with mallard flank fibers.
Thorax:	Tan synthetic dubbing.

This fine dressing by Shane Stalcup, author of *Mayflies: "Top to Bottom"*, (Frank Amato Publications, 2002) incorporates a segmented biot body with the realism and flotation of CDC. The combination is excellent, and works over some of the most selective trout. The fly as listed is a bit complex for most of us to tie in its smallest sizes. We recommend omitting all but the tails, body, and CDC wing, if that suits your tying abilities better, when you get to size 20 and below.

Presentation

Because they hatch so often on smooth-flowing waters, blue-winged olive duns present a special challenge. On such heavily fished waters as the Henry's Fork of the Snake, the Bow River in Alberta, or the South Platte in Colorado, hatches of these tiny insects can be especially frustrating, and the trout seem to have more education in entomology than we do. Even on lightly fished waters, trout set up a search image and become selective to what they desire to see. If your fly fails to look or behave like what trout are eating, you won't catch many selective fish, even on wilderness waters.

The same tackle and tactics used for emergers work as well for duns. Refine your gear to the most delicate. Use twelve- to fourteen-foot leaders, with at least three feet of fine tippet. You'll sometimes get away with fishing 5X over these hatches; most often you'll need 6X, and it's not uncommon to benefit from going down to 7X. Before you do, though, check out the length of what's left of your tippet, and be sure you haven't cut it shorter than a couple of feet. You need that extra tippet, no matter what diameter, to give your fly freedom to float without drag.

Pay close attention to your position in relation to rising trout, and the direction of your presentation. Quite often we'll go through a mildly panicked routine of changing tippets and then changing flies during a hatch, only to discover very near the end of it that we've been casting across some conflicting currents we've not noticed. Trout always notice the drag these cause. It's surprising how often moving from a downstream position into an across-stream or even upstream position, makes difficult trout suddenly easy. The move causes you to use a reach cast or wiggle cast, rather than an upstream presentation, and that alone often solves the situation. When you fish over blue-winged olive duns, and feel some stress on account of rejection by trout, tippet and fly pattern are no more likely to be the problem than position and presentation.

SPINNER IMITATIONS

Spinner falls of *Baetis* and the related genera vary in importance. In fact, we have a mild argument about their importance during a May trip to the Bighorn River some years ago. Rick says we got into big trout rising to *Baetis* spinners in a backwater channel, that we were together when it happened, and that he solved it and caught some nice fish on the flies he used to match the spinners. Dave doesn't recall any of this, but has photos of Rick holding nice trout on a Bighorn backchannel. That is evidence Rick is right and Dave is wrong, not unusual in matters of memory.

We do not doubt that blue-winged olive spinners are frequently important on most western rivers. They usually fall in mid- to late afternoon. We have also observed good spinner falls of *Acentrella* early in the morning along grassy banks of the Deschutes River. In some blue-winged olive species the spinners from the previous day's hatch return to water not long after the daily emergence of duns. Males swarm over the water or along the edges near it. Females fly into the swarm, mate, and return to vegetation to wait for their eggs to ripen. Some fly back over the water and deposit their eggs on the surface. Many crawl down the sides of rocks and sticks projecting from the water to lay their eggs on submerged surfaces. The nature of these two types of egg-laying presents opportunities for two types of fishing, one dry and the other wet. You'll need to be prepared with appropriate fly patterns. You'll always need to be very observant to tell which one to use.

When you're fishing such smooth water as the flats on the Henrys Fork of the Snake River, you'll have to refine your tackle and make most of your presentations downstream, on slack line casts, to fool many rising trout on *Baetis* imitations.

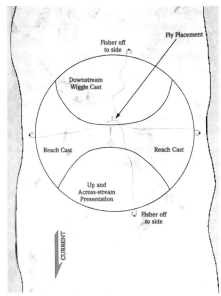

Quite often, when you're having trouble hooking trout feeding on *Baetis* duns, or any stage of any other insect, for that matter, the problem is less pattern and tackle than it is position and presentation. Try moving off to the side of the feeding trout for a reach cast, or upstream from it for a downstream wiggle cast, and you might find that your luck has suddenly improved.

Red Quill Spinner

Hook:	Standard dry fly, 1X fine, size 18-24.
Thread:	Brown 8/0.
Tails:	Brown hackle fibers, split.
Body:	Brown dyed hackle stem.
Wings:	Light blue dun hen hackle tips, tied spent.
Hackle:	Brown, clipped top and bottom.

Many species that are blue-winged olives when they emerge as duns become red or rusty spinners when they return to the water to lay their eggs and expire. The Red Quill Spinner fishes for about half of the BWO species in their final and fatal stage.

Blue Quill Spinner

Hook:	Standard dry fly, 1X fine, size 18-24.
Thread:	Gray 8/0.
Tails:	Blue dun hackle fibers, split.
Body:	Gray-dyed hackle stem.
Wings:	Light gray hen hackle tips, tied spent.
Hackle:	Blue dun, clipped top and bottom.

This gray-bodied dressing covers most remaining hatches that begin life as blue-winged olives. It's important to remember that few mayflies are the same color in the spinner stage that they were in the earlier dun stage. You can substitute polypropylene yarn, sparse, for the hen hackle tips as wings in both of these standard dressings. You'll then have polypro Spinners, which will work just as well as the listed patterns, and be just a little bit easier to tie. But they won't be quite so pretty.

Blue Quill Wet

Hook:	Standard wet fly, 1X or 2X stout, size 18-22.
Thread:	Gray 8/0.
Tails:	Blue dun hackle fibers.
Body:	Stripped peacock quill.
Rib:	Fine gold wire, counterwound over body.
Hackle:	Blue dun hen.
Wing:	Mallard primary or secondary feather sections.

This dressing represents female BWO spinners that lay their eggs beneath the surface, then are washed away on their way back toward the top.

Presentation

Most often during BWO spinner falls, you'll see trout sipping invisibles on flats like that Bighorn backwater. Try a floating imitation first. If that fails, swing a wet fly slowly in front of the trout and see if it moves them. If not, get out your handy aquarium net, hold it half in and half out of the current, and see what its meshes reveal.

You'll need to refer to that net often, during all stages of *Baetis* complex hatches. Recall through all stages of these small but far from minor hatches that your tippet, position, and presentation method can be just as important as the pattern you choose to match them.

Rick with a Bighorn River brown hooked on a tiny *Baetis* spinner imitation.

Chapter 7

Callibaetis (Speckle-Wings)

FAMILY: BAETIDAE

Genus: *Callibaetis.*

Western Species: 8; 4 restricted to the Southwest and 4 widely distributed across western states and provinces.

North America: 14.

Important Western Species:

Callibaetis ferrugineus hageni (synonyms *C. coloradensis, C. americanus, C. nigritus,* and *C. hageni*)

Callibaetis pallidus (synonym *C. semicostatus*)

Callibaetis pictus (synonyms *C. pacificus, C. doddsi, C. signatus,* and *C. vitrea*)

Common Names: Speckle-wing duns, speckle-wing quills, speckled duns.

When we wrote *Western Hatches* twenty years ago, there were fifteen species of *Callibaetis* distributed across the entire western United States and Canada. Current taxonomic revisions, which are ongoing, have lumped the three species you'd typically see listed as most important in angling references, *C. coloradensis, C. americanus,* and *C. nigritus,* into the single species *C. ferrugineus hageni.*

What were once thought to be separate species are now considered gradations of the same species as you move through the vast landscape over which this species is spread. However, the differences in size and color remain as they were, as you go from region to region, under the old classifications. Other species of *Callibaetis* are important locally. This is a group where identification to genus level is important because of the information it gives you about the insect's habitat and behavior. Having

Callibaetis   HATCH IMPORTANCE SCORE: 41.0

CRITERIA/SCORE	5		4		3		2		1	
Distribution: (within Western waters)	widespread	5.0	common		scattered		isolated		rare	
Abundance:	heavy	4.5	abundant		modest		trickling		individual	
Emergence type:	mid-water/slow	5.0	mid-water/fast		edges/slow		edges/fast		crawls out	
Emergence time:	mid-day	5.0	early and/or late over long period		early and/or late over short period		dawn or dusk		night	
Emergence duration:	multiple seasons per year	5.0	well-defined long hatch period		well-defined short hatch period		poorly-defined long hatch period		poorly-defined short hatch	
(Behavior/Availability) Nymph:	excellent		good		moderate	3.0	slight		poor	
(Behavior/Availability) Emerger:	excellent	5.0	good		moderate		slight		poor	
(Behavior/Availability) Dun:	excellent	5.0	good		moderate		slight		poor	
(Behavior/Availability) Spinner:	excellent		good	3.5	moderate		slight		poor	
Totals:		34.5		3.5		3.0		0.0		0.0

Note: *Callibaetis* are just as important in lakes as *Baetis* are in rivers, thus the score reflects their importance only if you fish lakes.

identified a *Callibaetis* hatch to that useful level, it's fine to go on from there into matters of imitation and presentation, without identifying specimens to species.

Emergence and Distribution

This is a predominantly western genus, with minor representation in the Midwest and East. For that reason, historical books on angling have rarely addressed *Callibaetis,* but more modern books with western information give them the importance they deserve. Some of the most useful and elegantly-written information on the genus to this day is in Ernest Schwiebert's *Matching the Hatch* (Macmillan, 1955), and his *Nymphs* (Winchester Press, 1973).

Callibaetis is largely a stillwater genus, and is found most often in lakes and ponds. However, it also has adapted to slow-flowing stream environments, especially in waters where vegetation takes root. You'll rarely find *Callibaetis* in freestone streams except where gentle sections enter or exit lakes and ponds, or meander through meadows. Spring creeks and tailwaters, where flows have been stabilized, at times offer excellent speckle-wing hatches.

Callibaetis can be collected from nearly any lake, pond, or beaver pond in the entire western U. S. and Canada, and are, without question, the most important stillwater mayfly to the western angler. We've also seen moving-water hatches, or had them reported, in the Henrys Fork of the Snake and Silver Creek in Idaho, the tailwaters of the Missouri in Montana, and the Bow River in Alberta.

In most stillwaters, *Callibaetis* complete two or three generations per year, each rousing the trout and producing excellent fishing. The first adults usually emerge in April, May, or as late as June, depending on altitude and lattitude, followed by a second brood in June, July, or August, and a third in September and on into October. In colder northern areas, and at high altitudes, *Callibaetis* are more likely to have just two generations in a season, the first in late spring, the second in late summer or early autumn. At altitudes and lattitudes where the warm summer break is brief, they might have just one generation, usually in late spring or early summer.

There is often overlap between peak periods of these generations of emergence on the same body of water. The spring brood might be tapering off when the first of the summer hatch appears; the summer brood might emerge right up until the fall hatch begins. On some western stillwaters there can be a fishable rise to speckle-wings on most days of the fly fishing season. On other waters the peaks are distinct, and you get little *Callibaetis* fishing between them.

CALLIBAETIS EMERGENCE TABLE

TIME	WINTER			SPRING			SUMMER			FALL		
	Dec.	Jan.	Feb.	March	April	May	June	July	Aug.	Sep.	Oct.	Nov.
7 a.m. - 10 a.m.												
10 a.m. - noon												
noon - 3 p.m.												
3 p.m. - 7 p.m.												
7 p.m. - 10 p.m.												

Nymph Characteristics

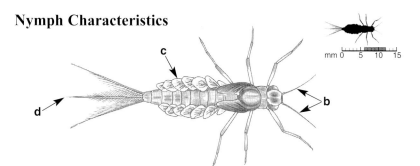

Callibaetis nymph.

a. Streamlined, swimmer shape. Middle area of thorax is wider than head. Abdomen tapered.

*b. Antennae long, two or more times longer than width of head.

c. Large heart-shaped gills on abdominal segments 1-7. Gills on segments 1-4 or 1-7 with small, recurved flaps, producing the appearance of double-plated gills.

d. Three tails of equal length, fringed with fine interlocking hairs.

e. Body pale to dark tan, olive, or olive-brown.

f. Length, excluding tails, 6-12mm (1/4-1/2 in.).

Note: *Siphlonurus* (Family: Siphlonuridae), can be collected at times from the same lakes and ponds as *Callibaetis*. This is the main genus with which you might confuse *Callibaetis* nymphs, and they are easily separated from *Callibaetis* by their short antennae compared to the long antennae of *Callibaetis*.

Dun Characteristics

Callibaetis dun.

a. Two tails.

b. Eyes of male large and divided.

c. Forewings mottled by distinct white venation.

d. Hind wings small, long, and narrow.

e. Top of body tan to brownish-olive or gray; usually a lighter shade mixed with olive on the underside.

f. Length, excluding tails, 6-12mm (1/4-1/2 in.)

Spinner Characteristics

Callibaetis male spinner.

a. Two tails.

b. Eyes of male large, divided, and slightly turbinate.

c. Forewings of female clear with speckled brown or gray markings on leading edge; male forewings entirely clear or occasionally mottled.

d. Top of body grayish-brown to almost black; underside pale gray to tannish-gray.

e. Length, excluding tails, 6-12mm (1/4-1/2 in.).

Callibaetis female spinner on the water, as a trout might see it.

Habitat and behavior

Callibaetis nymphs are almost always associated with vegetation, whether it's in a lake, pond, or very slow-flowing section of stream. In moving water, you find them only where winter and spring spates are tamed enough for plants to take root. That's why this group is associated with spring creeks, tailwaters, and meadow streams, the latter especially at alpine altitudes, and rarely found in freestone streams.

In lakes and ponds, look for speckle-wing nymphs near the shoreline and wherever you find beds of aquatic plants. They'll be as deep as sunlight strikes through to the bottom, because photosynthetic growth will take place there, and these nymphs will find vegetation to eat. In most wind-stirred and opaque desert lakes, light reaches a maximum depth of about fifteen feet. You won't find vegetation, or *Callibaetis*, beyond those depths. In high alpine lakes, usually as clear as air, light can reach the bottom twenty-five to thirty feet down, and you'll find these nymphs that deep.

How does this information translate into fishing importance? First, you'll fish *Callibaetis* nymph dressings out farther and down deeper in water that is progressively more clear. Second, you'll get hatches of duns farther out from shore, and less in association with it, on lakes with clear water, closer in toward shore and therefore shallower water, in stillwaters that have less clarity.

Don't let this mislead you into thinking you need to get far out from shore on waters that are clean and clear. If plant beds approach the shoreline, *Callibaetis* will be in close. We're thinking here about the dozens of mountain lakes that we fish by casting right from the edges or

Callibaetis nymphs prefer weedy shallows, but will be found at any depth with vegetation growth. When they're active and emerging, birds will be active over the water, and trout will be active down below.

by log-hopping along the shoreline. We're also thinking about lakes like Hebgen, near West Yellowstone, Montana, where open channels thread through acres of plant beds in six to ten feet of water. Large brown trout nose around in them, feeding on speckle-wing nymphs and emerging duns. That is true of any weedy lake, though the trout species might be different.

Callibaetis eggs hatch almost immediately after being deposited in the water, and the nymphs begin feeding at once. This is a major reason a single species is able to execute two or three generations in an annual cycle. The nymphs eat primarily diatoms and algae, and are a major converter of plant to insect and then trout tissue in lake ecosystems. The nymphs grow rapidly, molting nine to sixteen times during their development.

Shallow lakes rich with plant growth, such as Dry Falls Lake in central Washington, are hotbeds for *Callibaetis* hatches.

Quick flips of the abdomen and tails propel them in darting six-inch bursts. When at rest they arch their abdomens gracefully and fan their gills rhythmically. In as little as six weeks after hatching from the egg, the nymphs can display the dark wing pads that announce they're ready to emerge.

Prior to emergence, *Callibaetis* nymphs swim up and down between the safety of tangled plants and the surface. This restless activity can stir savage feeding by trout. Finally the nymph makes a steady, rapid swim to the surface, where the subimago bursts free from the nymphal shuck. If the weather is warm and the air still, the dun can be airborne in seconds. If it's overcast, drizzling, or the wind is brisk, as often happens on western lakes, duns might struggle in the film and then sit atop it for a minute or more before they're able to take wing and escape the eyes of cruising trout.

Trout at times concentrate on rising nymphs, ignoring the escaping duns, all the way through a hatch. Most of the time, though, they cruise and take whatever stage enters their gunsights. In our own analysis of stomach samples, most of them taken on a lake with no natural spawning and therefore all planted trout, we've found that the average feeding trout takes something like eight to twelve nymphs for every dun. That doesn't keep us from fishing dun dressings, though. When a trout feeding on *Callibaetis*, perhaps taking mostly nymphs, sees a dun or an acceptable imitation, it will usually whack it.

Daily emergence usually begins some time just before or after noon, and goes on through early afternoon and even into early evening. As with the earlier and closely related *Baetis* complex, the hatch is extended for hours on overcast days, truncated into an hour or less when the weather is sunny and warm. In spring and fall, hatches tend toward the warmest hours, in early afternoon. In mid-summer, hatches can creep toward the cooler hours of morning and evening.

Duns fly to lakeside vegetation, molt to spinners seven to nine hours later, and are ready to mate the next day. Large mating swarms of males congregate any time from early morning to mid-afternoon. The swarms may be four to twenty feet above the water, or over meadows near the water. Males rise and fall several feet at a time. Females fly into the swarm, where copulation occurs in the air. Fertilized females return to resting spots along the shore for up to five days, until their eggs are fully ripened and ready to hatch when they hit water.

Females begin to oviposit in mid-afternoon, dipping the tip of the abdomen to the water time after time to release 400 to 500 eggs. When finished they fall to the water and lie spent on the surface. It's easy to mistake the swarming males in the air, landing all over your shirt and hat, for the insect you want to imitate. Don't do that. Trout rarely eat them. Take time to snoop in the shallows, among protruding vegetation, and along fallen logs, on the downwind edge of the lake if the wind is blowing, and

Callibaetis male spinners often dot your shirt, but you want to capture a spent female from the water, and select your fly pattern based on it, because that is what trout will be taking.

find a spent female. Most males return to the shore to die in spider webs. It's the female *Callibaetis* you want to imitate.

Imitation

Some of the most exciting fishing on western stillwaters comes during frequent and heavy hatches of *Callibaetis*. These multiple-brooded mayflies offer a unique opportunity, but with it they present a unique problem. The same species is often available in early spring, in mid-summer, and again in late fall. Their hatches can prompt trout to feed and therefore provide good fishing for a large part of the season. But each generation requires less time to mature than the one before it, and you must notice that the individuals in each succeeding generation are a hook size or so smaller than those that went before them. If you don't notice this diminishment in size, your success might fall off as the season goes on.

In spring you might match a speckle-wing hatch, in each of its stages, with size-12 flies. During the second emergence, in summer, the same species might require that you drop your fly size down to 14. In fall the same hatch might diminish to a size 16. If it began in spring as a size 14, you'll need to descend to 16s and 18s as the season progresses. If you fish through the entire season with the same size-12 flies that worked in spring, you'll find your catch and your happiness dwindling as the season and the hatch progress.

NYMPH IMITATIONS

Callibaetis nymphs vary in color from pale tan and olive to a dark olive-brown, depending to a certain extent on their species, but to a greater extent on the color of the substrate upon which they've been living. They'll take on the color of their environment, as camouflage. You should always carry a few standard dressings in a medium tannish-olive shade. But with this group you will need to collect specimens from your home waters, or waters to which you travel, and match their colors as closely as you can. The differences will often be significant to trout.

Imitations of these swimmer nymphs should be tied slender and tapered. To elongate them, tie them on 2X or 3X long hooks, in sizes 12 for early season, through 16 or even 18 toward the end of it.

Olive Hare's Ear

Hook:	2X long, size 12-18.
Weight:	10 to 15 turns of undersized lead wire.
Thread:	Olive 6/0 or 8/0.
Tail:	Olive-dyed hare's mask guard hairs.
Rib:	Oval gold tinsel.
Abdomen:	Olive fur dubbing.
Wingcase:	Mottled turkey or dark goose feather section.
Thorax:	Brownish-olive fur dubbing, picked out.

The Olive Hare's Ear is an all-purpose nymph that you might carry for other reasons. It will work fine before and even during many *Callibaetis* hatches, and will work as the dressing you should carry and use until you've collected specimens and are ready to match them with size and color variations more precisely suited to them. If you run into tan to brown species, it's quite possible that the old standard Gold Ribbed Hare's Ear, parent to this olive variation, if tied slender and weighted slightly, will work as well as anything more exact. It has taken trout during speckle-wing activity many times for us.

Pheasant Tail Flashback

Hook:	2X or 3X long, size 12-20.
Weight:	Scant turns of undersized lead wire.
Thread:	Brown 6/0 or 8/0.
Tails:	Pheasant center tail fibers.
Rib:	Fine gold wire, reverse wrapped over abdomen.
Abdomen:	Pheasant center tail fibers, as herl.
Wingcase:	Pearlescent Flashabou.
Thorax:	Peacock herl.
Legs:	Pheasant center tail fiber tips, or omit.

This pattern is a slight variation on the standard Pheasant Tail Flashback mentioned earlier as an imitation of *Baetis* nymphs. It has peacock rather than pheasant herl for the thorax. There is something to be said for tying and carrying both versions, in a range of sizes from 12 to 22, and using it during both *Baetis* complex and *Callibaetis* hatches. We list it here not because it is an ideal imitation of the average *Callibaetis* nymph we've collected, but because we use it often during *Callibaetis* hatches and it catches a lot of fish for us. It's one of those matters in which we've let the trout have a say, and they've said they like the Pheasant Tail Flashback when *Callibaetis* nymphs are on the move.

Callibaetis Nymph

Hook:	2X or 3X long, size 12-20.
Weight:	8 to 10 turns of undersized lead wire.
Thread:	Olive 6/0 or 8/0.
Tails:	Olive-dyed partridge fibers.
Abdomen:	Tannish-olive to olive-brown fur dubbing.
Shellback:	Mottled turkey or dark goose feather sections.
Thorax:	Slightly darker fur dubbing than abdomen.
Legs:	Olive-dyed partridge fibers (omit in small sizes and pick out thorax fur).

This dressing is very similar to that listed earlier as the *Baetis* Nymph, and can be tied and carried as a size extension of the same pattern: in 12s and 14s in addition to the 16s through 24s already tied for the smaller genera. We advise you to collect *Callibaetis* and base the colors of this dressing on specimens from waters where you'll fish them. Always tie it slender. That seems to be the secret to it.

Presentation

Most often, we fish nymph imitations of *Callibaetis* mayflies in the period before a known emergence, in water three to six feet deep, near the shoreline, or in and around any weedbeds visible at those depths. In other words, we fish the nymphs where in our experience the duns will emerge a bit later. At times we continue fishing a nymph right through a scattered hatch. If trout turn their attention to duns, though, we sometimes switch even if the nymph is still fishing well, primarily to enjoy the sight of visible surface takes.

We generally fish *Callibaetis* nymphs on a floating, wet-tip, or intermediate line, with a long leader tapered down to 4X, 5X, or even 6X, depending on the size fly we're fishing. This is the same leader we'll use later when we switch to duns, which is one reason we almost always use floating lines as opposed to the wet-tip or intermediate that might be more efficient. It's one thing to change flies when the hatch starts and trout begin rising all around you; it's another thing to change lines. If you have two rods available, it's handy to rig one for nymphs and the other for dries when you expect speckle-wing activity.

When trout are actively in pursuit of *Callibaetis* nymphs, you can often do very well right from shore, even on such vast bodies of water as Yellowstone Lake.

After allowing the nymph some time to sink, a varied retrieve is set into motion. The fly is stripped so it swims in four- to six-inch bursts, then allowed to settle. Then it is stripped again. Trout take as often on the sink as they do the strip. Watch for signs of a visible take, or any twitch of your line tip or leader. More than half of the takes to *Callibaetis* nymphs are seen, not felt.

If we're armed with a nymph tied to our tippet, and a trout rises for a surface take to a dun within casting range, we do not take time to remove the nymph and tie on a dry. The trout would be long gone. Instead, a cast is made very near the rise, or in the direction the trout was headed if that can be plotted by previous rises. The fly is given brief seconds to sink, then a slow stripping retrieve is initiated. If the trout is still around it will usually turn back and take the nymph, though it's obviously just fed on a dun. Often the take happens almost as soon as the nymph hits the water, while it sinks in the moment before you begin your retrieve. In that case, you'll see the swirl of the take, as if you were fishing a dry. Set the hook.

When fishing speckle-wing nymphs over deeper water, especially where water clarity allows us to see weedbeds ten to fifteen feet and even deeper down, we use whatever sink-rate line it takes to get the fly down there. The countdown method becomes necessary, usually with a patient wait of between twenty seconds and a full minute. Of course trout might take the fly at any time on its way down, but they usually will not move far up from weed cover for it. Still, you must be watchful for signs of a take as you count your fly down.

When you're fishing in association with aquatic plants that you cannot see, you'll know when you're at the right depth if you retrieve tendrils of the plants on an occasional cast. Count the fly down a beat or two less, then intersperse short strips with pauses and a few feet of hand-twist retrieve. If nothing else, the slow hand-twist keeps your fly fishing in the right zone longer, which is beneficial after you've waited all that time for it to get down there. A faster retrieve might lift it up where trout don't notice it.

EMERGER IMITATIONS

When they attain size 12 and 14, *Callibaetis* nymphs have enough mass to break right through the surface film. You won't enjoy much emerger fishing over them, though on cold, gloomy days a few are crippled, and trout will rarely turn away from those. Emerger dressings will serve you most often when hatching *Callibaetis* are size 16 and smaller. The surface film becomes more of a barrier to them.

CDC *Callibaetis* Floating Nymph/Emerger
(Originator: René Harrop)

Hook:	Standard dry fly, 1X fine, size 12-20.
Thread:	Tan 6/0 or 8/0.
Tail:	Woodduck flank fibers.
Rib:	Fine copper wire.
Body:	Tan fur dubbing.
Legs:	Brown partridge fibers.
Wing:	White CDC, short.
Thorax:	Tan fur dubbing.

This emerger dressing, originated by René Harrop, is listed in Jim Schollmeyer's all-color guidebook, *Hatch Guide For Lakes* (Frank Amato Publications, 1995). Jim recommends fishing this fly on cloudy or rainy days, when the naturals struggle a bit in the surface film. Cast it to spotted rises and let it sit. Or cast it out in the area where trout cruise and rise. Fish it without motion, then give it an occasional twitch to entice trout.

Quigley Cripple (Originator: Bob Quigley)

Hook:	Standard dry fly, 1X fine, size 12-18.
Thread:	Tan 6/0 or 8/0.
Tail:	Light olive ostrich.
Body:	Light olive ostrich, as herl.
Thorax:	Dark olive fur dubbing.
Wing:	Tan deer hair, butts exposed.
Hackle:	Olive-dyed grizzly.

This great dressing was one of the first to imitate an emerging mayfly with its wings already out, but with the back end of the dun still struggling to escape the nymphal shuck, represented in a posture hanging down below the surface. As listed here in the original colors, the Quigley Cripple is excellent for many *Callibaetis*, and for some of the greater and lesser green drakes that will be covered later, as well. Fish the cripple dressing without movement most of the time. If trout are seen working around it, but are far enough away not to notice it, give it a nudge from time to time, just enough to send out tiny ripples and attract the notice of the trout.

Dun Imitations

On bright days *Callibaetis* duns usually escape the water quickly, and trout seem to focus on nymphs. However, on days with a chill in the air, some mist or rain coming down, or a slight wind riffling the surface, the duns have trouble getting airborne, and trout often take them as well as they will nymphs. Even when trout prefer nymphs, proved by body counts over the years, they'll still take duns, and will be fooled by imitations of duns. Since most fly-fishers are more satisfied by a rise to a dry than by a subsurface take, it's important to carry dun dressings not just for the fish they catch, but also for the fun they add to your fishing.

    Callibaetis dun patterns should be carried in sizes 12 through 18. Body colors range from pale olive to light brown. The wings range from pale tan to dark slate-brown, with those distinct white veins that you fortunately do not have to imitate. Always recall that mayfly dun bodies are a lighter color on the underside than they are on the back. It's the underside that a trout sees when it rises to take one. Collect a fresh dun on your own waters, during a hatch, and be sure you're matching what trout have an interest in eating.

Callibaetis Compara-Dun
(Originators: Al Caucci and Bob Nastasi)

Hook:	Standard dry fly, 1X fine, size 12-18.
Thread:	Olive or tan 6/0 or 8/0.
Wing:	Natural tan to brown Compara-dun deer hair.
Tails:	Ginger or brown hackle fibers, split.
Body:	Mixed dubbing to match belly color of natural.

This fine dressing was originally listed in Al Caucci and Bob Nastasi's *Hatches* (Comparahatch Press, 1975). We interpreted it, according to their instructions to vary the colors based on insects you collect, for a hatch on an Oregon lake. It fooled trout there, and continues to do so wherever in the West we take it.

    In our case, the fly has brown tails, a tannish-olive body, and tan wing. It's our standard *Callibaetis* dun dressing to this day. We do, however, like to have options. As with all dressings tied to match hatches, there are days when trout simply refuse one, but are willing to take a fly tied in a different style. Likely this seeming capriciousness is due to the different postures with which the fly styles sit on the water, but we won't know that for sure until we can interview trout. It would be nice if we could know in advance which would be their preferred posture and therefore pattern style for the day, but we haven't figured out a way to predict that yet. In the meantime, it's best to carry at least two or three pattern styles to match the duns of a hatch as important as the *Callibaetis*.

If you'd like to convert this Compara-Dun to a Sparkle Dun, and use it to represent the dun still stuck in its nymphal shuck, merely substitute clear Z-lon for the tails. Sometimes the emerger style fishes better, at other times less well.

Olive Hairwing Dun (Originator: René Harrop)

Hook:	Standard dry fly, 1X fine, size 12-18.
Thread:	Olive 6/0 or 8/0.
Tails:	Blue dun hackle fibers, split.
Abdomen:	Olive fur or synthetic dubbing.
Hackle:	Blue dun, five turns over thorax, clipped on bottom.
Thorax:	Olive fur or synthetic dubbing.
Wing:	Gray-dyed yearling elk body hair.

This is the same dressing listed in the previous section on *Baetis*, tied in a couple of larger sizes. You'll see this same dressing listed later in the larger sizes as an imitation of lesser green drakes *(Drunella* sp.). You might say, "Whoa, this is one fly I should carry in a full range of sizes!" You'd be right. That's what we do.

In size 12, on a July day in what was spring way up there, the Olive Hairwing Dun bailed us out during a *Callibaetis* hatch on Yellowstone Lake. Those cutts, which were supposed to be stupid, refused everything else. We were stupid enough to be carrying just two in the right size, which shortened our success to the time it took us to lose them.

Speckled-Wing Parachute (Originator: Pret Frazier)

Hook:	Standard dry fly, 1X fine, size 12-18.
Thread:	Tan or olive 6/0 or 8/0.
Wing post:	Mallard flank fibers, trimmed to shape.
Tails:	Ginger or blue dun hackle fibers, split.
Body:	Tannish-olive to brownish-olive fur dubbing.
Hackle:	Olive-dyed grizzly, tied parachute.

We've long used a parachute dressing as one of our options for the *Callibaetis* dun, to show a dramatically different silhouette from either the Compara-Dun or Hairwing Dun. The dressing we've used most often in the past is the one we tie for the western March brown *(Rhithrogena mor-risoni)*, left over from that earlier hatch. It works, but only mildly. This listed parachute pattern, tied specifically for *Callibaetis*, is a much more accurate imitation. In the dressing as listed in Randy Stetzer's *Flies: The Best One Thousand* (Frank Amato Publications, 1992), its originator, Pret Frazier, calls for tail, body and hackle all to match the natural. That's a good call. Use the colors we've listed as a starting point. Collect on your waters and vary the materials to suit what you find.

That is our best advice during all *Callibaetis* hatches. We've listed dun dressings that offer three distinct silhouettes on the water. Choose one, two, or all three of them, collect a few naturals, and vary the ties to get the size and color corresponding to your own hatches. That will allow you to offer feeding trout some options.

Presentation

If rises to duns are sporadic, cast to cover any that you can reach. Present the first cast just to the near side of the center of the rise rings. If the trout hasn't moved, by casting short of it you won't scare it off, and it's likely to come right back up. Make your next cast five to ten or so feet to one side of the rise, and your final desperation cast ten to fifteen feet to the opposite side. If the trout hasn't come to your fly by then, it has probably moved on, and you should, too. Look for another rise, and cast to that.

If a few to a bunch of trout are rising in a small area, it is always best to make your casts to rises on your side of the pod, placing the fly so the line won't sail over any observant heads. Let the fly sit and wait for cruisers in the pod to come to it. If that doesn't work, begin placing casts to individual rises, but be careful not to spook the whole pod by casting over it.

If trout seem to remain constantly just out of your reach, even as you move toward them in your float tube or whatever it is that's floated you out there, it's because you're frightening them a bit, and pushing them away from you. Sit still and let them get used to you. Then cast carefully, placing your fly in a way that doesn't alert the trout and cause them to drift away from you.

If the movement pattern of a cruising fish can be determined by observation of its previous rises, the fly should always be presented where the next rise is most likely to appear. This type of rhythmic feeding can be classic gulper feeding, in which a trout rides high and porpoises along, sipping insects in its path every two or three feet. It can also consist of a trout that rose once twenty feet to your right, then straight in front of you. Place your fly twenty feet to the left, then keep your gaze down off the distant view. You don't want the trout to sneak up, take your fly, and get away without your noticing that it happened.

SPINNER IMITATIONS

We wrote in *Western Hatches* that we had not found *Callibaetis* spinners important. We've learned a lot since then, though how to match speckle-wing spinners successfully every time out is not among our present collective knowledge. We've learned that *Callibaetis* spinners can be very important at times. And we now carry dressings that match them and fool trout most of the time when they are important. There are still times, however, when we wish we had that magic precise right fly.

Callibaetis males dance over the water in afternoon and evening swarms. Bodies of spent females, with their distinctive mottled forewings, can almost blanket the water where the wind pushes them against logs or shoreline debris. At times trout completely ignore them. There are two possible explanations: either the trout are already gorged on nymphs and duns from the hatch, or there is simply not enough nourishment left in the spent females to interest the trout.

Other times trout sip selectively and maddeningly on spent *Callibaetis* spinners. We used to try the traditional Adams, first clipped on the bottom, then clipped on both bottom and top if that didn't work. Most often it didn't work very well, though at times it took a few trout, and on rare occasions took a bunch. But now we carry specific dressings designed for these difficult still- and slow-water spinner moments.

When trout are cruising, rising to *Callibaetis* duns, you can usually get a bend in your rod by plotting a single trout's line of march, and placing your fly where the next rise is expected to appear.

Gulper Special (Originator: Al Troth)

Hook:	Standard dry fly, 1X fine, size 12-18.
Thread:	Brown 6/0 or 8/0.
Wingpost:	White or light gray polypropylene yarn.
Tail:	Grizzly hackle fibers, splayed slightly.
Body:	Dark beaver fur.
Hackle:	Grizzly, wound parachute.

This is the classic dressing for Gulpers, tied by master professional Al Troth, out of Dillon, Montana. It has been proved over time, on some of the most selective trout in the world.

CDC *Callibaetis* Biot Spinner
(Originator: René Harrop)

Hook:	Standard dry fly, 1X fine, size 12-18.
Thread:	Tan 6/0 or 8/0.
Tail:	Ginger hackle fibers, split.
Abdomen:	Brown goose biot.
Wings:	White CDC with brown Z-lon topping.
Thorax:	Tan fur dubbing.

You can use this dressing as listed, or vary the abdomen, wing, and thorax colors to match specimens of *Callibaetis* spinners that you collect. Most often, this one will work. The key to the dressing is the segmentation provided by the biot. The segmented bodies of the naturals, when they lie spent on the water, are distinctly marked. It's likely that trout get a critical look at them, since they're well aware that the natural has expended its energy, and is not about to escape into the air.

Presentation

There is little to add here about presentation of *Callibaetis* spinner patterns that has not already been covered in the emerger and dun sections. You won't turn to these imitative dressings unless you see trout working visibly on spent spinners. In that case, make sure your tippet is three feet long and fine, then make your most delicate cast, and be patient once your fly is on the water. Feeding on *Callibaetis*, in this last stage of their lives, seems to be sporadic most of the time. If trout are set up and gulping, which is rare, you know how to time their rises and place the fly where the next one is expected. If trout are cruising, taking one here and one there, all across the water, do your best to cover them, and your second best not to spook them.

    Callibaetis spinner fishing can be frustrating. It can also be miraculous. Once you've got the right pattern, and have the trout figured out, you can settle in for a long period of pleasant dry-fly fishing. Those spinners aren't going anywhere. Neither are the trout.

When naturals are present in enough numbers to interest trout, *Callibaetis* spinner falls must be solved if you're going to catch many.

Chapter 8

Siphlonurus (Gray Drakes)

FAMILY: SIPHLONURIDAE

Genus: *Siphlonurus*
Western Species: 4
North America: 20
Important Western Species: *Siphlonurus occidentalis,*
   S. columbianus, S. alternatus, and *S. spectabilis*
Common Names: Gray drake, black drake, yellow drake

Siphlonurus occidentalis, called either the gray drake or black drake depending on whether the person naming it is looking at the dun or the darker spinner, is by far the most important of the listed western species. However, distinguishing species of *Siphlonurus* requires a microscope, and is beyond the means of an angler standing in the stream. Malcolm Knopp and Robert Cormier suggest in their excellent book *Mayflies* (Greycliff, 1997) that *S. columbianus* and *S. alternatus* (*S. alternatus* occurs in the eastern U.S. and across Canada) are almost identical to *S. occidentalis.* That forces us to wonder how often we have collected a gray drake, glanced at it, called it *S. occidentalis,* and gone about fishing over it without ever realizing our mistake. Just a few faint markings on the underside of the nymphal abdomen set the species apart. Fortunately for us, trout do not notice the differences any more than we do.

The gray drake group, consisting of the three species *S. occidentalis, S. alternatus* and *S. columbianus,* can easily be lumped, and matched with the same patterns. The final species, *S. spectabilis,* has been called the western yellow drake by Ernest Schwiebert in *Nymphs* and also by the late Polly Rosborough in *Tying and Fishing the Fuzzy Nymphs* (Orvis, 1965, republished by Stackpole, 1988). Polly mistakenly classified *S. spectabilis* as an *Ephemera* in the first publication of his book, but observed it closely enough to remark, "Except for its color and slightly smaller size, it appears to be almost identical to the Black Drake." Because Polly imitated the spinner stage of *S. occidentalis,* he was among those who referred to it as the black drake rather than the gray drake, more apt for the dun stage.

You'll collect *S. spectabilis* far less often than the more important gray drake consortium. It's possible you'll be able to imitate the yellow drake, if you find it important in your fishing, with dressings for the more abundant gray drakes by modifying their colors slightly. We have not encountered the yellow drake in fishable numbers in our own expeditions, but that does not mean you will not.

Emergence and Distribution

The gray drake group is widespread but produces somewhat isolated hatches, scattered all across the West, mostly in streams but in some lakes as well. Heavy hatches are known on the meadow stretches of Oregon's upper Williamson River, from the Yellowstone River inside the park where flows are tamed by the outflow of Yellowstone Lake, and on the Bow River below Calgary, where the river is a tailwater.

CRITERIA/SCORE	5		4		3		2		1	
Distribution: (within Western waters)	widespread		common		scattered	3.0	isolated		rare	
Abundance:	heavy	5.0	abundant		modest		trickling		individual	
Emergence type:	mid-water/slow		mid-water/fast		edges/slow		edges/fast		crawls out	1.0
Emergence time:	mid-day		early and/or late over long period		early and/or late over short period		dawn or dusk	2.0	night	
Emergence duration:	multiple seasons per year		well-defined long hatch period		well-defined short hatch period	3.0	poorly-defined long hatch period		poorly-defined short hatch	
(Behavior/Availability) Nymph:	excellent		good	3.5	moderate		slight		poor	
(Behavior/Availability) Emerger:	excellent		good		moderate		slight		poor	1.0
(Behavior/Availability) Dun:	excellent		good		moderate		slight	2.0	poor	
(Behavior/Availability) Spinner:	excellent	5.0	good		moderate		slight		poor	
Totals:		10.0		3.5		6.0		4.0		2.0

The lower Henrys Fork of the Snake, the little-known part of the river where it exits the mountains and flows out onto the flatlands, produces a most interesting hatch. If our understanding is correct—we haven't fished that part of the river but have heard and read about it—gray drakes thrive in irrigation canals there. They hatch in great numbers, and send their spinners collapsing onto the main river nearby, where they bring up the biggest trout.

Wherever you find placid waters, especially if they have lots of rooted vegetation, you might find excellent populations of gray drakes. They have scattered importance from California to British Columbia, from New Mexico to Alberta.

Gray drakes and yellow drakes are also sprinkled in lakes throughout the West. Again, their populations are not consistent, as for example the *Callibaetis,* which will be found in nearly any western stillwater you examine. *Siphlonurus* will be found in lakes separated by hundreds of miles. In our own fishing, we have collected them rarely in stillwaters, and have found fish feeding selectively on them only a couple of times in British Columbia lakes.

In California and Oregon, gray drakes begin emerging in spring or early summer. In Washington and British Columbia the hatches tend toward mid to late summer. In the Rocky Mountain region they are late emergers, with hatches starting in late July and continuing heavy through September and at times on into early October.

S. spectabilis, the yellow drake, ranges up and down the Pacific coastal states and British Columbia, again with very localized abundance. We have not collected them in fishable numbers, but others report having good fishing over them. Yellow drake hatches can overlap those of the slightly larger and darker gray drakes. In a brief note in *Fuzzy Nymphs,* Polly Rosborough mentioned that given a choice between the two, trout pounce on the yellow drake and ignore gray drakes. Southern Oregon's gentle Williamson River has heavy hatches of gray drakes, minor hatches of yellow drakes. It was the great Polly's home river. Much of our knowldge about these hatches, and most of our patterns, are from his research and writings.

The wide geographical range and extended emergence dates of *Siphlonurus* are typical for western insects. The angler who is prepared to identify and match a hatch of gray or yellow drakes wherever he finds them will have a great advantage over the angler who depends on emergence tables and pattern lists to direct his fishing.

SIPHLONURUS EMERGENCE TABLE

TIME	WINTER			SPRING			SUMMER			FALL		
	Dec.	Jan.	Feb.	March	April	May	June	July	Aug.	Sep.	Oct.	Nov.
7 a.m. - 10 a.m.												
10 a.m. - noon												
noon - 3 p.m.								Pacific				
3 p.m. - 7 p.m.												
7 p.m. - 10 p.m.										Rocky Mountains		

Nymph Characteristics

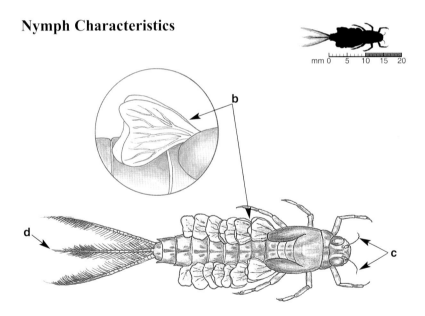

a. Swimmer nymph shape; thorax slightly wider than head or abdomen.

b. Gill plates large; double-plated gills on abdominal segments 1-2 or 1-7.

*c. Antennae short; less than 2 times width of head.

d. Three tails of equal length; fringed with interlocking hairs.

e. Body light to dark gray with darker markings on abdomen. *S. spectabilis* is pale tan to yellow.

d. Large, 10 to 20mm (3/4 in.) excluding tails.

*Note: The short antennae of *Siplonurus* nymphs make them easy to separate from the somewhat similar *Callibaetis* nymphs, which have long antennae.

Siphlonurus nymph.

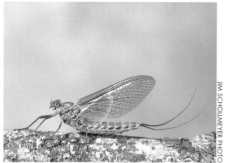
Siphlonurus dun.

Dun Characteristics

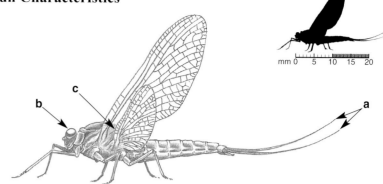

a. Two tails.
b. Males with pale band across middle of eyes.
c. Hindwings with rounded *costal angulation* on leading edge.
d. Wings light smoky-gray.
e. Color typically dark gray on top, light gray on underside, but may range from yellow-olive to almost black, usually with distinct markings on abdomen.
f. Large, body 10 to 20mm (3/4 in.).

Spinner Characteristics

a. Two tails.
b. Males with large eyes that meet on top of the head.
c. Males with pale band across middle of eyes.
d. Hindwings with rounded costal angulation.
e. Color typically dark wine-red on back, lighter on belly, but ranges from yellow-olive to almost black, usually with distinct banding on the abdominal segments.
f. Large, body 10 to 20mm (3/4 in.).

Siphlonurus spinner.

Habitat and behavior

Siphlonurus nymphs are most abundant in moving but slow water. Quiet pools and backwaters of freestone streams are occasional habitat. They can also be found along the margins of some lakes. These streamlined nymphs are usually found in fishable numbers only on peaceful streams with aquatic vegetation, plants and grasses that grow out of the water, or undercut banks where tangles of roots dangle in gentle currents. They can be found at times on open rock and mud bottoms, but usually when such areas are in association with nearby aquatic vegetation to which the nymphs can retreat.

Siphlonurus nymphs migrate from flowing water to quiet marginal areas as they mature. The first time we encountered a gray drake hatch, on southern Oregon's Williamson River, the numbers were overwhelming. Clouds of spinners swarmed over the river. The nymphs, however, could not be found. We swept nets through beds of plants, through grass growing along the edges of the stream, and beneath undercut banks, all in water deep enough to hold trout. The nets always came up empty.

A swale leading away from the river held a few inches of water that flooded some pasture grass. We dipped a net in it. The bottom came up squirming with hundreds of mature gray drake nymphs. They had migrated to such shallow water for emergence that fish could never follow them. That is typical of their behavior, though throughout most of their one-year life cycle, the nymphs live in water where trout can feed on them. Most intense feeding on the nymphs takes place when they migrate from their normal habitat to the edges in preparation for emergence.

Siphlonurus nymphs are excellent swimmers. Their three tails, with interlocking hairs, form an effective paddle. They dart in five- to ten-inch bursts across silty bottoms or among vegetation. They eat a variety of foods: algae, insect remains, and soft-bodied midge larvae are all part of their diet. We once had a *Hexagenia limbata* nymph expire in one of our aquariums that held gray drake nymphs as well. Before the big *Hex* was dead, *Siphlonurus* nymphs began grazing on its gills. The next morning they had consumed half of the big body.

As *Siphlonurus* nymphs mature, their wing pads become larger and darker. When ready to emerge, these nymphs are found in water where plant stems, rocks, or debris protrude from the surface. Emerging nymphs crawl several inches out of the water before molting into the dun. We have read references to *Siphlonurus* hatching in more typical mayfly fashion, out in open water and in the surface film, but have not observed this in our own fishing, though you might find it in your own.

Emergence may occur in the morning, early afternoon, or after dark. While on Oregon's Williamson River that first time, we searched for duns from morning until night, but saw none until the following dawn when we found them clinging to the grasses at streamside, covered with dew. They had apparently emerged at night. It is probable that most *Siphlonurus* hatches happen near or after dark, as defense against bird predation, but we have seen hatches of them on lakes on dark and cloudy afternoons. The duns are not available to feeding fish, unless they emerge out in open water, except when they are blown off their protruding emergence platforms and into the water by the wind.

After emergence, *Siphlonurus* duns molt to spinners in two to four days. Spinner flights form any time from mid-morning to late evening. A swarm might have hundreds of thousands of insects in the air at one time. After copulation and some time spent on streamside vegetation to let their eggs ripen, females fly back to the water and dip down to it, usually several times, releasing a cluster of eggs each time. When all eggs have been laid the females fall semi-spent or spent to the water.

At the peak of a spinner fall, the water is often covered by dead or dying females. Large rafts of them pile up in eddies like ice flows in the Arctic. At such times there is small hope that a trout will choose even the best artificial amid so many naturals. It might be a time to try mismatching the hatch with something like a Royal Wulff.

Imitation

Gray drake nymph dressings can be effective on waters with good populations of the naturals when fished in the days and hours prior to a hatch. Trout become accustomed to seeing the naturals migrating toward shore, and will not pass up an imitation of such a sizeable piece of protein. Duns are rarely available to trout, and you might consider yourself adequately armed with the size-12 Adams you surely carry for other reasons. We'll offer a dun dressing, but don't recommend you tie many unless you get into situations where trout request them. Then match the specimens you collect.

Gray drake spinners, often called black drakes, are the most important stage. They are so large that even when empty of eggs they make a good meal. Trout feed on them selectively when they're abundant on the water. If you encounter them, you'll need to match them.

Typical *Siphlonurus* habitat—in this case southern Oregon's Williamson River—is slow and stable, with rooted vegetation along the banks and on the bottom.

NYMPH IMITATIONS

Siphlonurus nymph patterns should be tied on 2X or 3X long hooks. The naturals range in size from 14, when immature, to 10 or 12 when migrating for emergence. You'll probably need imitations only in those largest sizes. Colors range from pale yellow for *S. spectabilis* through light to dark gray for *S. occidentalis* and related species. These swimming nymphs are streamlined; dressings for them should be slender and tapered.

Black Drake (Originator: Polly Rosborough)

Hook:	3X long, size 10-12.
Thread:	Gray 3/0 or 6/0.
Tail:	Speckled guinea fibers, short.
Body:	Beaver belly fur, with guard hairs.
Legs:	Speckled guinea fibers, tied in at each side.
Wingcase:	Small bunch of natural black ostrich flues.

Polly Rosborough described this pattern in his *Tying and Fishing the Fuzzy Nymphs*, still one of the most valuable references available to western fly fishermen. If you don't fish his hatches and therefore use many of his patterns, you'll still learn a lot from how Polly was able to *see*: collecting an insect, understanding its behavior in relation to trout, identifying and sometimes misidentifying it, but always matching it with a killing pattern and presentation.

Near Enough (Originator: Polly Rosborough)

Hook:	3X long, size 10-12.
Thread:	Gray 3/0 or 6/0.
*Tails:	Barred mallard flank dyed tannish-gray.
Body:	Light gray fox underfur.
Legs:	Barred mallard flank dyed tannish-gray.
Wingcase:	Butts of leg fibers.

*Note: Polly was a professional tier, known for his skills at dying fly-tying materials. He called for dying this tail material, "...in a very weak solution of half gray and half tan Rit." Do that if you'd like. If you're a more casual tier, and desire just a few of these flies, simply mark a mallard flank feather with a dark tan or light brown waterproof marking pen, or use a dark flank feather the way it arrives off the duck. Few trout will complain.

Polly tied his fuzzy fur bodies with what he called a *fur noodle*. The fur is clipped from the pelt, usually all guard hairs are removed, then a two- to three-inch length of fur is elongated in the palm of one hand. The skein is then rolled between the hands to form the noodle. It is tied in at the base of the tail, captured in a thread dubbing loop, and twisted tight enough to form a segmented body when wound. Polly roughed up the finished fly with the teeth of a hacksaw blade, hence the term *fuzzy nymph*.

Yellow Drake Nymph (Originator: Polly Rosborough)

Hook:	3X long, size 12-14.
Thread:	Pale yellow 3/0 or 6/0.
Tail:	Woodduck flank fibers.
Rib:	Working thread.
Body:	Pale cream yarn or fur.
Legs:	Woodduck flank fibers.
Wingcase:	Butts of leg fibers.

This dressing imitates *S. spectabilis*, which you might or might not ever encounter in numbers enough to need an imitation. If you do, this will do it.

If you don't, this will make an excellent searching nymph to tug slowly across gentle flowing waters, or to fish along the edges of a western still-water or meadow stream.

Presentation

The agile swimming of *Siphlonurus* naturals indicates the need to impart action to a nymph imitation. This can be done by casting down and across stream, letting the current activate the fly as it swings down and around. You may need to add a little life, especially in the slow water these insects often inhabit, with pulsing movements of the rod tip, or with short strips of line.

Most fish feed on *Siphlonurus* nymphs in slack water or eddies along the margins of streams, and in areas around the margins of lakes where aquatic plants grow. A cast that quarters out from a position on the bank, then is fished on the swing so that it swims back in toward shore, will mimic the behavior of the naturals. You can also wade a ways out and cast in toward the bank if the water is not too deep. If you do, make your casts upstream and retrieves downstream, keeping the nymph swimming near the bank as long as possible.

Flies for this sort of shallow nymph fishing should not be weighted. Rig with a floating line and eight- to ten-foot leader. If you desire to fish them near the bottom across a broader reach of water, use a wet-tip line to get them down, and shorten the leader to six or seven feet. You'll be doing this in slow to moderate currents, because that's where the naturals live. Cast a bit upstream from straight across. Give the wet-tip line plenty of time to tug the fly down there. Coax it across with rhythmic pulses of the rod tip. If the water is too slow to animate the fly, use the same stripping retrieve you'd use to fish it in a lake. That's the way Polly fished these favorite flies of his.

DUN IMITATIONS

Siphlonurus normally emerge by crawling out of the water on plant stems, sticks, and rocks. Duns are seldom available to trout. However, they are large and cruising trout will move long distances to take strays. A fly that looks a bit like them will suddenly have great value if you ever find a situation where duns are on the water where trout can get at them. If you fish waters where populations of gray drakes are heavy, be at least a little prepared. Carry the Adams, for which you already know the dressing, in size 10 and 12, or tie the following Gray Wulff in the same sizes.

Gray Wulff (Originator: Lee Wulff)

Hook:	Standard dry fly, size 10-12.
Thread:	Gray 6/0.
Wings:	Brown bucktail, upright and divided.
Tail:	Brown bucktail.
Body:	Bluish-gray wool yarn.
Hackle:	Blue dun.

If you tie the Gray Wulff just for this hatch, dress it sparsely. It won't have to float on any rough water. On rare days when gray drake duns are getting on the water, and being fed on by trout, it will be late afternoon, the sky will be dark, and the wind will usually be blowing at least a bit. Cast the fly to rises, of course, which will be in calm water right along the edges, usually just outside areas where grass, sedges, or cat-tail stalks protrude from the water. The trout might be large. Set the hook cautiously.

To their mild surprise, the authors recently discovered a fine population of *Siphlonurus occidentalis* in this low-gradient, farmland stream that they had fished for years. Trout thrashed Near Enough nymphs cast to the banks and coaxed into swimming along the grassy overhangs and undercuts.

SPINNER IMITATIONS

Gray drake spinners are more likely than duns to be available to fish. During the peak of a hatch period on water with good populations, spinner falls are at times too heavy to fish effectively. So many naturals are on the water that presenting an artificial seems futile. The following patterns are offered for days with light spinner falls, for fishing in the hour or so before spinners coat the currents, or for the early and late stages of the hatch. But don't give up even in the midst of a heavy hatch. Trout can always be singled out, and pestered until your fly arrives in front of them just at the moment they're ready to tip up and take one, if you're patient enough.

Black Drake Spinner (Originator: Polly Rosborougb)

Hook:	Standard dry fly, 1X fine, size 10-12.
Thread:	Black 6/0.
Tail:	Purplish-dun hackle fibers.
Rib:	Gray thread.
Body:	Purplish-brown synthetic yarn.
Hackle:	Purplish-dun.

Polly's patterns call for a lot of dyed hackle and body materials. You should study the exact colors of the naturals on your own waters before getting out the dying pots to match them. You might find different colors in demand. With the way materials have proliferated in recent years, you're also very likely to find precisely what you need in your nearest fly shop.

Spent Gray Drake (Source: Schollmeyer)

Hook:	Standard dry fly, size 10-12.
Thread:	Brown 6/0.
Tails:	Blue dun hackle fibers, split.
Wings:	Light dun hackle, tied spent.
Body:	Reddish-brown fur or synthetic dubbing.

This pattern is listed by Jim Schollmeyer in his *Hatch Guide For Western Streams.* It is excellent for many other rust-bodied spinners.

Yellow Drake Spinner (Originator: Polly Rosborough)

Hook:	Standard dry fly, 1X fine, size 12-14.
Thread:	Pale yellow 6/0.
Tails:	Pale ginger hackle fibers.
Rib:	Working thread, doubled.
Body:	Pale cream yarn or fur.
Hackle:	Pale blue dun.

This dressing is for those rare moments when you might enounter a fishable *S. spectabilis* spinner fall, and the even rarer time when it might be in daylight. The naturals are reported to return to the water most often well after dark, but might be early for you some cloudy late afternoon or evening.

Presentation

Spinner patterns should be presented on moving water with the usual drag-free drifts. During heavy spinner falls this requires spotting a fish carefully, timing its rise rhythm, and presenting the fly to it precisely. The best casting position is usually across from the trout and slightly upstream,

Big trout can happen in *Siphlonurus* water.
Dave caught this while fishing the Williamson River with his wife Masako and the great Polly Rosborough.

but be careful about sending wading waves down to spook the fish. Use either the downstream wiggle cast or cross-stream reach cast when you're positioned to the side or upstream from the trout.

Because of the precision needed to get a fly right in front of a trout at the moment it might be ready for the next take, during a very heavy spinner fall when lots of naturals are available to the fish, a case can be made for getting into position downstream from the trout, as near to it as you dare creep. At the precise right moment, after it has taken a natural and gone down for a moment, settle your fly gently on the water a foot in front of the trout's nose. Be prepared to try time after time, and be careful not to spook the fish.

We fished with Polly on his home Williamson River one final time when he was in his eighties. The gray drake hatch was sparse; just a few spinners drifted the currents that last afternoon. Not many trout were working, but Polly was able to get right up onto one that was feeding regularly. He took up his position on the bank above it and just a few feet downstream from it. When he made his cast, he smacked his spinner to the water several feet upstream from the trout, so hard that the dry fly sank.

We thought he'd made a mistake until the trout boiled the fly just inches beneath the surface. Polly played it out, released it, said, "That's how you fish my Black Drake Spinner."

He'd fished it wet on purpose. He'd never written that. It made us wonder what other secrets the great man knew about insects, fly patterns, and trout, and took with him to his grave.

Chapter 9

Ameletus (Brown Duns)

FAMILY: AMELETIDAE

Genus: *Ameletus*.
Western Species: 26
North America: 34
Important Western Species: *Ameletus cooki, A. oregonensis, A. sparsatus, A. velox*
Common Name: Brown duns.

Twenty-six western species are now listed in the genus *Ameletus*. Very few are found in the East and Midwest. When we list those above as important, it is with reservation. We have not found any species of *Ameletus* to be of major importance in trout fishing, though we collect them often, and know that trout feed on the nymphs at times, and that they probably take the duns as well, though we've never seen evidence that they do it selectively, thereby creating a hatch that you need to match.

Ameletus nymphs live almost entirely in waters that are not inhabited by trout, or on the margins of trout waters where fish have trouble getting at them. The nymphs crawl out to emerge, so duns are almost always safe from trout. Spinner falls are either too sparse to interest trout, or occur at night.

The entire genus retains footnote status in fishing terms until trout are observed to feed selectively on one of the stages of the natural. In our own experience, that has not happened yet. But they're present on western trout streams, and you'll collect them often enough that you'll wonder what they are, and wonder what their importance might be. You might even find them important on your own specific waters.

Ameletus **HATCH IMPORTANCE SCORE: 20.0**

CRITERIA/SCORE	5		4		3		2		1	
Distribution: (within Western waters)	widespread		common		scattered	3.0	isolated		rare	
Abundance:	heavy		abundant		modest		trickling	2.0	individual	
Emergence type:	mid-water/slow		mid-water/fast		edges/slow		edges/fast		crawls out	1.0
Emergence time:	mid-day	5.0	early and/or late over long period		early and/or late over short period		dawn or dusk		night	
Emergence duration:	multiple seasons per year		well-defined long hatch period		well-defined short hatch period		poorly-defined long hatch period	2.0	poorly-defined short hatch	
(Behavior/Availability) **Nymph:**	excellent		good		moderate		slight	2.0	poor	
(Behavior/Availability) **Emerger:**	excellent		good		moderate		slight		poor	1.0
(Behavior/Availability) **Dun:**	excellent		good		moderate		slight	2.0	poor	
(Behavior/Availability) **Spinner:**	excellent		good		moderate		slight	2.0	poor	
Totals:		5.0		0.0		3.0		10.0		2.0

Note: Overall importance is typically less than the modest ranking score because of limiting factors like availability and sparse abundance.

Emergence and Distribution

We have seen scattered *Ameletus* emergences in the opening and closing weeks of the trout season, and at almost all times in between. They seem to peak in early spring, then again in fall. Due to the large number of species and wide variety of habitats found in the West, hatches of *Ameletus* might occur on one water or another any time from February through October.

Usually their presence is given away by the sighting of a few duns on rocks at the edge of the stream or river, on cloudy and even rainy days. They are large, and easy to notice when they lift off and fly toward streamside vegetation. But their cast nymphal shucks, always at or just above the waterline of rocks or sticks and logs right along shore, are evidence that the nymphs have moved into the shallows and crawled out of the water before emergence. We have never noticed trout feeding on them, though no doubt they take such a large insect whenever they get a chance.

AMELETUS EMERGENCE TABLE

TIME	WINTER			SPRING			SUMMER			FALL		
	Dec.	Jan.	Feb.	March	April	May	June	July	Aug.	Sep.	Oct.	Nov.
7 a.m. - 10 a.m.												
10 a.m. - noon												
noon - 3 p.m.												
3 p.m. - 7 p.m.												
7 p.m. - 10 p.m.												

Nymph Characteristics

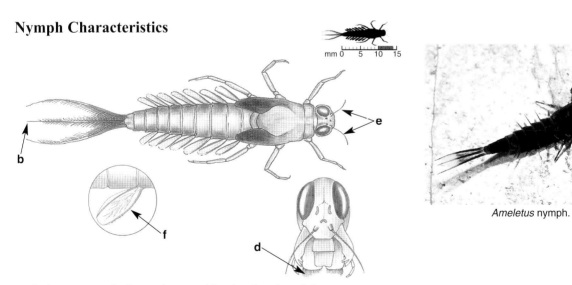

Ameletus nymph.

a. Swimmer nymph shape; thorax wider than head or abdomen.

b. Three tails with interlocking hairs.

c. Head is *hypognathus*, or postured downward.

d. Lower mouthparts (maxillae) have crown of comb-shaped spines.

e. Antennae short, less than 2 times width of head.

f. Small, single, oval gills on abdominal segments 1-7. Leading edge, and sometimes both leading and trailing edges, of gills with a dark, narrow *sclerotized* band.

g. Length, excluding tails, 10-14 mm (approx. 1/2 in.).

Ameletus dun.

Dun Characterstics

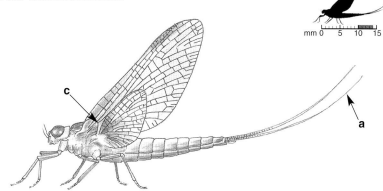

a. Two tails.

b. Males with large eyes that meet on top of head.

c. Hindwings with pointed projection on leading edge.

d. Brown, yellowish-brown, or pale olive bodies and wings. Some have distinct banding on abdomen.

e. Length, excluding tails, 10-14 mm (approx. 1/2 in.).

Spinner Characteristics

a. Two tails.

b. Males with large eyes that meet on top of head.

c. Hindwings with pointed projection on leading edge.

d. Wings hyaline, or clear, without darker markings.

e. Body brown, yellowish-brown, or pale olive.

f. Length, excluding tails, 10-14 mm (approx. 1/2 in.).

Ameletus spinner.

Habitat and Behavior

Ameletus are distributed throughout the western states, but fishable numbers occur very sporadically across this range. Some of the best populations are found in high mountain streams in the Rockies, where they have been collected at altitudes up to 11,000 feet.

Ameletus nymphs are commonly found in small, rapid streams, near but not in fast water. They rest on clean stones, vegetation, or debris, usually off toward the edges. They are not found in lakes. We have collected them from small coastal streams, clear and cold spring creeks, the big and placid Willamette River, and large desert rivers, in fact from almost all of the moving waters we fish. They often inhabit deep undercut banks, away from the main current, the same places inhabited by large trout. No doubt they're eaten by them, again just not selectively in our experience.

Ameletus nymphs can swim with minnow-like speed. Disturbances of their habitat will often send them scurrying for better cover. They have a one-year life cycle. The nymphs feed on algae or other plant material. When mature they select a quiet area near the water's edge to emerge. The nymphs crawl from the water on plant stems, twigs, rocks, or logs, like the related genus *Siphlonurus*, before emergence of the dun. Many times we've seen nymphs crawl just to the waterline, with the head and thorax just breaking through the surface tension, where emergence took place.

It might take ten to fifteen minutes for the dun to free itself from the nymphal shuck. Though of little fishing value, this type of emergence is a wonder to behold, and not difficult to observe. If you see a few duns at rest on streamside rocks, cease casting long enough to look around for a nymph at the waterline. Watch briefly and it will begin that magic transformation.

Ameletus nymphs are often found beneath undercut banks and among the vegetated tangles created by logs
fallen into spring creeks, such as Oregon's Fall River.

Spinner flights of *Ameletus* have not been recorded in either fishing
or scientific literature. Mating may take place far from the water or high
above it. Dave was sitting high atop a rim above the Deschutes River
once, looking far down over Beavertail flat, taking wide angle photos of
the river after a long hike in the early morning hours. A gorgeous male
spinner, about size 10, suddenly landed on his shirtsleeve. It sat long
enough to introduce itself, through a swift observation of its tail count,
size and color, and the shape of its eyes, as an *Ameletus*, then took off
again. A swallow appeared from nowhere and snatched the luckless insect
out of the air three feet in front of Dave's nose.

Twenty years ago in *Western Hatches* we wrote that there is still
much to be learned about this interesting western genus. That is still
true. It seems, however, that the importance to fly fishermen of *Ameletus*
species will remain minor because their lifestyles do not cause them to
constitute hatches that need to be matched.

Imitation

We offer little in the way of *Ameletus* imitations, first because few have
been devised by other writers, second because we have seen no need to
develop any ourselves. You will certainly collect them in your home
waters or on your travels throughout the West. You might find them in
fishable numbers and situations. The sparse information available about
Ameletus offers little help in the search for imitations. This is one case
where you'll get your chance to write your own book on the western
hatches.

We're quite certain that Polly Rosborough's *Isonychia bicolor* nymph is an imitation of an *Ameletus* species, since *I. bicolor* is not present in the West but is similar to many *Ameletus* we have collected in waters we know Polly fished. We collected some specimens once from Fall River in Oregon's Cascade Mountains. When we showed them to Polly, he said, "That's my *Isonychia bicolor!*" If you find these nymphs to be important in your waters we suggest you try Polly's pattern, or create your own variation based upon it.

TIED BY RONN LUCAS, SR.

Isonychia Bicolor (Originator: Polly Rosborough)

Hook:	3X long, size 8-10.
Thread:	Brown 3/0 or 6/0.
Tail:	Pheasant body fibers dyed dark brown.
Rib:	Yellow thread.
Body:	Fiery brown synthetic yarn.
Legs:	Pheasant body fibers dyed dark brown, tied in at throat.
Gills:	Tuft of marabou, one shade lighter than body, 2/3 length of body.
Wingcase:	Dyed seal brown hen hackle tip, 1/3 body length.

Polly states that the body color of the natural varies from purplish-brown to fiery brown, that imitations are successful within that range, and that body color is less important than size, shape, and action of the fly in the water. In our experience his statement applies perfectly to the *Ameletus* that we have collected.

Presentation

If you find need for *Ameletus* nymph imitations, present them along undercut banks and the margins of streams. They should be given swimming action either by the current or with a pulsing of the rod tip, just as you fish the more important *Siphlonurus* nymphs. There is little question *Ameletus* imitations will take trout. The only question is whether trout take them for *Ameletus.*

Duns and Spinners

The sporadic hatching of *Ameletus*, combined with their habit of crawling out to emerge, casts doubt on the usefulness of dun patterns for this genus. If you find that fish take *Ameletus* duns selectively on your waters, we suggest working out patterns along the lines of the traditional hackled style, or more accurate imitations based on hairwing duns or parachutes. Always base your imitations on collected specimens.

We offer no suggestions for *Ameletus* spinners. According to Edmunds, Jensen, and Berner's scientific work, *The Mayflies of North and Central America*, (University of Minnesota, 1976), *Ameletus* mating flights have never been observed. We have seen only sporadic returns of ovipositing females, none of them fed upon by trout.

Chapter 10

Isonychia (Great Western Leadwings)

FAMILY: ISONYCHIIDAE

Genus: *Isonychia*
Western Species: 5
North America: 17
Important Western Species: *Isonychia campestris, I. sicca, I. velma*
Common Names: Great western leadwing, slate drake.

Isonychia is a prominent genus in the East and Midwest, and causes fishable hatches in many waters there. They are not as common in the West, and trout do not get chances to feed on them selectively across most of our vast landscape. They are, however, fairly well represented in southern Oregon and northern California trout streams, and can be important at times on waters there. The genus reaches its greatest importance in waters that bound out of California's High Sierra.

These insects are large, especially *I. velma*, and trout that get the chance feed on them in the nymph stage. They crawl out of the water to emerge on rocks and protruding vegetation, so the dun is not as important as the nymph. California writers Ralph and Lisa Cutter report in the February, 2004 issue of *California Fly Fisher* that they've seen trout in the Little Truckee feeding selectively on duns cut in half by dragonflies. Those aerial predators caught the duns in mid-flight, ate the juicy abdomens, dropped the front halves to the water. Trout fed selectively on the remainders—the wings, legs, and heads—of the big insects. The Cutters used Quigley Cripples with the trailing shucks pinched off, and did well with them. Though we'll not list a dun dressing, you might keep that trick in mind.

Spinner flights tend to be sparse on most streams, but they're reported to be important on the Pit River in California, and are likely taken by trout at times in all waters where populations of the naturals are found.

Isonychia   **HATCH IMPORTANCE SCORE:**   **15.0**

CRITERIA/SCORE	5		4		3		2		1	
Distribution: (within Western waters)	widespread		common		scattered		isolated	2.0	rare	
Abundance:	heavy		abundant		modest	2.5	trickling		individual	
Emergence type:	mid-water/slow		mid-water/fast		edges/slow		edges/fast		crawls out	1.0
Emergence time:	mid-day		early and/or late over long period		early and/or late over short period	2.5	dawn or dusk		night	
Emergence duration:	multiple seasons per year		well-defined long hatch period		well-defined short hatch period		poorly-defined long hatch period	2.0	poorly-defined short hatch	
(Behavior/Availability) Nymph:	excellent		good		moderate		slight	2.0	poor	
(Behavior/Availability) Emerger:	excellent		good		moderate		slight		poor	1.0
(Behavior/Availability) Dun:	excellent		good		moderate		slight		poor	1.0
(Behavior/Availability) Spinner:	excellent		good		moderate		slight		poor	1.0
Totals:		0.0		0.0		5.0		6.0		4.0

Isonychia spinners are speedsters. They sprint in a smooth, straight-line flight from five to twenty feet above the water, giving even swallows a good run for their money. They're big bites, so it's likely that trout take them whenever the chance arises. But it's rare that trout feed on *Isonychia* spinners selectively.

Emergence and Distribution

Emergence of *Isonychia* in the Yellowstone area, notably on the lower Yellowstone River, begins in late May and continues until the first week of July. Its importance is often reduced to zero because it coincides with runoff. In the Pacific region, emergence is later in the year, normally beginning in August and continuing through October. Daily emergence is most often in early to late afternoon, or at dusk and after dark.

Isonychia campestris and *I. velma* both have Northwest distribution. *I. sicca* is found across most of the U.S., including hatches in the Southwest. *I. sicca* is also reported from the Yellowstone River in Montana. We have collected *I. velma* specimens from the Willamette and Rogue rivers in Oregon, and Polly Rosborough reported them from his home Williamson River in southern Oregon. Both *I. velma* and *I. sicca* are found in California waters such as the McCloud and Yuba Rivers. Because *Isonychia* crawl out to emerge, similar to the related *Siphlonurus* and *Ameletus*, nymphs of *Isonychia* are more important than either duns or spinners.

ISONYCHIA EMERGENCE TABLE

TIME	WINTER			SPRING			SUMMER			FALL		
	Dec.	Jan.	Feb.	March	April	May	June	July	Aug.	Sep.	Oct.	Nov.
7 a.m. - 10 a.m.												
10 a.m. - noon												
noon - 3 p.m.							Rocky Mountains		Pacific			
3 p.m. - 7 p.m.												
7 p.m. - 10 p.m.												

Isonychia velma

Nymph Characteristics

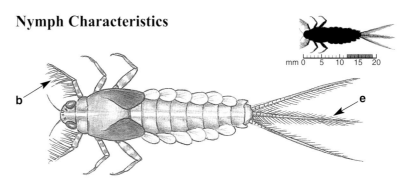

mm 0 5 10 15 20

a. Swimmer shape, thorax wider than head or abdomen.
b. Forelegs with double row of long hairs on femur and tibia.
c. Gills plate-like on abdominal segments 1-7.
d. Slender, finger-like gill tufts at base of gills and base of forelegs.
e. Three tails of equal length, fringed with fine interlocking hairs.
f. Body reddish-brown or purplish-brown to gray.
g. Mature nymphs large, from 12 to 19mm (1/2-3/4 in.) excluding tails.

Dun Characteristics

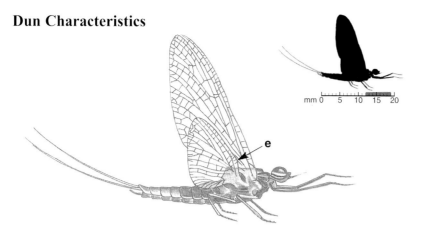

mm 0 5 10 15 20

a. Two tails.
b. Remnants of gill tufts remain at base of forelegs.
c. Middle and hind legs pale relative to front legs
d. Large hindwings; half the size of forewings.
e. Hindwing costal angulation rounded.
f. Forewings dark gray, often splotched or mottled.
g. Body reddish or purplish-brown to gray.
h. Body, excluding tails, 12 to 19mm (1/2-3/4 in.).

Spinner Characteristics

a. Two tails.
b. Males with large eyes meeting on top of the head.
c. Middle and hind legs pale relative to front legs
d. Hindwings with rounded costal angulation.
e. Wings clear.
f. Body reddish or purplish-brown to gray.
g. Body, excluding tails, 12 to 19mm (1/ 2-3/4 in.)

Habitat and Behavior

Isonychia nymphs prefer riffles in small to large streams. They often perch on tangled branches or other debris that trails in fast water. Rocks or flat ledges in swift currents may also harbor *Isonychia* nymphs. They will be found at times facing the force of a modest current, but typically shelter in niches between bottom stones.

They are extremely strong swimmers. Their tails, with interlocking hairs, form a large surface area and provide the major thrust. The nymphs can swim upstream in surprisingly swift currents. They are able to evade collecting nets with speed and agility, one reason that they show up less frequently than other insects in net samples. It's probable that when a trout sees an *Isonychia* nymph and attempts to take it, the prospective prey dashes off quite briskly.

The long hairs on the forelegs of an *Isonychia* nymph form a fil-ter-feeding basket. The nymph perches on a stick or rock, faces into the current anchored by its middle and hind legs and braced by its tails held against the substrate. The nymph holds this basket in front of its head. Diatoms, algae, and even tiny aquatic insects and other animals are all filtered from the current and then browsed off the hairs. The nymphs are at times predaceous, preying on smaller aquatic insect nymphs and larvae.

Isonychia nymphs mature in about one year. They crawl a few inches out of the water on rocks or plant stems to emerge. This occurs in late afternoon, evening, or just after dark. The restless movement of *Isonychia* nymphs toward shore prior to emergence provides the best fishing opportunity over these large insects. Open-water emergence near shore has been reported when the hatch happens during the flood cycle of a stream. This probably happens most often on waters like the lower Yellowstone River, where *Isonychia* have been obsrved to hatch during the typical runoff period that ends in July. We suspect that when open-water embergence takes place, rivers are typically out of shape for dry-fly fishing, but can't prove this from our own observations, which have been scant about this group.

Isonychia duns are not commonly available to fish. After twenty to thirty hours at rest in the terrestrial environment, the subimagoes molt into sexually mature imagoes or spinners. Spinners generally gather in late evening, although we have observed swarms active in the morning and the middle of the day. The large spinners are extremely strong flyers, for mayflies, and are even able to fight a strong wind in order to mate and lay their eggs. Fertilized females release a spherical egg mass several feet above the water or dip to the water's surface to release it. Not all female *Isonychia* end their lives lying spent on the water. Some return to the terrestrial environment and die there.

Imitation

Not many *Isonychia* patterns have been discussed in western fishing literature. A common thread runs through the two most famous flies. The late Charles Brooks wrote about his Velma May nymph in *Nymph Fishing for Larger Trout* (Crown, 1976). Its origins did not stem from any selectivity on the part of trout. Charlie ordered some black yarn and received purple. Rather than return it he fashioned a big nymph with it. He fished it and it took trout on a stream in Yellowstone Park that he didn't name. Then he researched his insect books and discovered that *I. velma* is a rare aquatic insect with a purplish body. Only then did he go out and find that *I. velma* was resident in that stream.

As Brooks summed it up, "It is sometimes poosible to work backward from a result in nymph fishing to identify a natural of which the artificial came first."

Polly Rosborough recounts the development of his *Isonychia velma* nymph in the 1988 edition of his *Tying and Fishing the Fuzzy Nymphs*. He and a friend were walking back to their car in moonlight after a hot *Hexagenia limbata* hatch. Polly heard the water being torn up near the trail, ran to it, cast and caught a two-pounder. Later he examined the trout's stomach, and found it crammed with *Hexs* in all stages. Among them, Polly wrote, "...standing out like a sore thumb was a giant nymph of a deep maroon-brown color. Counting its three half-inch tails, it was an easy inch and a half long." Polly based the creation of his *Isonychia velma* pattern, an effective one, on that one sighting of one specimen.

Though both of these dressings are imitations of the large *I. velma* nymph, neither were designed and tied in response to selective situations. There is little doubt about the effectiveness of either fly. There is also little doubt that a trout, living in water with even a small population of this big insect, would not be glad to give chase if it got a chance at a natural nymph, or a fly that resembled one. A few of these big dressings stuck into your nymph box, or possibly more appropriately your streamer box, might catch big fish for you. Those big fish might or might not be taking the fly for what you're tying it to imitate. You have to decide if that matters.

The placid stretch of the upper Williamson River where Polly Rosborough reported finding a specimen of *Isonychia velma*.

Nymph Imitations

Isonychia nymph imitations should be tied on 3X long hooks, in sizes 8 through 10. Colors range from purplish-brown to gray. The dressings for these powerful swimmers should be blockier than most swimmer patterns. The two following flies clearly reflect the personalities and fishing styles of their originators. Charlie was a stout and strong man, fished big and brutal water. Polly was slender and agile, fished smaller and more gentle streams.

Velma May (Originator: Charles Brooks)

Hook:	3X long, size 8-10.
Weight:	Lead wire, 12-20 turns.
Thread:	Olive 3/0 or 6/0.
Tail:	Grizzly hackle fibers dyed dark green.
Body:	Mottled brown wool.
Rib:	Purple wool, one strand, and gray ostrich herl.
Overrib:	Gold wire.
Hackle:	Grizzly, dyed dark green.

Brooks weighted this fly heavily, reflecting the rough Yellowstone area waters he fished, and his preference for thudding his flies right to the bottom. If you find *Isonychia* nymphs in heavy, fast water, consideration should be given to this weighted imitation.

Isonychia velma (Originator: Polly Rosborough)

Hook:	3X long, size 6-8.
Thread:	Brown 3/0 or 6/0.
Tail:	Three fibers of purple-dyed ring-necked pheasant center tail feather.
Rib:	Gold wire.
Body:	Deep purplish-brown synthetic yarn.
Legs:	Medium brown ring-necked pheasant body fibers tied in at throat.
Gills:	Purplish-brown marabou tied in over the body and extending two-thirds the length of the body.
Wingcase:	Dyed purplish-brown ring-necked pheasant body feather tied over the gills, extending one-third the length of the body.

Polly's patterns are shaped by the nature of his southern Oregon and northern California streams. These waters have less steep gradients and are not as boisterous as many western rivers. His unweighted flies fish such waters perfectly. He fished them on the swing, most often with a teasing rhythm of the rod tip. We recommend his pattern for *Isonychia* nymphs wherever you might find them in moderate to gentle water.

A. P. Black

Hook:	3X long, size 8-10.
Weight:	10-15 turns lead wire.
Thread:	Black 6/0 or 8/0.
Tails:	Moose body hair.
Rib:	Fine copper wire.
Abdomen:	Black rabbit fur mixed with black Sparkle Yarn.
Shellback:	Moose body hair.
Thorax:	Same as abdomen.
Hackle:	Two turns dark furnace hen.

Dick Galland, owner of the beautiful Clearwater House on California's Hat Creek, wrote a flyfisherman.com article in 2003 titled "California's Pit River." He mentioned the mid-September to early October *Isonychia velma* hatch on that river, and recommended a sparsely dressed A. P. Black with a soft-hackle collar, fished dead drift down seams or with jerky strips along slower edges. The same fly has long been a standard on the McCloud, probably in part because of its resemblance to the *I. velma* nymphs found in that river.

Presentation

Presentation of *Isonychia* nymph imitations should mimic their bold swimming. They should be given long strips with the line hand in slow water, or rhythmic action of the rod tip in fast water. In some situations, where the water is fast, it is best to tumble them along the bottom with no action except that given by the current.

Interestingly, both Brooks and Rosborough were advocates of wet-tip lines, but used them very differently. Brooks fished short upstream casts and used his line to help his heavily-weighted fly sink abruptly to the bottom and stay there. He fished his nymph almost under his rod tip until it passed below him. He fished out the drift, then let the current lift the heavy fly and wet-tip line toward the surface before lobbing the next cast upstream to fish a line of drift a foot or two from the first.

Polly made much longer casts out across the current, anywhere from straight across to a bit upstream or down from straight across. He then gave his unweighted fly some time to sink behind that wet-tip line, then began a pulsing swing, as if he were fishing a streamer.

Each of the two famous men fished their *Isonychia* nymphs deep, but in very different water types, with methods that suited the water and also their separate personalities.

Duns and Spinners

The *Isonychia* habit of crawling out on rocks or plant stems to emerge negates the effectiveness of dun imitations. To our knowledge none have been created for western hatches, and we have not bumped into situations that call for them in our own fishing.

In their comprehensive *Mayflies*, Knopp and Cormier recommend the Mahogany Spinner for the spinner stage of *I. sicca* and *I. campestris*. For *I. velma* they advise substituting a dark gray body material in the same dressing. We'll offer that advice, with our own that you should tie them only when you find *Isonychia* spinner falls that call for them.

Mahogany Spinner (Source: Knopp and Cormier)

Hook:	Standard dry fly, 1X fine, size 8-12.
Thread:	Brown 6/0.
Tails:	Pale dun hackle fibers, split.
Rib:	Tan Monocord thread.
Body:	Dark reddish-brown or dark gray fur or synthetic dubbing.
Wings:	White polypro fibers, spent.

Burgundy Spinner

Hook:	Standard dry fly, size 10-12.
Thread:	Red 6/0 or 8/0.
Tails:	Brown hackle fibers, split.
Body:	Burgundy fur or synthetic dubbing, or yarn.
Wings:	Brown hackle, clipped top and bottom.

Dick Galland recommends the Burgundy Spinner in size 10 for *Isonychia velma* spinner falls on the Pit River. Slight variations of it in size and color would likely fish for any *Isonychia* spinner activity.

Presentation

Trout are not often selective to the sparse spinner falls of this genus, which will usually occur at dusk or after dark except on overcast days. However, *Isonychia* patterns, because of the size of the naturals, can make excellent searching flies wherever the naturals are present on the water and a few are being seen by trout.

Part III

MAYFLY CRAWLERS

Introduction

Mayfly crawler nymphs, unlike streamlined swimmers, are generally robust and blocky in the body, though it's such a diverse group that the generalization gets tangled with the exceptions, most noticeable in the slender *Leptophlebia* and *Paraleptophlebia* genera. For the most part, however, crawler nymph stoutness reflects their mode of living. They live mostly in moving water, sometimes in the midst of the fastest water, but most often in slow to moderate currents, browsing about among bottom stones, spending most of their time on the undersides of rocks or in the cracks and crevices between them. At times, generally related to pre-hatch migratory activity or to behavioral drift, they can be found on the tops of rocks, exposed to the current, or even out swimming or drifting with the current.

The most common crawlers, and among those most important to western fly fishers, are in the Ephemerellidae family. These include the famous western green drakes, lesser green drakes, and pale morning duns. Some crawler groups live somewhat on the periphery of trout streams, and are less often important to anglers, though they do cause many fishable hatches. These include the above-mentioned *Leptophlebia* and *Paraleptophlebia,* the nymphs of which live in peaceful margin currents or even dead backwaters of streams and rivers, and at times along the edges of lakes. Their slender shapes seem to match their lives in such gentle waters. They do not need to fight strong currents, as the more common crawlers do.

The tiny *Tricos*, in the genus *Tricorythodes*, are far from marginal, though they do not live in typical crawler habitat. They produce massive hatches, most often in somewhat slow waters that flow over silted bottoms with aquatic plant growth. They are adapted to many trout waters that suffer from problems of impacted gravel, where most crawler nymphs would not find homes because the spaces between stones are plugged with silt. *Tricos* do well in such water, especially where plant growth becomes abundant as a consequence of the silting. But they also produce excellent hatches in such clean waters as Silver Creek in Idaho, a valley spring creek with modest gradient and therefore a silted bottom and excellent aquatic plant growth.

Crawler nymphs are typically flatter and more rectangular in outline than swimmers. They have three slender tails with sparse whorls of hair that typically do not interlock to form a paddle-like surface. Their eyes are located to the sides of the head, as opposed to the eyes of flattened clinger nymphs, covered later, whose eyes have migrated to the top surfaces of their wide heads.

Crawler nymphs are not as active as swimmer nymphs, and do not swim as well, though a few can propel themselves fairly well with up-and-down flips of the abdomen. Because their tails are slender, with little paddle-like surface, the abdominal segments must provide the thrust. Most often, crawlers spend their time moving slowly across the substrate. When dislodged from it, most of them struggle in the current with slow undulations of the abdomen, swimming feebly until contact is once again made with the bottom, or until their drift is punctuated by a trout.

Most of the crawler nymph diet consists of algae growing on bottom stones, or detrital vegetative material such as leaves caught among stones on the bottom. Some mayfly crawler nymphs, most prominently those of the green drakes and pale morning duns, are at home in both rocky freestone environments and in the rooted vegetation of well-oxygenated spring creeks and tailwaters.

Different members of this diverse and widespread group have adapted to nearly every trout fishing environment. You'll encounter them in nearly all moving waters you fish, and along the wave-washed edges of a few stillwaters as well.

The winged stages of crawlers, duns and spinners both, have three tails, while the duns and spinners of both swimmers and clingers have only two tails. This makes crawler mayflies easy to separate in the winged stages from swimmers and clingers. It is also the first identifying characteristic you should look for when examining any mayfly adult: count the tails! If it has three, you have instantly narrowed your search down to the crawler group. If it has two, you have at least eliminated them.

The taxonomic landscape has changed for crawlers over the last twenty years. Back then a single genus, *Ephemerella*, included the green drakes, lesser green drakes, pale morning duns, and a few other important crawler hatches. Since that time several sub-genera have been elevated to genus status. For example, the green drakes and lesser green drakes are now in the genus *Drunella*. Only the pale morning duns have stayed where they were, in the old genus *Ephemerella.*

Following is a list of the important crawler families and genera.

Important Crawlers
    Family: Ephemerellidae
      Genus: *Ephemerella*
            Serratella
            Drunella
            Attenella
            Caudatella
            Timpanoga
    Family: Leptophlebiidae
      Genus: *Paraleptophlebia*
            Leptophlebia
    Family: Leptohyphidae
      Genus: *Tricorythodes*
    Family: Caenidae
      Genus: *Caenis*

Chapter 11

Ephemerella (Pale Morning Duns)

FAMILY: EPHEMERELLIDAE

Genus: *Ephemerella*
Western Species: *12*
North America: *35*
Important Western Species: *Ephemerella inermis, E. infrequens*
Common Names: Pale morning duns, PMDs.

In our own experience, we rank the pale morning duns second in importance as a fishable hatch only to the *Baetis* complex of mayflies. Blue-winged olive hatches happen over almost all of the fly-fishing season, and can cause selective feeding throughout that entire period. The pale morning dun hatch, consisting of the two major species *Ephemerella infrequens* and *E. inermis,* lasts for six months, almost as long as the *Baetis* complex. Some writers rate the pale morning dun hatch higher than the blue-winged olive complex, as the single most important mayfly hatch. We don't have much quarrel with that. We've had excellent fishing over them, and often.

Pale morning dun hatches can go on and on for weeks and even months on the same stream, sometimes in great numbers but for a short daily period, more often trickling off, causing trout to feed for several hours each day. The hatch begins in May on some streams, ends in September or early October on others. You can predict their emergence dates with some certainty if you track their hatches over the seasons on your home waters.

Ephemerella inermis   **HATCH IMPORTANCE SCORE: 41.5**

CRITERIA/SCORE	5		4		3		2		1	
Distribution: (within Western waters)	widespread	5.0	common		scattered		isolated		rare	
Abundance:	heavy	5.0	abundant		modest		trickling		individual	
Emergence type:	mid-water/slow	4.5	mid-water/fast		edges/slow		edges/fast		crawls out	
Emergence time:	mid-day	5.0	early and/or late over long period		early and/or late over short period		dawn or dusk		night	
Emergence duration:	multiple seasons per year		well-defined long hatch period	4.0	well-defined short hatch period		poorly-defined long hatch period		poorly-defined short hatch	
(Behavior/Availability) **Nymph:**	excellent	4.5	good		moderate		slight		poor	
(Behavior/Availability) **Emerger:**	excellent	5.0	good		moderate		slight		poor	
(Behavior/Availability) **Dun:**	excellent	5.0	good		moderate		slight		poor	
(Behavior/Availability) **Spinner:**	excellent		good	3.5	moderate		slight		poor	
Totals:		34.0		7.5		0.0		0.0		0.0

EPHEMERELLA INERMIS/INFREQUENS EMERGENCE TABLE

TIME	WINTER			SPRING			SUMMER			FALL		
	Dec.	Jan.	Feb.	March	April	May	June	July	Aug.	Sep.	Oct.	Nov.
7 a.m. - 10 a.m.										Rocky Mountains		
10 a.m. - noon												
noon - 3 p.m.												
3 p.m. - 7 p.m.							Pacific					
7 p.m. - 10 p.m.												

Emergence and Distribution

Pale morning duns are far less complex than the *Baetis* group. They consist of two important species, *Ephemerella infrequens* and *E. inermis*, along with a couple of very similar and closely related species, *E. mollita* and *E. lacustris*, that are known from restricted locations. *E. lacustris,* for example, is known only from the Yellowstone and Jackson Hole area, which of course is an excellent angling address.

Distinguishing between these species, especially between *E. inermis* and *E. infrequens*, is not a reasonable option for the angler. Size, color, and other anatomical characteristics overlap to a degree that makes field identification impossible. To be sure which species you are imitating one must take a microscopic look at the gentalia of male spinners. If this sounds interesting, we recommend you pursue it at home, not while out on the water. Of these species, *Ephemerella inermis* is by far the most widespread and abundant, and is the species you'll be imitating during most hatches on western streams.

Hatches of the important pale morning dun species overlap and extend the season for several months, from May through early October. They begin earliest in California and southern Oregon, and extend into the season as you move north into cooler latitudes and east into higher altitudes. A couple of hatches that exemplify this are the famous PMD hatches in June on Oregon's Deschutes River and in July on Idaho's Henrys Fork of the Snake River.

Pale morning dun nymphs are well adapted to spring creeks and tailwaters. Because the temperatures of such flows are more stable than those of waters subject to spring runoff and normal warming trends, their PMD hatches can come off at somewhat unseasonal times. For example, on the unusual Firehole River it's a June hatch, while other streams in that region are still enduring high water from runoff, and the hatch will begin a month later in most area waters.

While some hatches of PMDs begin mid-morning, most start in the hour or so before noon. On very warm days, hatches may begin as early as 9:00 a.m., lending some validity to the *morning* portion of their name. If the weather is cool, they'll usually emerge during the warmest hours of mid-afternoon, from around 1:00 to 3:00 or 4:00 p.m. If the weather is bright and sunny, their hatches will be condensed into an hour or even less. If it is cool and overcast, they might be on the water for two or three hours. They are so varied that pinning down daily emergence times can only be done on a stream-by-stream basis, and is best left to studies on your home waters. If you're traveling, expect to see them at any time of day.

We've seen times on Oregon's Deschutes River when the hatch was very heavy, very brief, and ignored by trout, at least on the surface. It's odd to be standing in water that you know is full of fat redside rainbows, to see hundreds of hatching duns on the surface, and not see a single rise. Our guess is that the trout spend the pre-hatch and early hatch periods focusing on restless nymphs. In such a brief hatch, it's possible trout just don't get the time to turn their attention from the abundant and available nymphs to the duns floating overhead.

PMDs are distributed throughout the entire West. Hatches are excellent in California's famous spring creeks, Hat Creek and Fall River, as well as many of the Sierra Mountain freestone streams. Arizona and New Mexico waters that have appropriate habitat have good hatches. As you go north, the hatches get heavier and more famous. They are important on Colorado's Frying Pan River, and in Utah's Green River in the Flaming Gorge Dam tailwater and upstream from it. They are prolific in Montana's Bighorn tailwater, and in Alberta's famous Bow River.

Trout feed extensively on the nymphs, and also take emergers well. The dun stage of the hatch is most famous, largely because they float for some time while their wings dry. It's important, however, to watch rises carefully and be sure that trout are taking fully-formed duns, not trapped emergers. Spinner falls can occur in the morning and evening hours of the same day, and cause selective sipping by trout that is difficult to notice and difficult to solve even when you do notice it.

Nymph Characteristics

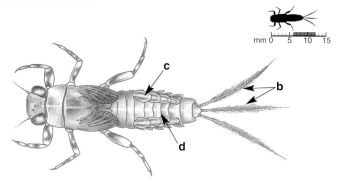

Ephemerella nymph.

Light and dark color phase nymphs of the same species, collected from the same spot.

a. Crawler shape; head and first segments of abdomen nearly same width as thorax.

b. Three tails of equal length, with dense fringe of *setae*, or fine hairs, along lateral margins of last 1/2 to 2/3 of their length.

c. Small, oval gills on abdominal segments 3-7, attached to the top edge of each segment.

d. Small paired *tubercles*, or projections, may or may not be present on posterior margins of abdominal segments. If present they are rounded and blunt.

e. Body reddish-brown to dark brown, sometimes with olive cast. Abdomen of some specimens with pale median stripe. Legs distinctly banded.

f. Body length excluding tails 6 to 9 mm, 1/4 to 1/2 in. (*E. inermis*)

g. Body length excluding tails 8 to 12mm, 3/8 to 5/8 in. (*E. infrequens*).

Dun Characteristics

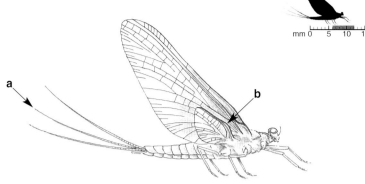

Ephemerella dun, female.

a. Three tails.

b. Hind wings with distinct rounded costal angulation.

c. Forewing pale yellowish-gray to pale gray, sometimes with yellowish tinting or mottling.

d. Body length 6-9 mm, 1/4 to 1/2 in., (*E. inermis*) or 8-12mm, 3/8 to 5/8 in., (*E. infrequens*), excluding tails.

*e. Body pale to bright olive-yellow; underside usually lighter color than back.

*Note: Body color is brighter and more olive-yellow when the dun first emerges, and slowly changes toward pale reddish-brown after the dun has been exposed to air for some time. PMDs vary so much in size and color, from stream to stream, and time-to-time, that anybody who pins its color down to precisely this or exactly that is going to be accurate in only one place, at one time. This explains why scientists rarely use color as an identifying characteristic in taxonomic keys.

Ephemerella dun, male.

Spinner Characteristics

a. Three tails.

b. Wings clear; hind wings with distinct rounded costal angulation.

*c. Body of females pale olive-yellow to brown; body of males typically darker, yellowish-brown to reddish-brown.

d. Body length 6-9 mm, 1/4 to 1/2 in. (*E. inermis*), or 8-12mm, 3/8 to 5/8 in., (*E. infrequens*).

*Note: Pale morning dun spinners display *sexual dimorphism*, meaning the males and females display different characteristics, in this case color. Both sexes may fall to the water after mating, though females typically outnumber males. Trout have been reported to be selective to one sex, turning away from the other, though we have not observed this in our own fishing over the hatch.

Ephemerella spinner, female.

Habitat and Behavior

Pale morning dun nymphs live on and among bottom rocks in the freestone stream environment, thriving in riffles and runs, where they shelter from the currents in the cracks and crevices between pebbles and stones. They browse on the thin layer of photosynthetic growth that covers bottom rocks where sunlight strikes, and on any decaying vegetation that gets trapped on the bottom.

These crawling nymphs have also adapted to the microniches in more stable stream environments where plants have been able to take root. This includes meadow reaches of freestone streams, spring creeks, and tailwaters wherever stable flows allow vegetation to set down roots.

Ephemerella spinner, male.

Great pale morning dun habitat on the lower Deschutes River.

Though hatches of pale morning duns on freestone streams can be heavy, the most prolific populations live in spring creek and tailwater currents that are both vegetated and well oxygenated. The nymphs do poorly in polluted waters, but come off in great numbers on clean waters with spring sources or below dams that reduce scouring spring floods without degrading water quality or allowing the water to become too warm. The lower Deschutes and lower McKenzie rivers, both in Oregon, both with dams, have heavy PMD hatches. The Bighorn and Bow rivers are also tailwater examples of excellent habitat for this hatch. But you might be foolish to seek out only famous waters on which to fish it. The hatch comes off in fishable numbers in nearly every stream and river in the western states and provinces.

Pale morning dun nymphs molt twenty or more times in the course of a one-year life cycle. Mature specimens have wing pads that are almost black when they're ready for emergence. If they've lived their nymphal lives in the fastest water of a riffle, PMDs will migrate toward less hectic water along the edges, or move upstream or downstream to where the fast water tapers off into a less boisterous run, before emergence to the dun stage takes place.

If they've lived in rooted vegetation, emergence will take place on the smooth flats of their preferred nymphal environment. Though you'll find occasional PMD hatches on fairly rough water, where flotation is needed in your imitation, most of the time they'll be found emerging on water that is calm to glassy, even on freestone streams. You'll need PMD emerger and dun patterns that show a realistic silhouette to trout.

When ready for emergence, pale morning dun nymphs release their hold on the bottom or the vegetation, and swim feebly or are buoyed slowly to the surface. The nymphal skin splits along the back in or a few inches beneath the surface film, so the dun must struggle through the film to the surface. They arrive on the surface with their wings wet, and must sit on the water for some seconds, or even a minute or more, before they're dry enough to allow flight.

Trout often concentrate on emerging duns struggling to make their exit from the nymphal exoskeleton and break through the surface film. Many hatching duns become crippled and fail to emerge. Trout take many more during their struggle. In either case, emerger fishing can be excellent during hatches of this group, especially on the smooth currents of spring creeks and tailwaters.

Pale morning duns remain vulnerable to trout predation in the dun stage until they leave the water. They fly to streamside vegetation, where they rest and make the final molt to the spinner stage one to two days later.

Mating swarms of males form over riffles and glides. Females fly into the swarm of males and mating occurs in the air. Females may return to streamside vegetation for a short period before beginning to lay their eggs by releasing egg clusters just above the water, or by touching the water with the tip of the abdomen while flying above the water. Spinner falls may occur in either the morning or evening. During warm weather, major spinner falls are usually in the morning. Spinner flights end with both males and females lying spent on the water, often arriving there suddenly and in great numbers.

Imitation

All stages of this important hatch, from nymph through emerger and on to the dun and spinner, can be important for imitation. *Ephemerella infrequens*, where it occurs, tends to be the earliest hatch of the two important species, and is slightly larger at size 14 or 16. The later and more abundant *Ephemerella inermis* is size 16 or 18. You can approach tying imitations for pale morning duns in one of two ways. The first is to consider the two species a single group and tie flies for both, on a continuum of sizes from 14 to 18 (because *E. infrequens* is rather rare, you might just tie flies in size 16 and 18 for the more common *E. inermis*). The second approach is to hold off tying any flies at all until you collect specimens and match them for the water you're fishing. This latter method has the advantage of supplying flies that match a specific hatch perfectly in terms of size and color, important in an insect that is so varied over its broad range. Of course the disadvantage of this method is that you may have no matching patterns when you first encounter the hatch.

Our preferred method for this hatch is to purchase a small, flat fly box with many compartments. In idle time we fill these with a selection of nymph, emerger, dun, and spinner patterns that range in size from 14 to 18, and that average out the colors of the various pale morning dun hatches we've collected in our fishing across the West. That has worked out to a dubbing mix of one part olive, two parts pale yellow. This color seems to take trout feeding on pale morning duns on most waters we've fished, and the selection of flies gives us a few options to offer trout when they capriciously refuse one fly and prefer another. That is a common happening with this important hatch.

A. K. Best, the famous Colorado fly tier and author, reports that the PMD hatch on the Frying Pan River has a pink cast due to iron salts in the water. A. K. is critical about color in all of his dressings. He imitates his Frying Pan PMD with a Pink PMD Quill Dun, and we've never fished with anybody who knows more about the relationship between color of the fly and satisfaction of the trout than the great A.K.

Nymph Imitations

Pale morning dun nymphs are typically reddish-brown to dark brown. Mature nymphs have well-formed black wingpads. Though you can get precisely imitative, most of our nymph imitation is done with standard patterns that we use to imitate other nymphs and some larvae as well.

Gold Ribbed Hare's Ear

Hook:	Standard nymph, 2X long, size 14-20.
Weight:	10 to 15 turns of fine lead wire.
Thread:	Brown 6/0 or 8/0.
Tail:	Hare's mask guard hairs.
Rib:	Oval gold tinsel, narrow.
Abdomen:	Light hare's mask fur.
Wingcase:	Mottled turkey or dark goose feather section.
Thorax:	Darker hare's mask fur, picked out for legs.

The Gold Ribbed Hare's Ear in size 14 through 18 is excellent for tumbling along the bottom during PMD prehatch periods. It's resemblance to the prolific nymphs of pale morning duns might be part of the reason for its almost constant success when fished as a searching pattern.

Beadhead Hare's Ear

Hook:	Standard nymph, 2X long, size 14-20.
Bead:	Brass or gold.
Thread:	Brown 6/0 or 8/0.
Tail:	Hare's ear guard hair.
Rib:	Oval gold tinsel, narrow.
Abdomen:	Light hare's mask fur.
Wingcase:	Mottled turkey or dark goose feather section (omit on smallest sizes).
Thorax:	Dark hare's mask fur.

When you expect a pale morning dun hatch later in the day, or when your kick net samples reveal a lot of the nymphs present in the water you're about to fish, try rolling a Beadhead Hare's Ear along the bottom in the appropriate size. This heresy might be more imitative than you think. The natural nymphs often exude a bubble of air between the exoskeleton of the nymph and that of the forming dun inside. As the two skins separate, preparatory to the rise for emergence, the bubble of air serves to work them apart so the dun can emerge quickly, and also to buoy the nymph toward the surface where emergence will happen.

We can't pin down the precise reason the Beadhead Hare's Ear works, but suspect it is rooted somewhere in the behavior of nymphs and the way trout see them. If you're among those who feel that bead heads should be banned, however, we agree that you should not use them.

Pheasant Tail (Originator: Frank Sawyer)

Hook:	Standard nymph, 2X long, size 14-20.
Thread:	Brown 6/0 or 8/0.
Tail:	Pheasant center tail fibers.
Rib:	Fine copper wire, counterwound over abdomen.
Abdomen:	Pheasant center tail fibers, as herl.
Wingcase:	Pheasant center tail fibers.
Thorax:	Pheasant center tail fibers.
Legs:	Tips of thorax fibers.

As the daily hatch activity begins to progress, switch to a Pheasant Tail, or Pheasant Tail Flashback, in the size that corresponds with the insects hatching. Fish it higher in the water column. Trout will often continue to focus on the nymphs even long after duns are afloat. Certainly most trout will continue to accept a nymph if they get a chance at one drifting helplessly toward them, even if duns are already on the water.

Deschutes PMD Nymph (Originator: Rick Hafele)

Hook:	Tiemco 2457 or similar style 1X short scud hook, size 14-18.
Thread:	Brown or olive 6/0.
Tail:	Light tan hackle fibers.
Underbody:	6 to 8 wraps of lead fuse wire.
Rib:	Heavy copper wire, wound over abdomen.
Abdomen:	Cinnamon dubbing.
Wingcase:	Dark turkey tail fibers.
Thorax:	Dark reddish brown dubbing or squirrel body hair picked out and with guard hairs left in.

Nymph Presentation

In the prehatch hours, when you're rolling nymphs along the bottom, rig with the split shot and strike indicator method. Fish with Gary Borger's *shotgun* method, described in his book *Nymphing* (Stackpole Books, 1979). Make your casts short and upstream, and fish out each drift. With each subsequent cast place your fly a foot or two farther out into the current from the one before it, so that you paint each bit of bottom with parallel brushstrokes with the fly, about one foot apart.

When the hatch begins, and fish move up in the water column, fish your nymph just a few inches deep. That's why the Pheasant Tail is listed here without weight. Rig it on a three- to four-foot tippet of 5X or 6X. Tie a tiny yarn indicator into the leader five to six feet above the fly, to help you detect takes. Don't hesitate to drop the nymph off the stern of the dry fly you've chosen to match the dun stage. Just tie a fine 20-inch tippet to the hook bend of the dry with an improved clinch knot, then tie the nymph to the other end with the same knot or a Duncan loop. You're fishing both stages, and will soon know whether trout prefer a nymph or dun.

Emerger Imitations

We once fished an eddy on the Bighorn River with photographer Jim Schollmeyer, when he suddenly began outfishing us a little more than was normal; it's usual for him to outfish us at least slightly. Jim waded at the edge of a large eddy that swirled around toward him from downstream, delivering the dregs of a pale morning dun hatch that the rest of us fished upstream and down from Jim, in the open currents instead of the eddy. We were catching a

PMD water on the Bighorn River in Montana.

At times trout become selective to crippled PMD duns.

few trout and were therefore happy until Jim began catching *lots* of fish, which is always a detterent to happiness if you're nearby and forced to watch it.

When we reeled up and waded over to investigate, we discovered Jim was casting over large lofting noses that were feeding on crippled PMDs stranded in the eddy. The rise rhythms of the trout were leisurely; their takes were confident. Jim invited us to fish alongside him. We tried our dun patterns and got refusals. Takes to whatever Jim was using were just as confident as those to the naturals.

When he finally allowed us a look at what he was using, it didn't make sense, but then again it did. His fly was a Gary LaFontaine Emergent Sparkle Pupa, size 16, pale yellow, tied for caddis. Jim dressed it with floatant and fished it in the film. The fly would land and lay on its side. A trout would see it and take it for a crippled PMD.

We won't offer that dressing here. But we will offer the advice to watch your feeding trout carefully during a PMD hatch. If they're taking on the surface, but you don't see fully-winged duns go down in the rises, try switching to something that represents a dun tangled up with its own nymphal shuck, awash in the surface film.

Pale Morning Emerging Dun
(Originator: Fred Arbonna, Jr.)

Hook:	Standard dry fly, 1X fine, size 14-18.
Thread:	Light olive 6/0 or 8/0.
Tails:	Ginger hackle fibers.
Rib:	Working thread.
Body:	Pale yellow fur or synthetic dubbing.
Wings:	Four turns light dun hen hackle.
Legs:	Two turns light ginger hen hackle.

This pattern for the emerging pale morning dun, from Fred L. Arbonna, Jr.'s fine book *Mayflies, the Angler, and the Trout (Winchester Press, 1980)* can be fished during the hatch, shallow and on the swing, as you would a standard wet fly. If trout are set up and feeding at the surface in a steady rise rhythm, then it's better to time your cast, and present the fly on a cross-stream reach cast, right down its feeding lane, just as you might a dry fly but sunk just a few inches deep.

This wet fly will float if you give it a couple of brisk backcasts, or if you treat it with floatant. Try fishing it in the surface film, as a tangled emerger, the same way Jim Schollmeyer fished the Emergent Sparkle Pupa in that Bighorn eddy.

Pale Morning Dun Emerger
(Originators: John Juracek and Craig Mathews)

Hook:	Standard dry fly, 1X fine, size 16-18.
Thread:	Yellow 8/0.
Trailing shuck:	Brown Z-lon.
Body:	Pale yellow dubbing.
Wing case:	Light gray Polycelon.
Hackle:	Two turns starling.

This pattern, from *Fishing Yellowstone Hatches*, is designed to float in the surface film, suspended from its Polycelon wing case. At times trout will favor this fly because it floats flush in the film as opposed to patterns that float just beneath it or ride up on top of it.

CDC PMD Floating Nymph/Emerger
(Originator: René Harrop)

Hook:	Standard dry fly, 1X fine, size 14-18.
Thread:	Yellow 6/0 or 8/0.
Tail:	Wood duck flank fibers.
Rib:	Fine gold wire.
Body:	Yellow fur or synthetic dubbing.
Legs:	Woodduck flank fibers.
Wing:	Light dun CDC fibers, short.
Thorax:	Yellow fur or synthetic dubbing.

This dressing, one of the best emerger styles, is designed to suspend the body beneath the surface, while the wings float on the surface film, representing the unfolding wings of a natural either trapped in the process of emergence, or merely starting to emerge and helpless while the transition is underway.

Presentation

All floating emergers should be rigged and fished just as you would rig for fishing a dry fly, with long leaders, fine tippets, light lines and delicate rods that allow the softest presentations. Work into position to present the fly just as you would a dry, casting up and across if your position is downstream from a feeding trout, with a reach cast if your position is across stream from it, and with a downstream wiggle cast if you are upstream from the trout. In any of these cases, you might have difficulty picking out your emerger and seeing it on the surface, because it will ride low in the film.

If necessary, use a small yarn or hard strike indicator to mark its location, and set the hook to any rise near it. It is also useful to use a dry fly that matches the dun as your marker, and the surface film emerger as a trailer two to four feet behind it. In that way you fish two stages. That doesn't mean you'll catch twice as many trout, but it does mean you'll catch some that would have refused either of the flies fished alone. And if all your takes are to the emerger, you'll notice them because they'll be so near the visible dun dressing.

Dun Imitations

Nearly every dry-fly pattern style ever invented has been applied against this famous hatch. You could simplify your life by fishing hackled dries in the Catskill tradition, for example the Light Cahill, originally tied to match the sulphurs of eastern streams. We did just that in our wayward youths, but switched to the Compara-dun style when Al Caucci and Bob Nastasi published *Hatches* in 1975. Our results on the smooth water where these insects typically hatch took a quick jump with that more imitative fly style. We realized then that hackled dressings are fine for a lot of our rumpled western waters, but flies for smoother water should show a better silhouette to the trout, and don't need the hackle for flotation.

We also used to follow the instructions in early hatch-matching books, and tie our delicate dun dressings on 4X fine-wire hooks. Such light hooks solved flotation problems, but caused others. We fished these fragile hooks over Deschutes redsides and Bighorn browns, lost fish, and got back hooks as straight as pins far too many times. Now we tie all of our dry flies on standard 1X fine hooks, and solve our flotation problems with better materials and dry-fly floatants. If you fish waters without any potential for big trout, don't hesitate to tie your flies on fine-wire hooks. But don't take them to average western waters. You'll land all the little trout you'd least care to, and lose all the big ones you'd really like to catch.

Jim Schollmeyer with a nice Bighorn River brown trout.

The kind of trout with the heft you'd most like to hold in your hands feed often, and often feed selectively, on pale morning duns.

Pale Morning Sparkle Dun
(Source: Juracek and Mathews)

Hook:	Standard dry fly, 1X fine, size 16-20.
Thread:	Pale yellow 6/0 or 8/0.
Wing:	Light or bleached Compara-dun deer hair, or yearling elk.
Tail:	Brown Z-lon.
Body:	Pale yellow or yellow-olive fur or synthetic dubbing.

This dressing represents the dun with the nymph shuck still trailing off the stern. Because it represents the emerger and dun in one fly, it's the first fly we turn to when trout begin to focus upward during a PMD hatch. This is one hatch, however, during which we would never like to be limited to a single dressing style. Too often trout will refuse what worked the day before, or the hour before, and accept something the same size and color, but tied in a different style.

Pale Morning Hairwing Dun (Originator: René Harrop)

Hook:	Standard dry fly, 1X fine, size 14-20.
Thread:	Pale yellow 6/0 or 8/0.
Tails:	Light ginger hackle fibers, split.
Abdomen:	Pale yellow or yellow-olive fur or synthetic dubbing.
Hackle:	Light ginger, five turns spread over thorax, clipped on bottom.
Thorax:	Same as abdomen.
Wing:	Natural light yearling elk body hair.

René's hairwing duns have come to be favorites because they lower the body into the surface film and fool trout on smooth water, but they also have enough flotation to fish well on riffles and runs. Another aspect of the Hairwing Dun is often overlooked: the wings slant back, in the posture of the natural mayfly dun on the water. Most dun dressings have their wings held upright. We have found that this wing silhouette is critical at times.

If you're ever fishing a hatch, and are not doing well, compare the posture of the fly you're using to a natural on the water, at casting distance. Look at it afloat, way out there, even though you know that trout see it close up. Try styles until you find one that looks as much like a pale morning dun as you can get it, at thirty or forty feet, and you'll be surprised how often you suddenly begin catching trout. Very often, the fly you end up with will be a Hairwing Dun.

Pale Morning Thorax Dun
(Originators: Mike Lawson and Vince Marinaro)

Hook:	Standard dry fly, 1X fine, size 16-20.
Thread:	Pale olive 6/0 or 8/0.
Wing:	Gray-dyed turkey flat.
Tail:	Light dun hackle fibers, splayed.
Body:	Pale yellow-olive Antron dubbing.
Hackle:	Light dun, spread on both sides of wing, clipped on bottom.

This pattern is by Mike Lawson, long-time owner of Henrys Fork Anglers and noted angler on that famous river. It's an interpretation, and simplification, of a pattern style originated by Vincent Marinaro and recorded in his *A Modern Dry Fly Code* (Putnam, 1950). This might be the most important American flyfishing book yet published. The thorax dun style, though not in use as much as it used to be, is still one of the finest for trout rising to insects on smooth waters. Once again, it floats with the proper posture, and will serve well as one of your options over PMDs, and many other mayfly duns as well.

PMD Quill Dun (Originator: A. K. Best)

Hook:	Standard dry fly, 1X fine, size 14-18.
Thread:	Beige 6/0 or 8/0.
Tail:	Medium ginger hackle fibers, splayed slightly.
Body:	Rooster hackle stem dyed tannish-olive.
Wings:	Pale grayish-cream hen hackle tips.
Hackle:	Medium ginger.

A. K. is so expert at dying materials that he wrote a book about it, *Dying and Bleaching Natural Fly Tying Materials* (Lyons & Bruford, 1993). For the hackle stem body of this dressing he recommends, "Dye first with light Rit tan then overdye with Rit kelly green or pink." If you're going to do that, the first step in the process is to buy A. K.'s book.

Quill stems, pre-dyed in an assortment of colors, can now be found in your local fly shop. You can buy BWO, PMD, and even stems dyed especially for A. K.'s Frying Pan PMD: pink.

A. K. also ties his PMD Quill in parachute style. We won't list it here, though it's very valuable. Substitute a turkey T-base feather or flat for the wings, and wind the hackle parachute around this post. Try both styles over trout during a hatch, and see which they prefer. Chances are when you've got your casting position and presentation worked out perfectly, they will accept either.

PMD Sidewinder No-Hackle
(Originators: Doug Swisher and Carl Richards)

Hook:	Standard dry fly, 1X fine, size 16-20.
Thread:	Pale yellow 6/0 or 8/0.
Tails:	Light blue dun hackle fibers, split.
Body:	Pale yellow-olive fur or synthetic dubbing.
Wings:	Pale gray mallard or teal wing sections.

Doug Swisher and Carl Richards swept anglers into the modern age of imitation with their *Selective Trout* (Crown, 1971). We don't use their Sidewinder No-Hackle duns a lot because they're tattered too easily by trout, and we don't like to tie something that gets chewed up so suddenly. However, No-Hackles don't take long to tie, once you master the steps in setting those difficult wings, so getting a few destroyed by trout is worth the trouble when this style is the only one trout will accept. No-Hackles actually continue to take trout long after their wings have decomposed. So the fault here is ours for not using them, and you should try them over the types of snotty trout that often feed on pale morning duns.

To master that winging, refer to a valuable little monograph called *Tying the Swisher/Richards Flies*, published by P. J. Dylan in 1977. The slender paperback was a response to the popularity of the fly style, and the difficulty in mastering the winging method. If you can't find a copy of the booklet, and have trouble locating directions elsewhere, the method is covered in Dave's *Trout Flies* (Stackpole, 1999). That reference has tying steps for almost all of the dressing styles listed in this book.

PMD CDC Biot Comparadun (Originator: Shane Stalcup)

Hook:	Standard dry fly, 1X fine, size 16-20.
Thread:	Pale yellow 6/0 or 8/0.
Tail:	Ginger hackle fibers, split.
Abdomen:	Yellow-olive goose or turkey biot.
Thorax:	Pale morning dun Superfine dubbing.
Wing:	Light gray CDC topped with mallard flank fibers.

This dressing combines the segmentation of biot for the body with CDC in the wing for flotation. Professional tier Shane Stalcup, fishing out of his Colorado home, fishes over some very selective trout, and designs many effective patterns to take them. This is an excellent example of his innovations.

Presentation

Most of the time you'll fish PMD dun dressings over selective trout, on water that is at least somewhat smooth. You already know you need to use delicate rods, light lines, and long leaders. You also know that you need to present your flies to the fish without alarming them with the sight of your line, leader, and fly sailing over their heads and smacking onto the water right in the middle of their window on the world. You also know that you must put that fly right onto the trout's feeding lane or the fish will not move to take it.

To solve these problems, think of the trout as being at the center of a circle: the hub of a wheel. You are somewhere around the periphery of that circle, at a moderate casting range, preparing to make your presentation. The position you take is critical. There is usually a single best place from which to cast to a trout, depending on the conflicting currents you'd like to get behind you.

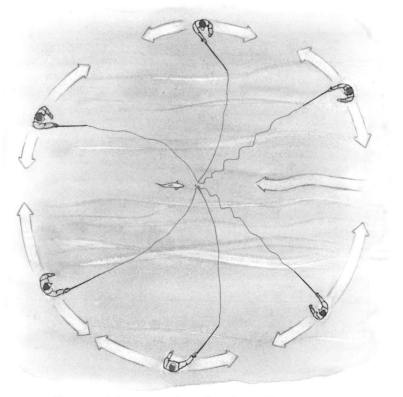

The presentation you use depends on the position you've taken
relative to the lie of a rising trout.

The presentation you make depends on the position you've taken. If you're in the downstream third of the circle, make your cast to the trout up and across stream. Try to increase the angle off to the side, or install a curve in the cast, so that the fly lands in the feeding lane of the trout but the line and leader lie alongside it. The trout sees the fly first, the line and leader just seconds after it has made its decision to take the fly, you hope. The downstream position is the hardest from which to accomplish a delicate presentation over selectively rising trout.

If you're in the portion of the circle directly across stream from the trout, on either side, then use the reach cast to present the fly. Aim the cast directly at the place you want the fly to land, two to four feet upstream from the trout. As the line unfurls in the air, tip the rod over in the upstream direction. When the fly lands, follow its drift with the rod tip. You'll keep drag from forming, and the fly will enter the trout's window ahead of the line and leader.

Perhaps the best casting position to take on smooth water is at an angle upstream from the trout, in the upper third of that imaginary circle. Be sure you're off to the side at least a little; you don't want to cast directly downstream to the fish. Use the wiggle cast, in which you aim at the trout's feeding lane, again two to four feet upstream from the trout's lie, and wobble your rod tip back and forth as the line lays out. The line and leader will land on the water in a series of serpentine curves. As the fly floats downstream toward the trout, those curves will feed out, and you will get a drag-free drift.

If the trout refuses, which it will many times before the cast becomes perfect, tip your rod to the side after the fly has passed the trout. Let the current tug your line well away from the fish before you lift the fly for the next cast. That is the reason you do not use the wiggle cast directly upstream from a rising trout, casting straight downstream to it. If you do, you'll get just one chance to send a fly down its feeding lane. If the fly is refused, the leader and then line follow, and you cannot lift them off the water without detonating the trout out of there.

We have found, time after time, that trout refusing all flies on upstream presentations take almost any flies fished with downstream presentations. Learn the reach cast and downstream wiggle cast. These two casts are worth at least a boxful of precise imitations.

Only a combination of the right fly pattern with the correct position and presentation will get your rod bent when trout are selective to PMD duns, no matter how much duct tape you wear on your waders.

Spinner Imitations

We've said it before: a lot of mayflies that begin as duns of one color or another end up as spinners that could be called red quills. It's true of most pale morning duns, though some seem to retain aspects of their pale yellowish-olive bodies. Most of the *Ehemerella inermis* and *E. infrequens* spinners we've observed, both male and female, are a light to dark brown that could be called rusty. It's no accident that the standard Red Quill Spinner, or Rusty Spinner, in a range of sizes from 12 to 20, is the most valuable spinner pattern you can tie and carry.

Red Quill Spinner

Hook:	Standard dry fly, 1X fine, size 16-20.
Thread:	Brown 6/0 or 8/0.
Tails:	Ginger or brown hackle fibers, split.
Body:	Ginger to brown dyed hackle stem.
Wings:	Light blue dun or white hen hackle tips, tied spent.
Hackle:	Ginger or brown, clipped top and bottom.

This dressing was listed earlier in the book for spinners of the BWO complex, and will fish as well for the PMDs. Try it during morning and evening falls of these insects that are nearly invisible when they get onto the water.

Rusty Sparkle Spinner (Source: Juracek and Mathews)

Hook:	Standard dry fly, 1X fine, size 16-18.
Thread:	Brown 6/0 or 8/0.
Tails:	Ginger or brown hackle fibers, split.
Body:	Rusty-brown fur or synthetic dubbing.
Wings:	White Z-lon, spent.

In *Fishing Yellowstone Hatches*, John Juracek and Craig Mathews recommend trying this spinner dressing in both the listed rusty color and pale olive as well. Collect specimens, and base your choice on the natural that trout are taking.

CDC Rusty Spinner (Originator: René Harrop)

Hook:	Standard dry fly, 1X fine, size 14-18.
Thread:	Orange 8/0.
Tails:	Light blue dun hackle fibers, split.
Abdomen:	Rusty brown goose biot.
Wings:	White CDC topped with gray Z-lon.

This dressing incorporates CDC, which always seems to add some magic to a fly. If it makes it no more imitative, it at least makes it more visible when it's afloat on the water. With these small and drab spent dressings tied for PMDs, visibility becomes an important factor. If you don't notice a take, it's difficult to set the hook.

Presentation

The key to fishing spinner falls of PMDs, and most other mayflies for that matter, is to know when they're happening around you. The spinners appear out of nowhere, collapse to the water, and trout begin feeding delicately but you can't see what they're taking. Stop casting and spend some time with your nose close to the water, or dip your aquarium net half in and half out of the surface currents and leave it suspended there for a few minutes. They'll show up then, their wings glassy and almost invisible, their bodies empty and nearly transparent. You wonder why trout would take these discarded hulls of the dying mayfly generation. But they do, and you need to match them with something almost as ethereal to take many trout.

Present these dressings with your most delicate gear. Position yourself as close to the trout as you can. Make every movement as slowly as you can. Cast with your rod tipped over to keep it from waving in the sight of the trout. When they're concentrating on spinners, or anything else floating flush in the surface film, it's surprising how close you can work to trout if you're careful not to alarm them.

Such close casting causes you to focus on your fishing; your own concentration increases your odds of catching trout, over PMDs or any other hatch.

Chapter 12

Serratella
(Small Western Dark Hendricksons)

FAMILY: EPHEMERELLIDAE

Genus: *Serratella*

Western Species: 7

North America: 14

Important Western Species: *Serratella tibialis* (previously *Ephemerella tibialis*)

Other Western Species of less importance include: *S. micheneri, S. levis*, and *S. teresa*

Common Names: Small western dark Hendricksons, little dark Hendricksons.

This small mayfly is overlooked in most regions, but is recognized as producing important hatches on a few waters, notably the Yellowstone River in Yellowstone National Park. The nymphs are most often mistaken by anglers for *Ephemerella inermis,* which is why we list it here following the more important pale morning duns.

We have collected *S. tibialis* from waters throughout the entire West, including our home Deschutes River and many Pacific coastal streams. Despite the common occurrence of this species, fishable hatches are relatively rare. The best hatch we have encountered was on a late-August afternoon while wading the Buffalo Ford reach of the Yellowstone River. It is likely that some good hatches of *S. tibialis* get misidentified as PMDs or are overshadowed by more pronounced hatches that occur at the same time of year. However, you might find it in fishable numbers, prompting trout to feed selectively, anywhere throughout its wide range.

Serratella tibialis **HATCH IMPORTANCE SCORE:** **24.0**

CRITERIA/SCORE	5		4		3		2		1	
Distribution: (within Western waters)	widespread		common		scattered	3.0	isolated		rare	
Abundance:	heavy		abundant		modest		trickling	2.0	individual	
Emergence type:	mid-water/slow		mid-water/fast	4.0	edges/slow		edges/fast		crawls out	
Emergence time:	mid-day	5.0	early and/or late over long period		early and/or late over short period		dawn or dusk		night	
Emergence duration:	multiple seasons per year		well-defined long hatch period		well-defined short hatch period		poorly-defined long hatch period	2.0	poorly-defined short hatch	
(Behavior/Availability) Nymph:	excellent		good		moderate		slight		poor	1.0
(Behavior/Availability) Emerger:	excellent		good		moderate		slight	2.0	poor	
(Behavior/Availability) Dun:	excellent		good		moderate	3.0	slight		poor	
(Behavior/Availability) Spinner:	excellent		good		moderate		slight	2.0	poor	
Totals:		5.0		4.0		6.0		8.0		1.0

Emergence and Distribution

Serratella tibialis has been reported from the Pacific states and provinces, and from Rocky Mountain waters as far north as the Castle River in

TIME	WINTER			SPRING			SUMMER			FALL		
	Dec.	Jan.	Feb.	March	April	May	June	July	Aug.	Sep.	Oct.	Nov.
7 a.m. - 10 a.m.											Rocky Mountains	
10 a.m. - noon												
noon - 3 p.m.												
3 p.m. - 7 p.m.									Pacific			
7 p.m. - 10 p.m.												

Alberta and as far south as New Mexico and Arizona. It occurs in a wide range of stream types, from large rivers to small headwater streams and spring creeks, at altitudes from sea level to over 10,000 feet. Cool streams with summer temperatures between 47°F and 60°F appear to be preferred.

Fred Arbonna, in his *Mayflies, the Angler, and the Trout*, reports *S. tibialis* hatches beginning in early July in California, from mid-July through mid-August in Colorado and Wyoming, and from early August to early September in Montana and Idaho. In Yellowstone Park the hatch typically begins in mid to late July and lasts until the end of August or the first weeks of September. Knopp and Cormier, in *Mayflies*, report *S. tibialis* on the Yellowstone, Missouri, and Castle rivers, noting that the peak of the hatch lasts from mid-August to mid-September.

Emergence is typically at midday, sometime between 11:00 a.m. and 3:00 p.m. In general, hatches will occur during the daily peak in stream water temperature. This occurs in late afternoon on small, cold, heavily shaded streams, and from late morning to mid-afternoon on larger, more open streams.

Nymph Characteristics

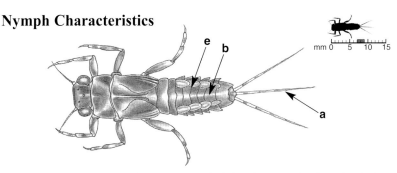

Serratella tibialis nymph.

JOHN JURACEK PHOTO

a. Three tails with alternating pale and dark bands, and whorl of fine hairs at apex of each segment. Tails without lateral fringe of fine hairs, as in *Ephemerella inermis*. This lack of a lateral fringe of hairs on the tails is the easiest and most effective way to distinguish *S. tibialis* from *E. inermis*.

b. Distinctive pale *dorsal stripe* usually (but not always) extending the entire length of the nymph's back.

c. Body ranges from dark purplish-brown to a dark bluish-black, with pale dorsal stripe.

d. Gills on segments 3-7.

e. A pair of small round *tubercles*, or projections, on the posterior margin of each abdominal segment.

f. Body length 7-9 mm, 5/16 to 7/16 in.

Dun Characteristics

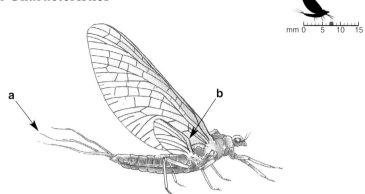

Serratella tibialis dun.

a. Three tails.

b. Distinct, slightly rounded, costal angulation on front margin of hind wing.

c. Wings gray to dark gray.

d. Body varies from brownish-olive to dark reddish-brown.

e. Legs cream color.

f. Body length 7-8 mm, 5/16 to 3/8 in.

Spinner Characteristics

a. Three tails.

b. Distinct, slightly rounded, costal angulation on front margin of hind wing.

c. Wings clear.

d. Body dark reddish-brown body.

e. Body length 7-8 mm, 5/16 to 3/8 in.

Habitat and Behavior

Serratella tibialis populations are usually found in the medium to fast sections of free-flowing streams at any altitude throughout their wide western range. They have adapted to a wide variety of habitats, but are most common where stream water is clean, temperatures not subject to extreme highs, and the currents are modest to brisk. These crawler nymphs live in niches either among bottom stones or on rooted vegetation, where they browse the fine layer of diatoms and algae that grows on rocks or leaves. The nymphs swim to the surface for emergence in or just beneath the surface film. Typical of members of the Ephemerellidae family, *eclosion*—emergence from the nymphal shuck—and escape through the surface film are struggles. During emergence a high percentage of individuals are crippled or stillborn, more on cool and overcast days than on bright and sunny days.

John Juracek and Craig Mathews, in *Fishing Yellowstone Hatches*, observe that trout usually prefer ascending nymphs over emerged duns during the hatch they fish on the Yellowstone River in the park. They credit this to the ease with which trout can intercept the nymphs, and the suspicion some trout have developed about dry flies by the end of the season on heavily-fished waters.

Spinner falls of *S. tibialis* usually occur in the evening, but they are not often concentrated enough to cause trout to feed on them selectively. Most often the spinners are mixed with those of related and unrelated species, so that neither you nor the trout can sort them out. You might match whatever is dominant, or use the generic Red Quill Spinner in the

The most famous hatch of *Serratella* is that of *S. tibialis* on the Buffalo Ford reach of the Yellowstone River.

appropriate small size. Juracek and Mathews recommend a size 18 Sparkle Spinner with either an olive or brown body.

Imitation

Trout generally feed selectively only on the ascending nymph, struggling emerger, or dun stages of *S. tibialis*. We will list a small range of patterns that are specific for it, but you should consider that when trout feed on such a small insect, they are often more selective to size, shape, and particularly presentation than they are to color. It's quite possible that you can match the nymph with the Pheasant Tail you already carry for other insects, the emerger with dressings listed for the *Baetis* complex, and the duns with a searching dressing such as the Parachute Adams, or with PMD patterns.

If you get into trout feeding on *Serratella* and they refuse these substitute patterns, then it's time to get out the tying kit and tie flies specifically for this small mayfly hatch. In that case, you should observe the colors of specimens that you've collected, and vary the following dressings to match your own specimens. The naturals will differ in size and color from stream to stream.

Nymph Imitations

Juracek and Mathews report that in their experience, color is not critical in nymph imitations of *S. tibialis* due to color variations in the naturals within the same river system. They call for medium brown nymph imitations, and also list the Pheasant Tail as suitable during this hatch.

Serratella Tibialis Fur Nymph
(Originators: John Juracek and Craig Mathews)

Hook:	Standard dry fly, 1X fine, size 16-18.
Thread:	Brown 8/0.
Tail:	Brown partridge fibers.
Body:	Brown dubbing.
Thorax:	Brown dubbing, picked out for legs.

This simple tie reflects the primary parts of the small natural perfectly. Vary the color to suit what you collect on your own waters. Note that Juracek and Mathews list the fly in sizes 16 and 18 for their Yellowstone River hatch, smaller than other writers report it on other waters.

Western Black Quill Nymph
(Source: Knopp and Cormier)

Hook:	Standard dry fly, 1X fine, size 14-16.
Thread:	Black 6/0 or 8/0.
Tail:	Black hackle fibers.
Rib:	Fine gold wire.
Body:	Bluish-black fur or synthetic dubbing.
Wing pads:	Black polypro.
Legs:	Dark brown partridge fibers.

This imitation, slightly larger and darker than that listed above, reflects the natural variations displayed by an insect that lives in many waters, over a widespread range. Regard this once again as a hint that you should collect on your own waters, and match what you find.

Presentation

Because of the widespread and common occurrence of *S. tibialis* nymphs, you may occasionally want to fish these flies as searching nymphs along the bottom. However, when trout feed selectively on nymphs of *S. tibialis*, they're typically taking them high in the water column, just inches deep, in the moments prior to their emergence into duns. You should rig as you would for dry-fly fishing over the same hatch, though it might help to dress your leader with floatant or line dressing to within a few inches of the nymph.

Present the nymph to visibly-feeding trout. When fishing nymphs just subsurface in this way, you'll have to watch your line tip, leader, and the area where your fly drifts for any signs of a take. Sometimes, however, trout will take with such vigor that the swirl breaks up to the surface. Though we haven't had enough opportunities over this hatch to have tried it ourselves, our suspicion is that the nymph fished as a dropper off the stern of a floating pattern selected to match the dun stage of the same insect would not hurt your chances at a few extra trout.

Emerger and Dun Imitations

Because these small insects have such a difficult time penetrating the surface film, getting free of their nymphal shucks, and drying their wings for flight, especially on smooth water, surface dressings can be quite effective during an emergence. Trout will likely be taking a combination of rising nymphs, struggling emergers, and fully-winged duns, though at times one trout will concentrate on one stage and others on a different stage.

Dressings such as Juracek and Mathews's Olive-Brown Sparkle Dun imitate the emerger and dun at once, and are especially effective. Patterns specifically for the duns are not likely to be ignored when the hatch is strong and trout are focused on it, feeding on all available stages.

Olive-Brown Sparkle Dun (Source: Juracek and Mathews)

Hook:	Standard dry fly, 1X fine, size 16-18.
Thread:	Olive 6/0 or 8/0.
Wing:	Natural dark Compara-dun deer hair.
Trailing shuck:	Brown Z-lon.
Body:	Olive-brown fur or synthetic dubbing.

Consider that there is very little difference between this dressing and the Sparkle Dun listed for the *Baetis* complex. Chances are that if you carry that fly for the more common blue-winged olives, and get into a less-common hatch of *S. tibialis*, you're already armed with a fly that will work.

Red Quill (Source: Knopp and Cormier)

Hook:	Standard dry fly, 1X fine, size 14-16.
Thread:	Dark brown 6/0 or 8/0.
Tails:	Light blue dun hackle fibers.
Body:	Reddish-brown dyed hackle stem.
Wings:	Gray-dyed mallard flank, upright and divided.
Hackle:	Cream.

This traditionally hackled dressing will not only imitate the winged *Serratella* dun, but will also support any small nymph that you desire to suspend beneath it. In that manner, you're imitating both stages of the insect on one cast.

S. Tibialis Dun Parachute (Source: Knopp and Cormier)

Hook:	Standard dry fly, 1X fine, size 14-16.
Thread:	Dark brown 6/0 or 8/0.
Wingpost:	Pale gray polypro yarn.
Tails:	Gray Micro Fibetts.
Body:	Brownish-olive to brown synthetic dubbing.
Hackle:	Cream, tied parachute.

Parachute dressings are excellent where you need a bit of flotation but also would like to suspend the body of the fly in the surface film, without hackle points to disrupt its silhouette. This pattern is good when you find *S. tibialis* hatches on less than the smoothest water. It will also support a nymph dangled on a fine tippet tied to the bend of the hook.

Presentation

Most of the time, when you find trout rising selectively to *S. tibialis* emergers or duns, you'll be fishing smooth currents. The Yellowstone River in the Buffalo Ford reach of Yellowstone Park is classic for this hatch, and a perfect example of the kind of water that produces excellent surface fishing over this and many other small insects.

You'll need your finest tackle for fishing such water. We rarely fish with light one- and two-weight rods, because they're too easily defeated by wind, but this is the place for them if you own them, or would like an excuse to buy one. Use ten- to fourteen-foot leaders, with three to four feet of tippet, 5X at a minimum and 6X more often. The reach cast and downstream wiggle cast will serve you better than the typical upstream dry-fly presentation on the kind of flat and heavily-fished waters where *S. tibialis* hatches are best known.

Spinner Imitations

There is little chance that you'll find yourself in desperate need of specific imitations for *S. tibialis* spinners. If you get into a spinner fall and find fish feeding selectively to it, try dressings that you already carry for other species before you tie anything specific for this insect. Juracek and Mathews recommend their Sparkle Spinner with a brown body, and we'll list it here in case you get into an emergency.

Brown Sparkle Spinner (Source: Juracek and Mathews)

Hook:	Standard dry fly, 1X fine, size 16-18.
Thread:	Brown 8/0.
Tails:	Brown hackle fibers, splayed.
Body:	Brown fur or synthetic dubbing.
Wings:	White Z-lon, tied spent.

Presentation

Rig fine and fish close, with slack-line casts from either off to the side or at an angle downstream. Single out a fish, time its rise rhythms, and make sure you drop the fly right into its feeding lane, at about the time it is ready to rise again.

Your biggest problem in this kind of spinner fishing will be micro-drag, caused by tiny conflicting currents that you are unable to see from casting distance. If you get up close enough, natural caution will cause you to concentrate and present your flies more delicately, which will help you fool trout in these situations.

Dr. Greg Lundmark with a nice Yellowstone cutthroat trout taken on a dry fly during the *Serratella tibialis* hatch.

Chapter 13

Smaller *Drunella*
(*Flavs*, Lesser Green Drakes)

FAMILY: EPHEMERELLIDAE

Genus: *Drunella*

Western Species: 6

North America: 13

Important western species of the smaller *Drunella*:

Drunella flavilinea (previously *Ephemerella flavilinea*)

D. coloradensis (previously *Ephemerella coloradensis*)

Common Names: *Flavs*, lesser green drakes, small western green drakes, dark slate-winged olives (*D. flavilinea*), slate-winged olives (*D. coloradensis*).

The genus *Drunella* contains a complex group of species that are well known to western anglers. These species fall neatly into two groups: the smaller *Drunella*, commonly called *flavs* or lesser green drakes, and the greater *Drunella*, commonly called western green drakes. Because both groups are distinct, produce excellent hatches, and are widespread and very important throughout the West, we discuss them in separate chapters, though they belong to the same genus: *Drunella*.

Drunella was until some years ago a sub-genus of *Ephemerella*, but has now been elevated to genus level. Because *Ephemerella* included the western green drakes and still contains the pale morning duns, the lesser green drakes were generally accorded no more than footnote status in discussions of the other *Ephemerella*. They deserve far more than that in any book about western mayfly hatches.

If you rate hatches according to the brief riot they instill in trout, causing fish to feed greedily for an hour or two for just a pandemonious week or

Smaller *Drunella*   **HATCH IMPORTANCE SCORE:**   **35.0**

CRITERIA/SCORE	5		4		3		2		1	
Distribution: (within Western waters)	widespread		common	4.0	scattered		isolated		rare	
Abundance:	heavy		abundant	4.0	modest		trickling		individual	
Emergence type:	mid-water/slow	5.0	mid-water/fast		edges/slow		edges/fast		crawls out	
Emergence time:	mid-day	5.0	early and/or late over long period		early and/or late over short period		dawn or dusk		night	
Emergence duration:	multiple seasons per year		well-defined long hatch period	3.5	well-defined short hatch period		poorly-defined long hatch period		poorly-defined short hatch	
(Behavior/Availability) **Nymph:**	excellent		good		moderate	3.0	slight		poor	
(Behavior/Availability) **Emerger:**	excellent		good		moderate		slight		poor	
(Behavior/Availability) **Dun:**	excellent		good	4.0	moderate		slight		poor	
(Behavior/Availability) **Spinner:**	excellent		good	4.0	moderate	2.5	slight		poor	
Totals:				10.0		19.5		5.5		0.0		0.0

two, but only on days when conditions are perfect, then you'll rate the larger but capricious western green drakes as more important than the lesser green drakes: *Drunella flavilinea and D. coloradensis.* They are called *lesser* because they are slightly smaller, not because there are fewer of them.

On the opposite hand, if you rate hatches on the way they come off dependably and daily for weeks and even months, for at least an hour on bright days but for several hours on cloudy days, drawing trout up to the surface to feed eagerly but selectively over long periods of time each season, then you'll rate these lessers as more important than their larger relatives. We do.

Lesser green drakes cause selective feeding on far more waters throughout the West, and for longer time periods, than the western green drakes. We have fished over heavy hatches of one species or the other—*Drunella flavilinea* and *D. coloradensis* are difficult to distinguish even for professional entomologists—on Fall River, a spring creek in Oregon, on the Frying Pan, a tailwater in Colorado, on the Logan River, a rushing freestone stream in Utah, and on Slough Creek, a placid meadow stream in Yellowstone Park, among a scattering of other places that are less well known but often more fun. If you travel much in the West, and enjoy fishing clean and cold streams, you'll run into this fine hatch.

Emergence and Distribution

Hatches of lesser green drakes tend to begin in the days and weeks just following hatches of the more famous and larger western green drakes. On many waters that means the middle to the end of June, but on other waters hatches are unrelated to their larger cousins and might peak at any time up until October. At times, the hatches of greaters and lessers seem to merge, the green drakes tailing off and the slightly smaller insects beginning just a few days later. The smaller *Drunella* species are actually large enough, at around size 10 or more often 12, to be mistaken for their size 8 and 10 relatives. They are so similar in appearance that without collecting specimens and taking a close look, you might never notice that one hatch has ended and another has started. Without question, mistaken identification of lesser green drakes has added to the fame of the greater green drakes.

Your fly pattern might even be right, as you fade from one hatch to the next, though most often it will be a size or so too large. On many waters that wouldn't matter to the trout. You'd keep right on catching them.

On most waters the lesser green drake hatch begins when water temperatures creep up toward a steady 55°F or a little higher. The progression logically moves both inland and north as you progress through

SMALLER *DRUNELLA* EMERGENCE TABLE

TIME	WINTER			SPRING			SUMMER			FALL		
	Dec.	Jan.	Feb.	March	April	May	June	July	Aug.	Sep.	Oct.	Nov.
7 a.m. - 10 a.m.												
10 a.m. - noon								Pacific		Rocky Mountains		
noon - 3 p.m.												
3 p.m. - 7 p.m.												
7 p.m. - 10 p.m.												

The alternating benches and drops of the upper Logan River form perfect habitat for nymphs of *Drunella coloradensis*. They hatch in great numbers in September.

the western season. But hatch progressions are never so simple in the vast and varied West. The lesser green drake hatch will be later at high altitudes in the southern Rockies than it will be at lower elevations in the northern Rockies, and it will be earlier on rivers warmed by the sun in Montana than on a frigid Oregon spring creek.

The best fishing we have experienced over this hatch, whether the more famous *flavs* or the widespread *D. coloradensis*, has been in September. It's a time when we enjoy traveling to the high Rockies, in part to see the gorgeous fall colors. The hatch is delayed there simply because the water does not warm to the temperatures these insects prefer for emergence until late in the season. To us, this hatch goes along with the change of colors in the mountains. For those who fish rivers at lower elevations, it is more often a midsummer hatch.

On cool and overcast days, hatches of the smaller *Drunella* tend to begin in early afternoon and go on until late afternoon or even into evening. Though fewer duns will be on the water at any one time, they'll be sufficient to keep trout up and feeding for hours. On bright, sunny days, unfortunately the average kind of weather in summer and fall in the Rockies, hatches tend to be condensed into an hour or less. On the Logan River in Utah we've seen the lesser green drake hatch compacted into half an hour, some time between 2:00 and 3:30 p.m. Trout go wild during the very brief time duns are on the water. Juracek and Mathews, in *Fishing Yellowstone Hatches*, report that these condensed hatches occur later in the afternoon and evening on streams in their West Yellowstone, Montana area.

Drunella flavilinea and *D. coloradensis* are distributed in every western state and province. It would be nice to break it down and say that the *flavs* are here and *coloradensis* there, but the truth is their populations overlap and are even thought to interbreed. The main factor separating populations of these two species is temperature, with *D. coloradensis* prefering slightly colder water (<55°F) than *D. flavilinea*. That is one reason it is dangerous for anglers, with limited experience in reading the finer details of the mayfly spinner's penile parts, to insist that every hatch be identified to species. Professional taxonomists have trouble doing that. In this group of just two species that are so similar, anglers should be content to lump them and get on with fishing. Until trout start lining up with their elbows on the counters of biological supply houses, ordering dissecting microscopes, you can match the two species wherever they are found, from Sierra streams in California to freestone streams in British Columbia, from the high mountain streams of New Mexico to the gentle Bow River tailwater in Alberta, with the same fly patterns.

Nymph Characteristics

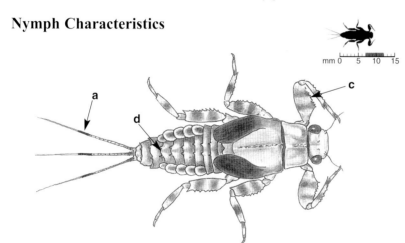

Drunella coloradensis nymph.

a. Three tails, with distinctive black band near center of each tail.
b. Blocky, crawler shape.
c. Stout femurs with serrated front edges.
d. Short paired projections, sharp to slightly rounded, along the posterior edge of each abdominal segment.
e. Gills on abdominal segments 3-7.
f. Reddish-brown to dark brown or olive brown.
g. Length, without tails, 7-12mm, 1/4 to 1/2 in.

The two species, *D. flavilinea* and *D. coloradensis,* are nearly impossible to separate to species in the nymphal stage. *D. flavilinea* nymphs typically have very rounded and poorly developed projections on their abdominal segments compared to *D. coloradensis* nymphs, but there is considerable overlap in the range of the features. As adults the only sure way to separate these species is by looking at the male reproductive organs under a good microscope. Since trout really don't care what species they eat, species identification is only necessary to satisfy your curiosity.

Dun Characteristics

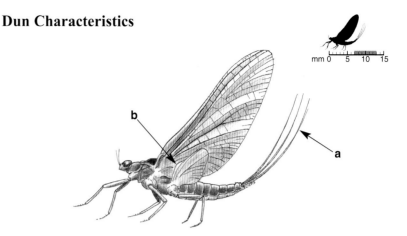

Smaller *Drunella* dun.

JIM SCHOLLMEYER PHOTO

a. Three tails.
b. Hind wings with distinct, slightly rounded costal angulation.
c. Bodies lack distinct segmentation by bright banding.
d. Wings pale to dark gray.
e. Length, without tails, 7-13 mm, 1/4 to 5/8 in.

If you find it difficult to identify a dun as belonging to the lessers or largers, you can easily associate it with nymphs by collecting from nearby streambed rocks, or by searching for cast shucks in quiet water. Mature nymphs, with darkened wingpads, will usually be easy to find by hoisting a few stones, and far easier to key than the duns.

The same is true for the following spinners. Their three tails tell you they're crawlers, and their size tells you they're either green drakes or lessers. Few characteristics jump out that separate them. If you can associate the duns with mature nymphs during a hatch, then rear a few duns to spinners, you will recognize all three stages as well as it can be done.

Spinner Characteristics
a. Three tails.
b. Hind wings with distinct, slightly rounded costal angulation.
c. Wings clear.
d. Body olive-brown to reddish-brown.
e. Body length 7-12mm, 1/4 to 1/2 in.

Habitat and Behavior
Both *Drunella flavilinea* and *D. coloradensis* nymphs demand clean, cold streams, usually with an abundance of gravel and cobble on the bottom. In some places, such as the Bow River and Henrys Fork of the Snake, they've adapted to niches among aquatic plants, which serve their needs for food and a place to hide from predators the same as niches among stones. They'll generally be found only in streams and rivers with moderate to fast flows. They will not be found in sluggish streams, nor will they be found in the still backwater areas of faster waters. The nymphs tend to live where currents are modest to brisk, then migrate toward the edges of the fastest water, to more peaceful places, just before emergence. That is why, even on brisk streams, you need imitations that are somewhat accurate: the nymphs might live in fast water, but the duns will usually be found floating on nearby water that is a bit less boisterous.

In the Rockies, the heaviest populations of these crawler nymphs occur in waters above 4,000 feet in elevation, but that is primarily because

Drunella flavilinea spinner.

JIM SCHOLLMEYER PHOTO

streams with clean, cold flows tend to be a bit higher up the mountain. In the Pacific Northwest, good populations can be found on streams near sea level. Wherever you find suitable conditions you'll find at least minor populations of the lesser green drakes.

The nymphs clamber among streambed stones, usually browsing on the thin layer of diatoms and algae that grows on surfaces struck by the sun, then retreating to niches on the undersides of the stones, and even far down into the gravel. If the nymphs live in rooted vegetation, then they browse the same thin layer of growth that forms on the leaves of underwater plants. They also graze detrital matter such as fallen leaves, though leaf packs are less common in the brisk flows these nymphs prefer than they are in marginal waters inhabited by other aquatic insect types.

When mature and ready for emergence, the wingpads of the nymph will extend over nearly half of the body length, and will be almost black. The nymphs become restless before emergence, migrating out of fast riffles and runs and into the flats and side-currents near the water that is more dangerous to emerging duns. This is excellent for you as an angler: the nymphs live in the fastest flows but you get to fish the hatch on the nearest smooth water. On Utah's bounding and beautiful Logan River, for example, we collected nymphs on the undersides of stones in some peaceful tailouts and sidewaters just four to six inches deep, preparing for their lift into aerial life. In normal circumstances this would have been meaningless, except that trout, in their eagerness during this feast, were right in there in the shallows after the duns that soon hatched from them, with their backs almost showing.

The nymphs let go their grip on the bottom and swim to the surface with a vigorous up-and-down thrusting of the abdomen that is not entirely efficient. They make a lot of movement, but not much progress. If it's a long trip to the surface, three to four feet or more, they might pause to rest during the ascent.

The nymphal exoskeleton splits either inches beneath the surface film, or in the film itself. Emergence for these large insects, as for most members of the Ephemerellidae family, is often difficult. They struggle to get out of the shuck, then the duns wait impatiently for their wings to become erect and to dry. They often sit on the water and drift helplessly for ten to twenty feet or more, then flutter, lift off, fall to the water again, and repeat the process several times before finally escaping into the air.

If they're emerging on the glides of stairstep mountain streams, many duns fail to get off the water before they're delivered to the next riffle or rapid downstream. These drowned duns quite likely form a major source of food for trout after the hatch is over, especially if it's a brief one, the kind most common on a bright, sunny day. It's probable that a wet fly such as a Leadwing Coachman or a soft-hackle such as the Partridge and Green would continue to take trout for an hour or so after a hatch, just as a dead-drifted nymph works in the hour or two before a hatch. We haven't tried extending the hatch with wet flies, but recommend that you do.

Emerger and dun fishing is excellent over lesser green drakes, and is quite clearly the core of the hatch. If it's the kind of hatch that trickles off for hours, then you can have surface fishing through that entire period. If it's brief, stretch it out with nymph fishing early, and try wet-fly fishing late if no other hatch comes off to interest the trout.

Lesser green drake spinners can be important at times. They are so large that trout do not ignore them if the naturals get onto the water in sufficient numbers to make feeding worthwhile. That will generally happen some time in the mid-morning hours during summer and early fall, though

Cobbly riffles separated by runs and flats provide the perfect combination of habitat for lesser green drakes.

it can happen in the evening when the weather is cooler. This, again, is one of those things that varies from place to place, and from time to time, throughout the vast West. You should be prepared with a few spinner dressings, and match the falls when you find them important. The naturals will usually gather in the air over riffles. The spent females, and males that fall as well, are taken most often by trout on somewhat smoother water just downstream from riffles and vigorous runs.

Matching most stages of the lesser green drakes requires mere extension through the size range of dressings that you tie smaller for the blue-winged olive complex and larger for the green drakes themselves. The size range of the lesser green drakes, almost always restricted to 12s and 14s, is the one most often absent in our continuum of olive dun dressings. We'd not like to confess to you the number of times we've been caught in a lesser green drake hatch well armed with patterns at both ends of the size range, but with none in that middle area that would have matched what was hatching.

Imitation

It's wise to carry a few imitations for all stages of the lesser green drakes, and to be well armed for the emergers and duns. This does not always require that you carry additional fly patterns, just that you know which ones to use when you suspect nymph activity, or observe emergers, duns, or spinners. For example, it's likely you already carry Pheasant Tail and Gold Ribbed Hare's Ear nymphs, and it's also likely those are all you'll ever need during the restless activity of *Drunella flavilinea* and *D. coloradensis* nymphs.

It's also possible that you already carry the traditional Blue Winged Olive dry fly in size 12 and 14, for the many hatches that hackled dressing will match over the course of a season. If you do, it will work fine during lesser green drake hatches on all but the smoothest and most heavily fished waters. It has the added advantage of all that hackle for flotation. In the typical high-mountain stream where these hatches are found so often, you'll need it. If you don't already carry René Harrop's Olive Hairwing Dun in its full range of sizes, you should.

It should become more and more clear that nature has adopted reddish-brown as the most common color for its various mayfly spinners. There are lively and valuable exceptions, especially the blue quills, but many mayflies start out as olives, sulphurs, and shades of brown but end the final stage of their reproductive lives spent on the water as red quills.

Nymph Imitations

We'll go out on a slight limb on this group, and advise you to carry your normal Pheasant Tails and Gold Ribbed Hare's Ears in regular and bead-head versions, in sizes 12 and 14, and that's about it. When you first fish any stream, if no insects are hatching and no trout are actively feeding on the surface, do some kicking around with a seine net. If you find lesser green drake nymphs dominant in samples, which will happen a surprising number of times, then use these standard nymph dressings as your searchers until the hatch begins and it becomes obvious that you should turn your attention to emergers or duns.

If these standards don't work for you, which will surprise us, then take time to collect some nymphs, and work out accurate imitations based on their size, shape, and color. All of those factors will vary slightly in *Drunella flavilinea* and *D. coloradensis* specimens observed from stream to stream throughout this unruly West of ours.

Pheasant Tail (Originator: Al Troth)

Hook:	Standard nymph, 2X long, size 12-16.
Weight:	10 to 15 turns fine lead wire, or omit.
Thread:	Brown 6/0 or 8/0.
Tails:	Pheasant center tail fibers.
Rib:	Fine copper wire, counterwound over abdomen.
Abdomen:	Pheasant center tail fibers, as herl.
Wingcase:	Pheasant center tail fibers.
Thorax:	Peacock herl.
Legs:	Tips of wingcase fibers.

This Al Troth version the the Pheasant Tail Nymph has a peacock herl thorax. Because the natural nymphs are somewhat stout, the weighting wire can serve two purposes: to get the fly down, and also to fatten it up. If you omit the weight, preferring to get the fly to the bottom with split shot on the leader, then use extra pheasant herl to construct a portly abdomen.

Pheasant Tail Beadhead

Hook:	Standard nymph, 2X long, size 12-16.
Bead:	Gold or brass.
Thread:	Brown 6/0 or 8/0.
Tails:	Pheasant center tail fibers.
Rib:	Fine copper wire, counterwound over abdomen.
Abdomen:	Pheasant center tail fibers, as herl.
Wingcase:	Mottled turkey or dark goose feather section.
Thorax:	Dark hare's mask fur with guard hair, picked out for legs.

Though the bead in a sense makes this a less imitative fly, it is often more effective during lesser green drake nymph activity. It's not certain whether the bead helps because it gets the fly down fast, or because the flash makes it more visible to trout, or because the added weight at the head causes a jigging action. Gary LaFontaine, famous for his underwater research, has sent skin divers down, or gone down himself, to observe the reaction of trout to beadhead nymphs. He concludes that the jigging movement of the fly, as it nods along on the current, is the primary attractant to trout. Gary doesn't draw conclusions casually. When lesser green drake nymphs are abundant and being eaten by trout, the beadhead likely works because of a combination of factors: excellent imitation of the natural nymph and movement that makes the fly look like it's alive and good to eat.

Gold Ribbed Hare's Ear

Hook:	Standard nymph, 2X long, size 12-16.
Weight:	10 to 15 turns fine lead wire, or omit.
Thread:	Brown 6/0 or 8/0.
Tail:	Hare's mask guard hairs.
Rib:	Medium oval gold tinsel.
Abdomen:	Medium hare's mask fur.
Wingcase:	Dark mottled turkey tail or goose wing feather sections.
Thorax:	Dark hare's mask fur with guard hair, picked out for legs.

This standard dressing probably owes some of its eternal success to its resemblance to the prolific lesser green drake nymphs, along with so many other insect types. We have found that the best searching patterns, whether nymph or dry, are based on some sort of trout food form. The Gold Ribbed Hare's Ear looks like a lot of them.

Hare's Ear Beadhead

Hook:	Standard nymph, 2X long, size 12 to 16.
Bead:	Gold or brass.
Thread:	Brown 6/0 or 8/0.
Tail:	Hare's mask guard hairs.
Rib:	Medium oval gold tinsel.
Abdomen:	Medium hare's mask fur.
Wingcase:	Mottled turkey or dark gray goose feather section.
Thorax:	Dark hare's mask fur with guard hair, picked out for legs.

Beadhead dressings have proved to be very effective for us over a number of years now, in searching situations, and also when a specific nymph is abundant and by its darkened wingpads can be pronounced about ready to hatch. While we agree with critics of beadheads that they are not imitative in a strict sense, we do feel that the Beadhead Nymph is imitative of the behavior of some naturals, many of which pump gases into the space between the nymphal shuck that is about to be cast and the skin of the dun that is just about to escape once the nymph reaches the surface. The bright bead can represent reflections off this trapped bubble of air.

Presentation

If you're fishing water more than three to four feet deep, you'll be able to get these dressings down most effectively with the split shot and strike indicator method. In that case make your casts upstream, usually into

When you're fishing typical benches over a *Drunella flavilinea* or *D. coloradensis* hatch, be sure to take up a position that allows you to get a drag-free drift on the water you're covering, whether you're using nymphs, emergers, or dun patterns.

broken water that is somewhat rough, or along the edges of such water. Let the flies tumble along the bottom naturally, with a dead drift, as if they were dry flies but fished inches above the bottom rather than on the surface. Watch your strike indicator carefully for any hesitation that indicates a trout has intercepted the nymph down below. Set the hook. The fly should be hitting bottom rocks now and then, so you'll get a lot of false indicator movements. But enough of those hesitations will be caused by trout to keep you happy. Use subsequent casts to cover all of the water.

In our own experience, we've fished these hatches most often in the glides and slicks between the brief riffles and drops of high-gradient streams. Such mountain waters are normally no more than two to three feet deep in the current lanes that hold trout. We have found that the best way to get a fly down to such modest depths, in such brisk water, is simply to drop a weighted nymph or beadhead off the hook bend of a dry fly, or to trail it behind an indicator on just two to four feet of tippet. The tippet to the nymph should be about as long as the water is deep. The dry fly or strike indicator must be buoyant enough to suspend the nymph without sinking.

You can use a searching dry, such as a Royal Wulff or Elk Hair Caddis, to serve as support for the nymph. But you're better off using a dry that will match the approaching lesser green drake hatch. Then trout will find an imitation of whichever stage they want as they turn their attention from natural nymphs to floating duns in the normal progression of the hatch.

In truth, in such shallow water, trout are often willing to strike up to the top and take the dry even in the pre-hatch hours. You'll normally find your catch about evenly divided between the nymph and dry, though it will run in spurts: several trout on the nymph, then a bunch on the dry. Refrain from removing one until the other has proved itself to be a mere appendage, in your way when you release trout hooked on the other fly. The trailing nymph, especially, gets to be a nuisance when trout begin focusing on the dry.

Emerger Imitations

We're tempted to throw in a soft-hackle, such as size 12 to 14 Partridge and Green, as a suggestion for the emerging dun. It should fish well when trout feed on those duns that either cast their shucks inches beneath the surface and make the final ascent without the nymphal shuck, or for those duns that make it to the surface but are then trapped in riffles and taken under again. But we have focused our own fishing on floating flies during the actual hatch, and have not taken time to perform the experiments necessary to prove the Partridge and Green.

This is in part due to the fact that we do not often get to fish for several days running over the same hatch, on the same water, and in larger part to our greed for the surface take. When dry flies are working, we have trouble swinging wets. You, however, might have more discipline, and we would like to assign you this bit of research.

A soft-hackle dressed with floatant would also make a fine emerger. But our own efforts have been directed toward either suspending a nymph body beneath a ball of synthetic that represents the emerging wings of the dun, or tying a dun dressing with some representation of the nymphal shuck still attached. Both styles are effective, though the latter, with their upraised wings, are much easier to fish in fairly rough water.

Flav Surface Emerger

Hook:	Standard nymph, 1X long, size 12-16.
Thread:	Brown 6/0 or 8/0.
Tails:	Brown partridge fibers.
Body:	Light brown or brownish-olive synthetic dubbing.
Wing pod:	Slate gray synthetic dubbing knot.
Thorax:	Dark brown or brownish-olive synthetic dubbing.
Leg:	Brown partridge fibers.

Use synthetic dubbing for the body of this fly, to help it float flush in the surface film. You can dress the entire fly with floatant, and the body will float. You can dress just the wing pod, and the fly will suspend from it with the body beneath the surface. It will be difficult to keep it suspended this way in rough water, but the method will work on the glides and slicks between riffles and drops on fast mountain streams. You will have trouble seeing the fly fished either way. Try a strike indicator tied into the leader four to five feet from the fly. You can also use emerger dressings as trailers behind dries that match the dun of the same insect.

CDC *Flav* Emerger

Hook:	Standard dry fly, 1X fine, size 10-14.
Thread:	Brown 6/0 or 8/0.
Tails:	Brown partridge fibers.
Body:	Brown or brownish-olive synthetic dubbing.
Wing:	Gray CDC, short.
Legs:	Brown partridge fibers.

This dressing suspends the nymph body beneath the bouyant CDC, and represents the emergent phase passing through the film. It is very imitative of the natural, but also very difficult to see on rough water. If you fish lesser green drake hatches over weedy spring creeks and tailwaters, you'll be able to follow the drift of this drab dressing. If you fish rougher water, add a strike indicator or a more visible dry fly a short way up the leader.

Olive Sparkle Dun (Source: Juracek and Mathews)

Hook:	Standard dry fly, 1X fine, size 12-16.
Thread:	Olive 6/0 or 8/0.
Wing:	Natural dark Compara-dun deer hair.
Trailing shuck:	Brown Z-lon.
Body:	Olive fur or synthetic dubbing.

This dressing represents the emerged dun with the nymphal shuck still trailing. It is excellent on smooth spring creeks and tailwaters, and also in the glides and slicks of mountain streams. You'll have no trouble following its float if you get up close and fish it at the ranges that give you the greatest advantage when fishing such hatches.

Presentation

On smooth water, you fish these dressings just as you would emerger or dun dressings for blue-winged olives and pale morning duns. Recall the circle, with the rising trout at its center and your position somewhere out on the circumference. Choose your position based on the currents you'd like to get behind you, and the best place from which to make your short cast, over a trout that is unaware of your presence. The reach cast and downstream wiggle cast will serve you well in these smooth-water situations. Your tackle should be delicate, your leader long and tapered to 4X, 5X, possibly even 6X, depending on the selectivity of the trout over which you're casting. The tippet itself should be at least two feet long, better three to four feet long, in order to give your emerger dressing the sort of free float you'd like to achieve.

If you're fishing typical stairstep streams during this hatch, then it's critical that you move up onto the bench just below the one you're fishing. Don't try to get a good drift from two or three benches downstream. Make your cast short, twenty to thirty feet. As soon as the fly lands, lift as much line as possible off the water. If the water passing swiftly over the stairstep at the end of the glide or run you're fishing catches your line, you'll get only a foot or two of drag-free drift before the fly begins to race. If you position yourself two or three stairsteps downstream from the one where your fly lands, you will not be able to hold enough line in the air to prevent drag.

We've often fished either emerger or dun patterns during lesser green drake hatches by getting right up onto the same bench as the trout. This requires that you stay either downstream, out of sight, or off to the side where the trout's view is obstructed by broken water. The fly can then be fished on very short casts with not much more than the leader out. High-sticking a surface-film emerger this close under your rod tip can provide quite a bit of excitement when a large trout leaves the bottom and rises visibly up through the water column to take your fly.

Sometimes a trout will arise with a dash, smack the fly, dive down with it. More often in the kinds of clear, clean, and shallow water where these hatches are most common, you'll see the trout lifting, rising slowly toward the fly, tipping and opening its white mouth, breaking the surface film with jaws agape, waiting for the fly to settle inside. If you haven't set the hook early after all that, you've got more discipline than we do.

Dun Imitations

You'll do most of your lesser green drake fishing, on typical boisterous mountain waters, with imitations of the fully winged dun stage. Trout might take more nymphs in the prehatch period, then lots of emergers when the hatch gets going. But they'll also accept dressings that look like portly, struggling duns trying to launch themselves into the air and to safety from trout. When trout will accept dry flies, they're the most fun to fish. Because you can place them accurately and moniter the drift so much better when you are able to see your fly, you'll often catch more fish on them than you would on imitations of the earlier stages.

Because lesser green drakes emerge on a variety of water types, you'll want dun dressings that offer excellent flotation, as well as some that float less well but show an unhindered silhouette on the water. Our own fishing over these hatches tends toward the Sparkle Dun if we can see it, and the Hairwing Dun where it's added flotation makes it easier to fish. Both work well where we've fished them, but you should choose your own pattern style, or better yet *styles*, based on the water types where you run into these hatches.

Blue Winged Olive

Hook:	Standard dry fly, 1X fine, size 10-16.
Thread:	Olive 6/0 or 8/0.
Tails:	Blue dun hackle fibers.
Body:	Olive fur or synthetic dubbing.
Wings:	Blue dun hen hackle tips.
Hackle:	Blue dun.

We list hook sizes from 10 to 16 because *Drunella flavilinea* hatches have been reported at the smaller end of that scale, and *D. coloradensis* has been reported at the larger end. Most of the hatches you encounter in this group can be matched with size-12 and -14 dressings.

The traditional Blue Winged Olive dry fly might be all you ever need for fishing this hatch. It will certainly be effective on the rougher mountain streams where the hatches are most common. But it won't serve you as well if you fish spring creeks or tailwaters, since such waters tend to get more fishing pressure, and their trout get more selective.

Frying Pan Biot Green Drake Dun (Originator: A. K. Best)

Hook:	Standard dry fly, 1X fine, size 12 to 14.
Thread:	Olive 6/0 or 8/0.
Tail:	Moose or dark elk body hair, slightly splayed.
Underbody:	Double and overwind the butts of tail material.
Body:	Green dyed turkey biot.
Wings:	Medium blue dun hackle tips.
Hackle:	One blue dun and one olive-dyed grizzly.

This A. K. Best dressing, from his book *A. K.'s Fly Box*, is excellent in the Rocky Mountain region where these hatches tend to be most prolific. It floats well on somewhat rough water, but we have seen A. K. bring fish to it on long stretches of smooth water downstream from the type of rough water where the nymphs make their homes. They migrate to the smoother flows before emergence begins, though duns can also come off in the slight windows of smooth water right in the pocket water that is so common on the famous Frying Pan.

Olive Hairwing Dun (Originator: René Harrop)

Hook:	Standard dry fly, size 12-16.
Thread:	Olive 6/0 or 8/0.
Tails:	Blue dun hackle fibers, split.
Body:	Olive fur or synthetic dubbing.
Hackle:	Blue dun, five turns over thorax, clipped on bottom.
Wing:	Gray-dyed yearling elk hair.

This dressing is an excellent compromise between flotation and the true back-wing silhouette of the natural. It will take trout on smooth water, and will float on rough water as well. If we were to have one option for the lesser green drake hatch, this might be it.

Dave was caught completely unprepared when he first fished the Logan River, in Utah, in the middle of September. He had no inkling that lesser green drakes would come off abruptly and in great abundance. He stood stunned in the pushy currents, surrounded by trout slashing at duns from below and swallows flashing at them once they got into the air above. Then he recalled a few Olive Hairwing Duns tied to match a size-12 *Callibaetis* hatch on Yellowstone Lake.

When the vest was frisked and these were found, and one attached to the tippet, those trout were suddenly easy. They were cutts, and were supposed to be stupid, but until the right fly was tried, the trout seemed to be a lot smarter than Dave.

Olive Parachute (Originator: Skip Morris)

Hook:	Standard dry fly, 1X fine, size 12-16.
Thread:	Olive 6/0 or 8/0.
Wingpost:	Yellow polypro yarn.
Tails:	White nutria guard hairs (substitute white Micro Fibetts).
Body:	Olive fur or synthetic dubbing.
Hackle:	Brown, parachute.

This fly is listed because it's a standard searching dressing that your authors use often, and it will serve you well if you get into a *flav* or *D.*

coloradensis hatch and have no proper match. We discovered it while fishing a small mountain stream with Skip Morris, author of *Fly Tying Made Clear and Simple* (Frank Amato Publications, 1992). Skip was using it because the parachute dressing floated well on rough water, and he was able to follow its drift because of the bright yellow parachute post.

It worked well for him that day in the absence of lesser green drakes, but has worked as well for the authors in later years when scattered hatches of these olive insects get trout up and watching the surface for hours at a time. If you don't try it for any other reason, that bright post will make it easy to see your fly. It's excellent as a searcher on small mountain waters, perhaps because it bears such close resemblance to the lesser green drakes that are so common on those rough streams.

Presentation

On smooth water, when trout set up and become selective to these large insects, you'll need to present your flies ahead of your line and leader, right down the feeding lanes of the trout. Take a position off to the side of a spotted and timed fish and use the cross-stream reach cast, or move into position upstream from the trout and use the downstream wiggle cast. Be prepared to present your fly time and again. It often takes several casts before the fly arrives perfectly timed over the trout, just when it's ready to rise.

On rough water, get right up onto the feeding trout, usually from downstream, and present the fly on a short cast. Hold your rod high to lift line off the water, to prevent drag, and watch carefully to notice the takes of trout. It's imperative, even on rough water, that you use a tippet long enough to give the dry fly a free float. If your tippet has been cut back to a foot or so, take time to extend it out to between two and three feet. The leader itself can be short, say the length of your rod or a bit longer. It needn't be fine, though 5X will typically fish far better than 4X on the glides and slicks of mountain streams.

Spinner Imitations

We've listed the Red Quill Spinner for almost every important group so far, and will list it again here in the appropriate sizes. That old traditional dressing does an excellent job imitating the final mating stage of the lesser green drakes. Carry it in a range from size 20 for the tiny blue-winged olives up to size 10 for the larger green drakes. In the middle of that range, size 12, 14, and sometimes 16, it fishes for the lesser green drakes.

We like René Harrop's CDC Rusty Spinner as well. For the smoother water on which many lesser green drakes emerge, it will be excellent. For rougher water, where the spinners fall on or just downstream from somewhat rumpled riffles, a parachute pattern, lofting its wingpost up where you can see it, is a better choice. It is less imitative, but the dry fly you cannot see is rarely the best choice for any type of water. On rough water, trout will not be as selective, will take the listed parachute dressing just fine, and you'll know about it because you can see it.

Red Quill Spinner

Hook:	Standard dry fly, 1X fine, size 12-16.
Thread:	Brown 6/0 or 8/0.
Tails:	Dark ginger hackle fibers, split.
Rib:	Fine gold wire, counterwound over body.
Body:	Reddish-brown dyed hackle stem.
Wings:	Light gray or white hen hackle tips, tied spent.
Hackle:	Dark ginger, clipped top and bottom.

This standard dressing will serve you well if you carry it in an extended range of sizes. It will be difficult to see on the water, but you can often use

On the rough and lightly-fished waters of small mountain streams, present your lesser green drake duns on upstream casts. Where the water is smoother, and the trout more often pestered, you'll be better served by the cross-stream reach cast and downstream wiggle cast.

a small yarn strike indicator to mark its position so you can follow its float, especially in low light.

CDC Rusty Spinner (Originator: René Harrop)

Hook:	Standard dry fly, 1X fine, size 12-16.
Thread:	Brown 6/0 or 8/0.
Tail:	Light blue dun hackle fibers, splayed.
Abdomen:	Rusty brown goose biot.
Thorax:	Rusty brown fur or synthetic dubbing.
Wing:	White CDC, topped with light gray Z-lon.

Try this excellent dressing if you find *flav* or *D. coloradensis* spinner falls on smooth water.

Brown Parachute Spinner (Source: Schollmeyer)

Hook:	Standard dry fly, 1X fine, size 12-16.
Thread:	Brown 6/0 or 8/0.
Wingpost:	Light gray Antron yarn.
Tails:	Light blue dun hackle fibers, splayed.
Body:	Brown synthetic dubbing.
Hackle:	Light blue dun, parachute.

This dressing, listed in Jim Schollmeyer's *Hatch Guide For Western Streams*, gives you a bright post to see, and helps you follow the float of the fly. You might try a white post, or even yellow, and see if it frightens trout. Chances are it will work just as well as light gray, and will be easier to see on rough water.

Presentation

Follow the prescription laid down for emergers and duns. If you're on smooth water, which is where you'll find spinner falls important most often, get into position to fish delicate gear, with presentations that show the fly to the trout ahead of the alarming line and leader.

If you're on rougher water, get up close to the trout, and fish carefully into the feeding lanes of rhythmic risers. If you miss the lane by more than a few inches, in rough water or on smooth currents, the trout might refuse to move for something with so little nutrition left as a lesser green drake spinner.

Chapter 14

Greater *Drunella*
(Western Green Drakes)

FAMILY: EPHEMERELLIDAE

Genus: *Drunella*

Western Species: 6

North America: 13

Important western green drake species: *Drunella grandis*
(previously *Ephemerella grandis;* 3 subspecies: *D. grandis
grandis*, *D. grandis ingens* [previously *Ephemerella glacialis*],
and *D. grandis flavitincta*)
Drunella doddsi (previously *Ephemerella doddsi*)
Drunella spinifera (previously *Ephemerella spinifera*)

Common Names: Western green drakes, lead-winged olives, great
lead-wing olive drakes.

This is the second and largest, in terms of individual insect size, of the two *Drunella* divisions, with the *flavs* or lesser green drakes covered in the previous chapter. Twenty years ago, when we wrote *Western Hatches*, western green drakes were considered the most important hatch on western waters. There were good reasons. It was a blitz of a hatch on the famous Henrys Fork of the Snake, at that time the single most famous trout stream in the West. It was a giant insect—still is—that covered the water and drew the largest trout up to feed on the surface. Anglers flew and drove and even hitchhiked from all over the country, and even the world, to fish the famed hatch on the more-famed river.

Two things happened. First, the Henrys Fork got drawn down and silted in for some years in the 1980s. Fishing deteriorated, and folks went elsewhere. The problem has been solved, and the river is returning to its earlier form, but fly-fishermen are fickle, and have turned their intense focus to other waters with less intense western green drake hatches. Second, smart anglers began to value more highly hatches that were less capricious, more widespread, and that went on for weeks instead of days, keeping fish up and interested in all those places, for all that time. While the week or two of the big hatch on the Henrys Fork was in one way rewarding, it was also crowded fishing, and the western green drakes only came off in their great numbers if the day was overcast, the wind was down, and at times it seemed, if the stars were aligned right. Some days everything seemed perfect and the big bugs still failed to show.

This unpredictability of the western green drakes in part helped shape our own philosophy that you should not aim all of your fishing toward taking trips timed to put you on famous waters during famous hatches, but rather should learn as much as possible about the broadest spectrum of aquatic insect hatches, and be prepared to match whatever hatch might happen on whatever water you find yourself fishing. If you happen to be on a well-known river during a well-known hatch, you'll be prepared to enjoy success over it. But you'll never be disappointed because the anticipated hatch fails to show, and something else takes its place.

That said, when western green drakes hatch, which they still do in great numbers and in many places, they're the most important insect in your world, at that moment. No trout will ever ignore them. You must be prepared to fish over them because trout won't take flies tied for anything else when these giants start popping.

Western green drakes hatch sporadically on many western trout streams, but in heavy numbers on only a few. The duns are so large, and suffer so severely from that common Ephemerellidae problem of taking a long time to get their wings erected so they can leave the water, that trout feed selectively on them wherever they occur in good numbers, and turn their attention to the top even when western green drakes hatch in scattered numbers.

Greater *Drunella*   HATCH IMPORTANCE SCORE: 32.0

CRITERIA/SCORE	5		4		3		2		1	
Distribution: (within Western waters)	widespread		common	3.5	scattered		isolated		rare	
Abundance:	heavy		abundant		modest	3.0	trickling		individual	
Emergence type:	mid-water/slow	4.5	mid-water/fast		edges/slow		edges/fast		crawls out	
Emergence time:	mid-day	5.0	early and/or late over long period		early and/or late over short period		dawn or dusk		night	
Emergence duration:	multiple seasons per year		well-defined long hatch period		well-defined short hatch period	3.0	poorly-defined long hatch period		poorly-defined short hatch	
(Behavior/Availability) Nymph:	excellent		good		moderate	3.0	slight		poor	
(Behavior/Availability) Emerger:	excellent		good	4.0	moderate		slight		poor	
(Behavior/Availability) Dun:	excellent	5.0	good		moderate		slight		poor	
(Behavior/Availability) Spinner:	excellent		good		moderate		slight		poor	1.0
Totals:		14.5		7.5		9.0		0.0		1.0

Note: Heavy hatches occur on some important waters (e.g. Henrys Fork of the Snake), but more often hatches are modest to sparse in abundance.

Emergence and Distribution

The western green drake hatch is typically an early- to late-June emergence, with some hatches in colder waters delayed to July and even into August. The hatch has been reported in September and even early October on some Rocky Mountain waters, and most of those reports are quite likely to be accurate. But there is also the chance that some reflect hatches of *Timpanoga hecuba* (see Chapter 17), similar in shape and color though somewhat smaller in size, which indeed emerge in those waters in autumn.

In our own experience, the western green drake hatch starts in scattered fashion on Pacific coastal streams, and in far-west rivers like the Deschutes and Yakima, in late May and early June. Numbers on the water are rarely enough to make trout hold stations and feed selectively on them, but the scattered big duns do get trout up and interested in large dry flies. It's heresy to say so, but the Royal Wulff, with its mayfly profile and colors that are a mix of olive and brown and not nearly so bright as you might think once they're wet in water, might owe a lot of its success to these scattered, rough-water hatches of western green drakes.

The hatch begins in early to late June on such famous waters as the Henrys Fork and South Fork of the Snake River. It can extend into early July in waters such as the Madison River, and is very important on the Yellowstone River in the park sometime in late July. Juracek and Mathews note in *Fishing Yellowstone Hatches* that western green drakes hatch two to four out of the last ten days in July, on the Yellowstone, and that a cloudy, rainy day should prompt you to drop everything and get to the river. It's one of the reasons those two famous anglers know so much about hatches and fly patterns: they live in West Yellowstone, Montana and can do just what they recommend for the rest of us.

Excellent western green drake hatches can be found on some British Columbia streams from early to mid-July until late September. This overlaps with the timing reported by Knopp and Cormier, in *Mayflies*, that green drakes hatch on Alberta's Ram River from late August to early September. This reflects the nature of all insect hatches to be delayed as you gain elevation and go north.

Drunella grandis and *D. doddsi* are distributed from California to New Mexico in the south, to British Columbia, Alberta, up to Alaska and the Yukon in the north. *D. spinifera* is more common on West Coast waters, though it can be found in isolated populations in such places as Rock Creek near Missoula, Montana. With such wide distribution, pinning down hatch dates for this group can be done to a certain extent on a local basis, but it's a danger to say that the western green drake hatch comes off in mid-June and leave it at that. Typically hatches start when water temperatures approach and pass the 50°F mark. That moment will vary with altitude and lattitude, and also with water source. A cold

The green drake hatch happens when mules ear sunflowers are in bloom along the banks of the Henrys Fork of the Snake.

GREATER *DRUNELLA* EMERGENCE TABLE

TIME	WINTER			SPRING			SUMMER			FALL		
	Dec.	Jan.	Feb.	March	April	May	June	July	Aug.	Sep.	Oct.	Nov.
7 a.m. - 10 a.m.												
10 a.m. - noon												
noon - 3 p.m.												
3 p.m. - 7 p.m.												
7 p.m. - 10 p.m.												

Choppy, boulder-strewn riffles provide perfect niches for the large green drake nymph.

spring creek might delay the rise in water temperature and therefore the emergence, while a nearby stream with more modest temperatures might move it up.

Al Caucci and Bob Nastasi sum it up perfectly in their fine *Hatches*, in which they remark that the western green drake hatch might be accelerated or delayed depending on how the sun strikes the south or north slopes of a mountain face high in the watershed, or when the annual snow melt makes its way out and allows the warmth of the sun to begin its work. Such variables make it difficult to pin hatch times down to a certain set of days, even on the same stream from season to season, and make it more rewarding to be prepared to recognize and imitate a hatch whenever and wherever you encounter it.

Wherever western green drake populations are heavy, the hatch cycle is typically short. A ten-day hatch period, with a three- to four-day peak, is quite common. The hatch begins with a trickle of duns, builds up for a few days, then gets pandemonious for a short time before tapering off to a trickle again. Exceptions occur, however, as evidenced by hatches of *Drunella doddsi* on a favorite small British Columbia trout stream that start in mid-July and continue in good numbers until mid-September. Trout retain their memory of such a big bite as a western green drake dun, and at times continue to take their imitations for days after the hatch has ended.

Such a short hatch cycle incited the old pandemonium on the Henrys Fork of the Snake, when everybody gathered there for the hatch, but lots of them got disappointed. The hatch there shifts around within a two- to three-week period in early to middle June. The peak is brief. You begin to understand why trying to be on the water when it happens requires an investment in time: you need to be able to stay on the river for a couple of weeks, or risk the frustration of missing the peak of the hatch.

On the more common streams with sparse hatches of western green drakes, duns will come off sporadically, with just a few scattered insects seen each day, but for a longer period of time. Sometimes such emergences will go on for three to four weeks. We got into these sorts of hatches on both the Deschutes River this past May and the Big Hole River in June. In neither case did we see more than a dozen insects in a day, nor did trout ever become selective to green drake duns. In both cases trout took duns when they got a chance at them, and were also willing to take our large imitations, though like the hatch, rises to naturals and responses to our casts were somewhat scattered.

Daily emergence usually begins in late morning to early afternoon, and goes on for one to three hours. As with most mayflies, it is brief on bright days, extended on cool and dark days. We have experienced heavy western green drake hatches at different times and on different waters, during all of the hours between 10:00 a.m. and 4:00 p.m., but rarely for more than two or three hours on any given day during that span of time. On days with trickling hatches, western green drakes might come off in ones and twos for five or six hours.

If the weather is bad, especially if it's windy, the hatch might abruptly cease even during the peak period. Since wind is common in the West, it's not unusual to miss a day or two of good fishing even when you get your timing right and hit the hatch at the moment it should be happening.

Drunella spinifera emerges most often in afternoon and into the evening, in the warmer parts of August and early September. In all stages, *D. spinifera* are nearly impossible to separate from hatches of the very similar *D. grandis*.

Spinner falls of western green drakes are typically sparse, and rarely cause selective feeding by trout, though when they do the insects are large enough that you might find it necessary to match them. Most guides and writers report that the spinners gather just before dark above riffles and runs, and that mating and egg-depositing flights take place after dark. In hot weather, western green drake spinners are also reported to hit the water around 4:00 a.m., not a time when most anglers are out looking for selective rising trout.

In our own experience, we've seen scattered green drake spinners on the water just three or four times in all of our years prowling western rivers, and have not observed trout feeding selectively on them.

Nymph characteristics
Drunella grandis:

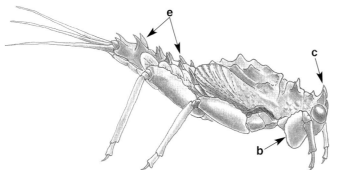

Drunella grandis nymph.

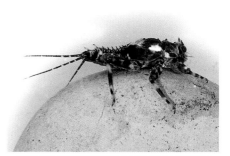

Drunella grandis nymph: side view showing spines on head, thorax and abdomen.

a. Blocky crawler shape. Three tails of equal length, with whorls of very short hairs.
b. Femurs of forelegs robust and well-developed; thicker than femurs of middle and hind pairs of legs. Leading edge of front femurs not toothed.
c. Pronounced rounded *tubercles* on top of head.
d. Plate-like gills on abdominal segments 3-7.
e. Abdominal segments 2-9 with pronounced paired tubercles or spines.
f. Body color yellowish-brown to dark brownish-black.
g. Body length 14-16 mm, 5/8 to 3/4 in.

Drunella doddsi nymph.

Drunella doddsi:

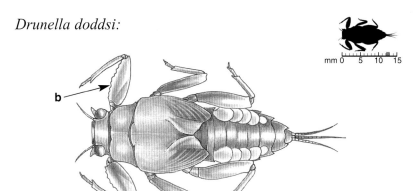

b

a. Very blocky, foreshortened crawler shape; almost like an obese crawler nymph. Three short tails of equal length, with whorls of short hairs.
b. Femurs of all three pairs of legs robust and well-developed. Leading edge of front femurs toothed.
c. Plate-like gills on abdominal segments 3-7.
d. Underside of abdomen with pad of dense short hairs that form sucker-like disk.
e. Body color olive-brown to dark brownish-black. Some specimens with distinct black and white mottling or banding.
f. Body length 12-13 mm, 1/2 to 5/8 in.

Drunella spinifera:

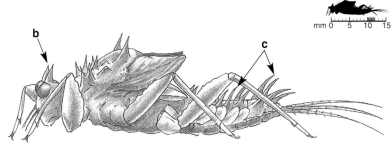

b

c

a. Blocky crawler shape. Three tails with whorls of fine hairs.
b. Prominent pair of pointed tubercles on top of head.
c. Abdominal segments 2-9 with long paired tubercles. Tubercles 1 1/2 times longer on abdominal segments 8-9 than 2-7.
d. Body length10-12mm, 3/8 to 1/2 in.

Drunella spinifera nymph.

The three important species of western green drakes are relatively easy to distinguish in their nymphal stage. *Drunella grandis* and *D. spinifera* are most similar, but *D. spinifera* is smaller and has longer and sharper spines than *D. grandis*. *D. doddsi* lacks the spines and has the suction-cup-like disk on its underside.

Dun Characteristics

Drunella grandis dun.

a. Three tails.
b. Hind wings with distinct, slightly rounded costal angulation.
c. Wings medium gray.
d. Body color, when fresh, is bright to dark green, usually with yellowish or brownish banding on abdominal segments.
e. Body length 13-16 mm, 7/16 to 3/4 in.

Drunella doddsi dun.

When just emerged, green drake duns are much brighter and show more green than they do after even short contact with the air. Within half an hour to an hour, most have turned an olive- to reddish-brown. It is critical to capture fresh specimens off the water, and to record their colors in your mind, your notes, or with your camera before selecting tying materials to match them.

It is very difficult to impossible, even for entomologists, to separate the species of green drakes in the dun stage. Size is the key characteristic separating the green drakes from the lesser green drakes, and is far from reliable. The best way to know what species dun you're dealing with, if you find that desirable, is to collect nymphs or cast nymphal shucks during a hatch, and associate the duns with the earlier stage from which they emerged.

Spinner Characteristics

a. Three tails.
b. Hind wings with distinct, slightly rounded costal angulation.
c. Wings glassy, clear.
d. Body color reddish- to blackish-brown.
e. Body 13-16 mm, 7/16 to 3/4 in.

Few reliable characteristics exist to recognize green drake spinners to species, or to separate them from the lesser green drake species. To confirm the species you need male spinners, a good microscope and a steady hand to dissect out the male reproductive organs. These organs are distinctly and uniquely shaped for each species. Once again, association of duns with nymphs, and then rearing of duns to spinners in hatch chambers—a closed paper sack works just fine—is the most effective way for anglers to know precisely what they have. While identification to species is educational, it is unnecessary to your fishing.

Greater *Drunella* spinner.

Habitat and Behavior

Drunella doddsi nymphs primarily inhabit fast-flowing sections of cold freestone streams and rivers of all sizes. They are often abundant in rushing mountain streams, from the Pacific Coast to the crest of the Rockies. They use the pad of fine hairs on their undersides to cling to

Nymphs of *Drunella doddsi* can hold on in the most brisk currents.

clean rock substrates in the fastest currents. Before emergence, however, they generally migrate out of the fastest flows to slightly calmer water either upstream or down, along the edges of the swift currents, or into pieces of pocket water where the duns, so helpless on the surface until their wings dry and they are able to fly, can get a short run of calm water. Many duns are drowned before making it into the air, and many more end up inside trout stomaches.

D. grandis nymphs occur in swift currents, but are also found in more peaceful edge currents, where they crawl among bottom rocks and wood debris, or in rooted vegetation. When you run into a heavy and therefore famous hatch of green drakes, it tends to be *D. grandis,* because trout set up and feed selectively on insects more often in the kind of water where this species tends to live in densest numbers.

D. spinifera nymphs are most common in cold Pacific coastal streams, where they inhabit water similar to *D. grandis* nymphs, from which they are difficult to separate.

Nymphs of all three green drake species are feeble swimmers, propelling themselves with vigorous but ineffective up-and-down flips of the abdomen. Their tails lack the fringed hairs that interlock on swimming nymphs and form flat paddle-like surfaces. Before emergence, these portly crawler nymphs often migrate to calmer water, where they may swim repeatedly to and from the surface before finally emerging as duns.

Actual emergence can take place in the surface film or a few inches below it. Many nymphs drift a foot or so deep, and for long distances, while the nymphal thorax splits open and the dun slowly escapes from the nymph shuck. Imitations fished just beneath the surface are effective on trout keying on this stage of the emerging natural.

Once the dun is free of the nymphal shuck, it is buoyed slowly to the surface by gases trapped within the folds of the wing tissue, the same gases that will inflate the wings when emergence is complete. If emergence takes place in the surface film rather than beneath it, the process can take a considerable length of time, causing the emerger to drift downstream with the currents for as much as fifty feet.

It takes some time for the fully emerged dun, once it is through the surface film, to pump up its wings and let them harden enough for flight. They often drift a long way, or get stuck in an eddy and get slowly shown around as if perched on a lazy Susan, until either trout take them or they manage to flutter away. During this period, whether on a current or an eddy, they will test their wings, sometimes scooting a few inches, at other times lifting off only to lose power and land on the surface again. Such difficult emergence behavior is an obvious cause of selective and greedy feeding by trout during even modest western green drake hatches.

Many western green drakes are crippled or stillborn during any emergence. Some trout concentrate on those stuck in the surface film, ignoring the fully formed duns that are able to make it through to ride on top. In cool weather, during heavy hatches, it is common for trout to focus on emergers and ignore the duns.

When emergence is complete, western green drake duns fly feebly to streamside vegetation, where their colors darken quickly. If you collect a dun from streamside rather than from the surface itself, you are likely to get a false impression of the color fly you should show to trout.

During a period of one or two days at rest in vegetation, western green drake duns molt to spinners. Then they join evening spinner flights, mate most often some time during the night, and lay their eggs in the early hours of the morning. Even if you observe a heavy flight of green drake spinners in the air, and notice trout feeding on the surface, be sure to observe closely to see whether the trout are taking what you see in the air, or some other insect that has gotten onto the water. It's rare to find a fishable fall of green drake spinners.

Imitation

While trout feed on all stages of the western green drake mayfly, they feed selectively on the emerger and dun, more often opportunistically on the nymph, and rarely on the spinner. We'll list dressings that match all stages, but you'll want to observe the feeding behavior of the trout over which you're fishing very carefully before deciding which imitation the trout might desire.

Nymph Imitations

Most of your fishing over populations of western green drake nymphs can be done with a few standard searching patterns. In truth, you'll probably never need to get imitative until the nymphs leave the bottom for emergence and trout begin taking them higher in the water column. However, the natural nymphs do make those migrations from fast water to slow, and also those false starts from the bottom toward the top. When your kick-net sampling reveals western green drake nymphs dominant, whether they're *D. grandis, D. doddsi, D. spinifera,* or you can't tell the difference, it will be advantageous to use a dressing designed specifically for those nymphs.

The kind of trout that feed on western green drakes often put a hefty bend in your rod.

Ida May (Originator: Charles Brooks)

Hook:	1X long, size 8-12.
Weight:	10-20 turns lead wire the diameter of the hook shank, or omit.
Thread:	Black 3/0 or 6/0.
Tail:	Grizzly hackle fibers dyed dark green.
Rib:	Peacock herl.
Counter rib:	Fine gold wire.
Body:	Black fuzzy yarn or fur.
Hackle:	Grizzly hen dyed dark green.

This dressing was designed by the great Charlie Brooks specifically for the *D. grandis* nymph in his West Yellowstone area. He did not call for weighting it, but fished it with a wet-tip line to get it down to the bottom. It would now be fished most often with split shot on the leader to help it sink, but a few wraps of lead will help deliver it to where you want it, right on the bottom. Brooks's book *Nymph Fishing for Larger Trout* (Crown, 1976) is still one of the finest gatherings of nymph-fishing methods, though it pre-dates the development of the split-shot and strike-indicator method, first detailed in Gary Borger's 1979 *Nymphing.*

Western Green Drake Nymph
(Source: Knopp and Cormier)

Hook:	Standard nymph, 2X long, size 4-10.
Weight:	10-20 turns lead wire the diameter of the hook shank.
Tails:	Dark brown partridge fibers, short.
Rib:	Medium gold wire.
Abdomen:	Dark olive-brown to brownish-black fur or synthetic dubbing.
Gills:	Olive-brown ostrich herl secured to sides of abdomen with ribbing wire.
Wing pads:	Black polypro yarn or goose quill segment.
Thorax:	Same as abdomen, teased out.

In *Mayflies*, Knopp and Cormier recommend collecting naturals, and varying the color of this tie to match what you find. In our own collecting we've seen these nymphs in quite an array of colors in the same bottom sample. We recall once seeing two mature *D. doddsi* nymphs on the same rock lifted off the bottom of a small Pacific coastal stream. One of the nymphs was almost black but speckled with tan spots, the other was tan and lightly speckled with black spots. Both were pretty. Trout would likely have taken a nymph tied to imitate either, though we don't know because trout were also happy to take a Royal Wulff that day, we think on account of the sporadic western green drake duns floating on the surface.

Presentation

Rig to fish these weighted nymphs with the split-shot and indicator method. Use a floating line, leader the length of your rod or a bit longer, and tippet just ten to twelve inches long. Place the indicator up the leader two to three times the depth of the water. Use the tippet knot to stop two or three split shot from sliding down to join the fly. Use a Duncan loop knot to tie the fly to the tippet. Make your casts upstream along current seams, and in pocket water, wherever you feel that green drake nymphs might migrate to get out of the faster water where they live most of their lives, and where trout might like to intercept them.

If you're fishing over a bottom where your net samples reveal numbers of *D. grandis*, fish the quieter water where the naturals gather for emergence. You'll be able to shorten the distance up to your strike indicator, and remove one or two of those shot from your leader. But always be sure that your nymph is near enough to the bottom to be seen by trout holding there.

Emerger Imitations

An old-fashioned wet fly such as the Lead-Winged Olive, in size 10 or 12, or a Partridge and Green soft-hackled wet in the same sizes, can do surprising execution during green drake hatches, simply because they resemble the duns making that transit from the nymphal exoskeleton just beneath the surface to the point where they begin their struggle through the surface film. Keep that transition in mind, and keep a few of those patterns in your fly boxes, for the many situations they might solve beyond these western green drake emergers.

A brief list of specific western green drake emerger imitations begins with a Tarcher-style nymph tied to represent the drifting natural, proceeds to a wet emerger, then to a CDC dressing tied to float in the film, and ends with an imitation of the dun with its wings unfolding but its abdomen still stuck and trailing in the nymphal shuck.

Tarcher-Style Western Green Drake Emerger
(Source: Knopp and Cormier)

Hook:	Mustad 31760, size 10-14, front 1/3 bent upward.
Weight:	10-15 turns fine lead wire.
Thread:	Dark olive 3/0 or 6/0.
Tails:	Dark brown partridge fibers, short.
Abdomen:	Yellowish-brown, dark olive, or brownish-black fur or synthetic dubbing.
Thorax:	Bright green Antron dubbing.
Wings:	Gray-dyed deer hair, short.
Legs:	Brown partridge.

This dressing represents the nymph drifting a foot or two beneath the surface film, waiting for the moment when it splits along the back and begins the release of the dun inside.

Green Drake Emerger
(Originators: John Juracek and Craig Mathews)

Hook:	Standard wet fly, 1X or 2X stout, size 10-14.
Thread:	6/0 or 8/0 olive.
Tail:	Moose body hair.
Rib:	Yellow thread.
Body:	Olive dubbing.
Hackle:	Grizzly hen dyed yellowish-olive.

This soft-hackle style emerger represents the dun, escaped from the nymphal shuck but still a few inches from the surface. Juracek and Mathews list it as their only western green drake dressing in *Fishing Yellowstone Hatches*: the only pattern they use throughout the hatch. They do not mention whether they fish it beneath the surface or dressed with floatant and in the film. When we use a soft-hackle in our own fishing during this hatch, we fish it subsurface, but try fishing it both ways and see which works best for you.

Green Drake CDC Emerger (Source: Schollmeyer)

Hook:	2X or 3X long, size 10-14.
Thread:	Olive 6/0 or 8/0.
Tail:	Brown partridge fibers.
Rib:	Fine copper wire.
Underbody:	White floss built up to tapered body.
Abdomen:	Light olive turkey biot.
Thorax:	Olive fur or synthetic dubbing.
Legs:	Brown partridge fibers to sides.
Underwing:	Dark gray CDC.
Wing:	Gray Z-lon.
Head:	Olive fur or synthetic dubbing.

This dressing is listed in Jim Schollmeyer's *Hatch Guide For Western Streams*. It is designed to fish for the dun emerged from the nymphal shuck but still struggling to get through the surface film.

Green Drake Quigley Cripple (Originator: Bob Quigley)

Hook:	Standard or up-eye dry fly, 1X fine, size 10-12.
Thread:	Olive 6/0 or 8/0.
Tail:	Olive-dyed grizzly marabou fluff.
Rib:	Yellow floss, single strand.
Abdomen:	Olive Antron dubbing.
Thorax:	Peacock herl.
Wing:	Deer hair, tips forward, butts back and clipped short.
Hackle:	Olive-dyed grizzly.

This excellent dressing represents the dun with its wings out of the nymphal shuck and extending, but the abdomen still stuck in the shuck. It floats with its wings in the film, the back end hanging down below the surface. Many naturals are taken by trout in this crippled position, especially during heavy hatches when trout can get choosy. It's an excellent design, and one we'd not like to be without when fishing western green drake hatches on smooth water.

Presentation

Rig any of these emergers on a floating line, long leader, and tippet at least a couple of feet long and in balance with the size fly you're fishing and the heft of the trout over which you're casting. That usually means 4X or 5X, but could be anywhere from 3X to 6X. You'll usually be casting western green drake emergers over edge currents near, but not in, more boisterous water. The trout will often be sophisticated because heavy hatches of these big insects attract anglers. The presence of the green drake hatch can often cause an increase in fishing pressure.

Fish the Tarcher-style nymph a foot or two beneath the film. Sometimes you'll want to dress all but the last foot or two of your leader. Cast upstream or across stream, and let the suspended nymph drift like a dead-drift dry to a specific rising trout, or down the length of a feeding pod of fish. Rig the soft-hackle style emerger the same, and fish it in the same manner, either cast precisely to the feeding lane of a spotted and timed trout, or with a longer drift through a pod of them.

Fish both the CDC Emerger and Quigley Cripple as you would a dry fly. Pick out a single selective fish. Locate its precise position and feeding lane, and try to time its rise rhythm. Make your presentation with a cross-stream reach cast or downstream wiggle cast, right into the feeding lane of the fish at the moment you expect it to be ready for the next rise.

If you have trouble following the drift of your fly using any of these methods, try a two-fly setup, using a dun as the marker for an emerger trailer. It's also possible to tie a small yarn indicator onto the leader four to six feet above the fly. Either rig will help you pinpoint the location of a fly that's difficult to see floating in the film or under it. This becomes especially important when numbers of naturals are on the water, trout are rising all around, and you need a way to know which rise is to your fly and which rises are not. If you set the hook to the wrong rise over sophisticated trout, and rip the fly off the water, you will put them down, ruining your own opportunity.

Dun Imitations

Many times trout feed on fully-formed and floating duns during a green drake hatch. As many times, they ignore them and concentrate on either rising nymphs, emerging duns beneath the surface, or emerging duns awash and struggling in the surface film. At rare times, individual trout will get choosy about different stages, and eat only one or the other. When you're fishing over these large insects, first you need to set up on an individual feeding fish. Second, you need to determine which stage it is taking.

That can be as easy as watching a few duns as they float down the feeding lanes of the trout. Binoculars help, but with such big insects they're not always necessary. If one or two winged insects disappear in swirls, you've got your smoking dun and know you can catch fish with a dry fly. If duns float over the top of the trout without drawing rises, you know you'll need to fish in the surface or under it.

If a visible riseform breaks the surface, for example revealing the lofted nose of the taking trout, then you know the fish took something in, not under, the film. If the rise ring is not so obviously on top, but a few bubbles are left when it's over, then you again know the trout broke the surface during the take, and took air down with it. Both a visible nose and bubbles are indications the insect eaten was awash in the film.

If the rise looks like it breaks the surface, but you see no sign of the trout and no bubbles left in the rise rings, it's an indication the take was just beneath the surface. The boil of the take may break the surface, but the take itself was anywhere from an inch to a foot down. Without very close observation, it's easy to mistake subsurface takes for rises on the surface.

The shape of a trout's rise, and whether or not there are bubbles left in the rise-rings, informs you about the level at which an insect was eaten.

You'll need to make all of these careful contemplations only during heavy hatches of western green drakes. If the hatch is sporadic, trout are usually eager to take any stage they can get. It's likely that you'll want to fish dry flies for the floating dun in that case, since it's usually considered to be more fun to catch a trout on a dry fly than something sunk.

Though we do not list them here for reasons of space and repetition, we quite commonly use large variations of ties we've already listed for the lesser green drakes and other mayfly duns as well. Hairwing Duns, Compara-duns, Sparkle Duns, Thorax Duns, and standard Catskill dries such as the Blue Wing Olive can all work well on suitable water types, when tied with olive bodies and gray wings, on hooks from size 8 to 12.

Montana Wulff

Hook:	Standard dry fly, 1X fine, size 8-12.
Thread:	Black 6/0 or 8/0.
Wings:	Black moose body hair, upright and divided.
Tail:	Black moose body hair.
Body:	Olive fur or synthetic.
Hackle:	Brown and grizzly, mixed.

This dressing is more specific than the Royal Wulff for western green drakes. It makes an excellent searching dry fly for those times when scattered naturals are seen on somewhat rough water from time to time throughout the day. Sporadic activity of large insects keeps trout looking upward, and they're usually willing to move quite some distance up through the water column for a chance at something so large. The same heavily-hackled fly is also fine for fishing riffles and rumpled runs when western green drakes are on the water in fairly heavy numbers, or even after a hatch. Trout seem to remember them.

Henrys Fork Green Drake Dun (Originator: A. K. Best)

Hook:	1X long, 1X fine, size 10-12.
Thread:	Green monocord.
Tail:	Dark elk hair, short.
Rib:	Brown UNI-Strand or single-strand floss.
Body:	Green fur or synthetic dubbing.
Wings:	Medium blue dun hen hackle tips.
Hackle:	One grizzly dyed green, one grizzly dyed yellow, clipped even with hook point on bottom.

A. K. also ties the same dressing in parachute style, using gray turkey flat or T-base for the wing post. For more specific instructions, and a few variations for the green drake hatch on A. K.'s home Frying Pan River, refer to his book, *A. K.'s Fly Box*.

Green Paradrake (Originator: Mike Lawson)

Hook:	Standard dry fly, 1X fine, size 10-12.
Thread:	Yellow 3/0 or 6/0.
Wing:	Dark gray elk hair.
Tail:	Black moose body hair.
Body:	Olive dyed elk hair, extended.
Hackle:	Grizzly dyed yellow, wound parachute.

This is the standard green drake dressing on the Henry's Fork of the Snake River. It works well there, and on other waters as well. It's a complicated tie, difficult to learn. But we've run experiments, fishing it against less imitative flies during hatches where the water is smooth and when the trout were clearly selective to western green drake duns. The difference in our catch, as compared to less imitative dressings, was dramatic. It's a fly style that is worth taking time to learn to tie.

Green Drake Natural Dun (Originator: Richard Bunse)

Hook:	Short shank, size 12.
Thread:	Yellow 6/0 or 8/0.
Body:	Ethafoam colored olive with waterproof marking pen.
Tails:	Mink, nutria, or beaver guard hairs.
Wing:	Gray coastal deer hair.

It takes a lot of time to learn to tie this style. After that, it takes a bit of time to tie each fly, though artist and our illustrator Richard Bunse ties

When you're fishing a sporadic green drake hatch on water like the Big Hole River, cover all the likely holding water with a big dry fly.

them a dozen at a time, production-line style. He also ties them down to size 18, for many mayfly hatches other than the western green drakes for which he conceived the design. We have not mastered them that small.

We have been in situations where western green drakes were hatching all around, big trout were rising to take them with detonations, and our standard patterns were failing while Bunse was standing next to us, busy playing trout after trout on his own creation. It's very effective. For the most detailed steps in tying it, see Skip Morris's *Tying Foam Flies* (Frank Amato Publications, 1994). Skip lists it as the Bunse Dun, which is what most of Richard's friends call it as well. He modestly calls his entire spectrum of foam mayfly imitations the Natural Duns.

Presentation

You'll encounter two types of western green drake activity: sporadic and concentrated. During the first type, fish your dun dressings more or less as searching flies, to cover the water. If you see a rise, naturally you'll want to cast to it. But most of your time will be spent setting up a disciplined pattern that shows your dy fly to all possible holding lies in a riffle, on a run, or over a flat. When fishing this way, rig with a nine- to twelve-foot leader tapered to a 4X or 5X tippet. Fish with upstream presentations, but recall that it's always wise to cast quartering across the current rather than directly upstream, to avoid lining the trout you'd like to take your fly.

When you're fishing a heavy hatch on the same kinds of water, generally a riffle or rough run, you can use the same presentation method, upstream and across, but will be better served by singling out a trout and casting specifically to it. Work on it until you've brought it up, caught it, or put it down. Then go on to the next.

You'll have to be careful of your rigging, position, fly pattern, and presentation—in fact of all aspects of the process of matching hatches—to get a bend in your rod during the green drake hatch on the Henrys Fork of the Snake River.

If you're fishing western green drake duns during a heavy hatch, over smooth water such as the famous Railroad Ranch section of the Henrys Fork of the Snake, you'll need to refine your gear and your methods, just as you do during blue-winged olive or pale morning dun hatches on the same water type. Be sure your tippet, no matter its diameter, is at least two to three feet long. Take up your casting position across from the trout or at an angle upstream from it, if you can. Make your presentation across to the trout with a reach cast, or downstream to it with a wiggle cast. Your goal is a drag-free float, though an occasional twitch or flutter might serve you well if trout refuse the fly fished without movement. The naturals, you'll recall, often struggle on the water and make aborted attempts to lift themselves off the surface.

In all cases, on smooth water over snotty trout, you'll need to place the fly right into the feeding lane of the trout. If it's possible, time the trout's rises and present your fly when you believe it's about ready to rise again. When you've got all this worked out, you'll be surprised to discover that pattern is at times less important than presentation during a western green drake hatch. But don't depend on that. This is one hatch in which the insects are so large, and the trout so selective to them, that exact imitation pays dividends, even on water that is not entirely smooth.

Spinner Imitations

Like the average mayfly adult that begins life as an olive dun, the western green drake ends life as a red quill spinner. Since it does that most often after dark or so early in the morning that they beat the sun, we won't bog down the book with a long list of dressings you'll probably never use. If you do get into a western green drake spinner fall, right at dark or just after dawn, try one of the dressings listed for the lesser green drakes, especially the Red Quill Spinner. If it's refused, and you get into the hatch consistently, try tying the same flies on larger hooks, size 8 and 10. If that fails, try the following dressing tied specifically for the western green drake spinner fall.

Green Drake Spinner (Originator: Sylvester Nemes)

Hook:	Tiemco BL 109, 1X fine, size 9-11.
Thread:	Olive 3/0 or 6/0.
Tails:	3 golden pheasant crest fibers.
Rib:	Fine gold wire, doubled.
Abdomen:	Dark green floss.
Thorax:	Dark brown fur or synthetic dubbing.
Wings:	Off-white rooster hackle, split.

This dressing is from Sylvester Nemes's book *Spinners* (1995), the only book-length treatment of that specific subject. To split the hackle and create spent wings, grasp all of the hackle tips on each side of the finished fly, between the thumb and forefinger tips of each hand, then tug them firmly outward in opposite directions until they are seated and retain the spent position.

Presentation

In the rare case that you encounter green drake spinners on the water, and find trout feeding selectively on them, refine your gear to suit the water type, and use your most delicate presentations to set Sylvester Nemes's spinner dressing, or any other, right into the feeding lane of a trout you've singled out and timed. Coax the fly into arriving in front of the trout on a drag-free drift, right when the trout is ready to tip up and take again.

Chapter 15

Attenella (Small Blue-Winged Olives)

FAMILY: EPHEMERELLIDAE

Genus: *Attenella*.
Western Species: 3
North America: 4
Important Western Species: *Attenella margarita.*
  (previously *Ephemerella margarita*)
Related Species: *Attenella delantala; Attenella soquele*
Common Names: Little blue-winged olive, small blue-winged olive.

Attenella margarita, the small blue-winged olive, is a late-season hatch that happens in most states and provinces in the West, but only on scattered cold but slow-flowing streams. We have rarely encountered it in fishable numbers, but where abundant it is a hatch that excites fish. It's possible you've already fished it and never known it. Without collecting it and observing it closely, it would be easy to fish through the hatch without ever noticing it was not a member of the *Baetis* complex.

Since *A. margarita* hatches on some important rivers, such as Hat Creek in California and the Yellowstone River in the Park, it's wise to be aware of this minor member of the Ephemerellidae family. When trout get a chance at them, they feed selectively, and you'll need to not only match them, but work out presentation techniques specifically for this hatch.

Emergence and Distribution

Attenella margarita are found on streams from Pennsylvania to California, and as far north as Montana and Alberta. The most famous western hatches of these tiny insects are on Hat Creek, the Henry's Fork of the Snake in Idaho, and the Yellowstone River in the Buffalo Ford area. All of these are cold but slow-flowing waters, ideal habitat for the nymphs of this species.

You might encounter *A. margarita* hatches on any western spring

Attenella   **HATCH IMPORTANCE SCORE:**   **19.0**

CRITERIA/SCORE	5		4		3		2		1	
Distribution: (within Western waters)	widespread		common		scattered		isolated	1.5	rare	
Abundance:	heavy		abundant		modest		trickling	1.5	individual	
Emergence type:	mid-water/slow		mid-water/fast	3.5	edges/slow		edges/fast		crawls out	
Emergence time:	mid-day		early and/or late over long period		early and/or late over short period	3.0	dawn or dusk		night	
Emergence duration:	multiple seasons per year		well-defined long hatch period		well-defined short hatch period		poorly-defined long hatch period	2.0	poorly-defined short hatch	
(Behavior/Availability) **Nymph:**	excellent		good		moderate		slight		poor	1.0
(Behavior/Availability) **Emerger:**	excellent		good		moderate		slight	2.0	poor	
(Behavior/Availability) **Dun:**	excellent		good		moderate	3.0	slight		poor	
(Behavior/Availability) **Spinner:**	excellent		good		moderate		slight	1.5	poor	
Totals:		0.0		3.5		6.0		8.5		1.0

TIME	WINTER			SPRING			SUMMER			FALL		
	Dec.	Jan.	Feb.	March	April	May	June	July	Aug.	Sep.	Oct.	Nov.
7 a.m. - 10 a.m.								Pacific		Rockies		
10 a.m. - noon												
noon - 3 p.m.												
3 p.m. - 7 p.m.												
7 p.m. - 10 p.m.												

creek or tailwater you visit in the morning hours from mid to late summer. Meadow stretches of some freestone streams may also produce the hatch in fishable numbers.

A. margarita hatches begin in early July in California, Washington, and Oregon, but are delayed until August and early September in Idaho and Montana. On the Yellowstone, Juracek and Mathews report the hatch from August 18 until October 4. Emergence is triggered, as with most Ephemerellidae, when temperatures reach and begin to exceed 50°F. Hatches on any stream, in any region, can be accelerated or delayed depending on the temperature of its water source. For example, an exceedingly cold spring creek in Oregon might have the hatch at the same time you would find it at a much higher-elevation freestone stream in Montana or Wyoming.

Daily emergence begins around 9:00 a.m. and continues until around noon. As always, duration of the hatch and numbers of insects coming off depend on the weather. On a cool, overcast day, the hatch might last three hours. On a bright sunny morning, expect the hatch to be concentrated into an hour or even less.

If you're ever on a favorite river in the morning in July, August, or September, and get into a hatch that has all the earmarks of a *Baetis*, capture a specimen and take a close look. If it has three tails, marking it as a crawler, in all probability it is a small blue-winged olive, or *Attenella margarita*.

Nymph Characteristics

Attenella nymph.

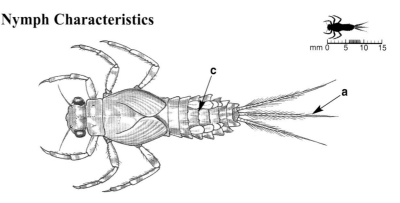

a. Three tails covered with fine, dark *setae*, or hairs.
b. Plate-like gills on abdominal segments 4-7.
c. Small, paired tubercles, or projections, on the dorsal rear margin of abdominal segments 2-9.
d. Abdominal segments 4, 5, and 8 often distinctly pale compared to other segments.
e. Body color light amber to dark brown.
f. Body length 6-9 mm, 5/16 to 3/8 in.

Dun Characeristics

Attenella dun.

JOHN JURACEK PHOTO

a. Three tails.
b. Wings medium gray.
c. Body bright to medium olive, or olive-brown.
d. Body length 6-8 mm, 5/16 to 3/8 in.

The presence of three tails separates this insect from members of the *Baetis* complex, the blue-winged olives, which have only two. The small size of this species separates it from the lesser green drakes, which otherwise share very similar characteristics.

Spinner Characteristics

a. Three tails.
b. Wings clear or white.
c. Females olive to brownish-olive, males with whitish to clear abdomen with black thorax.
d. Body length 6-8 mm, 5/16 to 3/8 in.

Habitat and Behavior

Attenella margarita nymphs crawl among bottom stones, or the roots of aquatic plants, in relatively slow-flowing water. They feed on plant material growing on rocks, or on the thin layer of algae and diatoms that coats the leaves of vegetative masses. Their numbers can be quite dense when the habitat is just right. They'll sometimes be found, but never in great numbers, in waters that are subject to runoff and scour.

When ready for emergence, the nymphs attach themselves to the riverbed or rooted vegetation. The next step is uncertain. Some observers have reported that duns escape from the nymphal shuck under water and are buoyed slowly to the surface by gases trapped in the wing folds. Others have reported that nymphs swim toward the surface and the dun escapes the nymphal shuck inches beneath it. Trout obviously applaud both types of emergence behavior, and you must be aware that during this hatch more insects are taken beneath the surface than on top of it.

These hatches almost always occur on flat-water stretches of slow water: the slicks and glides of spring creeks, tailwaters, and meadow streams. The naturals, because of their manner of emergence, are frequently crippled and stillborn. Fully-formed duns drift quite a distance on the surface before their wings are dry and they are able to fly. You must observe feeding trout carefully, however, to see if any duns are taken from the surface. It's quite common for trout to ignore the floating duns and continue feeding on those either still ascending through the water column, or trapped in the surface film.

Attenella emerge mornings on peaceful waters such as those in the Buffalo Ford reach of the Yellowstone River.

Spinner flights form over the same flat stretches of stream just before dark, and often collapse to the water at the same time darkness closes in. If the spinner fall is concentrated, trout will respond and feed on the naturals. If your state or province laws allow fishing after dark, and you're willing to stay out there and do it, you could turn this into an opportunity that you've got all to yourself.

Imitation

It's doubtful you'll ever encounter trout feeding selectively on *A. margarita* nymphs until the restless moments just prior to a hatch. When that begins, much feeding occurs at all levels of the water column, from the bottom to the top. Most rises that look like takes to duns on the surface itself are actually swirls to duns or nymphs just beneath the surface, in which case the riseform boils up to the top. During this hatch, use your binoculars to watch duns drifting down through pods of rising trout. If duns disappear, you know trout are taking them. It's more likely you'll notice that the duns are ignored, and know from that to select a subsurface imitation.

Nymph and emerger patterns are by far the most important for fishing this hatch. As its common name, the *small blue-winged olive*, might suggest, you can fish the hatch effectively with dressings tied for members of the *Baetis* complex. Dun and spinner patterns are less likely to be required, and again it's likely you'll already have what you need if you've fished *Baetis* hatches in spring and have a few flies left over for this summer and fall hatch.

As with most small hatches, size and shape are most important in your pattern, color a bit less so. Fishing the right stage of the hatch, and then presenting the chosen fly correctly, will usually be the critical factors if you get into an *A. margarita* hatch.

Nymph Imitations

As we've already noted, trout might feed on rising nymphs anywhere in the water column, from the bottom to the top, just before and during a morning *A. margarita* hatch. Your nymphs tied to match them should be tied without weight, or with very moderate weight, so that you can adjust the depth that you fish them without changing flies. Most often you'll fish these patterns to trout holding very near the surface and feeding visibly.

Pheasant Tail (Originator: Frank Sawyer)

Hook:	Standard nymph, 1X or 2X long, size 18-20.
Thread:	Brown 6/0 or 8/0.
Tail:	Pheasant tail fibers.
Rib:	Fine copper wire.
Abdomen:	Pheasant tail fibers.
Wingcase:	Pheasant tail fibers.
Thorax:	Pheasant tail fibers.
Legs:	Tips of thorax fibers.

You might try this version, or the Flashback Pheasant Tail that substitutes Pearlescent Flashabou for the pheasant tail fibers in the wingcase. The added flash might imitate gases trapped under the nymphal cuticle, and also because it's more visible, might attract an extra trout or two.

Cream Variant Nymph (Source: Knopp and Cormier)

Hook:	Standard nymph, 1X long, size 16-18.
Weight:	Few turns of fine lead wire, or omit.
Thread:	Tan 6/0 or 8/0.
Tails:	Amber-dyed mallard flank fibers
Rib:	Brown thread.
Body:	Amber fur dubbing.
Wingpads:	Light gray duck wing quill segment.
Legs:	Ginger hen hackle tips, divided to sides.

As with most effective nymph patterns for this hatch, this one represents the emerger as well as the nymph itself. If left unweighted, it can be dressed with floatant and fished in the film.

Presentation

Most of the time you'll want to fish a nymph dressing just subsurface during this hatch, on a leader dressed to within a foot or so of the fly, to suspend it inches deep. Your presentation should be drag-free, just as you would fish a dry fly.

Though our own experience with this hatch is minimal, we suggest you try suspending a nymph beneath an emerger or dun dressing of the same hatch. It's a way to offer trout a choice, and at the same time to suspend your nymph at the correct level for trout feeding just beneath the surface rather than on it.

Emerger Imitations

Because *A. margarita* suffers the fate of almost all ephemerellids, and has a difficult time emerging through the surface and into the fully-formed flying dun, the emerger stage is critical to fishing this hatch successfully. You should carry dressings designed to fish just under the surface, and also to fish in the surface film itself. Again, it's likely that you'll find what you need in the little box we advised you to stock specifically for the *Baetis* complex of hatches. If you don't find what you need there, the following patterns are designed to solve the *A. margarita* hatch.

A. Margarita Emerging Dun
(Originator: Fred Arbonna, Jr.)

Hook:	Standard dry fly, 1X fine, size 18.
Thread:	Light olive 8/0.
Tails:	Light brown hackle fibers.
Body:	Light olive-brown fur or synthetic dubbing.
Wings:	Four turns medium blue dun hen hackle.
Legs:	Two turns grizzly hen dyed olive-brown.

This soft-hackle style wet is designed to match the dun that has emerged on the bottom and must make its way to the top. It can be fished inches deep, or you can dress it with floatant and fish it in the film.

A. Margarita Emerger (Source: Knopp and Cormier)

Hook:	Standard dry fly, 1X fine, size 16-18.
Thread:	Light olive 8/0.
Tails:	Olive-dyed partridge.
Body:	Light olive-brown fur dubbing.
Wings:	Medium to dark gray wing quill segment or polypro fibers tied short over thorax.
Legs:	Olive-dyed partridge, divided.

This dressing, like the soft-hackle listed above, can be fished inches deep, or dressed to float in the film itself. Knopp and Cormier suggest weighting this emerger slightly and fishing it to trout winking just beneath the surface.

Presentation

These emerger dressings, whether fished a few inches deep or floating flush in the surface film, should be presented just as you would fish dry flies. It's rare you'll fish this smooth-water hatch and not be able to observe trout that are feeding on naturals. In most places they'll set up normal rise rhythms, in which case you should single out a trout and place your fly into its feeding lane when it's about to rise again.

Juracek and Mathews make the most thorough notes on fishing this hatch, in their *Fishing Yellowstone Hatches*. Their experience comes from the Yellowstone River on the smooth flats between Yellowstone Lake and the first falls. Trout there violate all the laws of being stupid cutthroats, on account of all the fishing pressure, and get very selective.

Juracek and Mathews point out the importance during this hatch of fishing over trout that you can see, and report that the most critical aspect of presentation is working into a position where the angle of the sun exposes feeding fish to your view. They write, "...because the fish feed largely beneath the surface on *A. margarita*, and move so much during feeding, it is imperative to fish to visible trout...they simply don't stay put..."

Dun Imitations

Most flies that you need to solve hatches of *A. margarita* will be found among those you tie for the *Baetis* complex. This is certainly true for the duns. We recommend you hold off tying for this hatch until you've had the opportunity to hold specimens in your hand, and observe them under your glass. Even then, you should have observed a few floating duns on the water with your binoculars to determine whether trout are even taking them. If not, the floating flies you use during this hatch are mere suspension systems for nymph and emerger dressings that you should drop off their sterns on twenty-inch tippets.

Your best dun dressings for smooth water will always float with the body flush in the surface film. We recommend such dressings as the following Sparkle Dun and Parachute because they might be taken for emergers as well as the duns they represent.

Little BWO Sparkle Dun
(Originators: John Juracek and Craig Mathews)

Hook:	Standard dry fly, 1X fine, size 16-18.
Thread:	Olive 6/0 or 8/0.
Wing:	Gray-dyed Compara-Dun deer or yearling elk hair.
Trailing shuck:	Brown Z-lon.
Body:	Olive to olive-brown fur or synthetic dubbing.

This would be our fly of choice for the lead fly of a dry-and-dropper combination. If it takes trout, and whatever fly you've tied beneath it does not, then nip off the nymph or emerger and fish with just the Sparkle Dun.

Little Blue-Winged Olive Parachute
(Source: Knopp and Cormier)

Hook:	Standard dry fly, 1X fine, size 16-18.
Thread:	Olive 6/0 or 8/0.
Wingpost:	Gray-dyed calf body hair.
Tails:	Three light gray Micro Fibetts.
Body:	Medium olive to olive-brown fur or synthetic dubbing.
Hackle:	Olive-dyed grizzly, wound parachute.

This parachute-style fly will float with its body flush in the film, and also will support a modestly weighted nymph fished beneath it.

Presentation

If trout are truly feeding on duns during this hatch, then refine your tackle to its finest, take up a position that places as many conflicting currents as possible behind you, and place your fly precisely down feeding lanes to visible trout. The methods used will be the same as those for any hatch that happens on smooth water, over trout that are heavily pestered and therefore difficult to fool. Use the reach cast and downstream wiggle cast, and any variations you can work on them, to achieve drag-free drifts without alarming the trout, or even alerting them to your presence.

Spinner Imitations

Spinner flights form at nightfall and often fall to the water after dark. If you desire to fish after dark, watch for rises below riffles and runs, and present your spinner dressings on the smoother water there. It's doubtful you'll ever need any specific dressings for this hatch. The ubiquitous Red Quill Spinner in size 18 will in all likelihood work fine. If it doesn't, more specific dressings are listed below.

Little Blue-Winged Olive Spinner
(Source: Knopp and Cormier)

Hook:	Standard dry fly, 1X fine, size 16-18.
Thread:	Olive 8/0.
Tail:	Three white Micro Fibetts.
Abdomen:	Working thread.
Wings:	White polypro fibers, tied spent.
Thorax:	Blackish-olive fur or synthetic dubbing.

A. Margarita Sparkle Spinner
(Originators: John Juracek and Craig Mathews)

Hook:	Standard dry fly, 1X fine, size 18.
Thread:	Olive or brown 6/0 or 8/0.
Tail:	Blue dun or brown hackle fibers, split.
Body:	Olive or rusty-brown fur or synthetic dubbing.
Wings:	White Z-lon, tied spent.

Presentation

You will have a difficult time following the float of any spinner dressing you fish for *Attenella margarita*, because of their near dark or after dark timing. Position yourself so the last faint light in the sky is reflected as a track of light on the water. You'll be able to see rises against this background. You'll never see your fly, but must be able to sense its position and set the hook to any rise you feel is in the same area. Sometimes you'll set into a trout, sometimes not. In either case, you'll get in some spooky fishing, experience a rare form of beauty, and possibly catch a trout or two as well. It might be the beauty that makes the fishing worthwhile.

If you get into a fishable hatch of *Attenella*, it will almost always be in the morning, in late summer or fall, on the kinds of smooth waters that furnish difficult problems to solve.

Chapter 16

Caudatella

FAMILY: EPHEMERELLIDAE

Genus: *Caudatella*
Western Species: 7
North America: 7
Important Western Species: None. The two species listed below are
    the species most commonly encountered:
        Caudatella heterocaudata
        Caudatella hystrix
Common Name: None.

This minor member of the Ephemerellidae family can be collected in some waters in the northwestern states and western provinces, but is not known to produce fishable hatches. We include it only so that if you collect it and try to identify it, you'll have a place to put it. If you find it in fishable numbers, with trout feeding selectively on any stage of it, we'd like to know it. No dressings will be listed to imitate it.

According to Knopp and Cormier, *Caudatella* hatch on the fast sections of scattered streams in July and August. They do not report fishing over it, nor do any other angling writers we've read. We have collected it in our travels, but only in the nymph stage, and never in fishable numbers.

Caudatella   **HATCH IMPORTANCE SCORE:**   **13.5**

CRITERIA/SCORE	5		4		3		2		1	
Distribution: (within Western waters)	widespread		common		scattered		isolated		rare	1.0
Abundance:	heavy		abundant		modest		trickling		individual	1.0
Emergence type:	mid-water/slow		mid-water/fast	3.5	edges/slow		edges/fast		crawls out	
Emergence time:	mid-day		early and/or late over long period		early and/or late over short period	3.0	dawn or dusk		night	
Emergence duration:	multiple seasons per year		well-defined long hatch period		well-defined short hatch period		poorly-defined long hatch period		poorly-defined short hatch	1.0
(Behavior/Availability) Nymph:	excellent		good		moderate		slight		poor	1.0
(Behavior/Availability) Emerger:	excellent		good		moderate		slight		poor	1.0
(Behavior/Availability) Dun:	excellent		good		moderate		slight		poor	1.0
(Behavior/Availability) Spinner:	excellent		good		moderate		slight		poor	1.0
Totals:		0.0		3.5		3.0		0.0		7.0

CAUDATELLA EMERGENCE TABLE

TIME	WINTER			SPRING			SUMMER			FALL		
	Dec.	Jan.	Feb.	March	April	May	June	July	Aug.	Sep.	Oct.	Nov.
7 a.m. - 10 a.m.												
10 a.m. - noon												
noon - 3 p.m.												
3 p.m. - 7 p.m.												
7 p.m. - 10 p.m.												

Caudatella nymph.

Nymph Characteristics

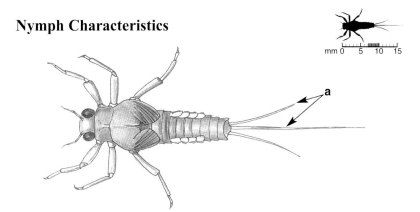

a. Outer two tails much shorter (1/4 to 3/4 in length) than center tail.
b. Moderate to well-developed paired spines on abdominal segments 1-10, 1-9, or 2-9.
c. Gills on abdominal segments 3-7.
b. Body length 7-10 mm, 3/8 to 1/2 inch, at maturity.

Dun Characteristics
a. Three tails, with outer two tails 1/4 to 3/4 the length of center tail.
b. Body length 7-10 mm, 3/8 to 1/2 inch, at maturity.

Spinner Characteristics
a. Three tails, with outer two tails 1/4 to 3/4 the length of center tail.
b. Body length 7-10 mm, 3/8 to 1/2 inch, at maturity.

The most unique and observable characteristic of *Caudatella* nymphs, duns, and spinners is the long center tail, with short lateral tails. Check specimens carefully to make sure the tails haven't been broken, thus obscuring this identifying characteristic.

The authors have collected scattered nymphs of *Caudatella* in their travels, including a few from Oregon's broad and pastoral Willamette River, but have never found them in fishable numbers, which doesn't mean you won't.

Chapter 17

Timpanoga
(Great Blue-Winged Red Quills)

FAMILY: EPHEMERELLIDAE

Genus: *Timpanoga*
Western Species: 2
North America: 5
Important Western Species:
    Timpanoga hecuba hecuba (previously *Ephemerella hecuba*)
    T. hecuba pacifica (previously *E. hecuba pacifica*)
Common Names: Great blue-winged red quill, great red quill,
    large dark Hendrickson, western green drake.

Timpanoga hecuba hecuba, and its subspecies *T. hecuba pacifica*, are quite commonly mistaken for the related western green drakes: *Drunella grandis, D. doddsi,* and *D. spinifera*. It's not an important mistake in angling terms. Flies that fish for one will catch trout over the other. But it's worth learning to recognize *Timpanoga*. It's a very large mayfly, has widespread distribution, and trout feed selectively on even a modest hatch. It's easy to separate this hatch from the green drakes once you take a quick look at the nymph, or even at a cast shuck. It's often helpful to know that you're fishing over one thing and not another, especially when it's as easy to establish as stooping to collect a cast shuck during a hatch.

In many places *Timpanoga* hatches are sparse, but it doesn't take many insects of such great size to get trout up and interested in feeding. In our own fishing, we have run into light to fairly heavy hatches from some small home streams in Oregon, to the famous lower Slough Creek in Yellowstone Park, where numbers of these big insects on the water were more than sufficient to cause selective feeding by large trout.

Timpanoga   **HATCH IMPORTANCE SCORE:**   **25.0**

CRITERIA/SCORE	5		4		3		2		1	
Distribution: (within Western waters)	widespread		common		scattered	3.0	isolated		rare	
Abundance:	heavy		abundant		modest	3.0	trickling		individual	
Emergence type:	mid-water/slow		mid-water/fast		edges/slow	3.0	edges/fast		crawls out	
Emergence time:	mid-day	5.0	early and/or late over long period		early and/or late over short period		dawn or dusk		night	
Emergence duration:	multiple seasons per year		well-defined long hatch period		well-defined short hatch period	3.0	poorly-defined long hatch period		poorly-defined short hatch	
(Behavior/Availability) Nymph:	excellent		good		moderate		slight		poor	1.0
(Behavior/Availability) Emerger:	excellent		good		moderate		slight	2.0	poor	
(Behavior/Availability) Dun:	excellent		good	4.0	moderate		slight		poor	
(Behavior/Availability) Spinner:	excellent		good		moderate		slight		poor	1.0
Totals:		5.0		4.0		12.0		2.0		2.0

Emergence and Distribution

Timpanoga begin hatching in early July on some low-altitude streams, and continue into September on many that are at higher elevations, especially in the Rocky Mountains. We enjoy a blitz of a hatch on a small valley stream just east of Oregon's Cascade Mountains in early August. But the best hatches we've fished are in the Yellowstone National Park area, peaking in late August through September.

We've seen *Timpanoga* described reliably as a sparse evening hatch, but have seen them coming off more often between 10:30 a.m. and 4:00 p.m. Some hatches will last that entire period, others will be much more brief, but will occur sometime during that period.

We once fished over a *Timpanoga* hatch with Nelson Ishiyama, owner of Henrys Fork Lodge. He left for Slough Creek after an early lunch and said on the way, "They'll start emerging about two o'clock." We got to the river and fiddled with gear for half an hour or so, then saw the first duns on the water and the first rises to greet them at precisely two o'clock. Rarely have we seen a hatch so precisely timed. Nelson stood up, waded in, began casting and catching trout as one might punch a time clock and go to work. He fished a Quigley Cripple.

Timpanoga hecuba hecuba is the more widely distributed of the two subspecies, with populations found from New Mexico north to Alberta, and from California north to British Columbia. *Timpanoga hecuba pacifica* populations are concentrated in the Pacific Northwest. The two subspecies provide fishable hatches in scattered waters throughout the entire West, wherever habitat is suitable to the nymphs. It's neither practical nor necessary for the angler to distinguish between them.

Nelson Ishiyama, owner of Henrys Fork Lodge, playing a Yellowstone cutthroat trout hooked in the gentle ripple in front of him, during a *Timpanoga* hatch on lower Slough Creek.

TIMPANOGA EMERGENCE TABLE

TIME	WINTER			SPRING			SUMMER			FALL		
	Dec.	Jan.	Feb.	March	April	May	June	July	Aug.	Sep.	Oct.	Nov.
7 a.m. - 10 a.m.										Rocky Mountains		
10 a.m. - noon												
noon - 3 p.m.												
3 p.m. - 7 p.m.												
7 p.m. - 10 p.m.								Pacific				

Nymph Characteristics

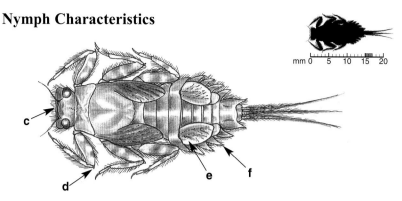

Timpanoga nymph.

a. Three short tails of equal length.

b. Body shape very flat for a crawler nymph; easily mistaken for a clinger, but head obviously narrower than the thorax.

c. Head with broad frontal shelf and eyes located on the posterior, outside margins of the head.

d. Distal end—farthest from the body—of each femur with a sharp pointed projection.

e. Gills on abdominal segments 4-7; those on segment 4 *operculate*, forming a covering over the remaining gills.

f. Abdominal segments with long lateral projections.

g. Body generally mottled brown with prominent mottling on the legs.

h. Body length 15-17 mm, 5/8-3/4 in.

The first time the lay half of us collected this nymph and tried to key it out, he assumed it was a clinger from its flattened shape, tried and tried to go through those keys, and was frustrated until he backed all the way up to "mayflies" and took it down from there. Then it fit easily into the correct family and genus.

Dun Characteristics

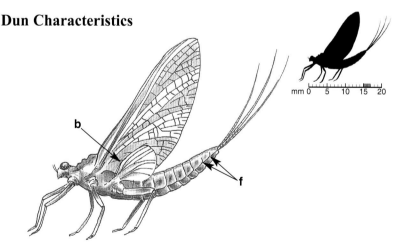

Timpanoga dun.

a. Three tails.

b. Hindwing with distinct rounded costal angulation.

c. Wings medium to slate gray.

d. Body olive to olive-brown.

e. Abdomen with remnants of nymphal gills on segments 4-7.

f. Abdominal segments 8 & 9 with well-developed lateral projections.

g. Body length 15-17 mm, 5/8 to 3/4 in.

Duns and spinners of *Timpanoga* have few reliable characteristics to easily separate them from other members of the western green drake group.

Association with the distinctive nymph, or its cast shuck, is the most dependable method of assuring that you're dealing with *Timpanoga* rather than *Drunella*. It is probable that some reports for green drakes, especially those occurring later in the season, are actually *Timpanoga*.

Spinner Characteristics
a. Three tails.
b. Hindwing with distinct rounded costal angulation.
c. Wings *hyaline*, or clear.
d. Abdomen with remnants of nymphal gills on segments 4-7.
e. Abdominal segments 8 & 9 with well-developed lateral projections.
f. Body olive-brown to reddish-brown.
g. Body length 15-17 mm, 5/8 to 3/4 in.

Few reliable characteristics exist to separate the spinners from related green drake groups until you begin dealing with wing venation and dissection of male reproductive parts. Association with the nymph and rearing from the dun are the most dependable methods, though that does not help you identify a spinner fall that descends from the sky and lands on the water in front of you while you're fishing.

Habitat and Behavior
Timpanoga hecuba nymphs occupy slow to moderate streams and rivers, often where some silting occurs. Their operculate gills, the first pair forming a lid over the others to keep them free from fine particles, are an indication of their adaptation to environments where silt settles. As a result they are better adapted to survive deposition of fine sediments from logging and overgrazing than many other fragile mayfly groups.

Lower Slough Creek in Yellowstone Park has an excellent hatch of *Timpanoga hecuba hecuba* in September.

One of our favorite trout streams has glacial origins. It often carries a slight to heavy load of silt, giving it a milky cast at times, but it holds a fine population of very nice trout. Because their operculate gills allow them to survive the silt, *Timpanoga* are by far the dominant mayflies in the stream.

Nature also creates environments where *Timpanoga* nymphs do well and other mayflies do not. For example the Lamar River in Yellowstone Park is laden with fine chalky silt after every summer thunder shower in its watershed, which can happen almost daily. *Timpanoga* are well adapted to surviving such silting. Hatches of them are excellent on the lower Lamar River in late August and September.

The most noted hatches of *Timpanoga* are found in the Lamar and its tributaries, Slough Creek and Soda Butte Creek. But it can be found in fishable numbers in populations scattered all around the West, where conditions are particularly suited to the nymphs.

The nymphs crawl on and between streambed stones, browsing on the thin layer of diatoms, called *periphyton*, the principle agent that causes you to slip on submerged rocks while you're wading. With their flattened shape, *Timpanoga* nymphs are well adapted to living in the faster parts of their slow- to moderate-moving streams. In our experience they are collected most often from the shallow and somewhat lazy riffles and long flats of valley-bottom streams. Most of the emergences we've seen are on flats downstream from shallow and barely rippled riffles.

At emergence, the duns release from the nymphal shuck either on the stream bottom or a few inches beneath the surface. In typical Ephemerellidae fashion, the duns have difficulty penetrating the surface film, then ride the currents for some distance before their wings are dry. A high proportion are crippled and stillborn. This should be reflected in the imitations you choose to fish for them. Nymphs and emergers fished just below the surface or in the film itself will be more effective over selective trout than nymphs tumbled along the bottom or dun dressings fished on top.

Since the bottom and top are the most common zones most of us fish during any hatch, the knowledge that you should concentrate your efforts beneath the surface and in it, not on top of it, will increase your take during this and any other hatch of mayflies in the large and important Ephemerellidae family.

We have found no reports of dun behavior after they've left the water, though we've kept specimens for photography, and clearly their colors darken. If you collect a specimen freshly hatched, it will be a softer olive than one observed a half hour or more out of the nymphal shuck. Though many reliable reports indicate *Timpanoga* duns with reddish-brown bodies, our own experience is that they're olive when they hatch, and change to the reported darker colors as time goes on. Trout see them afloat when they're fresh, not after they've escaped to streamside vegetation and had time to darken.

We have no reports of spinner activity, and have not observed *Timpanoga* spinners ourselves.

Imitation

It's doubtful you'll get into situations where *Timpanoga* are present or hatching in good numbers and you find it necessary to tie imitations specifically for them. Dressings you already carry for western green drakes will work well enough, as long as you recognize which ones to use. Do not tie dressings for this hatch until you've collected specimens and found the dire need for them.

Nymph Imitation

Some standard dressings that you already tie and carry, either as searching nymphs or specifically for the green drakes, will work fine. *Timpanoga* populations are excellent on many of our favorite Pacific coast and Cascade Mountain streams. One of our favorite searching nymphs is an

A. P. Beaver. It bears a remarkable resemblance to the *Timpanoga* nymph, which might account for some of its success, though these relationships are easier to speculate about than they are to prove.

A. P. Beaver (Originator: André Puyans)

Hook:	Standard nymph, 2X long, size 10-12.
Weight:	8-12 turns lead wire the diameter of the hook shank, or omit.
Thread:	Brown 6/0.
Tail:	Moose body hair.
Rib:	Copper wire.
Abdomen:	Beaver fur.
Wingcase:	Moose body hair.
Thorax:	Beaver fur, picked out.
Legs:	Tips of wingcase fibers.

If you tie this and carry it as a standard searching pattern, which we do, then weight it lightly so you can fish it a foot or two deep with no weight on the leader. If you tie it strictly as a *Timpanoga* imitation, then omit the weight so that you can fish it just inches deep before and during a hatch.

Hare's Ear Beadhead

Hook:	Standard nymph, 2X long, size 10-12.
Bead:	Gold or brass.
Thread:	Brown 6/0.
Tail:	Hare's mask guard hairs.
Rib:	Medium oval gold tinsel.
Abdomen:	Medium hare's mask fur.
Thorax:	Dark hare's mask fur.

This is obviously a searching dressing, but we find it effective whenever our kick net sampling reveals populations of *Timpanoga* nymphs.

Presentation

The most effective presentation for nymph dressings is dead-drifted right along the bottom when sampling proves a population of naturals, before they become active in preparation for emergence. In most of the shallow and slow waters the species inhabits, you will not need weight on the leader. Just rig with an indicator positioned a few inches more than the depth of the water up the leader. Make your casts upstream into the current, so the nymph has plenty of time to sink to the end of its tether.

If the water is deeper, or a bit swifter, rig with the normal split shot and strike indicator method. Employ Gary Borger's shotgun method, written about in *Nymphing*, to break the bottom into grids and cover each bit of it with a drift of the nymph.

Our favorite method for fishing these nymphs, either before the hatch or in the midst of it, is to suspend them on a 20-inch tippet tied directly to the hook bend of a searching dry-fly or dun imitation.

Emerger Imitation

Before tying any dressings specifically for this stage of the insect, collect a specimen and note whether the emerger dressings listed in the section on western green drakes, *Drunella grandis, D. doddsi,* and *D. spinifera*, will not match it as closely as anything you might tie. Any of them will usually do, as the adults of *Timpanoga* are normally almost indistinguishable from the greater *Drunella* species.

We will not repeat those listings here, but will mention that when Nelson Ishiyama fooled several highly selective trout on Slough Creek, he used a cripple dressing. The following is a Quigley Cripple varied for one of the colors you might encounter during this hatch. But be aware that you should collect your own specimens and base the colors of your dressing on what you find in your own waters.

T. Hecuba Quigley Cripple (Originator: Bob Quigley)

Hook:	Standard or up-eye dry, 1X fine, size 8-12.
Thread:	Olive.
Tails:	Olive-brown dyed marabou fluff.
Rib:	Single strand of yellow floss.
Abdomen:	Olive-brown Antron dubbing.
Thorax:	Peacock herl.
Wing:	Deer hair, tips forward, butts back and clipped short.
Hackle:	Grizzly dyed olive-brown.

This dressing reflects the brownish cast that many *Timpanoga* duns have to their generally olive bodies. They can be somewhat darker and reddish compared to the western green drakes. But be careful to observe fresh specimens, not darkened ones. If the specimens you collect on the water tend to these colors, your imitations should reflect that, though in truth, trout will probably take the standard tie listed earlier for the western green drake, even if its color is slightly off.

Presentation

There are no secrets here. You'll need to gear your presentation to the water type you're fishing over, more than to the insect species you're imitating. *Timpanoga* typically emerge in the tailouts of very mild riffles, in our own experience, and you'll do well enough with upstream-and-across presentations, so long as you're careful not to line the fish. On the long flats downstream from the same shallow riffles, trout will be far more spooky, and you'll need to use the cross-stream reach cast or downstream wiggle cast to keep from alerting the trout that you're around and after them.

Dun imitation

It's a terrible admission, but we've succeeded at times even during heavy *Timpanoga* hatches with size 10 and 12 Royal Wulffs. But that has always been over relatively eager trout that don't suffer a lot of fishing pressure. On waters where the trout are more sophisticated, you'll need to get more imitative. Don't neglect the western green drake dun dressings you've already tied. Trout will not normally snub them during *Timpanoga* hatches.

Blue-Winged Red Quill (Source: Knopp and Cormier)

Hook:	Standard dry fly, 1X fine, size 6-12.
Thread:	Brown 3/0 or 6/0.
Tail:	Moose body hair.
Body:	Reddish-brown dyed hackle stem.
Wings:	Dark gray dyed mallard flank, upright and divided.
Hackle:	Dark brown.

This dressing, listed in *Mayflies*, reflects the darker reddish-brown color and very large size sometimes reported for *Timpanoga* hatches, though we've never collected them ourselves bigger than size 10. This dressing will work well for the duns in almost all cases, and will also serve as excellent suspension for a nymph dressing fished inches deep, or as a strike indicator for an emerger fished in the film and therefore difficult to see.

Presentation

Whenever even a few of these large mayflies have been around, trout are aware of them and will usually rise to the surface for an imitation. While it's best to fish an emerger dressing during a heavy hatch and selective feeding, a dun pattern fished through a light hatch, or in the hours after a hatch, will do quite well. Use it as you would a searching dressing, covering likely lies in slightly riffled water, and of course cast it quickly to cover any rises you might notice. A trout that just succeeded in taking a large *Timpanoga* natural is a sucker for the sudden appearance of another in its window of vision.

Spinner Imitation

We have not found fishable spinner falls of this species in our own fishing. Knopp and Cormier, in *Mayflies*, report that a few days of hatches accumulate as spinners, swarm, and all fall on the same day. No mention is made of the time, but we suspect it would happen near nightfall, and that most spinner activity for this species takes place after dark. If you find need for a spinner dressing, Knopp and Cormier offer the following dressing in their excellent and reliable book.

Great Red Spinner (Source: Knopp and Cormier)

Hook:	Standard dry fly, 1X fine, size 6-12.
Thread:	Dark brown 3/0 or 6/0.
Tail:	Moose body hair, flared.
Body:	Dark reddish-brown dyed hackle stem.
Wings:	White polypro yarn, tied spent.
Hackle:	Coachman brown, clipped top and bottom.

This dressing reflects the dark color and great size of the natural found on some waters. If you ever find need for a spinner pattern tied specifically for this insect, this would be the one. We haven't found that need in our own fishing, but in the vast West we expect everything to happen at one time or another.

Presentation

It's often very near nightfall when spinners of all the larger groups of mayflies return to the water to lay their eggs. At such times trout will be seen feeding with very delicate rises, as if they know that the insect is fatally trapped and cannot escape. You'll need to make your presentations carefully, setting the fly softly to the water in or near the trout's position, but without alarming it. This presents challenges to both your ability to stalk fish on flats downstream from riffles, and to cast without smacking your fly to the water.

When you've solved these presentation problems, over trout rising late into the evening, then it's likely that your pattern will not matter so long as it is in some sort of near relation to the insect on the water. The old dependable Red Quill Spinner, listed so often already in this book, when tied in size 10 or 12, will likely catch as many trout as any other fly, especially since the spinners of *Timpanoga* are quite likely to be mixed up with others during these evening spinner falls.

Chapter 18

Paraleptophlebia (Mahogany Duns)

FAMILY: LEPTOPHLEBIIDAE

Genus: *Paraleptophlebia*
Western Species: 25
North America: 39
Important Western Species:
   Paraleptophlebia bicornuta
   P. debilis
   P. gregalis
   P. memorialis (previously *P. helena*)
   P. temporalis (previously *P. packii*)
Common Names: Mahogany duns, blue quills, blue duns, iron blue
   duns, black quills, red quills.

Paraleptophlebia emerge in the West in spring, summer, and fall, but most hatches are somewhat sporadic, and they become most important to fishermen when no other major hatch is happening to distract trout. As always there are exceptions. One of your authors was fishing a Britsh Columbia trout stream the first week of September. There was a moderate hatch of western green drakes, a good hatch of blue-winged olives, and good numbers of *Paraleptophlebia*. Around 3 o'clock all three species were on the surface at once, but the fat west-slope cutthroat had eyes only for the *Paraleptophlebia*. Once their emergence was over, the cutts homed in on the blue-winged olives. The green drakes floated along untouched all afternoon.

    Some *Paraleptophlebia* hatches are important in the spring, but almost never in summer. The most important western hatches happen in fall when *P. debilis* and *P. bicornuta* combine to offer trout enough numbers to cause selective feeding.

Paraleptophlebia　　　　　　**HATCH IMPORTANCE SCORE:**　**33.0**

CRITERIA/SCORE	5		4		3		2		1	
Distribution: (within Western waters)	widespread		**common**	4.0	scattered		isolated		rare	
Abundance:	heavy		**abundant**	4.0	modest		trickling		individual	
Emergence type:	mid-water/slow		mid-water/fast		edges/slow	3.0	edges/fast		crawls out	
Emergence time:	mid-day	5.0	early and/or late over long period		early and/or late over short period		dawn or dusk		night	
Emergence duration:	multiple seasons per year	5.0	well-defined long hatch period		well-defined short hatch period		poorly-defined long hatch period		poorly-defined short hatch	
(Behavior/Availability) **Nymph:**	excellent		good		moderate		slight	2.0	poor	
(Behavior/Availability) **Emerger:**	excellent		good		moderate	3.0	slight		poor	
(Behavior/Availability) **Dun:**	excellent		good	4.0	moderate		slight		poor	
(Behavior/Availability) **Spinner:**	excellent		good		moderate	3.0	slight		poor	
Totals:		10.0		12.0		9.0		2.0		0.0

Paraleptophlebia are much more important in the East, where their hatches are at times heavy. But trout on waters all over the western states and provinces get chances at them as well. Because they hatch in gentle edge currents, eddies, and pools, where trout get a good chance to examine them, when trout feed on *Paraleptophlebia* they often do it selectively. If you do not notice them, or are not able to match them, it's likely you'll do poorly during their hatches. They provide an excellent opportunity to fish over rising trout late in the season, when many other aquatic insects have hatched and terrestrials have all fallen.

Emergence and Distribution

Paraleptophlebia hatch on most famous western rivers, from Oregon's McKenzie and Deschutes rivers to Idaho's Henry's Fork, Montana's Rock Creek and Gallatin, Wyoming's Yellowstone, Colorado's South Platte and Frying Pan, and Alberta's Bow. Trout feed on *Paraleptophlebia* hatches in less-known waters from California to British Columbia, and New Mexico to Alberta. Though it's easy to overlook them because they hatch at the edges of streams and rivers most often, and are most important late in the season when many of us have tapered off our fishing, *Paraleptophlebia* often prompt large trout to move into the shallows and sip daintily. It's a prescription for excellent fishing whenever and wherever you find it happening.

Some western species, for example *Paraleptophlebia gregalis*, begin to emerge as early as March, with hatches common in April and May. These species grow through summer as nymphs, and overwinter as nearly mature nymphs before hatching the next spring. Other species, such as *P. debilis* and the largest species of all, *P. bicornuta*, hatch in the fall, starting in early September and continuing through October and even early November, providing excellent autumn fishing.

Daily emergence typically begins in the morning between 10:00 and 11:00 a.m., and goes on for two to three or more hours, ending between 1:00 and 4:00 p.m. As with most mayflies, hatches last longer on cloudy and even rainy days, and are condensed into a shorter time period on sunny days. Because the nymphs migrate right to the edges of the stream, and emerge in water just inches deep, or crawl out on rocks or vegetation, *Paraleptophlebia* hatches are easy to overlook.

PARALEPTOPHLEBIA EMERGENCE TABLE

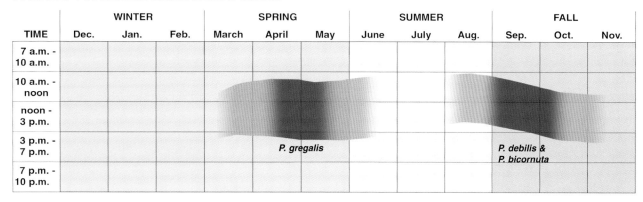

TIME	WINTER			SPRING			SUMMER			FALL		
	Dec.	Jan.	Feb.	March	April	May	June	July	Aug.	Sep.	Oct.	Nov.
7 a.m. - 10 a.m.												
10 a.m. - noon												
noon - 3 p.m.												
3 p.m. - 7 p.m.					*P. gregalis*					*P. debilis & P. bicornuta*		
7 p.m. - 10 p.m.												

Paraleptophlebia nymph.

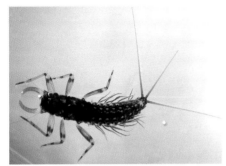

Paraleptophlebia bicornuta nymph.

Nymph Characteristics

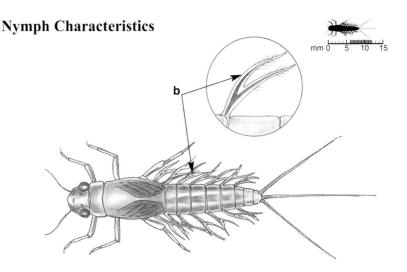

a. Body slightly flattened; square-shaped head.
b. Single, tuning-fork-shaped gills on abdominal segments 1 through 7.
c. Three tails equal length, as long as or longer than body.
d. Some important species (e.g. *P. bicornuta*) with prominent tusked mandibles. (see *P. bicornuta* photo at left).
e. Body normally uniform in color; shades of olive-brown to dark brown.
f. Body length 6-12mm (1/4-1/2 in.).

Dun Characteristics

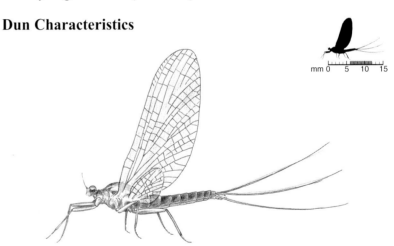

Paraleptophlebia dun.

a. Three tails of equal length.
b. Hind wings rounded and well developed, with no costal angulation on the leading edge.
c. Wings light smoky-gray.
d. Body light blue dun to deep reddish-brown.
e. Body length 6-12mm (1/4-1/2 in.).

Spinner Characteristics

a. Three tails, equal in length.
b. Hindwings rounded and well developed, with no distinct costal angulation on the leading edge.
c. Wings clear, occasionally tinted with amber.
d. Body of female uniform reddish- to purplish-brown; males with thorax and tip of abdomen brown, the middle of the abdomen white to almost clear.
e. Body length 6-12mm (1/4-1/2 in.).

Paraleptophlebia spinner.

Habitat and Behavior

Nymphs of *Paraleptophlebia* favor running water. They are most common in small- to medium-sized streams, though good populations are also found on many large rivers. Early instar nymphs are common in fairly fast riffles, usually resting on moss, debris, or coarse gravel. As the nymphs grow and mature they move to slower water. These larger nymphs are usually found in calmer areas where leaves and other detritus accumulates, or along undercut banks, where they rest on exposed roots and tangled branches. In rich spring creeks and tailwaters with moderate currents, they rest and browse on rooted vegetation.

Paraleptophlebia nymphs are poor swimmers. Their awkward side-to-side undulations do not result in much forward motion. When caught in the currents they may drift a long distance before regaining a hold on the substrate. This lack of swimming ability, and their common occurence in the drift, combine to make the nymphs important components of trout diets.

Emergence in spring is prompted when water temperatures reach and surpass 50°F for several days. The reverse is true in fall: hatches begin when summer water temperatures cool toward the same 50°F mark.

Paraleptophlebia nymphs that live in slow water leave the protection of river-bottom stones or debris and swim awkwardly to the surface. The duns escape the nymphal shuck in or just under the surface film. Species that live in fast water migrate to slower edge waters before emergence. An hour or so before emergence, the nymphs become restless, expose themselves with movement along the bottom, and in some cases make repeated trips to the surface and back to their resting places on the bottom, before making the final trip up for actual emergence. At other times nymphs may

No matter which western stream you fish when *Paraleptophlebia* are hatching, they'll almost always be most important right along the edges, where Darrell Martin fishes the otherwise broad and brawling Deschutes.

Artist Richard Bunse with a Yellowstone cutt caught on a dry fly during a *Paraleptophlebia* hatch in a September snowstorm.

crawl several inches above the water on sticks, rocks, plant stems, or other projections before the subimagoes work free of the nymphal shucks. On the Henrys Fork we have seen nymphs emerge on plant growth just under the surface. The duns quickly popped to the surface, then rode the currents several feet before their wings dried and they were able to fly.

When you see *Paraleptophlebia* duns fed on by trout, it will almost always be in the edge currents, within inches or scant feet of shore, usually in soft currents. Jim Schollmeyer, in his *Hatch Guide for the Lower Deschutes River* (Frank Amato Publications, 1994), noted that *Paraleptophlebia* are most important in the many eddies along the edges of that famous river. That is true on many other rivers as well. Montana guide Justin Baker, in his insightful anecdotal notes included in Knopp and Cormier's *Mayflies,* notes that he fishes his clients along the edges and in the eddies of the Clark Fork of the Columbia River in Montana during late-season *Paraleptophlebia* hatches.

Paraleptophlebia duns float for a long time in these eddies and calm edge currents. They are commonly on the water, sitting helplessly, for a minute or more, drifting tens of feet if there is much current to move them. It's no wonder that trout nose into the shallows to feed on them even when only a few are available.

The dun stage lasts from twelve to forty-eight hours before the final molt into spinners. In early spring or late fall, spinners are most active in the midafternoon or early evening. Summer mating flights occur in the evening just as the sun leaves the water. Spinner swarms fly at about eye-height, so it's one of the easiest mating flights to observe. A female flies into a dancing cloud of males, and is seized by a male. Copulation is completed in the time it takes the pair to fall only two or three feet. The female drops her eggs from a few feet high, or dips to the water several times, releasing a packet of eggs each time. Both males and females die shortly after mating, and fall to the water.

Male and female spinners differ significantly in color. The males have a dark brown thorax followed by a white, sometimes almost clear, section of abdomen that ends with a brown tip just before the tails. Female spinners have a uniform light to dark reddish-brown body. Both sexes have hyaline, or clear, wings. Tails of the males are considerably longer than those of females.

Paraleptophlebia spinners often land on the water with their wings either upright or semi-spent. At times the same dressing you use for the dun will work for spinners, because of this up-winged posture on the water. Trout may be selective to male or female spinners.

Imitation

Paraleptophlebia become very important wherever they emerge in open water rather than crawling out on sticks and stones. For example, there are excellent September hatches on the Yellowstone River and Henrys Fork of the Snake, where trailing vegetation reaches toward the surface, and where these insects hatch from the tops of the trailing weeds rather than migrating to shore. Nymph and dun imitations are most useful in such smooth currents.

In the rougher parts of streams, *Paraleptophlebia* nymphs migrate to the shallows and the duns emerge in calm water near shore or after the nymphs crawl out of the water onto streamside stones. On these types of streams, usually freestone in nature, the same nymph and dun patterns are useful when fished right at the edges, in water that is at times almost still, if trout are in there after the naturals. Almost any stream or river that has eddies and backwaters along its banks will present good opportunities to fish over autumn *Paraleptophlebia* hatches.

Nymph Imitations

Few nymph imitations have been created specifically for *Paraleptophlebia* species. In most situations a lightly-weighted Gold Ribbed Hare's Ear in size 14 or 16 is an excellent imitation. Justin Baker, in his notes in *Mayflies*, calls for a slim size 14 Pheasant Tail nymph when *P. debilis* hatch on the lower Clark Fork or the Bitterroot River. Patterns for these nymphs should be dressed on 1X or 2X long hooks, in sizes 12 through 18. The bodies should be slender and slightly tapered. Colors are usually olive-brown to reddish-brown or dark brown.

Pheasant Tail (Originator: Frank Sawyer)

Hook:	Standard nymph, 1X or 2X long, size 12-18.
Thread:	Brown 6/0 or 8/0.
Tails:	Pheasant tail fibers.
Rib:	Fine copper wire.
Abdomen:	Pheasant tail fibers.
Shellback:	Pheasant tail fibers.
Thorax:	Pheasant tail fibers.
Legs:	Tips of thorax fibers.

It's critical that you recognize situations in which you need to fish a *Paraleptophlebia* nymph imitation. Once you've arrived at that recognition, it's doubtful you'll ever need a more imitative pattern than this standard Pheasant Tail. It's a fly that you likely already carry to fish during other hatches as well.

Western Red Quill Nymph (Source: Knopp and Cormier)

Hook:	Standard nymph, 1X or 2X long, size 12-18.
Thread:	Brown 6/0 or 8/0.
Tails:	Brown partridge fibers.
Rib:	Fine gold wire.
Gills:	Pale gray marabou fibers along each side.
Abdomen:	Reddish-brown dyed hackle stem or dubbing.
Wingcase:	Black polypro fibers or dark goose quill section.
Thorax:	Reddish-brown fur or synthetic dubbing.
Legs:	Brown partridge fibers, divided.

Knopp and Cormier recommend this dressing in size 14 to 16 for western waters on the east side of the Rocky Mountain divide.

Western Blue Quill Nymph (Source: Knopp and Cormier)

Hook:	Standard nymph, 1X or 2X long, size 12-18.
Thread:	Dark brown 6/0 or 8/0.
Tails:	Dark barred woodduck flank.
Rib:	Fine gold wire.
Gills:	Pale gray marabou fibers along each side.
Abdomen:	Dark grayish-brown dyed hackle stem or dubbing.
Wing case:	Dark gray-brown goose quill segment.
Thorax:	Dark gray-brown fur or synthetic dubbing.
Legs:	Brown partridge fibers, divided.

Knopp and Cormier recommend this dressing for waters on the west side of the Rocky Mountain divide. This nymph also imitates species found in the Pacific Coastal region from California to British Columbia. Both red and blue quill nymphs are excellent imitative patterns and should be considered when you collect and match any nymph of the western *Paraleptophlebia* species.

Nymph Presentation

Nymph patterns may be fished with dry-fly tactics to dimpling or tailing fish. They also may be cast to cruisers along the shallow edges of streams. In a moderate current they can be fished with wet-fly tactics, on down-and-across-stream casts, a short drift while the fly sinks, then a gentle movement of the rod tip to activate the imitation as it makes its very slow swing across the soft currents.

Guide Justin Baker notes that he fishes the calm edge water with a nymph, from a boat moving just faster than the current at the bank. He has his clients cast at an angle behind the boat, tight to the rocks, then throw an immediate downstream mend. The nymph swims slowly downstream along the shore, just as a natural might. Baker cautions that the cast must be accurate, within inches of rocks or any bank structure.

In our experience, whenever duns are emerging either near shore or on it, it's a good time to suspend a Pheasant Tail or other nymph imitation on an 18-inch tippet beneath one of the following imitations listed for the duns. If we're fishing a nymph dressing without a dry, then we usually rig without any weight on the leader, but with a small yarn or hard strike indicator three to six feet up the leader from the fly.

Emerger Imitations

If trout are bulging along the shoreline during a *Paraleptophlebia* emergence, they're taking nymphs subsurface, and you should fish a nymph imitation. If they're breaking the surface and leaving bubbles in the rise ring, they're taking either emergers or duns. You can watch a few floating duns and quickly get an idea whether trout are willing to accept them or not. If the naturals pass undisturbed through rising trout, an unlikely scenario, you know the trout are feeding on emergers in the film or just beneath it. Even if they're not, an emerger dressing will usually take trout during these hatches.

Knopp and Cormier make the excellent suggestion that you simply convert your nymph dressing to a floating nymph or emerger dressing when trout are feeding in the surface but refusing to take duns. They offer a couple of ways to accomplish this, and we'll list their dressings here.

Western Red Quill Floating Nymph
(Source: Knopp and Cormier)

Hook:	Standard nymph, 1X long, size 12-18.
Thread:	Brown 6/0 or 8/0.
Tails:	Brown partridge fibers.
Rib:	Fine gold wire.
Gills:	Pale gray marabou fibers along each side.
Body:	Dark gray-brown to reddish-brown fur or synthetic dubbing.
Wing:	Dark gray polypro yarn ball or white closed-cell foam.
Hackle:	Medium brown, wound parachute around wing base.

Western Red Quill Emerger (Source: Knopp and Cormier)

Hook:	Standard nymph, 1X long, size 12-18.
Thread:	Brown 6/0 or 8/0.
Tails:	Brown partridge fibers.
Rib:	Fine gold wire.
Gills:	Pale gray marabou fibers along each side.
Body:	Dark gray-brown to reddish-brown fur or synthetic dubbing.
Legs:	Brown partridge fibers, divided.
Wing:	Gray-dyed deer hair or CDC, tied short.

Western Blue Quill Floating Nymph
(Source: Knopp & Cormier)

Hook:	Standard nymph, 1X long, size 12-18.
Thread:	Dark brown 6/0 or 8/0.
Tails:	Dark barred woodduck flank fibers.
Rib:	Fine gold wire.
Gills:	Pale gray marabou fibers along each side.
Body:	Dark gray-brown fur or synthetic dubbing.
Wing:	Dark gray polypro yarn ball or white closed-cell foam.
Hackle:	Medium brown, wound parachute around wing base.

Western Blue Quill Emerger (Source: Knopp and Cormier)

Hook:	Standard nymph, 1X long, size 12-18.
Thread:	Dark brown 6/0 or 8/0.
Tails:	Dark barred woodduck flank fibers.
Rib:	Fine gold wire.
Gills:	Pale gray marabou fibers along each side.
Body:	Dark gray-brown fur or synthetic dubbing.
Legs:	Brown partridge fibers, divided.
Wing:	Gray dyed deer hair or CDC, tied short.

These four dressings will serve you well wherever you find trout feeding on *Paraleptophlebia* emergers. In *Mayflies,* Knopp and Cormier list the Red Quill dressings as imitating *P. heteronea, memorialis, packii* (now *temporalis),* and *bicornuta.* The Blue Quill dressings imitate *P. gregalis* and *helena* (now *memoralis*). They are listed not because we think you will want to tie all of them, but so you will be able to choose the one that fits your needs when you've gotten into a situation where trout are picky about the *Paraleptophlebia* dressing they'll accept, and you've done some collecting to see what they're taking, and now know what you need to do to match it.

Emerger Presentation

If you ever find call for these *Paraleptophlebia* emerger dressings, it will be in the almost still currents right at the edge of the stream, or on smooth currents below trailing weed beds. Your rigging and presentation will have to be fine-tuned to those circumstances. Trout will be spooky when feeding in such exposed positions.

Most of the time you'll need to wade to a position out from the bank, in water where that's possible, and fish back in toward it. On such big rivers as the Clark Fork you'd drown doing that in most places so you must fish either from the bank or a boat. On the Deschutes River, fishing from a boat is not allowed and wading out from the bank is rarely possible, so you must fish its edges and eddies during *Paraleptophlebia* hatches while rock-hopping on shore.

Whatever position the water allows you to take, you must make delicate presentations, and you must get dead-drift floats. Slack-line casts, whether upstream, cross-stream, or downstream, are always the rule in this kind of fishing. You'll need to stalk your trout carefully, cast to them delicately, and watch your fly closely for the sipping rises you're sure to get.

On big rivers, *Paraleptophlebia* are almost always most important in the eddies and edge currents.

Dun Imitations

Paraleptophlebia duns are important because trout, getting a chance at one, will normally sneak up and sip it down. Because their hatches tend to be more sporadic, less intense than those of many other mayflies, trout feed more opportunistically on all stages of the insect, rather than keying in on one stage and ignoring the others. If trout will take a floating

Paraleptophlebia dun imitation, then it's wise to use one, because it will be so easy to see on the smooth edge currents where the naturals hatch.

While we normally avoid recommending hackled imitations for the smoothest flows, trout seem quite willing to accept them during *Paraleptophlebia* hatches. These high-floating dressings have the advantage of providing sufficient support to drop a nymph on a tippet tied to the hook bend.

Red Quill

Hook:	Standard dry fly, 1X fine, size 12 to 18.
Thread:	Brown 6/0 or 8/0.
Wings:	Blue dun hen hackle tips, upright and divided.
Tail:	Brown hackle fibers.
Body:	Reddish-brown dyed hackle stem.
Hackle:	Brown.

The traditional Red Quill is the accepted pattern for September *Paraleptophlebia* hatches on many western waters, even where trout are exceptionally selective.

Blue Quill

Hook:	Standard dry fly, 1X fine, size 12 to 18.
Thread:	Black 6/0 or 8/0.
Wings:	Dark blue dun or black hen hackle tips.
Tails:	Dark blue dun hackle fibers.
Body:	Stripped peacock herl stem.
Hackle:	Dark blue dun.

The traditional Blue Quill represents darker species of western *Paraleptophlebia.* One of these two traditional hackled dressings, the Blue or Red Quill, will probably solve all of your dun problems during any hatch of these insects that you encounter. If they fail, it will be because you need something slightly more imitative. If that happens, try the following Sparkle Dun or Thorax Dun, but remember that it's best to collect your own specimens and base the size of your fly and the colors of your materials on what you see.

Mahogany Sparkle Dun
(Source: Juracek and Mathews)

Hook:	Standard dry fly, 1X fine, size 12-18.
Thread:	Brown 6/0 or 8/0.
Wing:	Natural gray Compara-Dun deer hair or dyed gray yearling elk hair.
Shuck:	Brown Z-lon.
Body:	Brown Antron dubbing.

If you get into hatches of *Paraleptophlebia* that would be called blue quills rather than mahoganies, substitute gray Z-lon for the shuck and gray Antron for the body.

Mahogany Thorax Dun (Originator: Mike Lawson)

Hook:	Standard dry fly, 1X fine, size 12-18.
Thread:	Brown 6/0 or 8/0.
Wing:	Dark gray turkey flat.
Tails:	Dark blue dun hackle fibers, split.
Body:	Dark tan Antron dubbing.
Hackle:	Dark blue dun, spread around wings, clipped on bottom.

This dressing, interpreted for the selective trout on the Henrys Fork of the Snake River by Mike Lawson, and based on the work of Vincent Marinaro in *A Modern Dry Fly Code*, is one of our favorites. It fools trout feeding on duns, and also supports a nymph fished as a trailer behind it.

Dun Presentation

You'll be fishing these *Paraleptophlebia* dun dressings in the smooth edge currents of fairly boisterous streams, or you'll need them on the slickest currents of weedy spring creeks and tailwaters. Those are the only water types where trout will feed selectively on *Paraleptophlebia* duns. Refine your tackle to the most delicate you own. Lengthen your leaders to twelve to fifteen feet, three to four of that 5X or 6X tippet. Use the reach cast, wiggle cast, or whatever other cast shows the fly to the trout ahead of the line and leader, on a drag-free drift.

When fishing dun dressings over trout feeding at the edges, in thin water, never cast over their heads. Lining the trout in such a situation will send them fleeing.

No matter what imitation you use for *Paraleptophlebia* duns, or emergers for that matter, you'll find that trout rise deliberately to them, and sip them down slowly. You must learn to set the hook slowly to these unhurried rises, or you'll pull the hook away from the trout.

Spinner Imitations

Spinner falls of *Paraleptophlebia* can be important to the angler. They usually swarm in early evening and drop to the water about the time it gets difficult to see. Many of the mysterious rises that happen just about dark, when you see trout feeding but cannot see anything that might cause them to do that, are a result of these *Paraleptophlebia* spinner falls.

Blue Quill Spinner

Hook:	Standard dry fly, 1X fine, size 14-18.
Thread:	Gray 6/0 or 8/0.
Tails:	Blue dun hackle fibers, split.
Body:	Stripped peacock quill.
Wings:	White hen hackle tips, tied spent or semi-spent.
Hackle:	Light blue dun, clipped top and bottom.

This dressing, in combination with the following Red Quill Spinner that fishes for so many other hatches, will cover most *Paraleptophlebia* spinner falls.

Red Quill Spinner

Hook:	Standard dry fly, 1X fine, size 12-18.
Thread:	Brown 6/0 or 8/0.
Tails:	Brown hackle fibers, split.
Body:	Reddish-brown dyed hackle stem.
Wings:	White hen hackle tips, tied spent or semi-spent.
Hackle:	Brown, clipped top and bottom.

Don't tie either of these spinner dressings specifically for *Paraleptophlebia* spinner falls unless you encounter trout feeding on them selectively. That might not happen to you; it has yet to happen to us in all our travels, but as we've mentioned already our travels tend to be scattered. If you are lucky enough to fish more consistently on home waters, then these spinner falls might present themselves as a problem to you. It's a problem that is more difficult to notice than it is to solve once you've figured out what trout are doing.

We recommend these two dressings as a pair that, tied and carried in a range of sizes from 12 to 20, will cover most mayfly spinner falls you'll ever need to imitate. If you tie them and carry them in their own small fly box, you might find that solving many spinner falls becomes less the problem than it used to be.

Spinner Presentation

Though the nymph, emerger, and dun dressings are important primarily along the edges, with the exception of waters where weeds trail up toward the surface, spinners are more important out in open water. That is where the seeds for the next *Paraleptophlebia* generation get sown. It will almost always be right at evening. You'll almost always find trout feeding on them in smooth water, upstream or down from the riffles and runs where the nymphs might establish their little lives after the eggs are laid.

Refine your tackle and tactics to suit these smooth-water situations. You need do nothing different than you would do during any other mayfly spinner fall. The most difficult problem to solve will be following the drift of your fly in the failing light. You might use a strike indicator to mark the position of your fly on the water. Most often it's more effective to wade in close and present the fly with short casts, just twenty to thirty feet.

Wade carefully. Cast delicately. Be sure you get no drag. Watch your fly closely to see if it disappears in a delicate swirl. That is a prescription for almost all dry-fly fishing over insect hatches, and especially over spinner falls. Apply it wherever you find trout sipping any mayflies, in any stage of their ephemeral lives.

If you ever find *Paraleptophlebia* spinners important, it will be during the last of the day's fading light.

Chapter 19

Leptophlebia (Western Black Quills)

FAMILY: LEPTOPHLEBIIDAE

Genus: *Leptophlebia*
Western Species: 5
North America: 10
Important Western Species: *Leptophlebia cupida,*
 L. gravestella, L. nebulosa, L. pacifica
Common Names: Western black quills, black quills,
 early black quills.

The western importance of the scattered *Leptophlebia* species is marginal. They are more important in some sluggish trout streams in the Midwest and East, where they produce fishable hatches along the margins. We have encountered them infrequently in our travels and collecting in the West, and have yet to find them important in our fishing, with two exceptions from widely separated lakes. One was the southeast arm of Yellowstone Lake, where we once encountered an evening spinner fall of three-tailed mayflies, with trout rising all around. We took trout in that beautiful setting, fishing an Adams with the hackle trimmed off the bottom, until darkness forced us to row the boat toward our distant campsite. The second was from an interior British Columbia lake. Again a spinner fall of a large three-tailed mayfly, collected by our friend the late Dick VanDemark, and later identified and confirmed as *Leptophlebia,* provided a good rise of fish in late afternoon and early evening.

 While the spinners from Yellowstone Lake were not collected, it seems almost certain they were *Leptophlebia.* For a long time we did not associate *Leptophlebia* with lakes, but these two instances certainly point to their occasional importance there. In streams, *Leptophlebia* are found most often in almost still and marshy reaches, not exactly prime trout water.

Leptophlebia **HATCH IMPORTANCE SCORE:** **14.0**

CRITERIA/SCORE	5		4		3		2		1	
Distribution: (within Western waters)	widespread		common		scattered		isolated		rare	1.0
Abundance:	heavy		abundant		modest		trickling	1.5	individual	
Emergence type:	mid-water/slow		mid-water/fast		edges/slow	2.5	edges/fast		crawls out	
Emergence time:	mid-day		early and/or late over long period		early and/or late over short period	2.5	dawn or dusk		night	
Emergence duration:	multiple seasons per year		well-defined long hatch period		well-defined short hatch period		poorly-defined long hatch period	1.5	poorly-defined short hatch	
(Behavior/Availability) Nymph:	excellent		good		moderate		slight		poor	1.0
(Behavior/Availability) Emerger:	excellent		good		moderate		slight		poor	1.0
(Behavior/Availability) Dun:	excellent		good		moderate		slight	2.0	poor	
(Behavior/Availability) Spinner:	excellent		good		moderate		slight		poor	1.0
Totals:		0.0		0.0		5.0		5.0		4.0

CHAPTER 19: *LEPTOPHLEBIA* (WESTERN BLACK QUILLS) | 169

Fred Arbonna might have summed up the situation best when he wrote in *Mayflies, the Angler, and the Trout* that the fly-fisher, "...should first encounter a *Leptophlebia* hatch before going through the trouble of tying and carrying a specific artificial to imitate it..." We agree with that, and warn that you might never find a *Leptophlebia* imitation necessary. But you might collect the naturals in your own fishing, and wonder where they fit into the mosaic of other western hatches. You might also find trout feeding selectively on them in your own fishing, on your own western waters.

Emergence and Distribution

The various western *Leptophlebia* species are primarily spring emergers. Their emergence can begin as early as March or April in streams or lakes with waters that warm early, with peak emergence in May and June. In some cold waters emergence continues until early July. The hatch often coincides with heavy spring runoff, which combined with their preferred habitat makes them more marginal yet. Of course where good populations occur in lakes, runoff will not be a problem.

Daily emergence is typically sporadic throughout the day, beginning in late morning to early afternoon and peaking in mid-afternoon. If spinner activity is important it will begin in mid-afternoon, reaching a peak in late afternoon and going on into the evening.

Leptophlebia will be found in isolated populations throughout valley and foothill streams and rivers of the Sierras, Cascades, and Rockies. They are distributed from New Mexico to Alberta, and from California to British Columbia, but they will be found important only in very scattered locations where their favored habitat is at the same time suitable trout habitat. Most often that will be in the marshy, forested, and almost unwadeable downstream areas of stream systems, or in beaver pond sections of any waters that hold trout. They can also be found in lakes and ponds, most often in areas where very slow and shallow streams enter the stillwaters.

That spinner fall we fished on Yellowstone Lake occurred within a few hundred yards of the broad delta where the Yellowstone River branches out and enters the lake in a tangle of shallow, braided channels.

LEPTOPHLEBIA EMERGENCE TABLE

TIME	WINTER			SPRING			SUMMER			FALL		
	Dec.	Jan.	Feb.	March	April	May	June	July	Aug.	Sep.	Oct.	Nov.
7 a.m. - 10 a.m.												
10 a.m. - noon												
noon - 3 p.m.												
3 p.m. - 7 p.m.												
7 p.m. - 10 p.m.												

Nymph Characteristics

Leptophlebia nymph. Note: this is a preserved specimen; its colors are not true. See the separated gill for comparison to *Paraleptophlebia*.

a. Head squarish; body slightly flattened.

b. Gill *lamellae* double on abdominal segments 2 through 7, each gill terminating in a long filament. Gills on abdominal segment 1 forked and slender, distinctly different than remaining gills.

c. Three tails equal length; either with fine, sparse hairs, or hairs absent.

d. Color ranges from light yellowish-brown to dark chestnut brown.

e. Body length 7-15 mm (1/4-5/8 in.).

Dun Characteristics

a. Three tails, dark in color. Middle tail usually shorter than outer two.

b. Hind wings large and elliptical; no costal angulation.

c. Forewings dark slate-gray.

d. Body yellowish-brown through gray to dark chocolate brown.

e. Front legs dark, rear legs lighter.

f. Body length 6-14mm (1/4-1/2 in.).

Spinner Characteristics

a. Three tails, body length or longer with middle tail usually shorter than outer tails.

b. Hind wings large and elliptical; no costal angulation.

c. Forewings clear, or with brown markings.

d. Body light brown to dark slate-gray.

e. Body length 6-14mm (1/4-1/2 in.).

Habitat and Behavior

Leptophlebia nymphs are typically scattered in decaying leaf packs, decomposing vegetative material, and submerged woody debris such as limbs fallen to the water from streamside trees. Their populations are greatest in shallow and nearly still water, where they inhabit slow pools and eddies along the banks of western trout streams, and along the edges of ponds and lakes, especially where some wave action provides aerated water or a stream enters the stillwater.

If you ever find *Leptophlebia* important, most likely it will be on lakes and ponds with marshy creek inlets and outlets nearby. Beaver ponds often have fair populations of *Leptophlebia* nymphs, simply because beaver tend to build their dams toward the slower and more wooded stretches of streams, and also because the dams put the brakes on flowing water, increase submerged woody debris, and in general improve the habitat for *Leptophlebia* nymphs.

The nymphs tend to be nocturnal, remaining hidden in leaf litter or detritus during the day. They are exposed to trout predation only when

The only time the authors have found *Leptophlebia* in fishable numbers was a late-evening spinner fall on Yellowstone Lake, just off the braided entrance of the river. It was not clear if their nymph habitat was in the marshy areas of the river channels, or the wave-washed edges of the lake itself.

they come out to scavenge plant and animal remains under the cover of darkness. The nymphs grow rapidly through late summer and fall, over-winter as almost mature nymphs, and emerge in spring and early summer.

Before emergence the nymphs migrate from mild currents into side pools and shallow marshy areas. They swim awkwardly, with snake-like side-to-side undulations of the body. In the days and hours just prior to emergence, *Leptophlebia* nymphs begin to swim or crawl boldly in daylight.

A few days prior to emergence *Leptophlebia* nymphs gather in min-now-like schools in shallows and migrate as much as a mile upstream. Apparently this compensates for natural drift, which is increased due to their emergence during runoff. These migrations concentrate the sparse populations of nymphs, and might cause trout to move into the shallows and feed on them, especially if little other food is present in the stream.

In the hour or so before emergence, *Leptophlebia* nymphs make several restless trips from the bottom to the top. A few nymphs crawl out on rocks or protruding woody debris for emergence, but most emerge in the surface film in quiet backwaters. Emergence takes place on smooth, shallow water, almost always near the bank. Duns drift for long time periods—not distances because in such slow water they usually just sit—before they are able to become airborne.

Leptophlebia duns molt to spinners twelve to twenty-four hours after emergence. Spinners swarm and mate from mid-afternoon to dark. The female returns to the stream and lays her eggs by sporadically dipping the tip of the abdomen to the water. The eggs are generally deposited in running currents, but the tiny nymphs, upon hatching from the eggs, soon migrate toward their preferred marginal habitat.

Imitation

Most western fly-fishers will never need to imitate *Leptophlebia* nymphs, duns, or spinners. Even if you get into the rare circumstance where trout feed selectively on them, you'll usually be able to match them with patterns you already carry, or modifications of such patterns as the Adams that we trimmed to fish effectively during the *Leptophlebia* spinner fall on Yellowstone Lake.

We'll offer dressings and presentation methods in case you find a situation where trout are selective to the naturals, and you find it desirable to match them with patterns tied specifically for them.

Nymph Imitations

The naturals are slender. Tie your imitations on 2X or 3X long hooks, in tan to dark brown, size 12 to 16. The standard Gold Ribbed Hare's Ear, tied with very slight weight, might be all you ever need for *Leptophlebia* nymphs. If that doesn't do it, try the following specific imitation.

Western Black Quill Nymph (Source: Knopp and Cormier)

Hook:	2X or 3X long, size 12-16.
Thread:	Light brown 6/0 or 8/0.
Tails:	Pale barred woodduck flank fibers.
Rib:	Fine gold wire.
Body:	Grayish-olive fur dubbing.
Gills:	Grayish-olive marabou fibers along sides.
Wingcase:	Grayish-brown goose quill segment.
Legs:	Olive-dyed grouse soft hackle, half turn on underside.

Before tying this complex dressing, collect specimens from your own waters, and be sure to select materials that match the size and color of the naturals on which you've found trout feeding.

Nymph Presentation

You would fish such a specific dressing only over cruising fish that you've spotted feeding visibly on *Leptophlebia* nymphs, usually in the shallows along the edges of very slow water, or on beaver ponds. Use a slow hand-twist retrieve. If you see no trout working but suspect they are there and feeding on *Leptophlebia* nymphs, fish a slightly weighted nymph to the banks, and employ a slow retrieve with an occasional lift of the rod tip to mimic the restless trips to the top and back taken by the nymphs before emergence.

Dun Imitations

Before tying anything specific for *Leptophlebia* duns, try traditional patterns such as the Adams or Blue Dun in size 10 to 14. You might also do as well with any dressing you tied for the related *Paraleptophlebia*, though those would tend to be in slightly smaller sizes. If you find that you do need an imitation for the larger *Leptophlebia* duns, try one of the following dressings, or a color variation based on specimens you've collected.

Black Quill (Source: Schwiebert)

Hook:	Standard dry fly, 1X fine, size 10-14.
Thread:	Black 6/0 or 8/0.
Tail:	Dark blue dun hackle fibers.
Body:	Stripped badger hackle stem.
Wings:	Dark blue dun or black hen hackle tips.
Hackle:	Dark blue dun.

This dressing from Ernest Schwiebert's classic *Matching the Hatch* is difficult to improve upon for the rare *Leptophlebia* hatches you might need to match. He fished it most often over hatches on Colorado streams, but it will work throughout the entire West.

Leptophlebia Compara-Dun (Source: Knopp and Cormier)

Hook:	Standard dry fly, 1X fine, size 10-14.
Thread:	Black 6/0 or 8/0.
Wing:	Gray-dyed deer or yearling elk hair.
Tails:	Dark blue dun hackle fibers, split.
Body:	Dark brown or black fur or synthetic dubbing.

This dressing, from Knopp and Cormier's *Mayflies*, is one on which to base your own size and color variations. Since the naturals hatch on water that is still or nearly so, it might serve you better than a hackled dressing, which obscures the profile of the body and wings.

Dun Presentation

All dun dressings for this group will be fished in still or nearly still water, on the sit, waiting patiently for cruising and feeding fish. Refine your tackle to suit slow or still waters, and place your casts delicately, well ahead of the trout, in order not to spook them.

Spinner Imitations

You very likely will never need imitations of *Leptophlebia* spinners. If you do, our guess is that it will be on a beaver pond, or on the edge of a lake or pond very near the entrance or exit of a stream or river that is good habitat for *Leptophlebia* nymphs. The only situation we've encountered where the naturals fell in large enough numbers to cause selective feeding was on Yellowstone Lake, very near the entrance of the river in the southeast arm.

Black Quill Spinner (Source: Schwiebert)

Hook:	Standard dry fly, 1X fine, size 10-14.
Thread:	Black 6/0 or 8/0.
Tails:	Brown mallard breast fibers, splayed.
Body:	Stripped badger hackle stem.
Wings:	Medium blue dun hen hackle tips, spent.
Hackle:	Dark blue dun, clipped top and bottom.

If an Adams with the hackle clipped off the bottom won't work for you, try the standard Red Quill Spinner or Blue Quill Spinner that you carry for so many other more important mayflies before you tie this dressing specifically for *Leptophlebia* specimens you've collected.

Spinner Presentation

Fish the spinner dressing in early afternoon to evening over barely moving water in meandering forested streams, on the meadow stretches of freestone streams, and along the edges of lakes and ponds. In all cases you should fish it in response to trout working visibly to collected naturals, since it will be rare that you might actually see spinner falls of *Leptophlebia*.

Chapter 20

Tricorythodes (*Tricos*)

FAMILY: LEPTOHYPHIDAE

Genus: *Tricorythodes*

Western Species: 9

North America: 19

Important Western Species: *Tricorythodes minutus*
(synonym *T. fallax*)

Asioplax edmunsi (previously *Tricorythodes edmunsi*; the new genus *Asioplax* was created when this book was in its last stages).

Common Names: *Tricos*, trikes, white-winged curse, white-winged blacks, snowflake mayflies.

While nine species of *Tricorythodes* are found in the western states, only one, *Tricorythodes minutus*, is widespread and produces significant hatches for anglers to imitate. *Tricos* are the smallest mayflies in North America, but their hatches and spinner falls are so heavy that the largest trout in a stream, river, or in rare places lake, will move up to feed very selectively on the surface. Their principal importance is in the spinner stage, when they often coat the surface and set trout to gulping. But duns, especially females, can be important during dawn hatches. If you neglect them you might be missing out on the most fishable part of the hatch.

Tricos display sexual dimorphism: the males and females are slightly different in size and quite different in color. They can give the impression of two species hatching at once. The great A. K. Best might have summed up this hatch perfectly when he wrote in *A. K.'s Fly Box* that *Tricos*, "...can produce either fantastic fishing or utter frustration."

Emergence and Distribution

Tricos are usually multi-brooded, with the first generation hatching in June through August, the second in September and October. There is a

---

Trichorythodes   **HATCH IMPORTANCE SCORE:**   **33.0**

CRITERIA/SCORE	5		4		3		2		1	
Distribution: (within Western waters)	widespread		**common**	3.5	scattered		isolated		rare	
Abundance:	heavy	5.0	abundant		modest		trickling		individual	
Emergence type:	mid-water/slow	5.0	mid-water/fast		edges/slow		edges/fast		crawls out	
Emergence time:	mid-day		early and/or late over long period		early and/or late over short period	3.0	dawn or dusk		night	
Emergence duration:	multiple seasons per year	4.5	well-defined long hatch period		well-defined short hatch period		poorly-defined long hatch period		poorly-defined short hatch	
(Behavior/Availability) **Nymph:**	excellent		good		moderate		slight		poor	1.0
(Behavior/Availability) **Emerger:**	excellent		good		moderate	3.0	slight		poor	
(Behavior/Availability) **Dun:**	excellent		good		moderate	3.0	slight		poor	
(Behavior/Availability) **Spinner:**	excellent	5.0	good		moderate		slight		poor	
Totals:		19.5		3.5		9.0		0.0		1.0

Slow-flowing and moderately silt-impacted sections on many of our western trout streams have heavy hatches of *Tricos*.

great deal of overlap on most waters, with one brood tapering off as the other begins. On rich streams with heavy populations of nymphs, the emergence can seem to be one long continuous hatch, for weeks or even months, through most of summer and fall. Studies of *Trico* life cycles on some western spring creeks with near constant year-round water temperature found emergence occurring in every month of the year.

In less-rich rivers or streams with a wide range of seasonal temperatures, *Tricos* might have a single seasonal brood, in which case the peak of the hatch will come just once but last for two to four weeks. It will still produce some great fishing for those prepared to take advantage of this tiny insect in its incredible numbers.

Daily emergence reflects a two-stage hatch, with male duns emerging first. During hot summer weather this might be late in the evening or during the night. When the weather is cooler, in late summer or fall, male duns begin hatching close to sunrise, followed shortly by the female duns. Females almost always emerge in the morning, often beginning at dawn and continuing until 8:00 or 9:00 a.m. If the weather is exceptionally cool, hatches might begin at 9:00 a.m. and last until noon. Duns molt to the spinner stage very quickly, only one to two hours after emergence. As a result, spinner falls often begin as the last of the duns are still floating on the surface.

The *Trico* spinner fall attracts the greatest attention from fish and fishermen, but as A. K. Best points out, sometimes you can enjoy your best and most lonely fishing by getting on the water at daylight, when insects and anglers are both fewer than they will be later during the spinner fall, but trout are already up and feeding on duns.

Tricos are distributed across the entire continent. They inhabit slow-flowing rivers and streams, and portions of some lakes, in all western states and provinces where you might angle for trout.

Famous hatches of *Tricos* happen on Alberta's Bow River, Montana's Missouri, Big Hole, Bighorn, and Paradise Valley spring creeks, Idaho's Henrys Fork and Silver Creek, the Madison River in the Park, and the Madison Arm of Hebgen Lake. But one would be foolish to expect them only on famous waters. We encounter them every season on waters where we're not expecting them.

Just this past season we explored a wilderness section of an Oregon stream that we've fished in other sections for many years. It turned out that the wild and scenic area has been impacted by cattle grazing on a ranch upstream. The resulting siltation perfected the habitat for *Trico* nymphs, and the hatches were unexpected blitzes. Trout fed heavily on them when the spinners fell, and were disappointingly selective, since we'd not thought it necessary to carry our full range of fly boxes, including such tiny patterns, into such rough and remote country.

TRICORYTHODES EMERGENCE TABLE

TIME	WINTER			SPRING			SUMMER			FALL		
	Dec.	Jan.	Feb.	March	April	May	June	July	Aug.	Sep.	Oct.	Nov.
7 a.m. - 10 a.m.												
10 a.m. - noon												
noon - 3 p.m.												
3 p.m. - 7 p.m.												
7 p.m. - 10 p.m.												

Nymph Characteristics

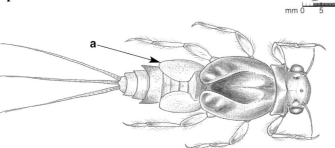

Tricorythodes nymph.

a. Gills on abdominal segment 2 triangular in shape and *operculate,* covering gills on segments 3 through 7.

b. Three tails, with center tail equal to or slightly longer than outer tails. Tails covered with *setae,* or fine hairs.

c. Hind wing pads absent.

d. Body light to dark brown, with many *setae,* or fine hairs.

f. Minute; body length without tails 3-10mm (1/8-3/8 in.)

Dun Characteristics

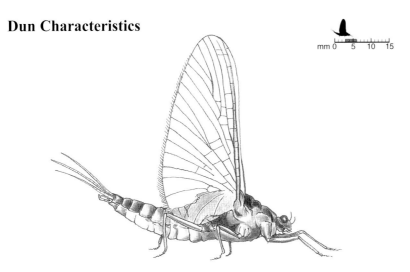

Female *Tricorythodes* dun.

a. Three tails. Male tails twice body length; female tails body length.

b. Stocky thoracic region.

c. Hind wings absent.

d. Front wings large, whitish-gray.

e. Female usually with light green abdomen and dark brown thorax; male with both abdomen and thorax dark brown.

f. Minute; body length without tails only 3-6mm (1/8-1/4 in.).

Spinner Characteristics

a. Three tails. Male tails twice body length; female tails body length.

b. Hind wings absent.

c. Forewings clear.

d. Female with pale to dark green abdomen and dark brown thorax; male with dark brown or black abdomen and thorax.

e. Minute; body length without tails only 3-6mm (1/8-1/4 in.)

Male *Tricorythodes* spinner.

Habitat and Behavior

Tricorythodes are found in streams of all sizes, from small creeks to large rivers. They inhabit both spring creeks and freestone streams. Populations

Female *Tricorythodes* spinner.

The broad, placid reaches of Silver Creek, with all of their rooted vegetation, have dense hatches and spinner falls of *Tricos*.

are heaviest where the currents are most gentle and aquatic vegetation most dense. They crawl in the vegetation or bottom silts in slow to moderately flowing stretches of rivers, and often in neglected side channels with meandering currents. They thrive wherever a thin layer of silt settles. Their populations can be heavy in the lower tailing ends of large pools in freestone streams, and in long, gentle flats in all sorts of streams. In river systems, *Trico* nymphs will be found in good numbers lower in the watersheds, where the gradient becomes less steep and silt is not washed out as readily as it is in the steeper and therefore more boisterous sections upstream. While it's not common, *Tricos* also turn up in lakes, sometimes in surprisingly large numbers. As in streams, the nymphs are fond of areas with rich aquatic plant growth. Large lakes, with significant wave action, or areas around inlet streams, provide sufficient motion to the water to keep these slow-water nymphs supplied with oxygen and thriving.

In rich waters that are warm during the summer season, *Trico* nymphs reach maturity within five to seven weeks. They emerge, the duns molt, the spinners mate and lay the eggs of a next short *Trico* generation. The generations begin to overlap, and that is why the hatch can seem to go on, unbroken, for almost the entire fishing season on some rivers.

Trico nymphs are feeble swimmers, always preferring to crawl unless they are dislodged from their holds on the bottom or in vegetation, or just prior to emergence. Even during emergence, many of the nymphs manage to avoid swimming.

Tricos emerge from nymphs to duns in one of three ways. Many hatch in open water, in the surface film, just as so many other mayflies do.

Others grip the bottom or vegetation, usually in very shallow water or on weedbeds that trail toward the surface; the dun leaves the nymphal exoskeleton beneath the water, and the dun floats slowly to the surface, probably buoyed up by gases trapped in the wing folds. Many *Tricos* emerge by crawling out of the water in the nymphal stage, on rocks or protruding vegetation, before the dun escapes the nymphal shuck.

None of these emergence techniques seem to stir selective feeding on the nymphs by trout. When the duns hatch through the surface film, however, trout often feed exclusively on them, especially on cripples.

Female *Tricos* typically emerge in early morning and molt to spinners from a few minutes to an hour after emergence. The timing is temperature dependant. On very cold days, and also very hot and windy days when the fragile insects might become dessicated, the final molt will at times be delayed until evening. On the average day, however, female duns molt very soon after emergence, and are ready to fly and mate immediately.

Male *Trico* duns that hatch in the evening or after dark remain in the dun stage until the following morning. They molt into spinners in the early morning, just in time for emergence of the day's females. The males form swarms either over the water or nearby, above the stream banks. You'll see them as smoky clouds hovering over the water, or over the banks near the stream.

Females enter the swarm, are mated in the air, and leave the swarm to rest briefly on streamside vegetation. Males generally fall spent to the water immediately after mating. This descent can be *en masse*, with that cloud suddenly gone from the air and hundreds or even thousands of insects suddenly appearing on the water. Stoop to examine the surface carefully and you'll see them pinned there. Trout notice them, too. The rise will begin abruptly, and unless you look carefully it will look like the trout are rising to nothing.

Male spinners collapse to the water ahead of females. Gravid female spinners fly to streamside vegetation, where they use a peristaltic movement of the abdomen to pump the eggs into an egg mass, or ball, attached to the outside of the abdomen. When this is ready to deposit, usually in half an hour or so, the female spinner returns to the water, dips her abdomen to the water to wash the egg ball off, then falls spent. Female *Tricos* often fly upstream some distance before depositing their eggs. Some researchers believe this is done to counter downstream drift during the nymph stage.

It sometimes appears that *Trico* duns molt to spinners in the air. It is likely, however, that some female duns are so eager to mate that they take off before completely freeing themselves from the dun *exuvia,* or cast skin. They take off with it stuck to their tails, and it shakes loose in the air and floats out of the mating swarm. When these cast skins are observed floating down out of a mating flight of *Tricos,* it appears that some of the insects have molted in the air.

This two-part spinner fall, with the males falling first and the females a bit later, after giving their eggs time to be fertilized, is important to recognize. Spinners of the two sexes are different colors, the females olive and the males dark brown or black. Begin fishing during a spinner fall with a pattern that matches the male, and switch to a female dressing only when trout cease accepting your darker pattern. You'll need to be very observant to notice when that happens. Quite likely, it won't.

Trico spinner falls generally commence when morning air temperatures reach around 68°F, though they still occur on cool fall days when

When the swarm of *Tricorythodes* males dancing in the air suddenly disappears, it's a sign they've hit the water, and trout will take notice even if you do not.

temperatures never get that warm. Typical times are from 9:00 a.m. to about noon. The spinner fall and continuing emergence from nymph to dun may overlap during heavy hatches. If dun emergence is later in the day due to cold weather, or if the weather is hot and windy, the mating flight and spinner fall might be delayed until early evening.

In hatches with mulitple generations, each succeeding generation is usually a bit smaller than the one before it. You might succeed with a size 18 or 20 imitation early in the season, but be forced to reduce your fly to a size 22 or 24 toward the end of the season, in order to continue catching selective trout on *Trico* imitations.

Imitation

We often carry what we call "experimental fly boxes", which are dedicated to various ties designed to fish for the stages of a specific hatch. *Tricos* definitely fall into the short list of hatches that deserve their own box. Fortunately it can be a tiny one, but it should have lots of separate compartments. You should buy such a box for your *Trico* fishing. Tie a small selection of flies for the hatch from the following list, and see which of them work best for you.

You won't need many flies for the nymph stage. It's easy to imitate them with the smallest sizes of almost any nymph you already carry, so long as it's approximately the right color. An emerger based on the female dun might be useful for those dawn hatches that A. K. Best likes to fish. You'll need imitations for the female dun, and for both female and male spinners. When you tie, keep in mind that the females are typically size 18 to 22, the males one size smaller at size 20 to 24.

Nymph Imitations

Nymphs are the least important stage of the *Trico* life cycle to anglers. However, they can serve as useful searching patterns wherever your collecting reveals large populations of the naturals. Trout will almost always accept something tiny if it's delivered near enough to their holding lies, on a natural drift. Try a *Trico* nymph as a dropper once in a while, off the stern of a larger nymph. You might get surprised by the size of the results.

Tricorythodes Nymph

Hook:	Standard wet fly, 1X or 2X stout, size 18-24.
Weight:	5 to 10 turns very fine lead wire, or omit.
Thread:	Brown 8/0.
Tails:	Three pheasant tail fibers, short.
Body:	Tan to dark brown fur dubbing, picked out at thorax.

This dressing is simple to tie, but very effective, and not just for *Trico* nymphs. Use optional lead wire to make sure the fly penetrates the surface film, if you need it. If you're going to fish the fly as a trailer behind a dry, omit the weight or use less.

Nymph Presentation

If you fish this fly by itself, do it in response to feeding activity, when you can see *Tricos* active on the water, or when you've collected, found good populations of *Trico* nymphs, and have reason to think that you'll be seeing a hatch soon. You'll want to present the nymph with upstream or cross-stream casts, to spotted trout or likely lies. Fish it dead drift a few inches to a foot or so deep. A tiny yarn or hard strike indicator two to four feet up the leader will help you detect takes that are sure to be subtle.

You can also fish a *Trico* nymph suspended beneath a dry fly that is both indicator and enticement. If you leave the nymph unweighted, it's possible to dress it with floatant and fish it in the surface film, as an emerger. But for that stage of the insect, you will improve your fishing by adding a polypro yarn knot to the fly, or some CDC, to represent the unfolding wings of the dun.

Emerger Imitations

At times trout feed on *Trico* emergers in preference to nymphs or winged duns. You'll have to watch the rise forms for bubbles, those sure indications of surface takes, then follow the float of a few duns to see if any disappear. If you see bubbles, but no duns go down, it's time to try an emerger pattern.

CDC *Trico* Emerger (Source: Schollmeyer)

Hook:	Standard dry fly, 1X fine, size 18-22.
Thread:	Olive 8/0.
Shuck:	Tan Z-lon, sparse.
Body:	Olive fur or synthetic dubbing.
Wing:	Gray CDC.
Thorax:	Dark brown fur or synthetic dubbing.

This dressing, listed in Jim Schollmeyer's *Hatch Guide For Western Streams*, will suspend in the surface film and fish perfectly for *Trico* emergers. It represents the female, which is what trout will see almost exclusively in their morning feeding during actual hatches. Be sure to collect specimens of naturals in order to fish the fly in the right size. As the season progresses, that will get smaller and smaller.

Emerger Presentation

You won't fish a *Trico* emerger except in circumstances where you're aware that trout are feeding on them, and doing it very selectively. In that case, you'll obviously need to single out a specific rising trout, locate its feeding lane precisely, and do your best to time its rise rhythms. Refine your gear to its most delicate, using light lines, leaders twelve to fifteen feet long, with three- to four-foot tippets of 6X or 7X.

Wade as close as possible so you can place your casts accurately into that very narrow feeding lane. Trout won't move far to the side to accept something so tiny. You'll need to use the cross-stream reach cast or downstream wiggle cast for drag-free floats. If you cannot get into any position except downstream from the trout, cast upstream to it, but place the fly just a foot or two above it, to minimize the amount of leader that goes over its head. This will be a common situation if you're wading, because *Trico* habitat is often in deep, weedy currents with soft, silty bottoms, the kind of water that can be treacherous to wade.

No matter what position you take and cast you use, place the fly close to the trout to reduce drag from invisible micro-currents. This also increases the chance that the fly will arrive in front of the fish at the moment it is ready to rise again. Even when you get everything just right, it might take twenty to thirty casts before the trout accepts the fly. If you can cast over a fish that many times without putting it down, you've succeeded in one sense even if you fail to ever hook it.

Dun Imitations

Two patterns are required to match the duns, one olive for the female and another dark for the male, due to their sexual dichotomy. But recall that they hatch separately. You're almost sure to need female dressings, but will find need for male dun dressings far less often. It's our experience with these tiny hatches that getting the size and then the presentation right solves the situation, even if the color of the fly is wrong. That won't be your experience in every case, though, so don't ever rely on it. We recommend that you carry duns in both olive and dark, and check to see exactly what trout are taking and match it.

We'll offer a few dressings to choose from, since trout seem to key to silhouette during this hatch, and might want one dressing style one time, and another an hour later. That's one reason we believe in the necessity of a separate experimental fly box for this hatch of diminutive insects. You need to carry a few options to please capricious trout.

Trico **Sparkle Dun**
(Source: Juracek and Mathews)

Hook:	Standard dry fly, 1X fine, size 20-24.
Thread:	Olive or black 8/0.
Wing:	Natural light Compara-Dun deer hair.
Shuck:	Brown Z-lon.
Body:	Olive or black fur or synthetic dubbing.

This dressing, as with all Sparkle Duns, represents both the dun and the trailing nymphal shuck, and could well be considered an emerger. It floats up where you can see it, and is an excellent dressing to fish with an emerger or nymph as a trailer. Note that it is listed with options for either olive or black. Tie both, but the olive is likely to be most useful to you.

Trico **No-Hackle Dun** (Source: Arbonna)

Hook:	Standard dry fly, 1X fine, size 20-22.
Thread:	Olive or black 8/0.
Tails:	Light blue dun hackle fibers, split.
Abdomen:	Grayish-olive dubbing.
Wings:	Pale mallard or teal quill segments.
Thorax:	Grayish-brown dubbing.

While we normally do not fish no-hackle dressings because their wings tatter on the first trout, we have had our best fishing during *Trico* hatches with a no-hackle similar to the above pattern, but with white wings and a black body. This would imitate the male dun, but we've fished it with fine success through the entire spinner fall on Silver Creek, where the trout are as snotty as they get. It's likely the fly worked because size and presentation are critical, color is often not. Trout continued to take these no-hackles long after the wings of the flies became tattered.

Trico **Male Dun** (Source: Knopp and Cormier)

Hook:	Standard dry fly, 1X fine, size 18-24.
Thread:	Black 8/0.
Wings:	Light blue dun hen hackle tips, upright and divided.
Tails:	Three white Micro Fibetts, 2-3 times body length.
Abdomen:	Dark brown or black fur or synthetic dubbing.
Hackle:	Light blue dun, sparse, over thorax.
Thorax:	Dark brown or black fur or synthetic dubbing.

Trico **Female Dun** (Source: Knopp and Cormier)

Hook:	Standard dry fly, 1X fine, size 18-24.
Thread:	Black 8/0.
Wings:	Light blue dun hen hackle tips, upright and divided.
Tails:	Three white Micro Fibetts, body length.
Abdomen:	Light green fur or synthetic dubbing.
Hackle:	Light blue dun, sparse, over thorax.
Thorax:	Dark brown fur dubbing.

In *Mayflies* Knopp and Cormier state their preference for hackled *Trico* dun imitations, first because they're easier to see, and second because they're easier to separate from the naturals during a heavy hatch. We've found that to be true and important in our own fishing, and also have found that trout will take the hackled dressings without hesitation when the presentation is right. If trout approach your hackled imitation but turn away from it with refusal rises, try clipping the hackle off the bottom before you switch to another dressing style.

The olive female of these two dressings will be more important in your fishing, but it won't hurt to have both.

We would like to mention mismatching the hatch as a tactic at this point, because it can be useful during *Trico* hatches, though it's not as satisfying as catching trout on imitations. It can mean catching trout when you might otherwise not, if you don't have any proper dressings during a hatch, or have difficulty following their drift on the water. We got into a heavy *Trico* hatch once on the Henrys Fork of the Snake River, with our illustrator Richard Bunse. Tiny duns were so thick on the water that it was impossible to pick out an exact imitation floating among them, even with a very short cast. Noses arose among all those naturals, sipping in very short, eager rhythms.

Bunse tied on a size 18 hackled dressing that stood out among the naturals like a sailboat in a fleet of rowboats. He cast it a couple of feet above a big and busy nose. When his fly got to the trout, that nose came up, the outsized fly went down, and the rest of the story gets long because that trout, when Bunse finally held it in his hands, was quite large.

Trico **Quill Dun** (Originator: A. K. Best)

Hook:	Standard dry fly, 1X fine, size 18-24.
Thread:	White 8/0, black 8/0.
Tail:	4-5 white spade hackle fibers, slightly splayed.
Abdomen:	Olive-dyed hackle stem.
Thorax:	Black fur or synthetic dubbing.
Wings:	White hen hackle tips.
Hackle:	Black.

This dressing from *A. K.'s Fly Box* can also be tied in parachute style, with white turkey T-base or flat feather sections for the wingpost. In either version the white thread is switched for black at the end of the quill body. Then a very short thorax of black dubbing is tied over the abdomen tie-off point, before the wings and hackle are tied in. For the parachute tie, the wingpost is tied in first. A. K. does not tie in the wings first on versions with hackle tip wings, considering the normal winging procedure, tying in the split wings first, to waste tying time.

Dun Presentation

Trout will be as selective as they get during dun hatches of tiny *Tricos*. Your casting position will be critical. It's also important to single out a rising trout, and to make your presentations precisely down its feeding lane, rather than scattering your casts to various rises, or trying to get a long drift through a pod of feeding trout. Trout will be focused on the fleets of duns coming down, making it easier to approach close without alarming them if you wade cautiously and make all of your movements slowly.

On lake arms and around stillwater edges, *Trico* duns will always be most important at dawn and just after it. They'll only be taken selectively when the water is smooth. If it's wind-riffled or rough, trout generally ignore such tiny insects.

When lake conditions are right, locate and single out a feeding trout, cast carefully into what you calculate to be its cruising lane, but place the fly five to ten feet ahead. Misses will be more common than hits, but be persistant. When a trout lines up on your fly, and you can see it homing in for the sipping take, discipline yourself to let the fly sit there until you know the trout has gone down with it. During such delicate feeding, takes will be deliberate. It's easy to jerk the fly out of there before the hook is secure in the trout's jaw.

Spinner Imitations

You'll need both male and female *Trico* spinner imitations, as the spinner fall is typically segregated by sexes, and trout are usually selective to one sex or the other. Use the male dressing first, and switch when females fall and trout shift attention to them, which, if it happens, is usually indicated by your success on rising trout suddenly falling off.

If you lack imitations and get into a fall of *Trico* spinners, with trout rising all around, don't surrender until you've tried your dun dressings. Or search your fly boxes for midge imitations. Trim whatever flies you have in the right size to what you consider the right shape. Trout will often take nearly anything if it's the right size and somewhat the right shape, when they're feeding on invisibles.

Clear Wing *Trico* Spinner (Originator: Gary LaFontaine)

Hook:	Standard dry fly, 1X fine, size 18-24.
Thread:	Black 8/0.
Tails:	Three medium blue dun hackle fibers, split.
Abdomen:	Dark olive synthetic dubbing.
Thorax:	Black synthetic dubbing.
Wing:	Clear Antron yarn.

The Antron wings on this spinner dressing serve the same function as the sparkle yarn overbodies on Gary LaFontaine's Sparkle Pupa patterns for caddis: they gather tiny bubbles of air, or reflect light that looks like them. Natural *Trico* spinners usually have bubbles trapped under their wings. This dressing is described in Gary's *The Dry Fly: New Angles* (Greycliff, 1990).

Trico Quill Spinner (Originator: A. K. Best)

Hook:	Standard dry fly, 1X fine, size 18-24.
Thread:	Black 6/0 or 8/0.
Tail:	4-5 white spade hackle fibers, splayed.
Body:	Black-dyed hackle stem, moose mane hair, or tying thread.
Wings:	White hen hackle tips.
Thorax:	Black fur or synthetic dubbing.

Use the various body options depending on the size hook on which you're tying. If it's size 18 or 20, use hackle stem. For, size 20 to 22, use moose mane. In size 22 or 24, use tying thread. The sizes overlap either to confuse you or to give you further options, depending on your point of view.

Trico **Sparkle Spinner** (Source: Juracek and Mathews)

Hook:	Standard dry fly, 1X fine, size 20-24.
Thread:	Black 8/0.
Tails:	White hackle fibers, split.
Body:	Black fur or synthetic dubbing.
Wings:	White Z-lon, spent.

This is the standard dressing for the male *Trico* spinner. If you were to tie it with an olive abdomen and dark brown thorax, you would have a female dressing.

Trico **Poly-Wing Spinner** (Source: Schollmeyer)

Hook:	Standard dry fly, 1X fine, size 18-22.
Thread:	Black 8/0.
Tail:	Gray Micro Fibetts, split.
Abdomen:	Olive fur or synthetic dubbing for females, black for males.
Wing:	White polypro yarn, spent.
Thorax:	Black fur or synthetic dubbing.

This is a favorite *Trico* spinner dressing, and can be varied to match the male or female simply by changing the color of the abdomen fur. It's a very practical approach to these important spinner falls, since both male and female patterns are needed at times.

Trico **Cluster Spinner** (Source: Knopp and Cormier)

Hook:	3X to 4X long, size 14-16.
Thread:	Black 8/0.
Tails:	Dark blue dun hackle fibers, split.
Wings:	White Antron or Z-lon fibers, tied spent, two pairs.
Body:	Black fur or synthetic dubbing, wound between wing pairs.
Forward tails:	Dark blue dun hackle fibers, split.

This dressing is generic for clusters of male *Trico* spinners. It can also be tied in olive to represent female duns or spinners. You could tie it with semi-spent wings to represent a couple of duns caught together by the currents, or in many other variations to suit your imagination. It has the advantage of being easier to see on the water than a fly tied to match a single *Trico*. You also get to play trout on a stouter hook. Try it; it's not the novelty it might seem at first glance. It catches selective trout.

Blue Dun Wet

Hook:	Standard wet fly, 1X stout, size 18-22.
Thread:	Gray 8/0.
Tails:	Blue dun hackle fibers.
Body:	Muskrat fur.
Hackle:	Blue dun hen, sparse.
Wings:	Mallard or teal wing quill sections.

This standard wet-fly dressing represents both *Trico* duns and spinners trapped under the water and drowned. Tie it very sparsely. Fish it on a very slow swing, either after a hatch and spinner fall are over, or during the hatch to trout feeding just under it. You can swing it through a pod of rising trout, and it will often be taken by fish that are feeding on the surface. Takes will be soft. Don't yank to set the hook with the size tippets you'll need to make this method work. You know what will happen if you do.

Soft-Hackle *Trico* Spinner
(Originator: Rick Hafele)

Hook:	Standard wet fly, 1X stout, size 18-22.
Thread:	Gray 8/0.
Tails:	Blue dun hackle fibers.
Body:	Muskrat fur.
Hackle:	Blue dun hen, sparse.

This simple soft-hackle pattern can sometimes save the day when trout seem to be extremely leader shy and even your 7X tippet looks like rope on a mirror. Fish it with the same method as your dry spinner patterns, but let it sink just below the surface film. During a heavy spinner fall some *Trico* spinners eventually get sucked under water. This pattern imitates that helpless fly, and trout sometimes seem much less critical of it than they are a dry.

Spinner Presentation
You'll fish *Trico* spinner patterns the same way you do emergers and duns. Single out a feeding trout, time its rises, cast just a foot or so upstream from it, right in its feeding lane. If the trout refuses, think about your gear and presentation before you get into a hectic scramble changing from fly to fly. A. K. Best advises you to ask two questions of yourself before changing flies: first, is your tippet fine and limp enough, second, are you putting the fly on the trout's nose? If the answer to both of those is *yes*, and trout are still refusing, then the problem might be your fly.

Idaho's famous Silver Creek is classic *Trico* water.
But a bit of advice: Don't wade, you'll scare the fish.

Chapter 21

Caenis (White-Winged Sulphurs)

FAMILY: CAENIDAE

Genus: *Caenis*
Western Species: 6
North America: 11
Important Western Species: *Caenis amica, C. latipennis*
Common Names: White-winged sulphurs, tiny white-winged curse.

Tiny *Caenis* mayflies, closely related to *Tricorythodes*, are far less important because they're not often found in habitat favorable to trout. When they do live and hatch in trout waters, their minute size and twilight emergence reduce their importance to a rarity. We mention them here because you will certainly collect them, and will at least want to know what they are. You might also encounter one of those rare cases where trout feed on them selectively when there is enough light to fish imitations of them.

Emergence and Distribution

Caenis live in both moving and still waters, most of the time those that are a bit too warm and silted for trout. We have collected them most often in habitat better suited to bluegill and bass, both of which, at least in their smaller sizes, feed on these tiny insects. However, *Caenis* are also known to hatch on Hat Creek and the Sacramento River in California, some waters in and around Yellowstone Park, and the famous seep lakes in Washington, where we've encountered them ourselves and found trout feeding on them.

Their geographical distribution is across all of North America, including all of the western states and provinces, wherever habitat is suitable to them. You will have to be on the water until dark and after it, on summer and early fall evenings, to ever notice them.

Caenis **HATCH IMPORTANCE SCORE: 18.0**

CRITERIA/SCORE	5		4		3		2		1	
Distribution: (within Western waters)	widespread		common		scattered		isolated	2.0	rare	
Abundance:	heavy		abundant	4.0	modest		trickling		individual	
Emergence type:	mid-water/slow		mid-water/fast		edges/slow		edges/fast		crawls out	1.0
Emergence time:	mid-day		early and/or late over long period		early and/or late over short period		dawn or dusk	2.0	night	
Emergence duration:	multiple seasons per year		well-defined long hatch period		well-defined short hatch period	3.0	poorly-defined long hatch period		poorly-defined short hatch	
(Behavior/Availability) **Nymph:**	excellent		good		moderate		slight		poor	1.0
(Behavior/Availability) **Emerger:**	excellent		good		moderate		slight		poor	1.0
(Behavior/Availability) **Dun:**	excellent		good		moderate		slight		poor	1.0
(Behavior/Availability) **Spinner:**	excellent		good		moderate	3.0	slight		poor	
Totals:		0.0		4.0		6.0		4.0		4.0

Caenis hatches begin in June, and continue right up until the weather cools in September. We've seen heavy hatches at both ends of that time frame on the same pond far out in the eastern Oregon desert. Unfortunately, it's a bluegill pond, though no doubt the daily and prolific hatches of *Caenis* contribute to the portly size of the handsome panfish in that spring-fed pond, which we find a good reason to go there.

Caenis hatches begin after the sun sets, and get heavy just about the time the last light is gone. In all the situations where we've found them emerging, our first clue was the sudden presence of cast whitish dun shucks all over our waders and vests. The emerging duns were flying right to the nearest solid object, which was us, and molting to the spinner stage there. Once you notice this happening, it's quite easy to watch the complete process of transformation from dun to spinner, right on your shirtsleeve. Most of the time, however, you'll need a flashlight to see it happen.

CAENIS EMERGENCE TABLE

TIME	WINTER			SPRING			SUMMER			FALL		
	Dec.	Jan.	Feb.	March	April	May	June	July	Aug.	Sep.	Oct.	Nov.
7 a.m. - 10 a.m.												
10 a.m. - noon												
noon - 3 p.m.												
3 p.m. - 7 p.m.												
7 p.m. - 10 p.m.												

Caenis nymph.

Nymph Characteristics

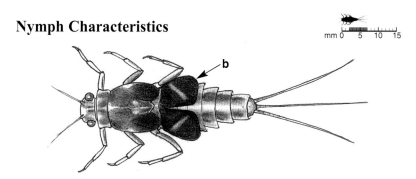

mm 0   5   10   15

a. Three tails, approximately equal in length.
b. Gills on abdominal segment 2 square-shaped and *operculate,* covering remaining gills.
c. Lacks the three prominent tubercles found on the front margin of the head of *Brachycercus.*
d. Nymph body veiled with microscopic hairs that entrap fine silt for camouflage.
e. Lack hind wing pads.
f. Body usually dark brown.
g. Minute; body length, without tails, 2-7 mm, (1/8-1/4 in).

The square operculate gill covers are distinct from the triangular shape of the operculate gills in *Tricorythodes. Brachycercus,* an even less important crawler that you might collect in warm and silted habitats, not trout habitat, will be similar to *Caenis* in almost all respects except the nymphs will have three obvious protrusions on the front of the head.

Dun Characteristics

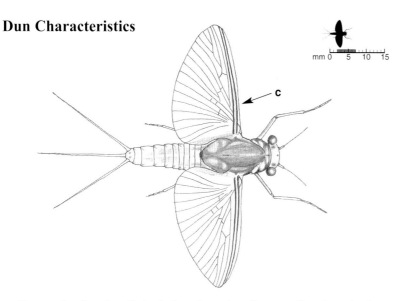

Caenis dun.

a. Three tails; female tails body length, male tails up to five times body length.
b. Lack hind wings.
c. Wings often with black stripe on leading edge.
d. Cream to whitish-tan abdomen, dark brown to black thorax.
e. Minute; body length, without tails, 2-7 mm, (1/8-1/4 in).

Spinner Characteristics

a. Three tails; female tails body length, male tails up to five times body length.
b. Lack hind wings.
c. Wings often with black stripe on leading edge.
d. Cream to whitish-tan abdomen, dark brown to black thorax.
e. Minute; body length, without tails, 2-7 mm, (1/8-1/4 in).

Habitat

Caenis nymphs prefer sluggish currents flowing over bottoms of silt mixed with detritus, fine sand, and gravel particles, or vegetative growth. They can be found most often in still pools, quiet backwaters, and along stream margins with almost no movement. They also thrive along lake margins, in the warmed shallows, and in stillwater weedbeds. We have collected the nymphs, massed prior to evening emergence, in water two to four inches deep with lots of protruding vegetation, right along the edges of Oregon's famous Davis Lake. The insects were in water no trout could navigate.

Caenis spinner.

Caenis spinner on the water, with its dun shuck still attached, as a trout might see one during and after a hatch.

   Caenis nymphs are cryptic insects, hiding or moving very slowly through their silted habitat. They almost bury themselves in silt, detritus, and mud on the bottom. The fine hairs on their bodies capture silt to cover them with camouflage.

   The duns begin to emerge just before dark, and the hatch continues after nightfall. The duns fly to the nearest vegetation or other object, and molt immediately to spinners, which fly away almost at once. The spinner flight and fall occur either during the night, or at daylight the next morning. These spinner flights are not known to be of interest to trout anglers, though it's possible that trout feed on them selectively at night or at dawn if the spinner fall takes place then.

If you get into a fishable *Caenis* hatch, it will be over a Western stillwater just as darkness falls.

Imitation

We have not seen situations where it was necessary to imitate these insects in order to catch trout. Part of that is because we are off the water most times before the hatch even starts, and are not necessarily enthusiastic about night fishing, especially when it involves size 22 to 26 flies and 7X tippets. However, it might also involve some large trout.

If this hatch interests you more than academically, or if trout in one of your home waters take *Caenis* selectively in a situation where you can see it happening and desire to match it, we recommend you fish it with your smallest *Trico* patterns. Recall that getting the size and silhouette right can be critical with insects this size, but that trout are rarely selective to color. This is especially true when it's dark and their eyes cannot register it, anyway.

If you get into a *Caenis* hatch and try to match it, you'll most likely want floating imitations, though a nymph dangled off the hook bend of your dry fly might also take trout. There is a substantial drop in size between the nymph and dun in this emergence, as the one casts its outer skin to become the other. Try a size 20 or 22 Pheasant Tail Nymph behind a size 22 or 24 hackled *Trico* dun dressing.

If you rig to fish this way, do it only in response to a hatch that you know is coming, based on previous experience on the same body of water, say you got into a hatch of these tiny white-winged curses the evening before, trout were sipping to take them, and you could not catch them. String a separate rod, long before dark, and tie on the necessary fine tippets and tiny flies while you can still see to do it. When night falls, *Caenis* duns suddenly appear all over your clothes, and trout begin to rise, unlimber that extra rod and have a go at it. Be patient; cast with wide open loops. It's easy to tangle such fine gear, and almost impossible to sort things out if a tangle happens.

If this kind of late-evening fishing works, and we've had it happen on ponds and lakes though we've not found it necessary to get so imitative to bring it off, you will probably add the most interesting moments to your day. You might also get to hold the day's nicest trout in your hands, though in truth, fishing such tiny flies and fragile terminal gear in so little light, you're more likely to have a *one that got away* story to brag about around the campfire that your friends started on shore about the time you noticed those first *Caenis* on your sleeves.

You'll run into late-evening *Caenis* hatches on many shallow, weedy western waters.

Part IV:
MAYFLY CLINGERS

FRONT WING VENATION OF HEPTAGENIIDAE

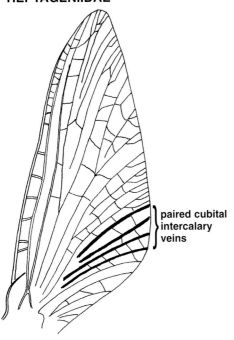

paired cubital intercalary veins

HIND LEG OF HEPTAGENIIDAE ADULT

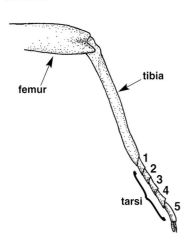

femur

tibia

tarsi

1
2
3
4
5

Introduction

Mayfly clinger nymphs are adapted to life in fast-flowing water. They are characterized by dorsal-ventrally flattened bodies, flat shovel-shaped heads that are wider than both the thorax and abdomen, well-developed lateral gills, and eyes that sit on the upper surface of their broad flat heads. Their flat shape allows them to cling closely to rocks and sticks on the bottom, avoiding the main force of the current, which passes above their thin bodies. The friction of water passing over any substrate creates a thin layer of slower water. The same principle partly explains why trout are able to hold along the bottom in brisk riffles and other water areas with fast currents. The bottom layer of current passing over cobble, stones, and boulders is slowed by friction, and trout find comfortable lies there, out of the way of water moving faster than they would be able to hold position against.

All clinger adults, duns and spinners, have two tails. They share this characteristic with swimmers and most burrowers, but it immediately eliminates all of the crawlers, which have three tails as adults. The adult clinger head retains some of the flat shovel-shape of the nymph. This helps distinguish clinger adults from the two-tailed swimmer adults, which have delicate, more rounded heads in the dun and spinner stages. All clinger adults have five distinct segments in the tarsi of the hind pair of legs. Their front wings are heavily veined and have two pairs of *cubital intercalary* veins.

Clinger mayflies are important only in streams and rivers, not in stillwaters. They thrive in fast, even torrential rapids, but also occur in slicks and eddies near fast water. They are well adapted to holding on in this habitat, but occasionally become dislodged from the bottom. The nymphs are poor swimmers, and float downstream rather helplessly until contact is again made with the substrate.

Important Clingers
The clinger group in the West consists of nine genera of various importance to Western fly-fishers, all in the family Heptageniidae. For purposes of clarity we will treat them in four chapters as separate sub-groups, some with more than one genera, because a few of the genera are very similar, and because others have been elevated from subgeneric status to full genus by taxonomists, but their relationships with trout and importance in angling terms have not changed.

Subgroups and Genera of Western Clingers
   Family: Heptageniidae.
      Subgroup 1-Genus *Rhithrogena*
      Subgroup 2-Genus *Epeorus* plus,
             Ironodes (previously *Epeorus*)
      Subgroup 3-Genus *Heptagenia* plus,
             Nixe (previously *Heptagenia*)
             Leucrocuta (previously *Heptagenia*)
             Stenonema
             Cinygma
      Subgroup 4-Genus *Cinygmula*

Chapter 22

Rhithrogena (Western March Browns)

FAMILY: HEPTAGENIIDAE

Genus: *Rhithrogena*
Western Species: 12
North America: 23
Important Western Species:
  Rhithrogena morrisoni (western March brown)
  R. hageni (western black quill)
  R. undulata (small western red quill)
  R. robusta
Common Names: Western March browns, western black quills,
  small western red quills.

Rhithrogena morrisoni, the famous western March browns, are the first large mayfly to emerge in heavy numbers during the western fly-fishing season. They are abundant and big enough, size 12 and 14, to get big trout up and feeding greedily. They hatch before spring runoff on many streams, when flows are still low and waters still in excellent fishing condition. The western March brown hatch defines the beginning of the fly-fishing season for many winter-bound anglers.

Rhithrogena have largely disappeared as fishable hatches in the eastern U.S. and eastern Canada. Nymphs of this genus demand unpolluted waters. It's a warning of what is possible in the West.

Rhithrogena **HATCH IMPORTANCE SCORE: 34.0**

CRITERIA/SCORE	5		4		3		2		1	
Distribution: (within Western waters)	widespread	4.5	common		scattered		isolated		rare	
Abundance:	heavy		abundant	4.0	modest		trickling		individual	
Emergence type:	mid-water/slow		mid-water/fast	4.0	edges/slow		edges/fast		crawls out	
Emergence time:	mid-day	5.0	early and/or late over long period		early and/or late over short period		dawn or dusk		night	
Emergence duration:	multiple seasons per year		well-defined long hatch period	4.0	well-defined short hatch period		poorly-defined long hatch period		poorly-defined short hatch	
(Behavior/Availability) Nymph:	excellent		good		moderate	2.5	slight		poor	
(Behavior/Availability) Emerger:	excellent		good	4.0	moderate		slight		poor	
(Behavior/Availability) Dun:	excellent	5.0	good		moderate		slight		poor	
(Behavior/Availability) Spinner:	excellent		good		moderate		slight		poor	1.0
Totals:		14.5		16.0		2.5		0.0		1.0

Emergence and Distribution

In the West Coast states and British Columbia, *Rhithrogena morrisoni*, the western March brown, begins to hatch as early as February after a mild winter. If the weather has been colder, or late-winter storms dump lots of cold water into the rivers, the beginning of the hatch will be delayed until March, or even to early April. Most years the hatch will go on for six to

RHITHROGENA EMERGENCE TABLE

TIME	WINTER			SPRING			SUMMER			FALL		
	Dec.	Jan.	Feb.	March	April	May	June	July	Aug.	Sep.	Oct.	Nov.
7 a.m. - 10 a.m.												
10 a.m. - noon												
noon - 3 p.m.												
3 p.m. - 7 p.m.				*R. morrisoni*				*R. hageni*		second hatch of *R. morrisoni*		
7 p.m. - 10 p.m.												

eight weeks, lasting until the end of April and on into May on many streams. On some rivers, such as Oregon's large Willamette system, there is an echo hatch of March browns in September. These late insects are usually smaller than the earlier hatches, around size 16.

R. hageni, the western black quill, is more abundant and important on waters farther inland, in the Rocky Mountain states and provinces. Hatches typically begin in late May, June, or July, and last for two weeks to a month or so. On some waters, these black quills emerge before runoff. On others the hatch comes during runoff or just after it. Our best fishing over this insect has been on the riffled sections of the Henrys Fork of the Snake River in Idaho, in the middle of June.

R. undulata, the small western red quill, is generally found in the gentler meadow reaches of high mountain streams, in most of the western states and provinces. Its emergences, because of the cooler temperatures at higher altitudes, are usually delayed into July, August, and even September.

R. robusta is a large and beautiful insect that we have collected in small numbers on many waters, but have never observed in numbers sufficient to constitute a good hatch. Fred Arbona, in *Mayflies, the Angler, and the Trout*, reports it ranging from Colorado to Canada and in fast mountain streams in California. We have collected it from the cold spring-fed Metolius River in the Cascade Mountains of Oregon. Its hatches are most common in May and June, though we confess to knowing little about their importance throughout the West. We suspect it is uncommon.

Daily spring emergences of western March browns and related species take place most often in the warmest part of the day. The best hatches are on cool and cloudy days, enhanced by light rain. The duns typically begin coming off sometime between 1:00 and 3:00 p.m., and continue to emerge on some days until 4:00 p.m. or even 5:00 p.m. These extended hatches are usually sporadic rather than heavy, which keeps the trout up and feeding eagerly and less selectively. If the spring day is sunny the hatch will usually begin around the same time, but will last only half an hour to an hour. Such a short hatch will often be heavy, and the trout can be fussy. If you neglect to capture a specimen early in the hatch, and find the correct pattern quickly, it might end abruptly about the time you solve it.

Summer hatches of *Rhithrogena* often begin an hour or so before noon, and usually last just one or two hours. If the day is cloudy, however, they will be extended into mid- or late afternoon. As always with mayflies, if the hatch is short it will be more difficult to fish, if it is spread out it will be easier to solve and will keep trout up and working less demandingly and for a longer period of time.

Fall hatches of *Rhithrogena* revert to the warmest hours of the day, from early to mid-afternoon, and are generally two to four hours in duration. Observe the size of the insects carefully when selecting a pattern to match them. Late-season duns will often be a size or two smaller than the same species emerging earlier in the season.

This widespread group of hatches, like many others that occur over the broad geography of the west, are difficult to pin down. You should be prepared to match them where and when you discover trout feeding on them. The important species of *Rhithogena* are distributed in all of the western states and provinces. One or another of them may be hatching somewhere during most days of the trout fishing season.

R. morrisoni typically prefer lowland streams, and are most important on the West Coast and at lower elevations farther inland. *R. hageni* are most often found in streams at elevations above 5,000 feet, and are more important in the Rocky Mountain region, from New Mexico in the south to Alberta in the north. *R. undulata* prefer streams at high altitudes but with gentle flows, and will usually be found in meandering waters at moderate to high elevations. It is difficult to distinguish between the species without professional knowledge and equipment. If you're able to recognize members of this group at genus level, that will tell you all you need to know in order to match it.

Nymph Characteristics

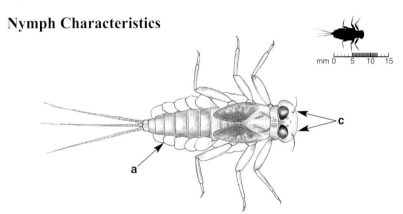

Rhithrogena morrisoni nymph.

a. Gills large; first and last pairs overlap under abdomen, forming a sucker-like disc.
b. Three tails body length or slightly shorter. Tails of mature *R. morrisoni* nymphs are distinctly white in color.
c. Eyes large; set on top of head rather than to sides.
d. Color: body ranges from olive-brown to dark reddish-brown with the underside often lighter in color.
e. Size: body length 5-12mm (1/4-1/2 in.).

Dun Characteristics

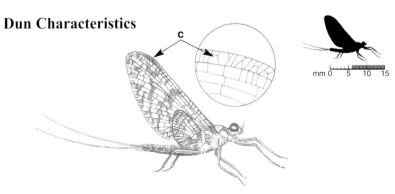

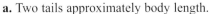

Rhithrogena dun.

a. Two tails approximately body length.
b. Head retains wide, flat appearance of nymph.

c. Wings well developed; mottled-brown, with *anastomosed veins* (heavily branched) at the upper leading edge of the forewings, forming a darkened area.

d. Color: body light- to reddish-brown or purplish-brown on back; underside much lighter, usually olive, cream, tan, or light brown.

e. Size: body length 6-15mm (1/4-5/8 in.).

Recognition of *Rhithrogena* duns to genus is not difficult using the listed characteriscs, but it is often easier to associate the duns with the nymphs from which they've emerged. Empty nymphal exoskeletons, or shucks, will be found floating in the side-currents where you stand casting to trout in the main currents, or you'll find the shucks drifting down toward you along with the duns. It is definitely worthwhile to capture a couple of nymphal shucks along with the duns you scoop into your aquarium net. By associating duns with their cast nymphal shucks, recognizing duns to genus will become much easier for the most common mayfly hatches.

Spinner Characteristics

a. Two tails body length or longer.

b. Eyes of male large and touching each other on top of head.

c. Forewings clear and heavily veined, with heavily-branched *anastomosed veins* at the upper leading edge of the forewings, forming a darkened area.

d. Color: body reddish-brown on top, tan to light brown on the underside.

e. Size: body length 6-15mm (1/4-5/8 in.).

Habitat and Behavior

Rhithrogena nymphs are clingers, adapted to living in the fastest water of riffles and even cascades. It is also common to find these nymphs, especially as they approach maturity, in medium velocity glides and runs adjacent to swift water. Their unique gills form a sucker-like disk, enabling them to cling with

Rhithrogena spinner.

Perfect *Rhithrogena* nymph habitat on a broad lowland river in Oregon.

Some *Rhithrogena* escape from the nymph shuck inches beneath the surface, and the vulnerable dun rises the rest of the way to the top, buoyed by gases trapped in the folds of the wings.

suction-cup tightness to the surface of smooth bottom stones. Their flat shape also helps them cling to stones, as it allows them to live in the thin layer of water slowed by friction along the surface of the stones. Thus, the faster current whisks over the top of these thin nymphs. The tenacity of their grip will be clear to you the first time you attempt to pull a *Rhithrogena* nymph off a wet rock in order to observe it closely.

Besides clinging to rocks tenaciously, these nymphs can also move across rocks with amazing speed. This was observed while laying in a riffle using a snorkel and wet suit, watching these and other nymphs up close. It was a sunny day, and a few *Rhithrogena* nymphs were grazing on top of some bowlingball-sized rocks. Casting a shadow over the nymphs with a hand resulted in the nymphs sprinting with remarkable speed to the underside of the rock. This was repeated several times; each time the nymphs ran to the underside of the rocks so quickly it was almost impossible to follow their movement. This suggested that any fish hoping for an easy meal of *Rhithrogena* nymphs would more often than not be disappointed.

Until mature and ready for emergence, flat *Rhithrogena* nymphs hide in small crevices between or even under stones, clinging tightly in the fastest currents, avoiding the main force of the water. They are seldom dislodged from the bottom. If dislodged, they are poor swimmers and tumble helplessly until they can regain their grip on the substrate.

Rhithrogena nymphs feed on the thin layer of diatoms and algae so common on the tops of stones in shallow riffles and runs. In the morning and evening, or on overcast days, they move to the tops of stones to feed. This foraging activity can expose them to the main force of the current, causing more to be cast into the drift.

The nymphs mature in about seven months. Several weeks prior to emergence *R. morrisoni* and *R. hageni* migrate to slower areas above, below,

Though most *Rhithrogena* nymphs live in fast water, they'll migrate to the nearest more peaceful water before emergence. So you'll often find the best fishing on flats upstream or down from well-oxygenated riffles.

or to the edges of their fast-water habitat. During these migrations more nymphs are washed off the bottom, making the pre-hatch days a good time to fish nymph imitations in streams with good populations of this group.

When ready to emerge, some *Rhithrogena* nymphs release their limpet-like grip on the bottom and rise quickly to the surface. Others, especially *R. morrisoni* and *R. hageni,* are reported to escape the nymphal shuck as duns while the nymph is still attached to the bottom. In this case the duns are buoyed to the surface by bubbles of exuded gasses trapped in the folds of the wings.

Some nymphs that leave the bottom and rise toward the surface pause a few inches beneath it, and the dun escapes the nymphal shuck there. Again, these individuals rise the rest of the way to the surface as duns, buoyed by bubbles trapped in the folds of the wings.

It is our observation that the majority of specimens during any *Rhithrogena* hatch swim all the way to the surface as nymphs, where the dun escapes the nymphal shuck in the film. Emergence is accomplished rather quickly, and there are not many cripples during a hatch of these insects.

Imitating this varied emergence activity with wet flies or nymphs fished a few inches deep produces some of the best fishing during a *Rhithrogena* hatch. Some trout will set up and feed consistently on the helpless rising nymphs and duns.

During hatches early in the year, when the air temperature is low, duns may float twenty or more feet before takeoff. This often provokes fish, which have just completed an appetizer of emerging nymphs, to start a main course of juicy duns. Dry-fly fishing can be excellent at this time. Since it is the first concentrated hatch of large insects in the average angler's trout fishing year, it's an exciting moment that your authors look forward to all winter.

Approximately two days after emergence, the newly-emerged duns molt to spinners. Mating swarms of males form in late afternoon or evening, often just after the day's emergence of duns. Females fly into the swarms and mating occurs quickly. After copulation in the air, females return to vegetation briefly to wait for fertilization of the eggs. Then they return to the water, drop to the surface, and release a cluster of eggs each time the abdomen touches the water. While we have seen mating swarms of *Rhithrogena* spinners near streams and rivers, often 40 or 50 feet above the water, we have not observed them on the water, nor have we seen trout feeding selectively on them. However, given the diversity of streams in the West, it is likely that spinners are important somewhere, sometimes. If you happen to be fishing when they are on the water, it will be important for you to imitate them.

Imitation

Rhithrogena nymph imitations are important during pre-hatch migrations of the naturals, and also when nymphs begin swimming to the surface for actual emergence. Flymph and emerger patterns have been effective for us during *Rhithrogena* hatches when both nymph and dun dressings have failed to take fish.

The floating dun can be the most exciting stage of the hatch to imitate, especially during hatches early in the season when cold weather keeps the naturals on the water for a long time. We have not seen feeding to *Rhithrogena* spinners, though it has been reported by reliable authors, and you might find situations in which spinner dressings serve you well.

NYMPH IMITATIONS

In any water where *Rhithrogena* nymphs are abundant, nymph patterns are most effective in the week or two prior to emergence of duns. Rarely do you need exact imitations. *Rhithrogena* nymphs can be imitated well enough with traditional patterns such as the Pheasant Tail, tied a bit portly, and the Gold Ribbed Hare's Ear. They should be tied on 2X long hooks, in sizes 12 through 16.

Pheasant Tail

Hook:	Standard nymph, 1X long, 2X stout, size 12 to 16.
Weight:	10-15 turns fine lead wire.
Thread:	Brown 6/0 or 8/0.
Tail:	Pheasant tail fibers.
Rib:	Fine gold wire.
Abdomen:	Pheasant tail fibers.
Shellback:	Pheasant tail fibers.
Thorax:	Pheasant or peacock herl.
Legs:	Tips of shellback fibers.

The Pheasant Tail Nymph is one you should carry in a range of sizes, since it matches so many things that trout eat. Tie it slender in the smallest sizes, 18 through 22, for the swimmer mayfly nymphs. As you get into the larger sizes, 12 through 16, use more herl fibers for the abdomen and thorax, to keep the fly in proportion. If you weight your Pheasant Tails in these sizes with wire one size finer than standard, what we call *underweighting*, you'll naturally puff them up a bit at the same time that you get them to fish at the level you'd like. Though you can get more imitative, we've never found it necessary. A Pheasant Tail tied somewhat portly captures the color and the widened shape of the natural *Rhithrogena* nymph almost perfectly.

Western March Brown Nymph (Source: Knopp and Cormier)

Hook:	Standard nymph, 1X long, 2X stout, size 12-16.
Thread:	Brown 6/0 or 8/0.
Tails:	Light brown hackle fibers or pheasant tail fibers.
Rib:	Fine coppper wire.
Abdomen:	Dark reddish-brown fur or synthetic dubbing.
Gills:	Dark gray ostrich herl along sides, captured under ribbing.
Shellback:	Dark brown turkey feather section.
Thorax:	Dark reddish-brown fur or synthetic dubbing.
Legs:	Brown partridge.

Knopp and Cormier, in *Mayflies*, recommend fixing a plastic template to the hook, or using soft lead wire that is flattened, to create a widened platform for the thorax of the fly. This better imitates the shape of the natural insect. One way to do this is to tie short strips of lead wire to each side of the hook shank in the thorax region, a method that has been called the *outrigger*. This serves to widen the body of the fly and also to sink it to the right depth to fish as a rising nymph. It's a bit slow to affix an outrigger. We usually just wrap the thorax region with a few turns of lead wire, then flatten it with pliers.

We have found that a simplified version of this fly, omitting the gills and the underlying template, works fine. A simple and fast way to accomplish a wide, flat body is to tie the abdomen and thorax with very loose, thick dubbing, then use your scissors to trim the fur from top and bottom. The result is a wide but thin nymph. In our experience such exact imitation of these nymphs is not nearly so important as fishing them correctly.

Nymph Presentation

When you're fishing imitations of *Rhithrogena* nymphs during their migrations, in the days and weeks before the hatch, or in the hours of the days on which they'll hatch later, present your patterns dead-drift right on the bottom or a very few inches above it. Trout at these times will be holding deep, and will not yet have any reason to focus their attention upward.

Rig with split shot on the leader ten to twelve inches from the fly, and with an indicator two to three times the depth of the water up the leader. Adjust the amount of shot and the length of leader between the shot and indicator until you know the fly is in that deadly zone just above those stones on which the naturals live. That's where trout will be waiting for them to arrive on the drift. Your fly should look like a helpless insect, washed off its home rocks.

Nymphs can be fished in fast water before the hatch period. Once emergence begins, the nymphs will be concentrated in calmer water, upstream, downstream, or off to the sides of riffles, near but no longer in the fastest flows. During the days of the hatch, fish these more peaceful edge currents, lightening up on the split shot and reducing the distance between shot and indicator. You still want to fish the bottom, dead drift, but it won't be so difficult to get the fly down there in the slower water.

When trout feed on ascending nymphs, during the hatch itself, you can continue to fish nymphs and do just as well, often better, than your friends who switch to emergers or dries. Take off the split shot, and fish the nymph on upstream casts to suspected lies or to observed rises. If the nymph is slightly weighted it will fish at the right depth, while a heavily-weighted nymph would plunge too deep. Leaving the indicator on the leader will not harm your fishing, and will help you detect takes.

EMERGER IMITATIONS

Rhithrogena often seem to display all of their emergence options during the same day's hatch. Some nymphs rise all the way to the top, emerge quickly to duns in the surface film. Other duns escape the nymphal shuck on the bottom and rise to the surface, buoyed by gases trapped in their folded wings. Many other nymphs rise to within a few inches of the surface, where the duns then leave the nymphal shuck and accomplish the last few inches, again buoyed by gases.

It's likely that more naturals are taken subsurface than floating during a typical *Rhithrogena* hatch. That's why imitations of the rising and emerging stage can be highly effective, and at times will work for an extended period of time both before and after a hatch. Emergers are also worth calling on when bright, sunny weather truncates the hatch. Trout will continue to be hungry after such a short, blitzing hatch, and eager to take imitations of emergers, which, not surprisingly, also resemble duns caught in the currents and drowned. The best emerger dressings look like both rising duns and drowned duns.

March Brown Spider (Originator: Sylvester Nemes)

Hook:	Standard wet fly, 2X stout, size 12-16.
Thread:	Orange Pearsall's Gossamer silk.
Rib:	Oval gold tinsel.
Body:	Hare's mask fur.
Hackle:	Brown partridge, sparse.

This dressing, from Sylvester Nemes's book *The Soft-Hackled Fly* (Chatham, 1975), is one of our favorites to fish during and after the western March brown hatch. It ofen accounts for as many trout as the dry flies that we'd rather fish when trout are willing to take them.

March Brown Flymph (Originator: Rick Hafele)

Hook:	Standard wet fly, 2X stout, size 12-16.
Thread:	Red Pearsall's Gossamer silk.
Tails:	Pheasant center tail fibers.
Rib:	Gold tinsel.
Body:	Dark hare's ear fur spun on red silk.
Hackle:	Furnace or brown hen.

This dressing, based on the notes of Pete Hidy and James Leisenring in their classic *The Art of Tying the Wet Fly and Fishing the Flymph* (Crown, 1971), was worked out early in our pursuit of this hatch, and continues to take trout to this day. If we were to be restricted to one fly to fish throughout a western March brown hatch, this might be it.

R. Morrisoni and *R. Hageni* Emerger
(Source: Knopp and Cormier)

Hook:	Standard wet fly, 2X stout, size 12-14.
Weight:	10 to 15 turns lead wire the diameter of the hook shank, or one diameter finer.
Thread:	Brown 6/0.
Tails:	Dark dun hackle fibers.
Rib:	Working thread.
Body:	Purple and black fur dubbing, mixed.
Wing:	Brown deer hair or Antron fibers, tied short.
Legs:	Brown partridge.

Knopp and Cormier call for weighting this fly heavily for *R. morrisoni* hatches and for most *R. hageni* situations, though some trout will feed higher in the water column on the latter species, and flies tied for them at times require less weight. If you fish an exact set of home waters, we recommend you work these things out, and weight your flies to fit your particular situations. If you travel and meet hatches wherever you happen to find them, as we do, then you'll be better served by weighting these emerger dressings just enough to deliver them through the surface film and sink them a few inches deep. That will cover the most common *Rhithrogena* situations. If you need to get them deeper, you can always add shot to the leader.

Emerger Presentation

You can present these emergers in one of two ways. The first, and usually most effective, is with the traditional wet-fly method, on the swing. But you must be careful to keep the swing slow or the fly will move far faster than any natural insect could ever swim. Remember that you're imitating a fragile and feeble insect being buoyed from the bottom toward the top by trapped gases. The direction of travel is vertical, with a downstream drift imposed by the current. Your fly will cut across the current on the swing, but you should mend or feed line wherever necessary to slow that swing.

The second method is upstream, and to rises, just as you would fish a dry fly. This type of presentation can be very effective, but has the one drawback that given the upstream dead-drift presentation, we'd rather be fishing a dry fly and get the visual take. If trout refuse the dry, however, a switch to the wet or emerger fished a few inches deep can at times hook trout that you would otherwise not be able to catch.

Dun Imitations

In *Mayflies* Knopp and Cormier point out that when *Rhithrogena* hatch on cool days, the duns get off the water slowly, and you will do best fishing

A soft-hackled wet fly or a flymph, fished on the swing in somewhat wrinkled water, will often take trout feeding on emergers during an early-spring *Rhithrogena* hatch.

floating imitations with a low profile, while on warm days the duns get off the water quickly, and you're better served by imitations with a high profile. Our own observations have not led us precisely to that point, yet we have noticed that during this hatch it is necessary to carry and try a variety of fly styles. One day a Compara-dun will take fish. The next it will fail entirely, and we need a parachute or hairwing dun to fool trout on the same water. We have never understood quite why. Perhaps their observations contain the solution. Your fly boxes should contain a variety of options for fishing over this widespread and prolific hatch.

We've already noted that the topsides of most mayflies are a different shade than their undersides, which trout see when they tip up to take them. The top of *Rhithrogena* dun bodies tend to be brown; their bellies are more often lighter tan with an olive cast. Keep that in mind when selecting dubbing for any floating imitation.

Western March Brown Compara-Dun
(Originators: Al Caucci and Bob Nastasi)

Hook:	Standard dry fly, 1X fine, size 12-16.
Thread:	Tan 6/0 or 8/0.
Wing:	Natural tan Compara-dun deer hair or yearling elk.
Tails:	Brown hackle fibers, split.
Body:	Tan to tannish-olive fur or synthetic dubbing.

This dressing is the standard for the hatch. It has a low silhouette, floats with the body flush in the surface film, and has an excellent wing profile. It will float very well on the gentle edge currents where most *Rhithrogena* duns emerge.

Western March Brown Parachute (Originator: Bob Borden)

Hook:	Standard dry fly, 1X fine, size 12-16.
Thread:	Tan 6/0 or 8/0.
Wingpost:	Natural brown deer body hair.
Tail:	Brown hackle fibers, split.
Body:	Tan to tannish-olive Hareline dubbing mix.
Hackle:	Brown, parachute.

This dressing, originated by Bob Borden, owner of the Hareline Dubbin' Company in Monroe, Oregon, is a standard on the Willamette River system, where the western March brown hatch is heavy. Bob's dressing offers an excellent silhouette of the natural, and floats with the proper posture necessary in all imitations for the dun. The parachute tie often takes trout when other dressing styles fail, but at rare times fails itself when one of the others works well.

Western March Brown Hairwing Dun
(Originator: René Harrop)

Hook:	Standard dry fly, 1X fine, size 12-16.
Thread:	Tan 6/0 or 8/0.
Tails:	Brown hackle fibers, split.
Body:	Cinnamon to tannish-olive fur or synthetic dubbing.
Hackle:	Brown, 5 turns over thorax, clipped on bottom.
Wing:	Natural brown deer hair or brown-dyed yearling elk.
Head:	Butts of wing hair.

This excellent René Harrop dressing has solved the March brown hatch when all other imitations were ignored by rising trout. Again, we don't know the reasons for the refusals, but now know that one dressing will never solve this hatch on every day that it happens. The hairwing style does have an advantage in that it floats well and shows an excellent silhouette of the natural body and wing on both rough water and smooth flats. It works well on all water types.

Western March Brown Biot Dun (Originator: A. K. Best)

Hook:	Standard dry fly, 1X fine, size 12-16.
Thread:	Tan 6/0 or 8/0.
Tail:	Brown hackle fibers, slightly splayed.
Body:	Tan dyed turkey biot.
Wings:	Tan dyed mallard flank fibers.
Hackle:	Brown and grizzly, mixed.

This dressing, from *A. K.'s Fly Box*, can also be tied as a parachute, using white turkey T-base for the wingpost. If you get into this hatch often, as we do, you'll want to experiment with both biot styles and possibly others. If your results are like ours, you'll wind up carrying most of the dressings we've listed and find days that you wish you had more. The western March brown is one of those major hatches for which we find it necessary to carry a separate fly box, filled with both tried and experimental imitations for *Rhithrogena* duns. Fortunately, in our own experience, dressings that fish well for *R. morrisoni* work as well for *R. hageni*.

Dun Presentation

You'll fish *Rhithrogena* dun patterns most often near the rough water where the nymphs live out their annual life cycle. But recall that the nymphs migrate to softer water before emergence, and that the duns come off in edge currents far more often than they do the rough stuff. If you were to look only at the nymphs, and ignore the duns, you would predict fast-water emergence and choose floating flies with lots of hackle, which would usually be a mistake.

Our own fishing is concentrated in the nearest flat water to the riffles and runs the nymphs call home. But the naturals often hatch on long, smooth flats as well. You should observe the duns, see where they hatch, and watch closely for trout feeding on them. Then fish the rises.

You'll fish *Rhithrogena* dun imitations most often with flat-water techniques. If the naturals are coming off in water that is at all wrinkled, you can get away with upstream presentations. If the water is smooth, try cross-stream reach casts or the downstream wiggle cast to solve such situations. The wiggle cast is especially effective when the natural nymphs have migrated upstream out of riffles to the tailouts entering from above. You must then approach the trout from the upper end of the tailout. If you do not throw some sort of slack line cast, you'll have instant drag due to the gathering speed of the currents. Your fly will leave a wake, and so will the trout as they scoot away from whichever dun dressing you've chosen to show them.

SPINNER IMITATIONS

We have yet to find a fishable spinner fall of *Rhithrogena*, which doesn't mean that you will not. If you do, there is every chance the Red Quill Spinner that we've already advised so often will serve you perfectly. If not, John Juracek and Craig Mathews list the following dressing in their book *Fishing Yellowstone Hatches*, indicating that you might get into a situation where the pattern will serve you in that area. The same dressing will work wherever you encounter spinner falls of *Rhithrogena* being fed on selectively by trout.

On the smooth flows where March browns often hatch, it pays to take up your position upstream from working trout, and cast downstream to them with a slack-line presentation.

***Rhithrogena* Sparkle Spinner** (Source: Juracek and Mathews)

Hook:	Standard dry fly, 1X fine, size 14-16.
Thread:	Tan 6/0 or 8/0.
Tails:	Brown hackle fibers, split.
Body:	Olive-brown fur or synthetic dubbing.
Wings:	White Z-lon, spent.

Like the Red Quill Spinner, this pattern is a standard that could be tied in a range of sizes and fished successfully over a wide array of mayfly spinners. In the sizes and colors listed, it is specific for falls of Yellowstone-area *Rhithrogena*.

Spinner Presentation

If you encounter spinner falls of this genus, it will be on flats below riffles or tailouts above them. Trout will feed deliberately and selectively on such water. You will need to refine your tackle to 5X and possibly even 6X tippets, long enough to give the flies freedom for a float without drag. Your casts should be gentle, presenting the flies softly to the water in position for drifts that show the fly to rising trout ahead of the telltale line and leader.

If you get into spinner falls of *Rhithrogena*, it will usually be on tailouts above fast and broken riffles.

Chapter 23

Epeorus (Pink Lady, Slate Brown Duns)

FAMILY: HEPTAGENIIDAE

Genera: *Epeorus, Ironodes.*

Western Species: *Epeorus:* 10   North America: 20
    Ironodes: 6   North America: 6

Important Western Species:
    Epeorus longimanus (slate brown dun)
    Epeorus albertae (slate cream dun, pink lady)
    Ironodes nitidus (slate maroon drakes, previously *Epeorus nitidus*)

Common Names: Slate brown duns, slate cream duns, pink ladies, slate maroon drakes, western Gordon quills, yellow quills.

Revision of this group has elevated *Ironodes* to full genus status from a subgeneric classification of *Epeorus*. Taken together—and it's very difficult to separate them—they are the only members of the clinger category to have just two tails in the nymph stage. All others have three.

Epeorus and *Ironodes* mayflies are quite common throughout the western states and provinces. The six species of *Ironodes* occur only in western states, while the genus *Epeorus* is widespread across the country, with ten western species and ten eastern/midwestern species. *Epeorus* are far better known and more important in the East, where *E. plueralis* is the base species for the famous Quill Gordon. You'll collect specimens of one genera or the other in bottom samples on nearly any brisk western trout water you fish. But they rarely hatch in densities that cause trout to feed selectively on them, and they are most often eclipsed in importance by more abundant hatches that emerge at the same time.

For practical fishing purposes, you rarely need to separate *Epeorus* and *Ironodes*. The chance exists that when you collect a two-tailed

Epeorus   HATCH IMPORTANCE SCORE: 25.0

CRITERIA/SCORE	5		4		3		2		1	
Distribution: (within Western waters)	widespread		**common**	4.0	scattered		isolated		rare	
Abundance:	heavy		abundant		modest		trickling	2.0	individual	
Emergence type:	mid-water/slow		**mid-water/fast**	4.0	edges/slow		edges/fast		crawls out	
Emergence time:	mid-day	5.0	early and/or late over long period		early and/or late over short period		dawn or dusk		night	
Emergence duration:	multiple seasons per year		well-defined long hatch period		well-defined short hatch period		poorly-defined long hatch period	2.0	poorly-defined short hatch	
(Behavior/Availability) **Nymph:**	excellent		good		moderate		slight		poor	1.0
(Behavior/Availability) **Emerger:**	excellent		good		moderate	2.5	slight		poor	
(Behavior/Availability) **Dun:**	excellent		good		moderate	3.0	slight		poor	
(Behavior/Availability) **Spinner:**	excellent		good		moderate		slight	1.5	poor	
Totals:		5.0		8.0		5.5		5.5		1.0

EPEORUS EMERGENCE TABLE

TIME	WINTER			SPRING			SUMMER			FALL		
	Dec.	Jan.	Feb.	March	April	May	June	July	Aug.	Sep.	Oct.	Nov.
7 a.m. - 10 a.m.												
10 a.m. - noon										Rocky Mountains		
noon - 3 p.m.												
3 p.m. - 7 p.m.												
7 p.m. - 10 p.m.					Pacific							

mayfly clinger nymph, and call it *Epeorus*, it might truly be a closely-related *Ironodes*. That minor mistake will make no difference to you, or the trout.

Seasonal emergence of this group begins as early as April in the West Coast region. If you fish early in the season, you'll find thumb- to wrist-thick sticks lodged in shallow riffles, completely debarked by beavers. Hoist one or two of them quickly from the water and you're likely to see several fairly large, thin, and dark nymphs shuttling to and fro, startled by this sudden access of light and absence of water. If they have two tails, which is quite likely, they are *Epeorus* or *Ironodes.*

In the same early season, you will see occasional bright-yellow points of light ascending toward streamside treetops. These are the duns that hatch from those dark nymphs you've collected from the riffles. If you can capture one, you will behold one of nature's most beautiful creations. However, you'll rarely see more than a single insect at one time, and you'll even more rarely notice one on the water, before it's lifted into the air. The chance to see this rare and beautiful mayfly should be among your reasons for fishing western streams and rivers early in the spring. That is probably the insect's only significance to your fishing. You could probably imitate it and catch trout. You'd be as well served by a standard searching dry, such as the Royal Wulff, and better served by an imitation of another insect if one happens to be hatching.

Summer hatches of two species, *E. longimanus* and *E. albertae,* can be less sporadic and more important to your fishing. They begin to emerge in late May or early June on low-elevation waters, and continue into September and even early October on streams at higher elevations. It's likely that you might see hatches at almost any time throughout the season, but even these are likely to be sporadic, and only in rare instances, for example when no other insects are around to interest trout, will they cause selective feeding and therefore be important in terms of imitation.

Daily emergence of both *Epeorus* and *Ironodes* tends to begin in mid-morning and trickle on all day, until late afternoon or evening. Again, at any one time, you are unlikely to see many individuals, or trout feeding exclusively on the naturals. When the hatches are concentrated enough to be important, it will usually be in late afternoon or evening. Juracek and Mathews report an important later-afternoon hatch of *Epeorus albertae,* their pink lady, in August on the Yellowstone River in Yellowstone Park.

Spinner falls occur in early to mid-afternoon in spring, in late afternoon or evening in summer. If daytime temperatures are unseasonably high, the spinner fall might be delayed from evening until the cool hours of the next early morning.

Ironodes nitudus, the slate maroon drake, can be of occasional importance on some British Columbia and Pacific coastal state waters. It hatches in June and July, usually in late morning or early afternoon. If you collect the insect and distinguish it from *Epeorus,* variations of dressings tied for related groups will fish as well for the nymph, dun, and spinner.

Members of the *Epeorus* and *Ironodes* genera are distributed in all western waters that remain cool through the entire year, and that have flows brisk enough to please clinger mayflies. They are not found in still-waters. In the warmer southwestern states, California, New Mexico, and Arizona, they will be found only in waters at higher elevations, where nights remain cool through summer and streams do not heat up excessively. As you move north in their range, *Epeorus* and *Ironodes* will be found at lower and lower altitudes. In British Columbia and Alberta they can be collected in lowland waters as long there are the swift riffles preferred by the nymphs. They need cobbled and rocky bottoms with abundant interstitial spaces just as much as they need cool, well-oxygenated flows.

In states between the northern and southern extremes of the Rockies, members of this clinger mayfly group will be found in some numbers in almost any moving water inhabited by trout. The brisker and cooler the water, the more abundant they'll be. If their hatches were as concentrated as those of other mayflies, they'd be as important to trout and anglers. Unfortunately, they are important only in scattered locations, and at rare times. But they are worth knowing about, and being able to recognize, because you will surely encounter them, and might find them in fishable numbers in some of your own waters.

Nymph Characteristics

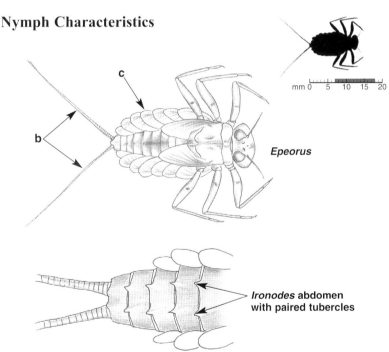

Epeorus

Ironodes abdomen with paired tubercles

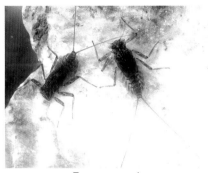

Epeorus nymphs.

Epeorus albertae nymph, pink lady.

a. Clinger nymph shape: head and body flattened, with head 1 1/3 to 1 1/2 times as wide as it is long; eyes in top of head rather than positioned to sides.

b. Two tails, body length or longer. *Epeorus* and *Ironodes* are the only mayfly clinger genera with two tails in the nymph stage.

c. Large lateral gills on abdominal segments 1 through 7, sometimes overlapping and producing a suction-cup effect.

d. Light brown to dark chocolate brown. Wing pads of mature nymphs black.

e. Body length 7-18mm (1/4-3/4 in.).

Ironodes is easily distinguished from *Epeorus* by the paired tubercles—small blunt spines—on top of each abdominal segment.

Dun Characteristics

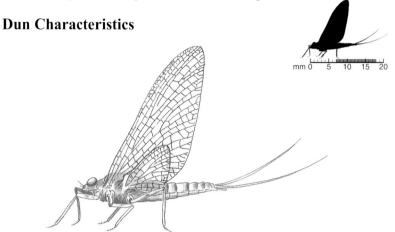

Epeorus dun.

Epeorus albertae dun, pink lady.

JOHN JURACEK PHOTO

a. Two tails approximately body length.

b. Head retains wide, flat appearance of nymph. Eyes of male duns are contiguous, meeting at the center on top of the head.

c. Wings pale gray, tan, to yellow, and well developed.

d. Body from pale cream or olive to distinct yellow. On some waters, body has a distinct pink cast.

e. Body length 7-18mm (1/4-3/4 in.).

The most consistent way to identify duns of this group is by association with the nymph from which they emerged. During a consistent mid-water hatch, collecting a cast nymphal shuck will not be difficult, though it will require that you cease fishing for a few moments and concentrate on collecting both a few dun specimens and the less visible two-tailed shucks awash just under the surface.

If the hatch is sporadic and confined to the area near the shoreline, you can often find cast nymphal shucks collecting in eddies. Before plunging in to scoop them into your aquarium net, watch the water for subtle rises. Trout often cruise a foot or two deep in eddies, waiting for the potpourri of insects that congest there. You might be able to catch one or two before you move in to collect what they've been feeding upon.

Spinner Characteristics

a. Two tails longer than the body.

b. Eyes of male large, almost touching on top of head; often black.

c. Forelegs of male are body-length or longer.

d. Wings clear, with distinct dark veins.

e. Body normally pale cream, yellow, to reddish-brown.

f. Body length 7-18mm (1/4-3/4 in.).

Habitat and Behavior

Epeorus spinner.

Epeorus and *Ironodes* nymphs are often present but not often abundant in the riffled reaches of lowland streams. They become more abundant as you move into the steeper gradients of foothill waters. They are most abundant in swift and cold mountain and headwater areas, where the types of flows to which they are best adapted are most common.

Nymphs of both genera require cold, clean, well-oxygenated water to survive. Their typical habitat is in fast, often turbulent riffles. They cling to the bottoms and sides of smooth, fist-sized or larger rocks, avoiding the strongest currents. They may also be found on tangled branches or logs that are caught in riffles.

These clinger nymphs are poor swimmers. Because of their fast-water habitat, a dislodged nymph will be carried some distance downstream before it can regain its grip on the substrate. But few of these nymphs are found in the drift, attesting to their tenacious grip. Just prior to emergence, however, the nymphs crawl restlessly to the upper surfaces of rocks, or migrate toward shore out of the fastest flows. This migration exposes them to the full force of the current, and many are dislodged and taken by trout during pre-hatch days. Such feeding by trout, deep along the bottom in or at the edges of fast water, is rarely selective.

At emergence, the duns of many *Epeorus* and *Ironodes* leave the nymphal shuck while still under water, either on the bottom or within a foot or so of the surface. The emerged dun, with its wings still compressed as they were in the wingcase and held back over the abdomen, is then buoyed to the surface by a bubble of gas. In other species, the nymph rises to the surface and the dun emerges in the surface film. While rising to the surface, whether as duns or nymphs, they are easy prey for waiting fish. Emerger patterns fished to imitate this behavior can provide excellent sport, at times even during very sporadic emergences.

Duns leave the water quickly on warm, dry days. If the weather is cold and wet, however, they might float several feet before getting airborne. After about one day the duns molt to spinners and mating flights begin to form. Swarms of some species are sparse, occurring in late evening or early morning. Other species form large swarms just as the sun leaves the water. After mating, the females return to shoreside vegetation for a short time so the eggs can be fertilized. Then they fly out over the water, dip down to it over fast riffles or very near them, releasing eggs each time the abdomen touches the surface.

Imitation

Epeorus and *Ironodes* nymph imitations are rarely necessary because of the firm grip the naturals have on the substrate. After heavy rainfalls they are tumbled in the currents more often, but fishing is seldom productive during such spates. In normal water conditions, when trout take nymphs along the bottom in fast water, it's rarely selectively, and searching nymphs bear enough resemblance to the naturals to fool most trout feeding on the drift. Their rough resemblance to *Epeorus* and *Ironodes* nymphs might be part of the reason for the consistent success of such nymphs as the Gold Ribbed Hare's Ear and Dave Whitlock's famous Fox Squirrel Nymph.

Epeorus and *Ironodes* are much more important at emergence than they are as nymphs. Duns that have left the nymphal shuck on the bottom, and nymphs rising toward the top for surface-film emergence, are both taken easily by feeding fish. Soft-hackle and flymph patterns imitate these rising emergers perfectly.

The floating dun can also be important, especially on cold, wet days when the naturals have difficulty leaving the water. High-floating patterns are perfect for picking pockets in fast runs and riffles during a swift-water clinger mayfly hatch.

Spinner flights of most *Epeorus* and *Ironodes* species are sparse and sporadic. Some species, however, form large enough swarms to be important at rare times.

Typical Rocky Mountain headwater stream with lots of clean water rushing over clean stones, the kind of habitat preferred by *Epeorus* nymphs.

Nymph Imitations

Most *Epeorus* and *Ironodes* nymph fishing can be done with traditional searching patterns such as the Gold Ribbed Hare's Ear, Fox Squirrel, or Pheasant Tail. These should be tied on size-12 to -16 hooks, and at least slightly weighted.

If you would like to tie specific imitations for *Epeorus* and *Ironodes* nymphs, try the following. Not surprisingly, they'll work very well as searching dressings, because they look so much like so many insects that get caught drifting in fast stream currents.

Epeorus Nymph (Originator: Poul Jorgensen)

Hook:	3X long, size 10-16.
Thread:	Olive 6/0 or 8/0.
Tails:	Two pheasant center tail fibers.
Abdomen:	Medium brownish-olive fur or synthetic dubbing.
Gills:	Abdomen dubbing picked out at sides.
Thorax:	Medium brown fur with guard hairs left in.
Legs:	Guard hairs of thorax fur.

This style is exceptional in its representation of the flat shape of the clinger mayfly nymphs. It comes from Poul Jorgensen's *Modern Fly Dressings for the Practical Angler* (Winchester Press, 1976). Jorgensen makes a very thick body by spinning the material on a thread loop, then roughing it up with a hobby saw. After wrapping the body on the hook, he trims the top and bottom, leaving the wide, flat shape of the natural. Not only is this concept excellent, it is easy and quick to execute. With minor variations in size and color, this style pattern will imitate any of the clinging mayfly nymphs. For the *Epeorus* and *Ironodes* you might tie it from the brownish-olive listed to a dark brown that is almost black. As always, if you're tying a fly as an imitation, be sure to collect and closely observe the natural insect you intend to imitate.

If you'd like to add weight to this style fly, you can take a few wraps of lead wire in the leading part of the abdomen and the thorax, then flatten it with pliers. This will enhance the wide and thin shape that you're after.

Epeorus Longimanis and *E. Albertae* Nymph
(Source: Knopp and Cormier)

Hook:	Standard or 1X long, size 10-12.
Weight:	10-12 turns lead wire, flattened.
Thread:	Brown 6/0.
Tails:	Light olive-brown hackle fibers, sparse and flared.
Rib:	Fine gold wire.
Abdomen:	Light to dark brownish-olive fur dubbing.
Gills:	Gray ostrich herl along sides, secured by ribbing.
Wing pads:	Black goose feather section.
Thorax:	Medium brownish-olive fur dubbing.
Legs:	Tan or olive-dyed soft-hackle fibers.

Once again, be sure that you've collected specimens from the water you're about to fish, and vary the color and size of this fly style based on what you observe. Compare the peripheral parts of the natural—gills, legs, wing pads, and tails—to the materials you're using to imitate them. No such imitative dressing is ever cast in stone because nymphs, even of the same species, vary in color from one water to the next.

Nymph Presentation

Epeorus and *Ironodes* nymph imitations should be tumbled along the bottom. Rig with split shot and strike indicator on the leader. Fish the flies upstream in riffles and runs, and down the seams between fast water and slow. Probe pocket water by wading up close, making short and accurate casts to the slight slicks and glides that form above and below boulders. Whenever you're fishing fast water, and notice a line of smooth water on the surface with no apparent cause, it likely denotes a trench down below, where the bottom has fallen away. Trout hold there and wait to intercept food from the drift. Be sure to fish your nymph so that it tumbles into such trenches.

Emerger Imitations

Some *Epeorus* and *Ironodes* rise to the surface as duns, buoyed up by gases trapped in the folds of the wings. Others rise as nymphs, buoyed to the surface by a bubble of gas that forms under the cuticle. Those that rise as nymphs emerge into the dun stage in the surface film. They are efficient emergers, and very few are crippled in the process.

The patterns you've already tied for nymphs will fish well for trout feeding on *Epeorus* and *Ironodes* that rise to the surface as nymphs. Remove the split shot from your leader and fish higher in the water column. You can remove the indicator as well, but it's often wise to leave it in place to help you detect takes to nymphs fished as emergers a few inches to a foot or two deep.

Soft-hackle patterns and flymphs, which imitate the working of the wings and legs of the ascending natural dun, are the most effective emerger patterns for those *Epeorus* and *Ironodes* that make their emergence on the bottom. These types of wet flies imitate the duns, not the nymphs, and should be dressed in a range of colors from pale creamish-olive to pale yellow, not the darker colors of the nymphs from which the duns emerge.

Partridge and Yellow Soft-Hackle
(Originator: Sylvester Nemes)

Hook:	Standard wet fly, 2X stout, size 12-16.
Thread:	Yellow Pearsall's Gossamer silk.
Body:	Two layers working thread, or one layer yellow floss.
Thorax:	Hare's mask fur.
Hackle:	Gray or brown partridge, sparse.

This pattern, from Sylvester Neme's *The Soft-Hackled Fly*, is suggestive of many *Epeorus* and *Ironodes* species rising to the surface as duns. The hackle fibers compress around the fur thorax when activated by the currents, giving the fly the wide front and quick taper of the natural. The working of the soft hackles as the fly is caught and released by turbulence represents the legs and unfolding wings of the emerged dun.

Pale Watery Dun Wingless
(Orignators: James Leisenring and Pete Hidy)

Hook:	Standard wet fly, 2X stout, size 12-16.
Thread:	Yellow Pearsall's Gossamer silk.
Hackle:	Pale honey dun hen.
Tail:	Pale honey dun hackle fibers, sparse.
Body:	Cream fur dubbing spun on yellow silk.

This wingless wet fly is tied in the style for which Pete Hidy coined the term *flymph*. The late Hidy co-authored the classic *The Art of Tying the*

Skip Morris trots a weighted generic nymph through small pools in a Cascade Mountain headwater stream. Part of the success of such stalking tactics are no doubt due to the presence of many *Epeorus* nymphs in the freestone habitat.

A soft-hackled wet fly such as the Partridge and Yellow can be devastating when fished upstream on a very short line during a sparse *Epeorus* hatch.

Wet Fly with James Leisenring in 1941. It was released in a new edition in 1971, under the title *The Art of Tying the Wet Fly and Fishing the Flymph*. The flymph style has the rough appearance of a dun that has emerged from the nymphal shuck on the bottom and must make its way to the top with its legs, tails, and wings all tossed by the currents. It's a perfect imitation for many *Epeorus* and *Ironodes* species. The style can be varied in size and color to match any of the species not imitated well by the given Pale Watery Dun dressing.

To form the rough flymph body, wax your tying silk well, spread dubbing loosely against the waxed thread, then capture the thread over the tip of your off-hand forefinger to form a dubbing loop. Twist this into a loose rope, and wrap it forward into a very loose, spiky body.

Emerger Presentation

Nemes recommends fishing his soft-hackled patterns just under the surface film. Constant mends are used to keep the fly moving at the pace of the current, without excess speed. Soft-hackles fished this way make excellent searching patterns, as well as imitating specific insects when a dressing in the right color and size is chosen.

Flymphs are also very effective when cast to visibly feeding trout. Take a position upstream and off to the side of an individual fish, or better yet a pod of fish working regularly. Cast just above and beyond the fish. Give the fly a little pull to pop it under water, or it will be caught in the surface film and float. Then let the current swing the flymph across the position of the fish. This method, used during an *Epeorus* or *Ironodes* hatch, will often bring bold takes from the most selective fish.

Dun Imitations

Occasionally *Epeorus* and *Ironodes* duns are the targets of selective surface feeding. More often they are taken sporadically and their imitations can be used as effective searching patterns when little other surface activity is apparent. The duns will ride the currents for at least a few feet, more if the day is overcast and cool.

Patterns for this stage must be selected with the habitat of the natural in mind. If the naturals emerge from fast water, it's possible that a searching dressing such as the yellow-bodied Grizzly Wulff will take trout just as well as a more specific imitation, and will have the advantage of floating better. If the naturals emerge from smoother water, which is common because the nymphs often migrate from fast water before emergence, then you will need to use a more imitative dressing.

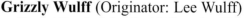

Grizzly Wulff (Originator: Lee Wulff)

Hook:	Standard dry fly, 1X fine, size 12-16.
Thread:	Brown 6/0 or 8/0.
Wings:	Red fox squirrel tail, upright and divided.
Tail:	Red fox squirrel tail.
Body:	Yellow floss.
Hackle:	Brown and grizzly mixed.

The Wulff series contains some of the highest-floating and best fish-taking flies available. While they are not often considered imitations for specific hatches, they do give the impression of many mayfly duns. The Grizzly Wulff is an excellent impressionistic pattern for many fast-water *Epeorus* and *Ironodes* duns, and is especially effective when fished during sporadic spring hatches of the bright yellow species.

Pink Lady Sparkle Dun (Source: Juracek and Mathews)

Hook:	Standard dry fly, 1X fine, size 12-16.
Thread:	Olive 6/0 or 8/0.
Wing:	Natural light Compara-dun deer hair or yearling elk.
Trailing Shuck:	Light brown Z-lon.
Body:	Pinkish-olive fur or synthetic dubbing.

This dressing, listed in Juracek and Mathews's *Fishing Yellowstone Hatches,* is specific for the hatch of *Epeorus albertae* in Yellowstone Park that happens on August and early September afternoons and evenings. The insect has a pink cast there, reflecting the nature of insects to vary in color on different waters, and causing the need to collect specimens and observe them closely before choosing imitations to match them.

According to Juracek and Mathews, the hatch emerges on the Yellowstone River in the evening on warm and bright days, in late afternoon on days that are overcast. Though cripples are rare, and trout feed on fully-formed duns, the listed sparkle dun, with its trailling shuck, works well on the smooth currents where they fish it.

Dun Presentation

If you're fishing *Epeorus* and *Ironodes* dun dressings on somewhat rough water, an upstream approach and cast are fine. As always, avoid lining the trout with a cast that causes the line and leader to fly right over their heads.

When you fish more imitative flies on smoother currents, be careful to make your approach from an angle off to the side, or from upstream. Let your position relative to a single rising trout dictate your presentation to it. If you're across stream from it, use the reach cast. If you're upstream, use the downstream wiggle cast, parachute cast, or some creative combination of the two types of casts that lets you place the fly in the feeding lane of the trout, and allow it to float downstream ahead of the line and leader, without any drag.

Spinner Imitations

In the event that you find a spinner pattern useful during an *Epeorus* or *Ironodes* spinner fall, it's likely that the dependable Red Quill Spinner will be close in color and precise in shape to the natural. In *Mayflies* Knopp and Cormier list a dressing for *Epeorus* spinners that can be tied either spent or semi-spent. It's an idea worth serious consideration, for this and for other groups of mayflies as well.

E. Albertae Spinner (Source: Knopp and Cormier)

Hook:	Standard dry fly, 1X fine, size 12-14.
Thread:	Gray 6/0 or 8/0.
Tails:	Olive-brown hackle fibers, split.
Body:	Pinkish-red fur or synthetic dubbing.
Wings:	Tan polypro fibers tied spent, or sandy dun hen hackle tips tied semi-spent.
Hackle:	Brown and cream, mixed (omit on spent version).

We can't recommend tying this dressing unless you get into a situation where your own fishing reveals a demand for it. Then we recommend you collect and observe your hatch closely, and adjust the color and size of your imitation accordingly.

Spinner Presentation

Male *Epeorus* and *Ironodes* spinners dance over fast, riffled sections of streams, usually at evening, but sometimes in the cool hours of the early morning. After mating females withdraw to streamside vegetation to allow their eggs to become fertilized. They return to the water, usually near the same riffles where they mated, and dip down to briefly contact the water, releasing a few eggs each time they touch the water. Then they rise and repeat the process several times before falling spent. Some *Epeorus* and *Ironodes* females might rest on the surface between rounds of egg-laying, usually in the semi-spent posture.

Trout take the spent and semi-spent females, most often with sipping rises, but at other times with vigorous and splashy rises. Present your spinner imitations to the rises with standard tactics, always taking your position and making your cast in order to achieve a drag-free drift.

The Yellowstone River inside the park has one of the best-known *Epeorus albertae*, pink lady, hatches.

Chapter 24

Heptagenia (Pale Evening Duns)

FAMILY: HEPTAGENIIDAE

Genera: *Heptagenia, Nixe, Leucrocuta, Cinygma.*
Western Species: *Heptagenia*: 3 western species   North America: 13
                 Leucrocuta: 3   North America: 10
                 Cinygma: 3   North America: 3
                 Nixe: 6   North America: 15
Important Western Species:
    Heptagenia elegantulata: Pale evening dun
    H. solitaria: Gray fox
    Nixe simplicoides (previously *Heptagenia simplicoides*):
         Western ginger quill
    N. criddlei (previously *Heptagenia criddlei*): Little
         slate-winged dun
    Cinygma dimicki: Western light cahill
Common Names: Pale evening dun, gray fox, western ginger quill,
little slate-winged dun, western light cahill.

With the exception of the genus *Cinygma*, which is rare and has scattered importance, all genera of this group were previously classified as *Heptagenia*. For practical angling purposes, that works as well today. Entomologists distinguish the nymphs by minor differences in the width of the labrum or the shape of the tarsal claws, things that trout do not normally notice when they're about to inhale an insect. If these distinctions concern you, however, refer to the drawings of the parts that separate the genera of what we will from now on refer to as the *Heptagenia,* or pale evening dun, complex.

Heptagenia complex   HATCH IMPORTANCE SCORE: 26

CRITERIA/SCORE	5		4		3		2		1	
Distribution: (within Western waters)	widespread	4.5	common		scattered		isolated		rare	
Abundance:	heavy		abundant		modest	3.0	trickling		individual	
Emergence type:	mid-water/slow		mid-water/fast	3.5	edges/slow		edges/fast		crawls out	
Emergence time:	mid-day		early and/or late over long period		early and/or late over short period	3.0	dawn or dusk		night	
Emergence duration:	multiple seasons per year		well-defined long hatch period		well-defined short hatch period		poorly-defined long hatch period	2.0	poorly-defined short hatch	
(Behavior/Availability) **Nymph:**	excellent		good		moderate		slight	2.0	poor	
(Behavior/Availability) **Emerger:**	excellent		good		moderate	3.0	slight		poor	
(Behavior/Availability) **Dun:**	excellent		good		moderate	3.0	slight		poor	
(Behavior/Availability) **Spinner:**	excellent		good		moderate		slight	2.0	poor	
Totals:		4.5		3.5		12.0		6.0		0.0

Emergence and Distribution

Though some coastal hatches begin as early as late May, the most important hatches of the *Heptagenia* group are in June, July, and August. At their highest elevations, for example in waters in and around Yellowstone Park, hatches peak in September, and continue on some waters into October. We were fishing a desert tailwater in far eastern Oregon one warm day in the middle of November, and came across a sporadic hatch of size 16 pale evening duns just after the sun went down. Trout had nosed into shallow edge waters and were sipping them contentedly.

The best pale evening dun hatches are typically in June and July in far-west waters, July and August in inland interior waters, and August and September in the higher elevations of the Rockies.

Daily emergence in cool weather is during the warm part of each day; early to late afternoon. In warmer weather, typical of summer, hatches are delayed until evening. We have experienced hatches heavy enough to prod trout into feeding selectively all during the afternoon, and at times just as the last light fades over the evening stream. Because we are on streams more often during the midday hours, we have fished *Heptagenia* hatches more often then than closer to dark. They are called pale evening duns, but don't fail to watch for their hatches during the afternoon.

Members of the complex are distributed throughout the entire West, wherever water flows briskly over bottoms of somewhat clean stones. While clingers are often thought of as being adapted only to fast water, some species in this group are just as abundant in the lower ends of large river systems, where flows have slowed and some siltation occurs, as they are in the upper ends with their steeper gradients and faster, cleaner water. Species of *Leucrocuta* are particularly fond of these lower and slower river sections.

HEPTAGENIA EMERGENCE TABLE

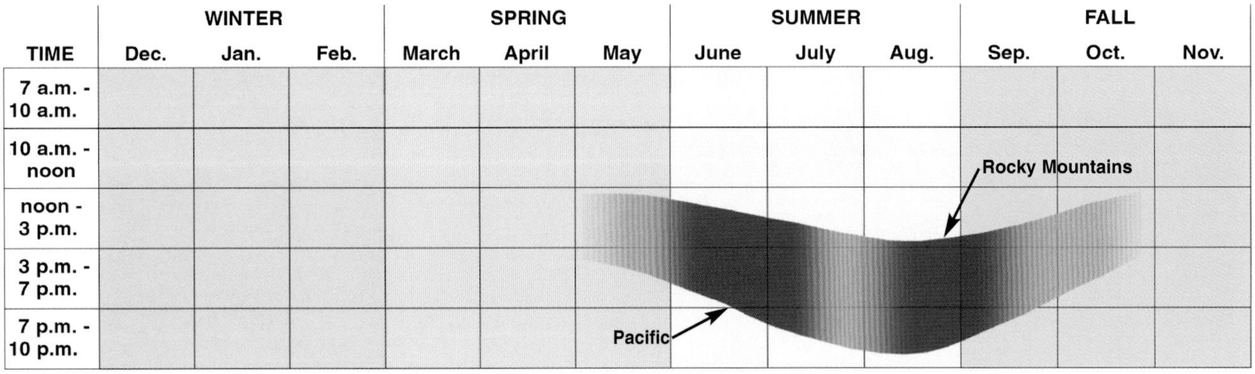

TIME	WINTER			SPRING			SUMMER			FALL		
	Dec.	Jan.	Feb.	March	April	May	June	July	Aug.	Sep.	Oct.	Nov.
7 a.m. - 10 a.m.												
10 a.m. - noon												
noon - 3 p.m.												
3 p.m. - 7 p.m.												
7 p.m. - 10 p.m.												

Rocky Mountains

Pacific

Nymph Characteristics

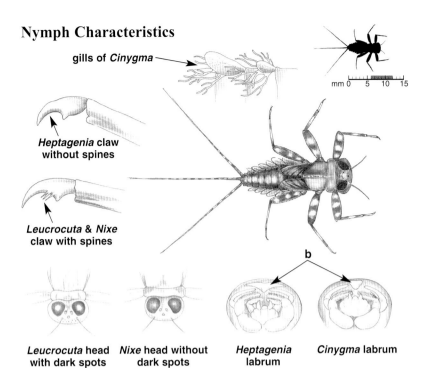

gills of *Cinygma*

Heptagenia claw without spines

Leucrocuta & *Nixe* claw with spines

b

Leucrocuta head with dark spots | *Nixe* head without dark spots | *Heptagenia* labrum | *Cinygma* labrum

Heptagenia nymph.

a. Body and head with flattened clinger shape; head 1 1/3 to 1 1/2 times as wide as it is long.

b. *Labrum* is wide, 1/2 to 3/4 the width of the head, in *Heptagenia*, and narrow, less than 1/3 the width of the head, in *Cinygma*.

c. Three tails, body length.

d. Color ranges from light olive-brown to amber or dark brown.

e. Body length 6-12mm (1/4-1/2 in.).

Dun Characteristics

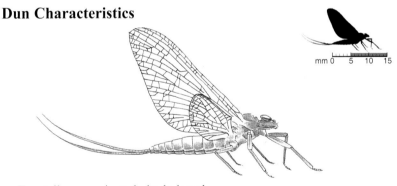

Heptagenia dun.

a. Two tails approximately body length.

b. Head retains wide, flattened appearance reflective of clinger nymph.

c. Wings well developed, with many veins; pale cream to pale tan or gray in color.

d. Body creamish-white to reddish-brown.

e. Body length 5-15mm (1/4-5/8 in.).

Spinner Characteristics

a. Two tails body length or longer.

b. Eyes of male large and nearly touching on top of head (in *Cinygma* and *Leucrocuta*, eyes of male are widely separated).

c. Wings clear.

d. Body pale cream or tan to reddish-brown.

e. Body length 5-15mm (1/4-5/8 in.).

Heptagenia male spinner.

Heptagenia female spinner.

Habitat and Behavior

Nymphs of the *Heptagenia* complex are adapted for clinging to the substrate in fast water. However, they commonly inhabit the slow to moderate reaches of the same streams and rivers where other clingers, such as *Epeorus*, live in the midst of the fastest water. *Heptagenia elegantula*, the pale evening dun and one of the most common species in the complex, is found most often in large river systems. We have fished over these hatches on the broad Willamette River, always at evening, where the duns sit in almost still shallows, and also on the brawling Deschutes, usually in the afternoon, where the duns drift slowly along in modest currents within ten feet of the banks.

Heptagenia complex nymphs will be found in all cool, clean streams, at almost all lattitudes and elevations throughout the West. They will be abundant, however, only in those reaches where the water backs away from being boisterous.

The nymphs are able to get a strong grip on the bottom, and are rarely found in the drift until the days preceding a hatch. When they do get swept into the current, they have limited ability to swim. They make quick up-and-down flips of the abdomen, but it doesn't help them make much forward progress.

A few days before emergence the nymphs migrate from water with moderate current speeds toward side pools, eddies, and shallow runs. During these migrations trout might feed heavily on the nymphs, though we've never noticed that they do this selectively. It's possible, however, that they will focus on them, and it's certain that trout feeding on bottom drift when *Heptagenia* and related clinger nymphs are on the move will not refuse an imitation that looks even a little like one.

Hatches in these peaceful edge currents begin when water temperatures reach 50-55°F. Some nymphs release their grip on the bottom and swim to the surface with those quick flips of the abdomen. Emergence takes place in the surface film. The duns escape the nymphal shuck quickly, and there are few cripples. Other nymphs rise toward the surface, pause, and the dun emerges from the nymph shuck within inches of the surface. These duns are then buoyed up to the surface by gases trapped in the wing folds.

Heptagenia complex duns tend to escape the water quickly on warm days. On cool days they often sit on the surface in still edge waters, or drift slowly along in relatively gentle side currents. They sometimes float forty to fifty feet, but time is more important than distance with these mayflies, because the current often is so slight where they hatch that trout must move to the insects rather than wait for the current to deliver the insects to them. Trout often key on these helpless duns, and feed heavily and selectively when they do. Fishing dry flies to imitate duns of the *Heptagenia* group is almost always done within a foot to at most ten or fifteen feet out from the banks.

Juracek and Mathews, in *Fishing Yellowstone Hatches,* relate fishing over cutthroat trout, on the Yellowstone River in the Park, that were feeding on *Heptagenia* duns in edge waters just a few inches deep. This reflects our own experience on many widespread western waters. As Juracek and Mathews tell it, even stupid cutts become quite wary when they're exposed to predation in water that shallow. Of course, cutts on the Yellowstone River between the lake and the first falls see so many fishermen and flies that they break all the rules about cutthroat stupidity. A few weeks into the season, they're among the most selective trout we've ever seen.

No matter where you find *Heptagenia* and related genera important in the broad span of the West, their emergences will always take place along the edges, within a few feet, or a few inches, of shore.

Male *Heptagenia* complex spinners gather in late afternoon or evening over the stream banks, hovering a few feet above the water. When females arrive, mating takes place in the air, and mated females return to rest on streamside vegetation for a brief time. Then they return to riffles or to water near riffles, dip briefly to the surface at intervals, releasing a cluster of eggs each time the abdomen touches the water.

When finished laying their eggs, the exhausted females fall to the surface and drift spent on the currents.

Imitation

If you prowl western streams much at all, you're very likely to get into *Heptagenia* complex hatches that are well worth imitating. It does not necessarily follow that you will need specific dressings to accomplish the imitation. We have been able to meet most pale evening dun nymph situations with the common run of Gold Ribbed Hare's Ears and other non-imitative nymphs we carry. In emerger situations we have discovered ourselves armed with nothing more than traditional Light Cahill wets and done very well. During many dun hatches on the Deschutes River and along the edges of many other western rivers and streams, the same dressings we use for pale morning duns have served very well when chosen in appropriate sizes.

You might find *Heptagenia* complex species more important in your own fishing, and decide you need to match them precisely. Or you might just prefer to fish a hatch with dressings specific for it. Whatever your reasons, if you find the need for imitations designed for the group, the following should fish for all stages.

Nymph Imitations

We like the approach taken by Knopp and Cormier in *Mayflies*, offering a light and dark version of a nymph for the group. If you move beyond meeting *Heptagenia* situations with whatever is in your box at the time, we suggest you try one of the following nymph dressings.

Heptagenia **Nymph, Dark** (Source: Knopp and Cormier)

Hook:	Standard nymph, 1X long, size 12-16.
Weight:	8-10 turns lead wire, flattened (optional).
Thread:	Brown 6/0 or 8/0.
Tails:	Dark brown hackle fibers, splayed.
Body:	Dark olive-brown fur mixed with trace of gray.
Wingcase:	Dark mottled brown turkey feather section.
Legs:	Brown partridge, divided.

Heptagenia **Nymph, Light** (Source: Knopp and Cormier)

Hook:	Standard nymph, 1X long, size 12-16.
Weight:	8-10 turns lead wire, flattened (optional).
Thread:	Olive 6/0 or 8/0.
Tails:	Gray hackle fibers, splayed.
Body:	Light olive-brown fur dubbing.
Wingcase:	Light or dark gray goose feather section.
Legs:	Gray grouse fibers, divided.

It's our recommendation that you always tie these nymphs lightly weighted. Flattening the lead wire will help you achieve the wide appearance of the naturals. It will also cause the flies to penetrate the film and sink a few inches if you desire to fish them in the slow and shallow water where the

You'll usually want to fish *Heptagenia* complex nymphs along the gentle edges of streams that also have brisk riffles and runs.

naturals often migrate for emergence. If you want to fish them in deeper and faster water, during the migration toward the shallows, you can always escort them down to the bottom with split shot attached to the leader.

Nymph Presentation

When you're fishing *Heptagenia* nymphs deep, rig for the standard split shot and strike indicator method, and cover the water according to Gary Borger's *shotgunning* method, using a disciplined casting regimen to show your fly to any potential lies. It's likely you'll fish pale evening dun nymphs more often, at least imitatively, in the shallows, where trout at times follow the naturals and feed on them, especially at evening. In that case, rig with an indicator but omit the split shot. Or leave off the indicator and dress your leader with dry-fly floatant to within a foot or so of the fly.

A fine way to fish nymphs during or just before a *Heptagenia* hatch is to suspend the subsurface fly on a fifteen- to twenty-inch tippet, tied right to the hook bend of a dry fly that imitates the dun that either is emerging, or will soon. This will double the chance that you'll solve the hatch, and show trout what they want. Not incidentally, it will fish the nymph at just the right depth.

Emerger Imitations

Many of the naturals escape from the nymphal cuticle a few inches beneath the surface, and rise to the surface as emerged duns. When they emerge this way, their wings are still folded but beginning to unfurl, and contain bubbles of gas within the folds. An emerger dressing is effective whenever trout feed on this stage of the insect. You can be fairly sure that whenever a hatch in the *Heptagenia* complex is in progress, an emerger dressing fished among rising trout will fool at least a few of them. Our standard solution, effective at a rate of around 50% or so, is the traditional Light Cahill wet fly that we always carry for other reasons.

Knopp and Cormier recommend imitating emergers by replacing the wingcase of the nymph imitations listed previously with short and fine deer hair, synthetic yarn, CDC, or hackle tips tied short. The colors should be tan to pale gray. It's a fine way to imitate *Heptagenia* complex emergers.

Though pale evening duns rarely emerge as cripples, Juracek and Mathews recommend fishing a Sparkle Dun through pale evening dun hatches. It's a tossup whether trout take it for an emerger or dun, but we'll list it here as an emerger.

Heptagenia Sparkle Dun (Source: Juracek and Mathews)

Hook:	Standard dry fly, 1X fine, size 14-16.
Thread:	Brown 6/0 or 8/0.
Wing:	Light tan Compara-dun deer hair or yearling elk.
Shuck:	Light brown Z-lon.
Body:	Grayish-brown Antron dubbing.

Emerger Presentation

Subsurface emergers fished for the *Heptagenia* complex can be presented in all of the ways that nymphs are fished in the shallows: with an indicator two to four feet up the leader, without an indicator but with the leader dressed with floatant down to the final foot or so, or as a dropper beneath a dry fly fished for the dun. They can also be fished on the swing, the traditional method for wet flies. But you must find a way to swim them in near the banks, where the naturals emerge and trout feed on them. You can

take your position on the bank upstream from working fish, cast out, and let the fly swing in to the trout. Or you can wade out—be careful of sending wading waves over the trout in this type of water—and cast right to the shoreline. Let the slow current tease the fly out, on the swing around and down below you.

To fish the *Heptagenia* Sparkle Dun as an emerger, simply cover rises. Tactics used with floating emerger dressings are covered more thoroughly in the following section on duns, and will be the same.

Dun Imitations

You'll almost always fish over hatches of the *Heptagenia* complex on somewhat smooth, quiet waters, along the edges. Quite often, on large river systems, the duns get caught in eddies and backwaters. At times they drift, at other times they simply sit, waiting for their wings to dry so they can lift off the water and fly out of danger from trout.

You would think that such water types would always favor low-floating imitations. Knopp and Cormier, however, report they've done better with high-floating, hackled dressings on warm days, when duns lift off the water quickly. We haven't encountered that ourselves, but can't discount it. We have had some success fishing traditional Light Cahill dries along the edges during pale evening dun hatches. Perhaps the quick liftoff of the naturals accounts for it.

Knopp and Cormier recommend dun dressings that lower the body into the surface film for days when the duns leave the water slowly. Our own fishing over *Heptagenia* complex duns is done most often with Compara-duns. A thorax-style tie, with hackle for flotation but clipped on the bottom to lower the body to the surface, might be the best compromise.

Light Cahill

> **Hook:** Standard dry fly, 1X fine, size 12-16.
> **Thread:** Tan 6/0 or 8/0.
> **Wings:** Woodduck flank fibers, upright and divided.
> **Tails:** Light ginger hackle fibers.
> **Body:** Cream badger underfur.
> **Hackle:** Light ginger.

This is an excellent eastern dry fly that translates well to many western hatches. The *Heptagenia* group is the most obvious, but the Light Cahill will also take trout during *Epeorus* and pale morning dun hatches, especially when those naturals are hatching on somewhat riffled water. Use it for *Heptagenia* in warm weather, when duns leave the water quickly.

Pale Evening Thorax Dun (Originator: Vince Marinaro)

> **Hook:** Standard dry fly, 1X fine, size 12-16.
> **Thread:** Tan 6/0 or 8/0.
> **Wing:** Pale gray or white turkey flat.
> **Tails:** Light ginger to brown hackle fibers, split.
> **Body:** Cream to reddish-brown fur or synthetic dubbing.
> **Hackle:** Light ginger to brown.

Thorax dun dressings always float on the water with the posture of the natural mayfly dun. If you tie them in a range of colors and sizes, they can be used to cover any of the hatches in this book. Preference in fly pattern styles is always a personal choice. Those who choose thorax duns won't be making many mistakes.

Vincent Marinaro originated the style, and recorded it in his *A Modern Dry Fly Code* (Crown, 1950), certainly the most original and perhaps the most important American book on dry-fly fishing. The style was subsequently modified by Mike Lawson, for his hatches on the Henrys Fork of the Snake River in Idaho. We tie it and fish it in Lawson's style, simply because it is easier to tie but just as effective over trout as the Marinaro original.

Pale Evening Compara-Dun
(Originators: Al Caucci and Bob Nastasi)

Hook:	Standard dry fly, 1X fine, size 12-16.
Thread:	Tan 6/0 or 8/0.
Wing:	Pale Compara-dun deer hair or yearling elk.
Tails:	Ginger, split.
Body:	Cream to tan fur or synthetic dubbing.

The Compara-dun style, from Al Caucci and Bob Nastasi's *Hatches*, has become pretty much our own standard for fishing over *Heptagenia* complex and many other mayfly hatches that happen most often on smooth currents. The Compara-dun style is based on Fran Betters's Haystack, from his book *Fran Betters' Fly Fishing, Fly Tying, and Pattern Guide* (by the author, 1985). The Compara-dun changes the deer-hair tail of the Haystack to split hackle fibers. Craig Mathews's Sparkle Duns are based on Compara-duns, replacing the split hackle fiber tails with Z-lon to represent the trailing shuck of the natural. Most successful pattern styles go through similar transformations over time, and the originations become tangled. The effectiveness of the changes reflects the durability and viability of the originator's concepts.

Dun Presentation
The secret to fishing imitations of *Heptagenia* complex duns is patience. Not patience to cast the fly and wait for a take, but instead patience to watch the water until a trout reveals itself feeding on the duns before a cast is made. Trout are extraordinarily cautious when feeding in the kinds of shallow waters into which hatching pale evening duns lead them. They often take naturals with such delicate sips that the merest dimple reveals the death of an insect.

Your first mission is to notice the insects in the first place. It is easy to wade past them and even through them, your focus out on the central currents where you expect insects and trout to be, your back turned to the shallow and at times almost still bank waters where trout are more rare, but where pale evening duns most often emerge.

Your second mission, after you've spotted the insects, is to move close but cautiously, focus tight, perhaps with binoculars, and watch for those rises. Once you've acquired a watchfulness, you'll notice trout feeding in many places where you had never noticed them before. That is true on all types of water, over all types of insects, not just pale evening duns, and not just at the edges.

Your final accomplishment will be to settle the fly gently to the water without spooking the trout you've spotted rising among the naturals. This will require fine rigging, with long tippets of 5X and sometimes 6X. You must work out your approach, position, and presentation carefully so that you do not alarm the trout. You'll have to cast delicately. You'll have to avoid the temptation to lift your fly off the water and set it down again when another trout rises nearby. If you rip your line

Where the water is shaped right for it, it's always best to wade out away from the bank and cast back in toward it, over rising trout, during a *Heptagenia* hatch.

off the water and spook one trout, in such water, it's likely you've spooked them all.

Spinner Imitations

We have fished over hatching duns of this group far more often than we've fished over falling spinners. Other writers report the opposite: that the duns are of minor importance, the spinners more often prompting selective feeding. You should be prepared to fish all stages of the hatch. That does not necessarily mean you need to tie dressings specifically for spinners of the *Heptagenia* complex, just that you notice when they're in the air and on the water, and know how to select and fish an imitation for them. At times, the same dressing you've used for other mayfly spinner falls, for example *Epeorus* or pale morning duns, will work as well for this one.

Though the Red Quill Spinner that we've recommended so often will work at times during *Heptagenia* complex spinner falls, the naturals most often have very pale bodies, and you'll need something with softer colors. We'll list two dressings from Fred Arbona's *Mayflies, the Angler, and the Trout* because they are elegant, and because he places emphasis on the importance of this stage of the hatch.

Western Pink-Quill Spinner, *Heptagenia elegantula*
(Originator: Fred Arbona, Jr.)

Hook:	Standard dry fly, 1X fine, size 10-12.
Thread:	Rusty reddish 6/0.
Tails:	Light ginger hackle fibers, split.
Abdomen:	Pale gray fur or synthetic dubbing.
Hackle:	3 turns light ginger, clipped top and bottom.
Wing:	Light dun hen feather tips, tied spent.
Thorax:	Rusty reddish fur or synthetic dubbing.

Western Ginger-Quill Spinner, *Heptagenia simplicoides*
(Originator: Fred Arbona, Jr.)

Hook:	Standard dry fly, 1X fine, size 14-16.
Thread:	Beige 6/0 or 8/0.
Tails:	Medium ginger hackle fibers, split.
Abdomen:	Pale cream fur or synthetic dubbing.
Hackle:	3 turns light ginger, clipped top and bottom.
Wing:	Light dun hen feather tips, tied spent.
Thorax:	Pale yellow fur or synthetic dubbing.

These two dressings, in the colors and sizes listed, will in all likelihood cover any *Heptagenia* or related spinner fall you encounter. However, as we've emphasized all along, when you get into a spinner fall that trout feed on selectively, collect your own specimens and select your own materials to match them.

Spinner Presentation

Spinner falls of *Heptagenia* and related genera will generally occur over or near riffles, at or near dusk. They are hard to notice if they occur in failing light. The dry flies listed above will be difficult to see on the water, where and when you'll usually need to fish them. If you are unable to follow the drift of the fly, consider using a strike indicator to mark it. In any case, move up close, and present the fly with casts as short as you can without alerting the trout to your presence.

If you fail to catch rising trout when *Heptagenia* spinners are in the air and on the water, try switching from a dry to a sparse wet fly. The Pale Watery Dun Wingless listed for *Epeorus* and *Ironodes* emergers makes a fine imitation of drowned *Heptagenia* complex spinners.

Fish this or a similar wet fly on the swing, through and just downstream from riffles above which the naturals are dancing. You might be surprised at the number of times you feel a soft, slowly increasing resistance to the progress of your fly as it drifts across the current. That is a trout interviewing it. Refrain from setting the hook with a jerk. Let the trout set the hook itself.

When pale evening dun spinners are present, fishing a pale wet fly or flymph on a gentle swing through a slight riffle can fool fish feeding on drowned naturals.

Chapter 25

Cinygmula (Dark Red Quills)

FAMILY: HEPTAGENIIDAE

Genus: *Cinygmula*
Western Species: 10
North America: 11
Important Western Species:
    Cinygmula ramaleyi (dark red quill)
    C. reticulata (pale brown dun)
Common Names: Dark red quill, blue-winged red quill, pale brown dun, small western Gordon quill.

Cinygmula is primarily a western genus, with only a single species found east of the Rocky Mountains. Even in the West, while widespread, it is generally of scattered and minor importance. However, as Ernest Schwiebert points out in his notes on the genus in his classic *Nymphs*, species of minor importance overall can be the most important thing locally if they hatch when you're on the water and trout become selective to some stage of them.

This is not a hatch you will find important very often. If you fish the type of cold meandering mountain waters the nymphs prefer, however, you're likely to find yourself in situations where being able to recognize and match them will help you catch trout that you otherwise might not.

Emergence and Distribution

Cinygmula ramaleyi begins hatching as early as May in Sierra Mountain waters. Their primary hatches are in June in the coastal states and provinces, and continue through June and July in the inland areas of the West. They peak in mid-July in waters both in and around Yellowstone National Park. *Cinygmula reticulata* emerges from late July through

---

Cinygmula **HATCH IMPORTANCE SCORE:** **23.0**

CRITERIA/SCORE	5		4		3		2		1	
Distribution: (within Western waters)	widespread		common		scattered	3.0	isolated		rare	
Abundance:	heavy		abundant		modest	2.5	trickling		individual	
Emergence type:	mid-water/slow		mid-water/fast	3.5	edges/slow		edges/fast		crawls out	
Emergence time:	mid-day	4.5	early and/or late over long period		early and/or late over short period		dawn or dusk		night	
Emergence duration:	multiple seasons per year		well-defined long hatch period		well-defined short hatch period		poorly-defined long hatch period	1.5	poorly-defined short hatch	
(Behavior/Availability) Nymph:	excellent		good		moderate		slight		poor	1.0
(Behavior/Availability) Emerger:	excellent		good		moderate		slight	2.0	poor	
(Behavior/Availability) Dun:	excellent		good		moderate	3.0	slight		poor	
(Behavior/Availability) Spinner:	excellent		good		moderate		slight	2.0	poor	
Totals:		4.5		3.5		8.5		5.5		1.0

August and into early September in cold-water streams at high altitudes in the Rockies and Pacific Coastal mountains.

Daily emergence typically occurs during the warmest period of the day, from late morning to late afternoon. The hatch will usually be sporadic and last two to four hours on cool and overcast days, but might last an hour or less if the weather is hot and the sun is bright.

Geographic distribution is over the entire West, but restricted to waters that retain cool water temperatures through the heat of summer. That means they will be most abundant in streams draining the Pacific Coastal mountains, higher-elevation interior streams, and spring creeks that maintain cold flows even at lower elevations. *Cinygmula ramaleyi* has the widest distribution, with fishable numbers in waters from New Mexico to Alberta, and from the High Sierra to British Columbia. *Cinygmula reticulata* is restricted to the more northerly portions of the West, with good populations extending from Oregon, Idaho and Wyoming in the south to British Columbia and Alberta in the north.

We have fished over *Cinygmula* hatches on the Metolius River in Oregon, the upper Skagit River in British Columbia, and the South Fork of the Boise in Idaho. The Metolius River is a spring creek with very cold water emerging from springs to flow through long, meandering meadow sections, over bottoms of fine gravel. The upper Skagit River is a cold mountain stream with fast choppy riffles separated by smooth glides and deep pools. The South Fork of the Boise is a tailwater stream with cold flows maintained through the summer by releases of water from Anderson Reservoir. These three different streams all have the presecription for fishable hatches of this insect: cold water, moderate stream flows, and clean gravel bottoms. Wherever you find such habitat, kick around in the gravel with a screen net. You'll probably turn up numbers of these small flattened clinger nymphs. The greater the population density your collecting reveals, the more likely you'll find trout feeding selectively on the naturals at some time during the summer season.

CINYGMULA EMERGENCE TABLE

TIME	WINTER			SPRING			SUMMER			FALL		
	Dec.	Jan.	Feb.	March	April	May	June	July	Aug.	Sep.	Oct.	Nov.
7 a.m. - 10 a.m.												
10 a.m. - noon							*C. ramaleyi*		*C. reticulata*			
noon - 3 p.m.												
3 p.m. - 7 p.m.												
7 p.m. - 10 p.m.												

Nymph Characteristics

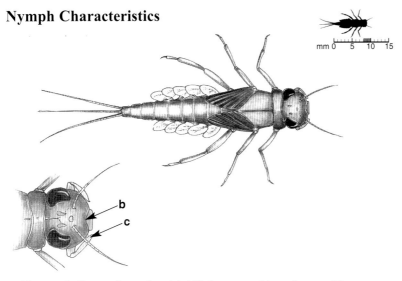

Cinygmula nymph.

a. Flattened clinger shape; head 1 1/5 times as wide as long, with eyes on top rather than to sides.
b. Front margin of head with distinct *emargination* or median notch.
c. Maxillary palpi visible, protruding to each side of head, when nymph is viewed from above.
d. Three tails.
e. Color light tan to dark reddish-brown to almost black.
f. Body length, when mature, 8-10 mm (3/8 to 1/2 in.)

Dun Characteristics

Cinygmula dun.

a. Two tails.
b. Head retains the flattened aspect of the clinger nymph.
c. Basal segment of the fore tarsi 2/3 to 5/6 the length of the second.
d. Wings gray or amber.
e. Body pale cream to olive-, orange-, red-, or grayish-brown.
f. Body length, without tails, 7-10 mm (5/16-1/2 in.).

Spinner Characteristics

a. Two tails.
b. Head retains the flattened aspect of the clinger nymph.
c. Eyes of male large and separated dorsally.
d. Basal segment of the fore tarsi 2/3 to 5/6 the length of the second.
e. Fore legs of male longer than body; forelegs of female body length.
f. Wings often with tan to yellow cast.
g. Body rusty- to reddish-brown, with darker thorax.
h. Body length 7-10 mm (5/16-1/2 in.).

Cinygmula spinner.

Habitat and Behavior

Cinygmula nymphs live under stones and in the crevices between pieces of cobble and gravel. Meandering meadow reaches and smooth glides below riffles in streams that retain cool temperatures throughout the entire year provide ideal habitat. This usually means freestone streams at altitudes over 5,000 feet, or spring creeks at lower elevations but with cold water sources. Forested coastal mountain streams from British Columbia to California also provide the needed cool temperatures for good *Cinygmula* populations.

Cinygmula nymphs are typically more abundant on streambeds of gravel or pebbles than they are where the substrate consists of larger cobble. They are rarely found where the streambed is silted from excess erosion, a frequent problem in areas of logging or the return of agricultural runoff.

Cinygmula nymphs are poor swimmers. Unlike most clingers, they are often found in the drift, probably because of their preference for the kinds of bottoms over which they must constantly clamber between small stones. They are revealed often in trout stomach samples, even during non-hatch periods. Unlike most other clingers, they do not migrate from their midstream habitat to slower edge currents prior to emergence. This is likely due to their selection of moderate flows to begin with.

Individual *Cinygmula* emerge from the nymph to dun stage anywhere between the stream bottom and the water's surface. Most swim weakly to the top as nymphs and emerge in the film. When rising for emergence in this way, the nymphs drift a fair distance before reaching the surface, and trout get an extended chance at them. Others emerge to the dun stage on the bottom and are buoyed to the surface by gases trapped in the folds of the forming wings.

The best *Cinygmula* populations are found in the headwater areas of river systems.

Duns float for a short distance on warm days, up to twenty to fifty feet in cooler weather. Hatches are typically more sporadic than concentrated. Trout tend to take stations and accept whatever stage of the insect shows up within their windows of opportunity: now a nymph, then a dun, next an emerger.

Spinner flights occur during the day, are generally sporadic, and have not been reported to be fishable in any reference that we have read. That agrees with our own experience; we have not fished over spinner falls of this genus.

Imitation

Cinygmula is a hatch you will not encounter often, and in all likelihood will be able to solve with dressings that you carry for more common hatches. The Pheasant Tail Nymph will often serve for nymphs both along the bottom, when fished with split shot and a strike indicator during periods of behavioral drift, or for the mid-depths and subsurface, when fished without weight during emergences. A western March brown imitation, selected in the appropriate size and tied with grayish-yellow wings, will fish for the duns, as will the traditional Dark Cahill dry fly. The faithful Red Quill Spinner will likely be all you need if you ever encounter such a fall of the egg-laying females that it's necessary to match them.

Nymph Imitations

During a *Cinygmula* hatch, trout often feed on nymphs just below surface. If you are tying specifically for this genus, then your nymphs should be lightly weighted. This will help them penetrate the surface film without taking them too deeply toward the bottom. If you want to fish them along the bottom, use split shot on the leader to get them there.

If you desire a specific nymph imitation, the following dressing from Jim Schollmeyer's *Hatch Guide For Western Streams* should meet your needs. You can vary its colors, if necessary, to match specimens you collect on your own waters.

Marabou Pheasant Tail Nymph (Source: Schollmeyer)

Hook:	Standard nymph, 1X long, size 12-16.
Weight:	8-12 turns fine lead wire.
Thread:	Brown 6/0 or 8/0.
Tail:	Pheasant tail fibers, flared.
Rib:	Fine copper wire.
Body:	2-4 brown or red-brown marabou fibers, as herl twisted with dubbing loop.
Wingcase:	Pheasant tail fibers.
Thorax:	Peacock herl.
Legs:	Tips of wingcase fibers.

With the action inherent in marabou, this pattern is effective for either the rising nymph or the dun buoyed up by gases. As Jim Schollmeyer notes, trout feeding during this hatch will likely take any stage of the insect they can get.

Nymph Presentation

If trout refuse your dry flies during a *Cinygmula* hatch, try fishing a nymph dressing to them just as you would the dry. Dress the leader with floatant within a foot or two of the fly. Then use upstream, cross stream, or even downstream casts to drift the fly drag-free through the lies of the rising trout. At times they'll take the subsurface fly even when it looks like they're feeding on top.

It is also effective to drop a nymph dressing off the stern of the dun used to imitate the same insect. Use this method when you see trout feeding visibly at or near the surface, but notice that some duns manage to float through the rises untouched. It's the surest sign that trout are feeding on nymphs, and that you should fish one on a dead-drift presentation, up near the surface. The two-fly setup is an excellent way to accomplish this, and to offer trout a choice in case they suddenly decide they desire duns.

A nymph can also be fished on the swing, just like a wet fly, to imitate the naturals as they are swept downstream during their rise to the surface. This method is especially effective for covering the water when a hatch is sporadic and feeding fish are spread down a fair length of stream. In the usual moderate, smooth flows these insects prefer, the wet fly method can be an effective way to cover trout without lining them, or alarming them with your wading as you move into position on them. Just move slowly downstream, casting patiently, mending to slow the swing, edging down a foot or so between casts.

Emerger Imitations

Few individuals end as cripples during a *Cinygmula* hatch, but you might find that a fly fished in the film works better than a fly floating on the surface. The following emerger might serve to take trout at such times. Collect the natural, and vary the colors of the imitation you tie according to what trout are taking on the stream you are fishing.

SRI CDC Emerger, Brown (Originator: Bill Black)

Hook:	Standard dry fly, 1X fine, size 12-16.
Thread:	Brown 6/0 or 8/0.
Tail:	Pheasant tail fibers.
Rib:	Black Krystal Flash.
Body:	Brown fur or synthetic dubbing.
Wingcase:	Dark dun or olive-yellow CDC, looped.
Thorax:	Brown fur or synthetic dubbing.
Legs:	Butts of wingcase fibers.
Head:	Brown fur or synthetic dubbing.

Emerger Presentation

You'll fish emergers for this insect on slow to at most moderate currents. Your tackle will have to be delicate. Your presentation will have to be calculated to show the fly to the trout ahead of the alarming line and leader.

Dun Imitations

It's likely that you'll be able to match the dun stage of this hatch with flies you already carry. For example Knopp and Cormier, in *Mayflies*, list the traditional Dark Cahill as an excellent imitation for the *Cinygmula reticulata* dun. It's not unreasonable to expect that the Adams would fool fish during an emergence of either that species or the more common *C. ramaleyi*. Another effective fly is the March Brown Compara-dun, or any of the other matches for the western March brown dun that we listed in the section on that insect. A couple of dressings tied specifically for the hatch follow. The wings of *Cinygmula* duns are often a yellowish-olive or amber color, so imitations might need to be adjusted accordingly.

Dark Red Quill (Source: Knopp and Cormier)

Hook:	Standard dry fly, 1X fine, size 14-18.
Thread:	Tan 6/0 or 8/0.
Wings:	Dark gray or olive-yellow calf body hair, upright and divided.
Tail:	Medium blue dun hackle fibers, flared.
Body:	Stripped reddish-brown hackle stem.
Hackle:	Brown and grizzly, mixed.

This dressing, from *Mayflies*, is tied to imitate *C. ramaleyi*. If you'd like a fly that fishes flush in the film, you could easily alter it to a Compara-dun style by using the same body and tail with a wing of deer hair or yearling elk tied in a 160-degree arc over the body. As with all hatches that are not important until you're suddenly faced with them, the more creative you get, the more often you'll solve them.

Cinygmula Parachute Dun (Source: Schollmeyer)

Hook:	Standard dry fly, 1X fine, size 12-16.
Thread:	Tan 6/0 or 8/0.
Wingpost:	Gray or amber poly yarn.
Tail:	Medium blue dun hackle figers, split.
Body:	Light reddish- or olive-brown fur or synthetic dubbing.
Hackle:	Medium blue dun, parachute.

Jim Schollmeyer lists this imitation in his *Hatch Guide For Western Streams*, one of the best sources for information about this hatch, patterns to match it, and methods with which to present them.

Dun Presentation

Cinygmula duns emerge out in open water, not off to the edges, but on slow to moderate currents. When fishing such water, always take a position relative to rising trout that puts as many conflicting currents behind you as you can. Then choose the presentation method that does not alert the visible feeding fish to your presence, and that shows the fly ahead of the line and leader. Your tackle and tactics will have to be tuned to their finest to fish successfully over any hatch on the kind of water inhabited by *Cinygmula*.

Spinner Imitations

Spinner falls of this genus have not been noticed to cause selective feeding by trout. If you get into a situation in your own fishing where an imitation is important, you can rely on the traditional Red Quill Spinner, which by now we hope you have tied to match a variety of other spinner falls. If that fails you, capture a natural and select or even create a dressing that matches it. Fish it with the same smooth-water tactics you use for any other hatch or spinner fall on the same kind of gentle water.

The Metolius River is a classic spring creek with the kinds of constant cold flows that encourage good *Cinygmula* populations.

Part V:
MAYFLY BURROWERS

Introduction

Two species of burrowing mayflies are of major importance in the West, another one minor. All are among the very largest mayflies, hatch in great numbers, but most often at night, get trout working greedily, but not always in conditions that allow you to take advantage of such heavy and selective feeding. When they hatch during daytime, usually in late afternoon on dark, gloomy days, you must be able to recognize them and be prepared with flies to match them, or you'll harvest some of the finest frustration that angling offers. Big trout will be frolicking, and you won't be able to do much about it. Because the insects are so large, even big, pisciverous trout feed on them eagerly.

Burrowers are found in both rivers and lakes. Their primary habitat requirement is a suitable substrate in which the nymphs can excavate their four- to five-inch-deep U-shaped burrows. The bottom must be soft enough to dig in, but not so soft that the burrow might collapse. Such bottoms are widely scattered throughout the entire West, usually with great spaces between: one here, another one a hundred miles to the south, a third alongside the highway on your trip up to Canada. Wherever conditions are correct, great populations of the nymphs thrive, and hatches can be extremely heavy. All important burrower hatches occur over bottoms of firm silt, soft mud, fine sand with solid enough composition to hold a burrow, or gravel fine and loose enough for the nymphs to tunnel through.

Burrowing nymphs can tolerate relatively low oxygen levels, but they are very susceptible to pollution. They are now gone from many areas where they enjoyed the original seat of their fame, in the Great Lakes and

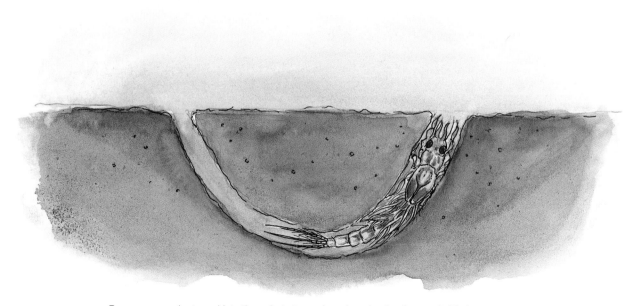

Burrower nymphs tunnel into the substrate, and are found only where suitable bottoms are soft enough for the nymphs to dig in, but firm enough to prevent their burrows from collapsing.

the Mississippi River basin, because of water degradation in those areas. Fortunately efforts to clean up areas of the Great Lakes are beginning to pay off, and large numbers of burrowers are starting to emerge once again. In the West, most waters that historically had them still support abundant nymphs, and have excellent hatches.

The large nymphs remain cryptic and hidden in their burrows during the day, and come out to crawl or swim across the bottom to forage at night. They have robust legs, for digging, and exaggarated mandibles, in the shape of tusks, again for excavation. Their rows of feathery gills, along the length of the abdominal segments, wave in rhythmic succession, causing a minor current to flow constantly through their burrows. This allows them to live in some waters so low in oxygen that they are marginal for trout.

Burrowing nymphs are excellent swimmers, moving briskly with snake-like up-and-down movements of the abdomen. When it's time to emerge, the nymph leaves the bottom, dashes to the surface, and emergence takes place in the film. Often the biggest trout working a hatch of burrower mayflies never get near the surface. They remain on the bottom, and capture the nymphs as they scuttle out of their burrows.

It takes some time for the duns to struggle free from the nymphal shuck, and then more time for fluid to pump through the veins of their large wings, stiffening them for flight. When lots of these large insects are awash or afloat on the surface, most trout, and at times even the very largest ones, turn their attention to the top.

Most burrower emergences take place at dusk or after dark, as a defense against predation from birds. This does not protect them from trout, but it does make it difficult to fish over their hatches, especially in the western states that do not allow fishing after dark. When clouds darken western skies, however, the insects will often begin to emerge in the hour or two before dusk.

These late-afternoon and early-evening hatches are the ones for which you should be prepared, especially if your bottom sampling has revealed populations of one of the burrower species in the water you're about to fish. If you find them, let that be your signal to linger until dark, or after nightfall if the law allows it.

If you enjoy getting off the water early for dinner, you'll rarely fish over a burrower mayfly hatch.

Important Western Burrowers

FAMILY: EPHEMERIDAE
Genus: *Hexagenia.*
Species: *Hexagenia limbata.*
Genus: *Ephemera.*
Species: *Ephemera simulans.*

FAMILY: POLYMITARCYIDAE
Genus: *Ephoron.*
Species: *Ephoron album.*

Chapter 26

Hexagenia (Hex)

FAMILY: EPHEMERIDAE

Genus: *Hexagenia*
Western Species: 2
North American Species: 7
Important Western Species: *Hexagenia limbata*
Common Names: Big yellow may, Michigan caddis, *Hex*, great
lead-winged drake.

The *Hexagenia limbata* mayfly produces the famous but misnamed Michigan Caddis hatch in the Midwest. The hatch is not nearly so well known in the West as it is in the north-central states, in large part because the flat lands of the Midwest produce slow-moving streams that naturally accumulate the soft bottom substrate needed by this burrowing mayfly. Western streams with the ideal conditions are more scattered and less common.

The huge mayflies of the *Hexagenia* genus have two habits that keep them hidden from anglers. First, they burrow in the mud of lake and stream bottoms as nymphs, and are rarely collected unless you have a hunch they are there and use methods that dig them out. Second, the duns begin to emerge at twilight and the hatch goes on well into the night. The spinner fall is usually concurrent with the hatch, taking place at and after nightfall. The adults are often not noticed because fishermen have usually gone home before the adults appear. On cloudy days, *Hexagenia* duns may begin to emerge an hour or two before dark.

Hexagenia limbata　　　　**HATCH IMPORTANCE SCORE:　28.0**

CRITERIA/SCORE	5		4		3		2		1	
Distribution: (within Western waters)	widespread		common		scattered		isolated	2.0	rare	
Abundance:	heavy		abundant	4.0	modest		trickling		individual	
Emergence type:	mid-water/slow	5.0	mid-water/fast		edges/slow		edges/fast		crawls out	
Emergence time:	mid-day		early and/or late over long period		early and/or late over short period		dawn or dusk	2.0	night	
Emergence duration:	multiple seasons per year		well-defined long hatch period		well-defined short hatch period	3.0	poorly-defined long hatch period		poorly-defined short hatch	
(Behavior/Availability) **Nymph:**	excellent		good		moderate		slight		poor	1.0
(Behavior/Availability) **Emerger:**	excellent		good	4.0	moderate		slight		poor	
(Behavior/Availability) **Dun:**	excellent		good	4.0	moderate		slight		poor	
(Behavior/Availability) **Spinner:**	excellent		good		moderate	3.0	slight		poor	
Totals:		5.0		12.0		6.0		4.0		1.0

Emergence and Distribution

Seasonal emergence begins in late May and early June on lowland lakes and streams in California across to New Mexico. The peak of the hatch in most Cascade, Rocky Mountain, and foothill regions starts in June and progresses, as you go up in elevation and north in latitude, into early July. The 4th of July is the perfect time for *Hexagenia* fireworks on many western streams and lakes where they occur. At high elevations in the northern states, or in Alberta and British Columbia, the hatch doesn't begin until early August. Knopp and Cormier, in *Mayflies*, report the peak of the *Hexagenia* hatch in late July and early August on Alberta's North Raven River.

The timing of the *Hex* hatch is spread across many months throughout the West, and the hatch on any given body of water, stream or lake, may last one or two weeks to five or six weeks.

Daily emergence usually begins at twilight and continues for two to three hours after dark. If the day is overcast, not an unusual occurrence in regions prone to afternoon thunderstorms, the hatch might begin in late afternoon. It can go on until and even after dark, but peak while you are still able to see well enough to fish, especially given the large size and bright color of the flies you'll be using.

Well-known hatches are widespread across the West at such locations as Flathead Lake in Montana, Hayden Lake in Idaho, the San Joaquin, Sacramento, and Fall rivers in California, and the Williamson River in southern Oregon. The hatch is spread through all of the western states and provinces, and is known even in Alaska.

The Williamson was the late Polly Rosborough's home river. His notes on the *Hexagenia limbata* hatch, in *Tying and Fishing the Fuzzy Nymphs,* are based on many years of experience, and are among the best informed.

HEXAGENIA EMERGENCE TABLE

TIME	WINTER			SPRING			SUMMER			FALL		
	Dec.	Jan.	Feb.	March	April	May	June	July	Aug.	Sep.	Oct.	Nov.
7 a.m. - 10 a.m.												
10 a.m. - noon												
noon - 3 p.m.												
3 p.m. - 7 p.m.												
7 p.m. - 10 p.m.												

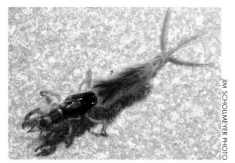

Hexagenia nymph.

Nymph Characteristics

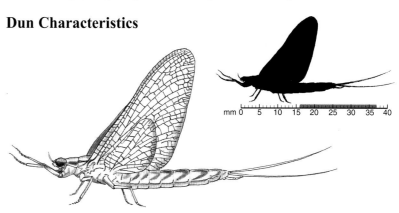

a. Head with large mandibular tusks; forelegs stout, designed for burrowing.

b. Frontal process widest at its base, its leading edge truncated, conical, or rounded.

c. Gills on segment one small and forked; those on segments 2 through 7 large and fringed, overlapping on top of the abdomen.

d. Three tails heavily fringed with fine hairs.

e. Body pale yellowish-brown.

f. Insect large; body length 12-37mm (1/2 to 1-1/2 in.).

Dun Characteristics

a. Two tails.

b. Forewings large and well developed; yellow to pale brown, with distinct cross-veining.

c. Hind wings large, half the height of forewings.

d. Body from light tan to bright yellow with distinct dark markings.

e. Body large; 16-37mm (3/4-1 1/2 in.) excluding tails.

Hexagenia dun.

Spinner Characteristics

a. Two tails, body length or longer.

b. Wings clear or tinged with yellow or brown; some veins may be darkened.

c. Body of female tan to yellowish-brown; male yellowish-brown to reddish-brown.

d. Insect large; 16-37mm (3/4-1 1/2 in.).

Habitat and Behavior

The Midwest has the perfect landscape for *Hexagenia limbata,* with low-gradient streams and lots of marl bottoms or areas layered by depositions of

Hexagenia spinner.

Polly Rosborough's home Williamson River is prime *Hexagenia limbata* habitat.

silt. The West, however, is a landscape scattered with mountain ranges, resulting in steeper-gradient streams. Silt deposits are washed out annually. Streambeds are cleaned down to stone. Burrowing mayfly nymph populations cannot take root in such typical western habitat. Wherever western streams meander, however, and allow the buildup of silt on the bottom, *Hexagenia* have a chance to get established. Their populations are scattered, confined to places with the proper consistency on the bottom.

Lakes and ponds are far more likely than streams to have mud and clay bottoms, even in steep country. That is why many of the best western *Hexagenia* populations are found in stillwaters instead of streams. Half of your authors grew up in Astoria, Oregon, less than ten miles upstream from the point where the vast Columbia River enters the Pacific Ocean. The water there is heavily brackish, the bottom mud. No trout live in such water, but an annual *Hexagenia* hatch happens there, and would tempt trout if they did.

Hexagenia nymphs feed primarily on detritus: decaying plant and animal matter, like the bodies of plankton and zooplankton that die and descend slowly to compact on the bottoms of lakes, or leaf material that gathers in the peaceful parts of streams or covers the bottoms of stillwaters. *Hexagenia* nymphs prefer cool water, but can live in somewhat warm water with low oxygen content. They are often found in waters more suited to warmwater species than to trout.

The nymph stage of the life cycle lasts one to three years, with the rate of development largely dependent on water temperature. During their growth, *Hexagenia* nymphs progress through as many as forty to fifty instars.

The nymphs dig burrows four inches to a foot deep in soft but firm mud and silt bottoms. They avoid light, remaining in their burrows during the day. They come out to forage on bottom debris at night. While in the burrow their plume-like gills ripple lengthwise in a rhythmic movement that causes a slight current through the narrow tunnel, delivering a constant flow of oxygenated water over the gills. This efficiency at extracting oxygen out of water that is not charged with it allows them to survive in waters where trout could not.

A book about western hatches implies that the subject is trout. But it's legal almost everywhere to fish for bass, bluegill, and crappie at night. A *Hexagenia* hatch might be your best opportunity to fish over selectively rising game fish of another sort aside from trout.

Hatching takes place at twilight, when the nymphs begin to feel comfortable about leaving their burrows. When they are ready for emergence, they come out of their retreats and move restlessly for a short time across the lake or streambed. Then they swim toward the surface. This is accomplished with brisk up-and-down undulations of the body, propelled in part, no doubt, by the fringed tails. When they swim, the front legs are held forward, the middle and rear legs tucked along their sides.

We have reared *Hexagenia limbata* nymphs in aquariums, and have been able to observe them swimming. They move surprisingly fast, suggesting that a stripping retrieve is at times needed to mimic their movement. Fly patterns that capture the undulating manner of the natural look more realistic than rigid dressings that move through the water like sticks.

Some nymphs pause to rest on the way to the surface, or in some cases perhaps to wait for the biological news that their nymphal skin is ready to split and allow the release of the dun at the surface. The longer the distance from the bottom, of course, the more likely the nymph will pause on the way to the top. When they rise through several feet of water, they are easy prey for feeding trout.

Transformation from the nymph to the dun, in the surface film, is accomplished quite quickly. However, the large duns, once emerged, often sit on the surface for some seconds or even minutes, often struggling to fly or fluttering to test their wings, before they are able to lift into the air. Trout at times key on the duns, and locate them by their movement on the surface. If you see or hear trout feeding in front of you, but they refuse your floating pattern, try twitching your rod tip intermittently to send out some ripples. It might attract trout rather than frightening them away.

Duns that manage to avoid the ravages of feeding fish fly to vegetation not far from the lake or stream, and rest for one to four days before shedding the subimaginal cuticle and becoming reproductive spinners. Flights of male spinners begin to gather at dusk or just after dark, either low along the edges of a stream or lake, or, at times, high above the water. Females enter the swarm, are mated, and retreat to rest briefly on nearby vegetation to allow their twin yellow sacs of eggs to fully ripen.

Ripe female spinners return to the water and ride the current or sit on the stillwater surface while extruding both egg masses into the water at the same time. Their wings are upright, and often fluttering, as ovipositing begins, but slowly collapse to the spent position when the eggs are jettisoned or soon thereafter. They die not long after all of the eggs are gone. Trout take them as targets of opportunity, in all of the postures the insects take on their way to depositing the seeds of the next mayfly generation.

On overcast days, spinner flights and even egg depositing might take place during daylight. But that will be rare. The spinner fall usually begins after dark, and often coincides with the daily—more likely nightly—emergence of duns.

Imitation

The biggest lunkers of a stream or lake may remain on the bottom during this hatch, to feed on the nymphs as they leave their burrows and scuttle over the bottom, before that dash toward the surface. You'll need imitations of the nymphs for these fish, and for pre-hatch times when you'd like to fish deep in waters with such large populations of *Hexagenia limbata* that you're pretty sure trout are taking them occasionally. Nymph imitations of such big insects can make good searching patterns, almost like streamers, because trout remember them even when it's been awhile since they've eaten them.

Trout feeding at or near the surface might be taking nymphs just before they reach the top, emergers in that brief struggle in the film, or duns on the surface itself, waiting for that moment of lift-off. One trout might concentrate on one stage, the next trout on another. Most trout will feed opportunistically on any *Hexagenia* they can get. Since spinner falls often overlap with dun emergence, trout will take spinners along with everything else. When spinner falls occur after dun emergence has finished, you may find that trout become selective to the flat-winged posture of the spinners.

If you fish waters that have this hatch, or you travel extensively and are therefore likely to come upon it by surprise, you should carry imitations of the nymph, emerger, dun, and spinner. The true key to fishing the hatch is noticing it in the first place. If you hear rumors about it on the body of water you're fishing, whether stillwater or stream, or if you suspect its presence, stay on the water late and watch for it. You'll have no trouble noticing these big, lumbering mayflies. You'll also have no trouble hearing the awesome rises of trout feeding on them.

Nymph Imitations

All nymphs tied for these large insects should have some sort of feature that captures the movement of the natural. They swim with those undulating movements, and it's not likely that trout take them when they're not swimming. They're not found in the drift, placidly riding the currents, like many other mayfly nymph forms. When one of them senses that a trout is on its tail, it will turn on its afterburners. That is why a rapid retrieve can work well with their imitations.

The movement of the naturals can be captured with such materials as marabou and rabbit fur strips. Another method is to use the wiggle nymph concept, hinging the fly in the middle. One caution with the wiggle nymph: it takes movement to bring out its action. If you fish it on the sit or with a slow retrieve, the aft half will hang down, and the fly will look more like a broken stick than a living insect.

While it's heretical to say so, and we'll not list it here as an imitation, it's likely that a size 8 or 10 Woolly Bugger, tied in yellowish-brown, would be as effective as anything during a *Hexagenia* hatch. That is speculation; we haven't had a chance to prove our theory. The following flies have been proved on trout.

It's the motion, as much as the body size, shape, and colors, that you must match with *Hex* nymphs.

Big Yellow May (Originator: Polly Rosborough)

Hook:	3X long, size 6 to 8.
Thread:	Yellow 3/0 or 6/0.
Tail:	Barred lemon woodduck fibers.
Shellback:	Lemon-dyed teal flank fibers.
Ribbing:	Yellow synthetic yarn.
Body:	Antique gold yarn.
Legs:	Lemon-dyed teal flank fibers tied in at the throat.
Wingcase:	A small bunch of lemon-dyed woodduck teal flank fibers tied in over the body, extending one-half the length of the body.

According to Polly's original instructions, in *Tying and Fishing the Fuzzy Nymphs,* the dyed teal fibers for the shellback should have a lighter cast than those for the wingcase and legs. In practical terms, trout about to wallop one might not notice that fine detail. If you're as concious of color as Polly, we recommend that you collect a few naturals and base your material selections on what you find. It's likely you'll notice some variation among the specimens, and that the trout are used to seeing the same inconsistencies.

Hexagenia Limbata Wiggle Nymph
(Originator: Fred Arbona, Jr.)

Abdomen hook:	Long-shank ring-eye hook cut to 15mm.
Thorax hook:	Standard wet fly, 2X stout, size 12.
Weight:	Thorax hook weighted with 10-15 turns lead wire the diameter of the hook shank
Thread:	Tan 3/0.
Tails:	3 strands tan ostrich herl.
Ribbing:	Fine gold wire, abdomen only.
Gills:	Dark slate ostrich herl, captured under ribbing wire.
Abdomen:	Olive-brown fur or synthetic dubbing.
Hinge:	Piano wire or 15-pound-test monofilament.
Wingcase:	Dark mottled turkey tail segment over thorax.
Thorax:	Olive-brown fur or synthetic dubbing.
Legs:	Light brown partridge fibers.

This dressing is listed in Arbona's *Mayflies, the Angler, and the Trout,* which also contains directions on how to tie it. Briefly, tie the abdomen section on a long-shank hook, and clip the barb off the hook when it's finished. Tie the hinging material in at the bend of the thorax hook, run the tag end through the eye of the abdomen hook, and tie the tag down, forming a loop. Cement this tie-in point to hold the loop firmly. Tie the thorax on the forward hook and the fly is finished.

Hexagenia Strip Nymph (Originator: Gary Borger)

Hook:	Standard wet fly, 2X stout, size 6-8.
Thread:	Tan 6/0.
Abdomen:	Gold-tan rabbit hide strip.
Wingcase:	Peacock herl.
Thorax:	Olive hare's mask dubbing with guard hairs, picked out to sides, trimmed on bottom.

This pattern, originated by Gary Borger and listed for western *Hexagenia limbata* hatches in Jim Schollmeyer's *Hatch Guide for Western Streams,* captures the look and the movement of the natural. If you buy your rabbit strips precut and in the right color, it is also easier to tie than the Wiggle Nymph.

Nymph Presentation
When fished in lakes, *Hexagenia limbata* nymph imitations should be fished deep, on the appropriate sink-tip or full-sinking line to get them to the bottom. Fish them from their position on the bottom with a stripping retrieve. You might also want to try a steady lifting motion of the rod tip, swimming the fly straight up. Pause to lower the rod and gather the line you've taken in, letting the nymph imitate a resting period of the natural. Then lift again.

In streams, fish the nymphs on or near the bottom, on the swing. Use a rhythmic pulsing of the rod tip to impart a swimming action to the fly.

If trout are feeding on nymphs, but up near the surface, in either streams or stillwaters, fish them on a floating or intermediate line. Cast them to rises, and begin the retrieve right away. If you're fishing in typical *Hexagenia* circumstances, you'll cast them to the *sounds* of rises.

Emerger Imitations

You can tie any of the listed nymphs without weight, and add a short clump of light gray or yellow-brown dyed deer or elk hair over the thorax, and you'll have a fine emerger dressing. The following fly is specific for the emerger of this insect.

Hex Foam Emerger (Source: Schollmeyer)

Hook:	TMC 206BL, size 10.
Thread:	Brown 6/0.
Tails:	Three elk-hair fibers.
Body:	Segmented yellow foam.
Wing:	Light tan deer or yearling elk hair.
Thorax:	Yellow fur or synthetic dubbing.

This dressing, from Jim's *Hatch Guide for Western Streams*, is tied with an extended body, formed with the tails attached and segmented with thread, on a needle before being transferred to the hook. These methods are listed and photographed in Ted Leeson and Jim Schollmeyer's heroic *The Fly Tier's Benchside Reference* (Frank Amato Publications, 1998).

Emerger Presentation

Rig with stout tippets, 2X or 3X, to turn over these big flies. Cast them to rises, or to the sounds of rises, and let them sit if you're on a lake or pond, and let them drift if you're on a stream. If a dead float doesn't draw any trout, try giving them a wiggle by drawing the line tight, then twitching the rod tip. The fly will send out ripples, just like a struggling natural. Most often you'll be doing this in low light, or no light at all. The coarse leader will not hurt your chances of hooking trout, and will help you land some of the largest of them.

Dun Imitations

Trout don't pass up many chances at the floating stage of an insect as large as this one. If you run into it, you'll need imitations. They hatch universally from water that is either still, or flowing slowly, because bottoms that are proper for them do not form in fast water. So your imitations not only must float, which can be difficult with such a large amount of steel in the hook, but also must look a lot like the natural. That is why some patterns are heavily hackled, and others use extended bodies of hollow hair or foam.

Though we'll not list its dressing here, the Grizzly Wulff might be an acceptable emergency pattern for the *Hex* hatch if you've got one large enough on you, and nothing nearer to the natural. Or the old but not outdated Bucktail Caddis, in size 6 or 8, might fool some fish. It's quite possible, however, that trout will demand something more imitative for such a giant insect.

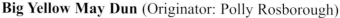

Big Yellow May Dun (Originator: Polly Rosborough)

Hook:	3X long, size 8.
Thread:	Yellow 3/0 or 6/0.
Wings:	Pale yellow hackle tips tied upright and divided.
Tail:	Barred lemon woodduck flank fibers.
Shellback:	Lemon-dyed teal flank fibers.
Rib:	Yellow working thread.
Body:	Yellow synthetic yarn with a good full taper.
Hackle:	Yellow and light ginger, mixed.

Use ten full turns of each color hackle, of high-quality saddle, to properly float this fly.

Bunse *Hex* Dun (Originator: Richard Bunse)

Hook:	Short-shank, dry fly, size 6 to 8.
Thread:	Yellow 6/0 or 8/0.
Tails:	Two mink tail, nutria, or beaver guard hairs.
Body:	Ethafoam, extended, colored with yellow waterproof marking pen.
Wings:	Bleached coastal deer hair or natural yearling elk.

The Bunse Duns, Natural Duns, or as we used to call them when Richard first started tying them, the Wonder Duns, are an unusually useful series of flies. They are not easy to learn to tie, but when you get the hang of it, and perfect the patience required to form the separate body on a needle and transfer it to the hook, with tails attached, they are not so difficult.

We've listed them in this book only for hatches in large sizes: green drakes and the *Hex*. But Richard ties them down to size 18, and uses them for hatches that include the pale morning duns and blue-winged olives. We have urged him for many years to write a monograph on the style, because we consider it an important fly style. He's an excellent artist, knows the insects, knows how to imitate them, and how to fish those imitations. He also would rather go fishing than write a monograph, so we haven't gotten anywhere with our prodding.

The steps in tying Bunse's Natural Duns are listed in Skip Morris's *Tying Foam Flies* and in Schollmeyer and Leeson's *The Fly Tier's Benchside Reference*.

Hexagenia limbata Paradrake (Originator: Fred Arbona, Jr.)

Hook:	2X long, 2X fine dry fly, size 8.
Thread:	Yellow 3/0.
Body:	Olive-brown dyed elk hair, extended.
Wing post:	Dark gray deer hair.
Hackle:	Tannish-yellow dyed grizzly saddle, parachute.
Tails:	Two dark moose body hairs.
Rib:	Working thread.

The Paradrake style, originated by Mike Lawson and listed for the *Hex* hatch in Arbona's *Mayflies, the Angler, and the Trout*, seems complex until you get the sequence of steps worked out. The body hair is tied in first, sticking out beyond the eye of the fly. Then the wingpost is tied in with the hackle fixed in at the base of it. After the tails are tied in, the body hair is reversed and the working thread used to capture and segment it to the length desired for the extended body. The hackle is then wound and tied off, and the excess body hairs trimmed away from the tail fibers. It's not the easiest style to tie, but it is one of the best when you're imitating large insects.

Dun Presentation

Rig with stout gear to propel these large flies. Lines should be in the 6- and 7-weight class. Leaders, which need not be long, since you'll be fishing most often in low light or even at night, should be tapered to tippets of 2X or 3X.

Make your casts, as always, to sighted or sounded rises. If the fly does not attract trout on the sit on stillwaters, or on a dead-drift float on moving water, try twitching your rod tip. The imparted ripples will imitate the fluttering movement of a natural testing its wings, and might incite a trout to erupt on it.

Spinner Imitations

The first consideration when you get into a spinner fall of *Hexagenia limbata* is to use the same dressing you'd use for the dun. Quite often the spinner fall and dun emergence overlap. Most often trout feed on whatever stage of the insect gets into danger in front of them. If you're fishing a dun dressing and see spinners begin to fall—you might have to flick on your flashlight and frighten a few fish to make that observation—then keep on fishing the dun dressing unless you clearly know you're getting refusals to it.

If you know you're going out to meet a *Hex* hatch, we recommend arming yourself with flies to match all stages. You might choose one of the following, or tie them all and compare them against each other to see which performs best in a fishing situation. It is the kind of opportunity that comes up too seldom in our own fishing over hatches: the chance to compare one dressing against another and see which works best. We have not been able to do that during hatches of this insect. Or maybe we'll confess to an excess of excitement when we get into one, so that we forget we're supposed to do that, and just go on laughing and fishing.

Big Yellow May Spinner (Originator: Polly Rosborough)

Hook:	3X long, size 8.
Thread:	Tan 3/0 or 6/0.
Tails:	Barred lemon woodduck flank fibers.
Body:	Yellow synthetic yarn.
Wings:	Dyed yellow deer hair, semi-spent.
Hackle:	Yellow and ginger, mixed.

TIED BY RONN LUCAS, SR.

Use high-quality hackle to keep this big dressing afloat. If you feel it improves it, you can wet your thumb and fingertips and draw the hackle fibers vigorously out to each side, parallel to the wings. They'll hold that position. This will allow the fly to float lower in the water, and might make a difference if the trout are particular about such things. In truth, this fly as Polly Rosborough tied it might be mistaken by trout for either the emerging dun or the egg-depositing spinner.

Big Yellow May Hairwing Spinner (Source: Schollmeyer)

Hook:	Standard dry fly, 1X fine, size 8-10.
Thread:	Brown 6/0.
Tail:	Pheasant tail fibers.
Body:	Yellow-dyed deer hair, extended over tail fibers.
Wing:	Light deer hair, tied spent, topped with Pearl Krystal Flash.

This fine dressing, listed in Jim's *Hatch Guide for Western Streams*, imitates the natural perfectly. Again, the steps for tying the extended body are given in Leeson and Schollmeyer's *The Fly Tier's Benchside Reference*.

Bunse's *Hex* Spinner (Originator: Richard Bunse)

Hook:	Standard dry fly, 1X fine, size 8-10.
Thread:	Yellow 6/0.
Tail:	White Micro Fibetts.
Body:	Ethafoam, extended, colored yellow with waterproof marking pen.
Wing:	White polypro macramé yarn, two strands tied spent, combed out.

The basic steps for tying the extended body for this fly are the same as those for his dun dressing, and are covered in *The Fly Tier's Benchside Reference* or *Tying Foam Flies*. Tie such exact imitations if you get into the hatch and are dissatisfied with your success. They are sure to improve it.

Spinner Presentation

It is normally after dark when the spinners begin to fall. A few minutes of fishing might be sandwiched into the last legal moments of the fishing day, in states or provinces where your fishing ends an hour after sunset. In places where night fishing is legal, this dramatic fishing period might last two or three hours. Always be sure to carry a flashlight in the back of your vest when following this elusive hatch.

Polly Rosborough worked out a system for fishing the *Hexagenia limbata* hatch with his nymph, dun, and spinner patterns. He would begin fishing in the pre-hatch period with a nymph and a three-pound-test tippet. As soon as the hatch started and duns appeared, he switched to a pre-tied four-pound-test leader with a dun dressing already attached. The change was sped by the use of connecting leader loops. The effectiveness of the dun lasted about half an hour, Polly told us, and then he switched again, taking off his entire leader and quickly looping on a five-pound leader with his spinner dressing tied to the tippet. With this he fished out the last legal light.

This system let the late Polly change flies and step up his tippet size without tying any knots in the heat of battle. It is still a good system wherever *Hexagenia limbata* hatches are found. If your laws allow you to fish at night, of course, you do not need to deal with such frenzied fly changes, since you'll be able to continue fishing as long as the hatch and spinner fall last. With such large insects, you can often continue to fish successfully for some time after the last insects are gone. Trout remain on the prowl, and they don't forget such big bites soon.

You'll have to fish in the dark to get the fullest pleasure from the average *Hex* hatch.

Chapter 27

Ephemera (Brown Drakes)

FAMILY: EPHEMERIDAE
Genus: *Ephemera*
Western Species: 1
North America: 7
Important Western Species:
    Ephemera simulans
Common Names: Brown drake.

The brown drake, like its related species the big yellow may, *Hexagenia limbata*, is more important in the Midwest than it is in the West, because low-gradient streams with the proper bottom composition for burrowers are more abundant in that flatter region. However, populations of brown drakes are heavy in western waters with appropriate bottom structure. Because of their large size, trout will pay rapt attention to them wherever they are found.

Bottoms suited to brown drakes are composed of gravel, sand, or silt rather than the firm mud or clay preferred by *Hexagenia limbata* nymphs. Populations of the two species rarely overlap. Where bottoms right for either of the two species are found, numbers will be great and trout will be attentive.

Brown drakes are rather scattered in the West, like the *Hex*, but they occur on some very important waters, and therefore are considered to constitute a more important western hatch than the big yellow mays, which though larger and locally more numerous, tend to hatch on fewer well-known waters. Brown drake hatches happen, for example, on the Henrys Fork of the Snake, the upper Gibbon in Yellowstone National Park, and on the graceful Bow River in Alberta. All of those rivers have lots of trout and large trout. Brown drakes cause them to lose caution.

Ephemera simulans   HATCH IMPORTANCE SCORE: 21.0

CRITERIA/SCORE	5		4		3		2		1	
Distribution: (within Western waters)	widespread		common		scattered		isolated		rare	1.0
Abundance:	heavy		abundant		modest	3.0	trickling		individual	
Emergence type:	mid-water/slow		mid-water/fast	3.5	edges/slow		edges/fast		crawls out	
Emergence time:	mid-day		early and/or late over long period		early and/or late over short period		dawn or dusk	2.0	night	
Emergence duration:	multiple seasons per year		well-defined long hatch period		well-defined short hatch period		poorly-defined long hatch period	2.0	poorly-defined short hatch	
(Behavior/Availability) Nymph:	excellent		good		moderate		slight		poor	1.0
(Behavior/Availability) Emerger:	excellent		good		moderate	2.5	slight		poor	
(Behavior/Availability) Dun:	excellent		good	3.5	moderate		slight		poor	
(Behavior/Availability) Spinner:	excellent		good		moderate	2.5	slight		poor	
Totals:		0.0		7.0		8.0		4.0		2.0

Oregon's Owyhee River is typical *Ephemera simulans* habitat. It holds more smallmouth bass than trout, but those few trout are often wallopers.

Emergence and Distribution

The heaviest hatches on the waters most famous for brown drakes, in the Rockies from Alberta down to the Yellowstone region, occur in late June through July. In lowland areas in the far west, they might begin emerging as early as late May. In cold streams at high altitudes in the Rockies, the hatch is often delayed until August or early September. Hatches have been reported as late as October in high elevation waters at the northern latitudes of their range.

Brown drake hatches often overlap with the tail end of the western green drake hatches, or start shortly after them, sometimes on the same waters. The size is similar, and both groups have three tails. But the similarities end there. Green drakes are midday hatches, while brown drakes emerge in the afternoon only on days with the darkest of thunderstorm conditions. Most days, brown drakes hatch at dusk or after dark.

Temperature is the dominant factor controlling emergence. The hatch period lasts for one to two weeks, beginning with light hatches when permanent water temperatures reach around 50°F, and then peaking when temperatures climb into the middle and high 50s.

Daily emergence typically begins at twilight, and continues on through evening and after dark. If the weather is overcast and cool, it might advance into late afternoon. Jim Schollmeyer suggests that you nose around the eddies and backwaters of streams and rivers known to have populations of brown drakes, looking for the large cast shucks of the nymphs. This is an indication that the hatch has started. On finding such evidence, then you should hang around until dark, rather than departing early.

Ephemera simulans is the only western species of this genus, and is distributed from the Rocky Mountains to the Pacific Coast, and from Northern California to the Yukon. It dwindles west of the Cascades, however, and the best populations are found in the Rocky Mountain states.

The hatch occurs on many waters that are not suitable habitat for trout, as you would suspect of a hatch that requires low-gradient flows for the deposition of appropriate bottom types. For example, we have collected it from the desert Owyhee River, at the corner of Oregon, Idaho, and Nevada, but that river, while holding some trout, is better habitat for smallmouth bass. The lower Yellowstone River, near the confluence of the Mussleshell River, is populated with brown drakes, but is far downstream from the most productive trout water.

Brown drakes are also known from lakes, though more often in the Midwest than the West. Once again, the bottom must have the correct composition for the burrowing nymphs. We have not collected them ourselves from western stillwaters, and have seen no reference to specific lakes with important hatches. Like the slightly larger *Hex*, it's a hatch for which you need to be on the lookout, with a few flies in your boxes in case you run into it.

EPHEMERA EMERGENCE TABLE

TIME	WINTER			SPRING			SUMMER			FALL		
	Dec.	Jan.	Feb.	March	April	May	June	July	Aug.	Sep.	Oct.	Nov.
7 a.m. - 10 a.m.												
10 a.m. - noon												
noon - 3 p.m.												
3 p.m. - 7 p.m.												
7 p.m. - 10 p.m.												

Nymph Characteristics

Ephemera nymph

a. Head with prominent mandibular tusks; forelegs designed for burrowing.

b. Frontal process forked rather than rounded; widest at apex.

c. Gills on segment 1 small and forked; gills on segments 2-7 large, fringed, overlapping above abdomen.

d. Three tails fringed with fine hairs.

e. Body pale yellowish-brown.

f. Body length, without tails, 12-20mm (1/2-3/4 in.).

Dun Characteristics

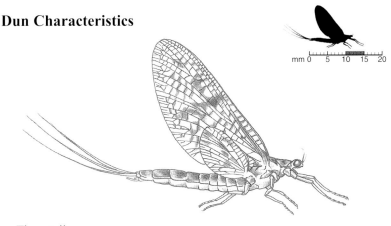

Ephemera dun.

a. Three tails.

b. Wings well developed; pale brown with dark markings.

c. Body long and slender; yellowish-tan to brown with dark markings on the back of the abdominal segments.

d. Body large, 10-15mm (3/8-5/8 in.).

Spinner Characteristics

a. Three well-developed tails.

b. Wings with dark markings.

c. Body yellowish-tan to brown with dark markings on the back of the abdominal segments.

d. Body large, 10-15mm (3/8-5/8 in.).

Habitat and Behavior

Ephemera simulans nymphs inhabit the slow-flowing areas of cool to cold streams, rivers, and scattered lakes with appropriate bottoms to allow their burrowing. Their most common habitat is found in meandering meadow-type streams with fine gravel bottoms. They are not found in higher-gradient freestone streams with brisk currents that scour the bottom of fine particulate matter. The nymphs emplace their U-shaped burrows, from four inches to a foot deep, in bottoms of fine sand, gravel, or silt, but not in the mud and clay bottom types where *Hexagenia limbata* prefer to dig their burrows.

Unlike the scavenger-feeding *H. limbata*, the nymphs of *E. simulans* are thought to be mostly carnivorous, capturing insects and other small animals. They normally mature in a single year; two years may be required in areas where the water remains cold the entire year.

Brown drake nymphs remain in their burrows during daylight hours, speculated to be a response to photo-sensitivity as much as to avoid trout predation, though who knows how the cart got harnessed to the horse; it might be that the photo-sensitivity developed because those individuals that trotted around on the bottom during daylight got eaten by trout, and failed to pass their genes along to any progeny.

While in the burrow during the day, brown drake nymphs constantly wave their plume-like gills along their backs in a rhythmic pulse that creates a minor current through the burrow. This washes the gills with aerated water. The nymphs come out to forage across the bottom when light levels fall at dusk. They continue to feed during the night, and return to their burrows at or before the first light of the next dawn.

When mature and ready for emergence, brown drake nymphs leave their burrows and make a rapid ascent to the surface. They swim with up-and-down undulations of the abdomen. Fly patterns that match them are more effective when tied with materials that capture this movement. The brown drake is most available to trout during this rise from the bottom for emergence, and it's probable that a lot more nymphs are taken during a hatch than duns, even when the latter become available to trout. The nymphs sometimes mass for emergence around lake shorelines or in slow areas of streams, causing even the largest trout to move into areas where they are vulnerable to anglers.

The ascending nymph pauses a few inches to a couple of feet beneath the surface film. The nymphal shuck is cast there, and the dun finishes the rise to the surface, assisted by bubbles trapped in the wing folds. Emergence through the film is fairly swift for so large an insect, and few are crippled during emergence. The duns usually drift just a short distance before they are able to leave the water and escape the threat of trout predation.

The final molt to the spinner stage takes place during either the first or second night after emergence, and the fully mature insect is then ready for mating and egg laying. Males gather in flights over stream margins at twilight, flying in somewhat circular patterns low over the edges. At nightfall the males elevate, swarms of females move in under them, and the males descend into their midst to mate. The spinners are exceptionally good flyers for mayflies, flying with a quick darting dance rather than the slow up-and-down flights of other species.

When mating is complete, both sexes fall spent to the water, often still connected. They separate, the females extrude their egg masses, and both sexes die spent on the water. These dense spinner falls can offer good fishing if you're able to notice them in the dark, and if you're allowed by fishing regulations to fish late enough to imitate them.

Some portions of the Henrys Fork of the Snake River are excellent habitat for brown drake nymphs.

Imitation

Trout seem to consume brown drake nymphs in large proportion over duns and spinners, which might be due to the greater availability of the nymph stage. Duns get off the water quickly. Spinner falls are elusive, and happen most often after dark, which makes it difficult to observe precisely when trout are feeding on them.

That does not mean that you'll always catch more trout on nymphs. We appreciate the admission in John Juracek and Craig Mathews's book *Fishing Yellowstone Hatches* that the nymph patterns they've tried look right but underachieve for them. They conclude that, "...this is one hatch that can still use more study."

When trout feed on insects of this size, especially in low light, they are often opportunistic. Though they take more nymphs, again because the nymphs are more available, there is a good chance they'll take your dry imitation of the dun, which is easier to fish effectively. With this and many other large hatches, when a nymph doesn't work, try a dry and see if trout will accept it.

Fish nymph imitations in the hours before a hatch. If you have the right pattern and fish it the way trout want it, it can be effective right through the hatch. But carry imitations for all stages, and be prepared not only to switch until you find what works, but also to try various methods of presentation until you find the one that pleases the critical eye of the trout.

You won't fish imitations of brown drakes on anything but smooth water. Because their populations are heavy on some waters that are heavily pestered by anglers, you'll not often get a chance to fish them over foolish trout.

Nymph Imitations

Trout feed on brown drake nymphs along the bottom, in the mid-depths when the naturals are on the rise, and just subsurface during emergence. The naturals are long, slender, and only slightly tapered. Their imitations should be tied on 2X or 3X long hooks. Keep in mind the undulating movement of the nymph as it swims. You'll want to imitate that motion, with whatever you tie, as much as the exact shape of the insect.

Brown Drake Nymph (Source: Knopp and Cormier)

Hook:	3X long, size 6-10.
Weight:	10-20 turns lead wire, diameter of the hook shank.
Tails:	Three light olive-brown ostrich herls.
Rib:	Fine gold wire.
Gills:	Pale gray ostrich herl on top of abdomen, secured by ribbing wire.
Abdomen:	Light yellowish-tan fur or synthetic dubbing.
Thorax:	Light yellowish-tan fur or synthetic dubbing.
Wing pads:	Mottled dark turkey feather segments tied along sides of thorax.
Legs:	Olive-dyed partridge fibers.

Knopp and Cormier, in their *Mayflies*, note that this dressing can be tied in traditional style, as it is shown, or as a wiggle nymph, by installing a hinge between the abdomen and thorax.

Ephemera Simulans Wiggle Nymph
(Originator: Fred Arbona, Jr.)

Abdomen hook:	Ring-eye hook, cut to 12mm.
Thorax hook:	Standard wet fly, 2X stout, size 16.
Weight:	8-10 turns lead wire on thorax hook.
Tails:	Light brown mini ostrich herl fibers.
Rib:	Fine gold wire.
Gills:	Gray ostrich herl along top sides of abdomen.
Abdomen:	Light yellowish-tan fur or synthetic dubbing.
Hinge:	Piano wire or 15# monofilament.
Wing pads:	Mottled brown turkey feather section.
Thorax:	Light yellowish-tan fuzzy dubbing blend.
Legs:	Olive-brown dyed grouse or partridge fibers.

This dressing, listed in Fred Arbona's *Mayflies, the Angler, and the Trout,* can be tied in what Arbona terms the streamlined standard tie, or as the wiggle nymph shown here. You should likely dress this one and the one above it in both wiggle and standard form. If you get into enough chances over brown drakes, you can fish one style against the other and compare your own results. We haven't had that many chances, or the discipline to do that when we did.

Brown Drake Strip Nymph (Originator: Gary Borger)

Hook:	Standard wet fly, 2X stout, size 6-8.
Weight:	10-20 turns lead wire, diameter of the hook shank.
Thread:	Tan 6/0.
Abdomen:	Gold-tan strip of tanned rabbit hide.
Wingcase:	Peacock herl.
Thorax:	Olive hare's ear dubbing.
Legs:	Thorax fur picked out, clipped flat on bottom.

This Gary Borger dressing is listed for the brown drakes in Jim Schollmeyer's *Hatch Guide for Western Streams*. It captures the movement of the natural insect with the inherent motion of the material. It is possible that a Woolly Bugger, tied in size 8 or 10, with yellow-brown marabou, chenille, and hackle might turn the same trick, though we haven't tried it.

Nymph Presentation

During pre-hatch days, or even weeks, fish weighted brown drake nymph imitations along the bottom, preferably at dusk and after dark. Let them sink, then retrieve with twitches of the rod tip that give the fly a darting swimming motion. You might need to use a sink-tip or wet-head line to get them down. This method is effective in eddies, backwaters, and the slow sections of streams, and also along the edges of lakes or ponds where populations of brown drakes are known to exist.

During emergence, fish the same nymphs with an active stripping retrieve. Try to swim them a foot or two under the surface if you see trout actively taking the naturals, which will be evident by broad-shouldered swirls. If no trout are visible, but a few scattered duns are on the water, you might need to fish the nymph dressings deeper.

Ephemera nymphs leave their burrows and swim swiftly to the surface for emergence. You can simulate this fast rise to the surface by giving your fly time to sink, then by using the current to lift the fly, or by lifting the rod tip to bring the fly up toward the top quickly.

The nymph stage is available to fish longer than the dun or spinner. The importance of nymph patterns is greater than that of dun patterns in many situations. This is especially true when you're after large trout, which tend to confine their feeding to the ascending nymphs while smaller fish feed on the surface.

Emerger Imitations

Not much is made of brown drake emerger dressings, mostly because of their swift way through the surface film and high success ratio making it to the dun stage. Few are crippled. But trout do feed on those that pause to release from the nymphal exoskeleton beneath the surface, and then complete the trip to the top as duns buoyed by gases trapped in the wings. Juracek and Mathews list a dressing for this stage in *Fishing Yellowstone Hatches.* It is based on their nymph pattern for the same hatch.

Brown Drake Emerger (Source: Juracek and Mathews)

Hook:	2X long, size 8-12.
Thread:	Brown 8/0.
Tails:	Tan Z-lon.
Rib:	Brown polyester thread.
Gills:	Gray pheasant aftershaft feather, counterwound length of abdomen.
Abdomen:	Light brown fur or synthetic dubbing.
Wingcase:	Gray polycelon, enlarged as emerging wings.
Thorax:	Light hare's mask dubbing, picked out.

This dressing captures the appearance of the insect in the process of making the transition from nymph to dun.

Emerger Presentation

The Juracek and Mathews pattern is designed to be fished floating in the surface film. Your presentation should be based on standard dry-fly practice for smooth waters. If you're fishing in light too low to see it, consider adding a strike indicator a few feet up the leader.

Dun Imitations

When you begin to hear splashes, or if you're fishing in enough daylight that you begin to see them, and see or suspect duns on the water, you've got all the indication you need that trout have switched to floating duns, or at least are taking them opportunistically when they get a chance at them. Trout might continue to take rising nymphs, but floating patterns are often easier to fish, especially if you see rises to which you can cast them, or if you've encountered one of those frequent times when trout are obviously feeding on brown drake nymphs but refusing your imitations of them.

Dun patterns can be important in the last minutes of legal light, or if you're allowed to fish them after dark, far into the night. During the height of a heavy hatch even the largest trout might switch to feed on the surface.

Brown Wulff (Originator: Lee Wulff)

Hook:	Standard dry fly, 1X fine, size 8-12.
Thread:	Black 6/0.
Wings:	Brown calf tail or bucktail, upright and divided.
Tails:	Brown calf tail or bucktail.
Body:	Brown or cream fur or yarn.
Hackle:	Brown.

The Wulff series of patterns make good suggestions for many of our large western mayfly hatches. The style can be altered quite readily in color and size to represent any of naturals over which you find yourself fishing.

Brown Paradrake (Originator: Mike Lawson)

Hook:	Standard dry fly, 1X fine, size 12.
Thread:	Brown 3/0.
Wingpost:	Medium brown deer hair.
Hackle:	Grizzly dyed olive-brown, parachute.
Tails:	Three moose body hairs.
Body:	Yellowish-tan dyed elk hair, extended, ribbed with working thread.

As with all dressings in the paradrake style, tie in the post first, the hackle at its base, then the tails. Bring the thread forward to the hook eye, and tie in the clump of body hair there. Rib it to the back, then return it to the front. Wind the hackle, and tie it off in front of the wing. Clip out the excess body hairs without cutting the tail fibers.

Bunse Brown Drake Dun (Originator: Richard Bunse)

Hook:	Standard dry fly, 1X fine, size 10-12.
Thread:	Brown 6/0.
Wing:	Natural Compara-dun deer hair.
Tail:	Brown Micro Fibetts, split.
Body:	Ethafoam colored yellow-brown, extended.

This dressing in Bunse's natural dun style is listed in Jim Schollmeyer's *Hatch Guide for Western Streams*. Directions for tying the style can be found in Skip Morris's *Tying Foam Flies*, though this dressing is not listed, so you'll have to interpret to get the right colors. Basic steps can also be found in Schollmeyer and Leeson's encyclopaedic *The Fly Tier's Benchside Reference*.

Dun Presentation

The brown drake is a smooth-water hatch, but occurs only in low light. You will have to strike a balance in terms of refining your gear, so that your leader is stout enough to turn over the large flies, but the tippet is fine enough that trout will not turn up cold wet noses at what you're trying to get them to take. The ideal combination might be a rod balanced to a 5- or 6-weight line, a ten- to twelve-foot leader tapered to 3X or 4X. The critical presentation criteria will be the position you take in relation to the rising trout, so that you do not need to line them, and your ability to set such a large fly delicately onto the water. You'll have to wade into your best position and execute your best cast, or more likely many casts, in low light or even total darkness.

Spinner Imitations

To fish the brown drake spinner fall we would first suggest trying one of the dun patterns, since duns and spinners are often on the water at the same time, and most trout feed at will on whichever stage they can get. If you find that spinners are falling and trout are selective to them, then it will become true that a more exact imitation is needed. The dun may overshadow this stage during some *Ephemera* hatches. If you find fish feeding selectively on the spinners, however, one of the following patterns should be tried.

Montana's Smith River has fishable populations of *Ephemera* that reveal themselves only after the campfires have been lit, except on cloudy, heavily overcast afternoons.

Brown Drake Spinner (Source: Knopp and Cormier)

Hook:	Fine dry fly, size 8-12.
Thread:	Brown 3/0 or 6/0.
Tails:	Three dark brown Micro Fibetts or moose body hairs.
Body:	Reddish-tan to dark tannish-yellow fur or synthetic dubbing.
Wings:	Light brown or tan polypro fibers, spent.

This dressing, from *Mayflies*, is listed for the intrepid angler willing to fish after dark. It will be difficult to see on the water. You might find it possible to take a position where you can look down the track of the fading light of the sky reflected on the water. The fly floats down this bit of brightness as a black outline, but it's enough to follow its drift and notice takes to it. Rises will not often be subtle to a fly this large. If you can't see the fly, perhaps you'll be able to hear the take.

Ephemera Simulans Spinner (Originator: Fred Arbona, Jr.)

Hook:	Fine dry fly, size 8.
Thread:	Tan 3/0.
Tails:	Three moose body hairs.
Rib:	Working thread.
Body:	Reddish-tan fur or synthetic dubbing.
Wing:	Light tan hen or partridge body feathers, tied spent.

This fly is not far removed from the reliable Red Quill Spinner, which might work if you tie it on long-shank size 8 and 10 hooks.

Spinner Presentation

The same rules apply that are listed above for duns. You'll be on the same water, at the same time. Position will be the critical factor, with the addition of the knowledge that these low-floating flies will be very difficult to see on the water. When looking for the proper position from which to make your cast, keep an eye on reflected sky light, and line yourself up so that you're casting onto it, and can see your fly as a black silhouette against it. If you position yourself to cast onto water that reflects only blackness, you'll have no chance to see your fly.

Of course, you'll often not be able to take a position that allows you to silhouette your fly against bright water. In that situation, you'll have to fish by feel and sound rather than by sight. That will be the most common case when you're fishing over a brown drake hatch.

Chapter 28

Ephoron (White Drakes)

FAMILY: POLYMITARCYIDAE
Genus: *Ephoron*
Western Species: 2
North American: 2
Important Western Species:
    Ephoron album
Common Names: White drakes, white fly.

Two species of this burrowing genus occur across the continent: *Ephoron album* and *E. leukon*. The most common in the West is *E. album*, but even this species is quite uncommon in trout waters. The combined experience of your authors with this species is one observation. Rick found it in abundance gathered around the lights of an all-night gas station not far from the lower Snake River in Idaho. Trout were not part of that equation. However, it does exist in waters where trout are found, and you might run into it in your travels and fishing throughout the West, especially if you fish at dusk and after dark.

The white drake, *Ephoron album,* is closely related to the white miller of deserved eastern fame. Hatches in the East are more often on waters inhabited by trout. Out West, the species tends toward warmer waters inhabited by other types of fish. However, it has been reported from fishable sections of the Missouri River in Montana, and no doubt occurs in other trout waters as well. Where it occurs, hatches are heavy. If you do run into it, you'll need to know what to do about it.

Ephoron are classed as small burrowers. They are found only in slow-flowing sections of rivers, usually downstream from the prime trout fishing areas of the same river systems.

Ephoron album   **HATCH IMPORTANCE SCORE:**   **13.5**

CRITERIA/SCORE	5		4		3		2		1	
Distribution: (within Western waters)	widespread		common		scattered		isolated		rare	1.0
Abundance:	heavy		abundant	3.5	modest		trickling		individual	
Emergence type:	mid-water/slow		mid-water/fast		edges/slow	3.0	edges/fast		crawls out	
Emergence time:	mid-day		early and/or late over long period		early and/or late over short period		dawn or dusk		night	1.0
Emergence duration:	multiple seasons per year		well-defined long hatch period		well-defined short hatch period		poorly-defined long hatch period		poorly-defined short hatch	1.0
(Behavior/Availability) Nymph:	excellent		good		moderate		slight		poor	1.0
(Behavior/Availability) Emerger:	excellent		good		moderate		slight		poor	1.0
(Behavior/Availability) Dun:	excellent		good		moderate		slight		poor	1.0
(Behavior/Availability) Spinner:	excellent		good		moderate		slight		poor	1.0
Totals:		0.0		3.5		3.0		0.0		7.0

Emergence and Distribution

Seasonal emergence typically takes place in August and early September when water temperatures are at annual highs. Hatches begin when waters reach and maintain temperatures of 65°F to 70°F. If temperatures drop, the hatch will hold off, and fishable emergences are not often predictable in the West because of changeable weather patterns. The preferred water temperatures of *Ephoron* approach or exceed the maximum highs that trout can tolerate. That is why their populations are found more often in waters holding warmwater fish.

Daily emergence begins in early evening, with a scattered hatch at first. Numbers increase through dusk and usually peak after dark. The hatch and egg-laying flight are almost abrupt, ending about an hour after they begin, though adults might be found on the water for some time after activity ends.

Ephoron have a unique mating behavior among mayflies. The males molt quickly into spinners and mate within half an hour to an hour after emergence. Females do not ever molt to spinners, rising right from the water to swarm and mate as duns, in which stage they lay their eggs and collapse spent to the water. The legs of females are atrophied, and cannot support the insect either on the water or on vegetation. These are the only mayflies in which the females mate as duns.

Geographic distribution of *Ephoron album* is scattered throughout the west, but fishable populations have only been reported to us from the Missouri River in the region of Holter Dam. It is quite likely that many smaller slow-flowing but clean waters hold the insect and trout as well. It is also probable that the lower fishable areas of some large river systems, such as the Snake and the Yellowstone, also have the white drake in waters where trout, if they do not thrive, at lease survive.

EPHORON EMERGENCE TABLE

TIME	WINTER			SPRING			SUMMER			FALL		
	Dec.	Jan.	Feb.	March	April	May	June	July	Aug.	Sep.	Oct.	Nov.
7 a.m. - 10 a.m.												
10 a.m. - noon												
noon - 3 p.m.												
3 p.m. - 7 p.m.												
7 p.m. - 10 p.m.												

Nymph Characteristics

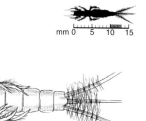

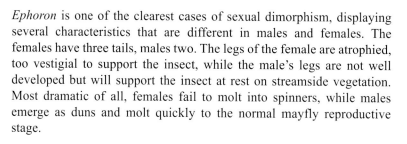

a. Burrowing tusks curved in, almost touching at ends, covered with tiny spines.
b. Long branched gills held over abdominal segments 1-7.
c. Conical-shaped frontal prominence.
d. Short, stump-like femora on fore and middle pairs of legs.
e. Three tails fringed with hairs.
f. Body tan to grayish-brown.
g. Body length, without tails, 10-13mm (1/2-5/8 in.).

Dun Characteristics

a. Females with three tails; males two.
b. Females with atrophied legs; male legs feeble but functional.
c. Wings pale gray to white with a purple cast on the leading edge of the forewing.
d. Body white, often with a gray cast.
e. Body length 11-13 mm. (1/2 to 5/8 in.)

Ephoron is one of the clearest cases of sexual dimorphism, displaying several characteristics that are different in males and females. The females have three tails, males two. The legs of the female are atrophied, too vestigial to support the insect, while the male's legs are not well developed but will support the insect at rest on streamside vegetation. Most dramatic of all, females fail to molt into spinners, while males emerge as duns and molt quickly to the normal mayfly reproductive stage.

Spinner Characteristics

a. Only males reach spinner stage.
b. Two tails.
c. Eager males often trail dun cuticle into the air.
d. Clear wings.
e. Body pale to white, with some darkening of abdominal segments 9-10.
f. Body 9-12mm (1/2 to 5/8 in.).

Ephoron male dun.

Habitat and Behavior

Ephoron nymphs make their burrows in soft clay or fine silt bottoms, usually in slow, warm, but unpolluted rivers. They leave these burrows only in low light, at dusk or after dark, to forage on the bottom. The nymphs are good to excellent swimmers.

In the hour or so before they are ready to hatch, the nymphs leave their burrows and prowl restlessly over the river bottom. Then they swim briskly toward the top. Within a few inches to a foot of the surface, the nymph pauses, and the nymphal shuck splits. *Ephoron* often drift for long distances during this process in which the dun escapes the nymph exoskeleton. Once the dun escapes and reaches the surface, it passes through the film without hesitation and quickly flies off. Females are particularly quick to leave the water, because their legs won't support them on the surface.

In the course of the hatch, male duns emerge first and fly to streamside vegetation, where they molt quickly to the spinner stage. About half an hour later most of the females emerge and fly into the air swiftly. Females do not molt. Instead, they mate as duns just above the water immediately after emerging. Mated females gather in swarms and fly upstream just inches over water. The entire flight will swirl and switch directions every fifty to one hundred feet as they fly upstream. They can fly as much as two or three miles before depositing their eggs and dropping to the water spent. This is a response to behavioral drift, ensuring that an annual downstream movement, pushed by current, does not eventually sweep the entire species out to sea.

The flight ends as soon as temperatures drop with full nightfall. Usually, scatterings of naturals remain helpless on the water. Emergence, male molting, and the swirling egg-laying flight of the females all take place within a hectic hour. During the brief and chaotic process of this hatch, with so many insects flying so low over the water, trout often jump and try take them out of the air.

Imitation

Your first clue to this hatch will usually be the sight of drowned adults in side eddies or washed onto riverbanks in the morning. If you find such evidence of a night hatch, stay on the water until dark, and carry a few imitations. During the hatch, trout will take drifting nymphs until duns begin to get thick, and then turn their attention to the top to take the floating male spinners, and later to the dying female duns.

We will offer just a single nymph and dun dressing for the hatch. If you get into a spinner fall, it's likely the dun pattern will continue to take trout. If it doesn't, try clipping out the wings and trimming the hackle from top and bottom. The result will be a spent-wing dressing that might work well. If it doesn't work, collect and observe specimens, and match them with variations on standard spinner themes.

Nymph Imitation

The nymph listed below is from Knopp and Cormier's *Mayflies.*

White Fly Nymph (Source: Knopp and Cormier)

Hook:	3X long, size 12-14.
Thread:	Light gray 6/0.
Tails:	Light grayish-brown mallard flank fibers.
Body:	Grayish-brown fur dubbing.
Wingcase:	Dark mallard wing quill section.
Legs:	Light grayish-brown mallard flank fibers, divided.

Weight this fly heavily to fish it deep along the bottom prior to a hatch, and tie it without weight to fish it just subsurface in imitation of the drifting nymph. Or average it out, and underweight the fly so you can fish it deep with weight on the leader, or with a sink-tip line, and shallow on a floating line.

Nymph Presentation

Fish a weighted nymph deep on a strip retrieve just before dusk. During emergence, when the natural nymphs drift with the current just beneath the surface, fish a moderately weighted nymph on upstream casts, just as you would a dry fly. Use a strike indicator to help follow the drift of the fly and to report takes to it.

You might also fish the nymph on a traditional wet fly swing. Or cast it across stream, let it sink a couple of feet or more, then stop the rod to swim the nymph toward the surface.

Dun and Spinner Imitation

Because you are so unlikely to run into this hatch in a fishable situation, we will offer only the traditional White Wulff dressing to imitate both the dun and spinner stages.

White Wulff (Originator: Lee Wulff)

Hook:	Standard dry fly, 1X fine, size 12-14.
Thread:	White 6/0.
Wings:	White calf body hair.
Tail:	White calf body hair.
Body:	White fur or synthetic dubbing.
Hackle:	Badger.

To convert this to a spent pattern, consider drawing the hackle and wings out to each side with your fingers. If you pull them hard enough, and the fly is tied well enough, they will hold their position, and at least look like a semi-spent fly. If that doesn't work follow the above prescription: cut the wings and both bottom and top hackle fibers from the fly.

Dun and Spinner Presentation

Fish the fly dead drift, recalling that you'll be doing it in the dark, or very near it. If that doesn't work, then Knopp and Cormier report in *Mayflies* that a dry fly fished with drag, or skittered, works well when these erratic insects are in the air and on the water.

Conclusion: Much Ado About Mayflies

When we first set out to revise *Western Hatches*, it was primarily so it could be done in all color, with updated fly patterns reflecting changes in pattern styles and materials available in the last twenty years. Our guess was that the book would be somewhat expanded, with the addition of a few new sections to account for taxonomic revisions.

What we encountered was an infinity of new sources, in both angling and entomology. What we also ran into were many more fine distinctions among the insects that we knew must be covered, simply because anglers have studied western insect hatches more closely, and know much more about them, at ever lower levels of classification. As an example, the *Ephemerella* mayflies were treated as a single group in the first edition of *Western Hatches*. In this second edition, taxonomic revisions and angler knowledge required that the same material be covered in seven sections, each with more information and therefore at more length than the original single section.

At the end of the mayfly portion of the revision of *Western Hatches*, a short way into the new millennium, we counted up and discovered we had more than 500 pages of manuscript, over 300 photos and 75 illustrations. That amount of news, when compiled, amounted to the book you're holding in your hands. We were forced to recognize that the material had shaped itself: the book had to be about *Western Mayfly Hatches* alone, or it would run over two thousand manuscript pages, more than a thousand photos and two to three hundred illustrations. That would create a book far too large to hold in your hands.

One reviewer, a friend of caddisflies, criticized the first edition of *Western Hatches* for saying too much about mayflies, and too little about other insects, including guess which ones. We explained then, and do now, that two reasons made that happen. First, mayflies hatch out in open water, in daring daylight, with a defense against predation of massing their numbers, more often than any other group of aquatic insects. Second, the mayflies are more complex than most other groups—we'll except caddisflies—and require a wide variety of patterns and tactics.

What do those two things mean? First, mayfly emergence behavior leads to trout feeding on them selectively far more often than any other insect group, caddisflies included. Second, the finer divisions require more pages and photos to cover them.

The result: no apologies this time. We've covered mayflies in this single volume because they're more important to the Western angler, more often, than other aquatic insects, and because the material it took to cover the subject shaped itself into this single book about them.

Glossary

A

abdomen. third, or posterior, division of the insect body normally consists of nine or ten apparent segments.

algae. one-celled, many-celled, or colonial plants containing chlorophyl and having no root.

ametabolous. insects that do not change form during lifetime.

anastomosed. as used in *Western Mayfly Hatches,* densely-branched wing veins forming discernible dense, or darkened, area in wing.

apex. that part of any joint or segment opposite the base by which it is attached; that part of the wing farthest removed from the base.

B

basal segment. segment closest to base or attachment point to the body.

burrowers. non-scienic classification of a group of mayfly nymphs that burrow into or bury themselves in the bottom material of streams and lakes.

C

clingers. non-scienic classification of a group of mayfly nymphs that are flattened in aspect, adapted to living in swift water.

costal. thickened anterior margin of a wing.

costal angulation. angle in the leading edge of the wing; in *Western Mayfly Hatches* usually refers to the leading edge of the hind wing.

crawlers. non-scienic classification of a group of mayfly nymphs that move from place to place in most cases by crawling rather than swimming.

cripple. an emerging insect that fails to free itself from the nymphal (or pupal in insects with complete metamorphosis) cuticle.

cubital intercalary veins. supplemental veins to the fifth (cubital) longitudinal wing vein.

cuticle. outer covering of an insect.

D

diatoms. microscopic algae whose walls consist of two parts or valves and contain silica.

distal. near or toward the free end of any appendage.

dorsal. pertaining to the upper surfaces.

dorsal stripe. stripe on the upper surface, usually of a mayfly nymph's back (see median stripe).

dorsal-ventrally. top and bottom; refers to flattening of clinger nymphs.

dun. intermediate winged stage of mayfly, between nymph and sexually mature spinner. Also called *subimago.*
    color: light, medium, or dark gray.

E

emargination. a cut-out place in an edge or margin.

eclosion. the act or process of hatching from the egg.

exoskeleton. the outside skin in insects, to which the muscles are attached.

exuvia. cast skin of nymph or dun.

F

femora. plural of femur.

femur. the thigh; usually the stoutest segment of the leg, articulated to the body through the trochanter and coxa and bearing the tibia at its distal end.

flymph. wet fly tied to imitate an insect in the stage described by Pete Hidy as, "...no longer a nymph but not yet a fly."

fore wings, forewings. forward pair of wings; large flight wings of mayfly adults.

frontal process. projection or outgrowth from the front of the head.

fur noodle. method of segmenting a fly body by catching the fur in a loop of thread and twisting them together tightly before the body is wound.

G

gill lamellae. gills in the form of thin plates or leaf-like processes.

H

hemimetabolous. insects with incomplete metamorphosis; have only egg, nymph, and adult stages.

hind wings, hindwings. rear pair of wings; smaller and sometimes absent in mayfly adults.

holometabolous. insects with complete metamorphosis; have egg, larva, pupa, and adult stages.

hyaline. transparent or partly so; glassy.

hypognathus. posture of having the head verticle and the mouth directed downward.

I

imago. mayfly spinner; sexually mature mayfly adult.

instar. period or stage between molts in nymph or larva.

L

labrum. the upper lip, which covers the base of the mandibles and forms the roof of the mouth.

M

mandibles. the first pair of jaws in insects.

mandibular tusks. long protrusions from the mandibles, used by burrowing nymphs for digging.

maxillary palpi. one- to seven-segmented finger-like appendages attached to the maxilla, an insect's second pair of jaws.

median stripe. pale central line; in *Western Mayfly Hatches* describes pale line running all or part of the length of the back surface of a nymph (see dorsal stripe).

mesothorax. middle thoracic segment.

metathorax. third and rear-most thoracic segment, closest to abdomen.

molt. to cast off or shed the outer skin; in the mayfly, to shed the nymph or dun exoskeleton.

O

operculate. lid or cover; in *Western Mayfly Hatches* refers to the first gill forming a protective cover over the remaining gills.

outrigger. a method of weighting a hook by affixing a length of lead wire along each side of the shank.

oviposition. depositing of eggs.

P

periphyton. thin layer of algae and diatoms growing on the surface of submerged rocks and debris.

plumose. feathered; like a plume.

posterior margins. hind-most trailing edges.

previously. an insect name that has been replaced by a more current revision of the taxonomy.

prothorax. first thoracic segment, closest to head.

proximal. that part of an appendage nearest the body.

S

sclerotized. hardened in definite areas by deposition or formation of other substances than chitin.

semi-spent. spinner on the water with its wings held at an angle, generally around 45°, to the surface.

serrated. saw-like; with notched edges.

setae. slender hairs often creating a fringe along the edge of legs or tails.

sexual dimorphism. sexes occurring in two distinct forms; in mayflies, usually in different colors.

shuck. the exoskeleton of the nymph stage of the mayfly, left behind when the dun escapes it (same as exuvia).

spent. spinner on the water with its wings flattened in the surface film.

spine. thorn-like process or out-growth of the cuticle.

spinner. final stage of mayfly adult life; sexually mature adult; also called *imago.*

subimaginal cuticle. outer covering of subimago, or dun.

subimago. mayfly dun; intermediate stage between nymph and sexually mature spinner.

substrate. bottom material of stream or lake.

swimmers. non-scientic classification of a group of mayfly nymphs that are active, moving from place to place by swimming.

synonym. a different name given to a species or genus previously named and described.

T

tarsi. plural of tarsus; feet of an insect; jointed appendages attached at the apex of the tibiae.

taxanomic. scientific system of naming organisms.

thorax. second or intermediate region of insect body, between head and abdomen, bearing the legs and wings of the insect.

tibia. fourth division of the insect leg; articulated at the proximal end to the femur and bearing on the distal end the tarsi.

tubercles. rounded to pointed lobes or processes.

turbinate. top-shaped; nearly conical.

U

underweighting. weighting a nymph less than normal by using weighting wire one size finer than the diameter of the hook shank.

V

vein. riblike support strengthening the membranous wings of an insect.

veinlet. small vein.

venation. the complex system of veins of a wing.

W

whorl. a ring of hairs set about a joint or center like the spokes of a wheel.

Bibliography

—Arbonna, Fred L. Jr.: *Mayflies, the Angler, and the Trout*. New York: Winchester Press, 1980.

—Atherton, John: *The Fly and the Fish*. New York: The MacMillan Co., 1951.

—Best, A. K.: *Dying and Bleaching Natural Fly Tying Materials*. New York: Lyons & Burford, 1993;
    A. K.'s Fly Box. New York: Lyons & Burford, 1996;
    Advanced Fly Tying. Guilford, CT: The Lyons Press, 2001.

—Betters, Fran: *Fran Betters' Fly Fishing - Fly Tying and Pattern Guide*. Wilmington, NY: AuSable Wulff Products, 1986.

—Borger, Gary: *Nymphing*. Harrisburg: Stackpole, 1979.

—Brooks, Charles: *The Trout and the Stream*. New York: Crown, 1974;
    Nymph Fishing for Larger Trout. New York: Crown, 1976;
    Larger Trout for the Western Fly Fisherman. Piscataway, NJ: Winchester Press, 1983.

—Caucci, Al and Bob Nastasi: *Hatches*. Woodside, New York: Comparahatch Press, 1975;
    Fly-tyer's Color Guide. New York: Comparahatch, Ltd., 1978.

—Cutter, Ralph: *Sierra Trout Guide*. Portland: Frank Amato Publications, 1991.

—Edmunds, George F. Jr., Steven Jensen, and Lewis Berner: *The Mayflies of North and Central America*. Minneapolis: University of Minnesota Press, 1976.

—Gierach, John: *Trout Bum*. Boulder: Pruett, 1986.

—Hafele, Rick and Dave Hughes: *Western Hatches*. Portland: Frank Amato Publications, 1981.

—Hafele, Rick and Scott Roederer: *Aquatic Insects and Their Imitations*. Boulder: Johnson Books, 1995.

—Hafele, Rick and Steve Hinton: *Guide to Pacific Northwest Aquatic Invertebrates*: Oregon Trout, 2003.

—Hellekson, Terry: *Popular Fly Patterns*. Salt Lake City: Peregrine Smith, Inc., 1977;
    Fish Flies (Volume One and Two): Portland: Frank Amato Publications, 1995.

—Hughes, Dave: *Handbook of Hatches*. Harrisburg: Stackpole, 1987;
    Western Streamside Guide. Portland: Frank Amato Publications, 1997;
    Trout Flies. Mechanicsburg: Stackpole, 1999.

—Jorgensen, Poul: *Dressing Flies for Fresh and Salt Water*. Rockville Center, NY: Freshet Press, 1973;
    Modern Fly Dressings for the Practical Angler. New York: Winchester Press, 1976.

—Juracek, John and Craig Mathews: *Fishing Yellowstone Hatches*. West Yellowstone: Blue Ribbon Flies, 1992.

—Kaufmann, Randall: *Fly Patterns of Umpqua Feather Merchants*. Glide, OR: Umpqua Feather Merchants, 1998.

—Knopp, Malcolm and Robert Cormier: *Mayflies*. Helena, MT: Greycliff, 1997.

—LaFontaine, Gary. *The Dry Fly, New Angles*. Helena, MT: Greycliff, 1990;
    Trout Flies, Proven Patterns. Helena, MT: Greycliff, 1993.

—Leeson, Ted and Jim Schollmeyer: *The Fly Tier's Benchside Reference*. Portland: Frank Amato Publications, 1998.
    Tying Emergers. Portland: Frank Amato Publications, 2004.

—Leisenring, Jim and Vernon S. "Pete" Hidy: *The Art of Tying the Wet Fly and Fishing the Flymph*. New York: Crown, 1971.

—McCafferty, W. Patrick: *Aquatic Entomology*. Boston: Jones and Bartlett, 1981.

—Marinaro, Vincent: *A Modern Dry Fly Code*. New York: Putnam, 1950;
    In the Ring of the Rise. New York: Crown, 1976.

—Martin, Darrell: *Fly-Tying Methods*. New York: Nick Lyons Books, 1987;
    Micropatterns. New York: Lyons & Burford, 1994.

—Meck, Charles R.: *Meeting and Fishing the Hatches*. New York: Winchester Press, 1977.

—Merritt, R. W. and D. W. Cummins: *An Introduction to the Aquatic Insects of North America*, Third Edition. Dubuque:
    Kendall/Hunt, 1996.

—Morris, Skip: *Fly Tying Made Clear and Simple*. Portland: Frank Amato Publications, 1992;
    Tying Foam Flies. Portland: Frank Amato Publications, 1994.

—Nemes, Sylvester: *The Soft-Hackled Fly*. Old Greenwich, CT: Chatham Press, 1975;
    Soft-Hackled Fly Imitations. Bozeman: by the author, 1991;
    Spinners. Bozeman: by the author, 1995.

—Proper, Datus: *What the Trout Said*. New York: Alfred A. Knopf, 1982.

—Rosborough, E. H. "Polly": *Tying and Fishing the Fuzzy Nymphs*. Harrisburg: Stackpole, 1988.

—Sawyer, Frank: *Nymphs and the Trout*. New York: 1958. Crown

—Schollmeyer, Jim: *Hatch Guide for the Lower Deschutes River*. Portland: Frank Amato Publications, 1994;
    Hatch Guide for Western Streams. Portland: Frank Amato Publications, 1997;
    Hatch Guide for Lakes. Portland: Frank Amato Publications, 1995;
    Nymph Fly-Tying Techniques. Portland: Frank Amato Publications, 2001.

—Schwiebert, Ernest: *Matching the Hatch*. New York: MacMillan, 1955;
    Nymphs. New York: Winchester Press, 1973;
    Trout. New York: E. P. Dutton, 1978.

—Stalcup, Shane: *Mayflies: Top to Bottom*. Portland: Frank Amato Publications, 2002.

—Stetzer, Randy: *Flies: The Best One Thousand*. Portland: Frank Amato Publications, 1992.

—Swisher, Doug and Carl Richards: *Selective Trout*. New York: Crown, 1971;
    Fly Fishing Strategy. New York: Crown, 1975;
    Tying the Swisher/Richards Flies. Eugene: P. J. Dylan, 1977.

—Torre-Bueno, J. R. de la: *A Glossary of Entomology*. New York: New York Entomological Society, 1973.

—Usinger, Robert L. et. al.: *Aquatic Insects of California*. Berkeley: University of California Press, 1956.

Index

Index

Other books by the Authors

Dave Hughes

Books:

Western Hatches (with Rick Hafele)
An Angler's Astoria
American Fly Tying Manual
Handbook of Hatches
Reading the Water
Tackle & Technique
Tactics for Trout
Strategies for Stillwater
Dry Fly Fishing
Nymph Fishing
Fly Fishing Basics

Deschutes: River of Renewal
The Yellowstone River and Its Angling
Big Indian Creek
Wet Flies
Western Streamside Guide
Trout Flies
Essential Trout Flies
Taking Trout
Trout from Small Streams
Matching Mayflies

Rick Hafele

Books:

The Complete Book of Western Hatches – Rick Hafele and Dave Hughes, 1981, Amato Publications.
An Angler's Guide to Aquatic Insects and Their Imitations – Rick Hafele and Scott Roederer, 1995 (2nd Ed.), Johnson Books, Boulder, CO.
Guide to Pacific Northwest Aquatic Invertebrates – Rick Hafele and Steve Hinton, 2003 (2nd Ed.), Oregon Trout

Videos:

Anatomy of a Trout Stream – Scientific Anglers, 1986
Fly Fishing Large Western Rivers: Spring, Summer, Fall, Winter – Laughing River Productions, 2003 (www.laughingrivers.com)